Enterprise-Grade Hybrid and Multi-Cloud Strategies

Proven strategies to digitally transform your business with hybrid and multi-cloud solutions

Sathya AG

Enterprise-Grade Hybrid and Multi-Cloud Strategies

Group Product Manager: Preet Ahuja

Publishing Product Manager: Preet Ahuja

Book Project Manager: Uma Devi Lakshmikant

Senior Editor: Sujata Tripathi

Technical Editor: Irfa Ansari

Copy Editor: Safis Editing

Proofreader: Sujata Tripathi

Indexer: Hemangini Bari

Production Designer: Joshua Misquitta

DevRel Marketing Executive: Rohan Dobhal

Senior DevRel Marketing Executive: Marylou De Mello

First published: April 2024
Production reference: 1280324

Published by Packt Publishing Ltd.
Grosvenor House
11 St Paul's Square
Birmingham
B3 1RB, UK

ISBN 978-1-80461-511-9

www.packtpub.com

To my mom, Geetha, for infusing the love of reading at an early age.

To my dad, Annamalai, who instilled the sense of freedom to explore fearlessly.

To my wife, Sangeetha, my biggest supporter, critic, and believer.

To my little angels, Athulya and Aadhya, for inspiring me every day.

To all my gurus, for their wisdom and guidance.

I also would like to thank the technical reviewers and the Packt team for their dedication and support in bringing this book to life.

Foreword

The appeal of the hybrid cloud is undeniable. It offers the best of both worlds – the flexibility of public cloud services and the control of private infrastructure. However, this flexibility comes at a cost – *complexity*. It poses unique sets of challenges that require careful consideration, innovative solutions, and change management.

Whether you are jumpstarting your cloud transformation journey, trying to understand hybrid cloud paradigms, or designing a scalable and open foundation for a cloud-first IT organization, this book is your guide to navigate through the complexities and find meaningful solutions and actionable guidance to maximize your returns on investment.

Sathya has done a brilliant job of highlighting the critical aspects of how an enterprise can transform their hybrid cloud from a complex maze into a powerful engine for innovation. This book empowers you to build a robust hybrid cloud foundation, enabling agility, scalability, and a competitive edge in the digital landscape.

I am extremely hopeful that this will serve as a trusted companion for any enterprise that is embarking on their cloud journey, guiding them toward success in an increasingly hybrid and interconnected world.

—*Kunal Das, SVP, Chief Data and Analytics Officer, Advance Auto Parts*

Contributors

About the author

Sathya AG is a principal architect at Google, where he leads digital transformation initiatives. In this capacity, Sathya works with large enterprise customers to digitally transform, innovate, and scale their businesses through the adoption of modern technologies. Prior to his current role at Google, Sathya served as an enterprise architect at Oracle, spearheading go-to-market and digital-native strategies for retail and healthcare industries. He is a tech evangelist, regularly writes on emerging technologies on various forums, and can also be found speaking at industry events and conferences. Sathya holds a postgraduate degree in business administration and a bachelor's in electronics engineering. In addition to his professional endeavors, Sathya serves as an advisory board member of the CDAO circle, mentors young graduates, and volunteers for humanitarian causes. Sathya lives in Apex, North Carolina, with his wife and two daughters.

I would like to thank my mentors at Google for their guidance and support. I would also like to extend my thanks to my wife, Sangeetha, and my daughters, Athulya and Aadhya, for their patience, support, and encouragement, without which this book wouldn't have been possible.

About the reviewers

Naresh Kumar Miryala is a highly experienced engineering leader with nearly 20 years of industry experience and a strong background in the cloud, platform engineering, and artificial intelligence. He leads high-performing cloud data platform teams in his current role at Meta Platforms, Inc. He has a proven track record of carrying out cloud transformations, infrastructure implementation, database management, ERP solutions, and DevOps deployments. His expertise spans multiple domains, such as database systems, large-scale backend infrastructure, security, multi-cloud deployments, cloud infrastructure, DevOps, and artificial intelligence.

I'd like to thank my family and friends, who understand the time and commitment it takes to research. I am grateful for your unwavering belief in me and for always pushing me to be my best self.

Charith Hettige has worked in the IT infrastructure domain for over 21 years and has specialized in cloud solutions architecture and cloud operations for over 10 years. He has worked for multinational organizations that operate infrastructure services to provide internet-scale products around the globe. He holds multiple certifications from the industry in the areas of the cloud, security, infrastructure, and IT service management. He obtained his Master of Science in information technology from Cardiff Metropolitan University in Cardiff, Wales. He also serves as a technical advisor to the CompTIA SME Technical Advisory Committee. He has also been a freelance Microsoft Certified Trainer for 10 years.

I am humbled by the opportunity to provide technical expertise and contribute to the success and growth of the industry by sharing my learning and experiences. I would like to thank the author for the opportunity to collaborate and every person who has supported me in this process.

Anant Dimri brings decades of expertise in guiding customers through transformation journeys. He has worked at Microsoft for 16 years, helping major financial, manufacturing, and pharmaceutical companies, and currently works at Google, helping their biggest customers with their digital transformation journeys. He has a master's in computer science and has been a speaker at several cloud events.

My heartfelt gratitude goes to my beloved wife and my two boys for their unwavering support. I'm also deeply indebted to Sathya for inviting me to collaborate on this remarkable project.

Table of Contents

Part 1: Challenges with Cloud Adoption at an Enterprise Scale

1

2

3

Enterprise Challenges with Cloud Adoption   57

Part 2: Succeeding with Hybrid Cloud and Multi-Cloud

4

Building the Foundations for a Modern Enterprise   91

5

An Enterprise Journey to Cloud Transformation   119

6

Building an Open and Nimble Cloud Framework   151

7

Part 3: Lead and Transform Your Business with Cloud

8

Architecting a Cloud-Ready Enterprise   229

9

Facets of Digital Transformation   261

Preface

In the last decade, **cloud technology** has evolved from just another deployment platform into an engine for digital disruption. As modern technologies, such as artificial intelligence, augmented reality, virtual reality, edge computing, and quantum computing, continue to build on the foundations laid by cloud agility, scale, and resiliency, the cloud has become an indispensable platform that powers not just IT transformation but also business transformation. Embracing the cloud empowers enterprises to innovate faster, deliver new capabilities more efficiently, and maintain a competitive edge in the dynamic global marketplace.

Cloud adoption at an enterprise scale is a journey and can bring with it several challenges, including where to start, identifying the right workloads, and choosing the right cloud strategy. There are several resources that offer an opinionated view of cloud strategies from a target cloud platform perspective. This book aims to take a provider and platform agnostic perspective and will present a prescriptive framework, strategies, and best practices, which will help enterprises build an open, nimble, and modern cloud-ready enterprise.

Based on my extensive experience working with several enterprises across multiple industries on digital transformation initiatives, this book will provide a deeper insight into the various facets of cloud transformation and how enterprises can leverage the cloud as a vehicle to lead and drive innovation.

Who this book is for

This book is written for enterprise IT leaders and architects responsible for driving business transformation through cloud adoption. With cloud migration strategies, prescriptive frameworks, and practical real-world examples, this book will serve as a guide to lead and innovate with the cloud, from setting up the IT organization framework to architectural best practices and ESG.

The target demographic for this book is as follows:

- IT leaders: Leaders responsible for defining the organization's cloud strategy, vision, and setting up a cloud center of excellence
- Enterprise architects: Enterprise architects and solutions architects are responsible for designing the organization's future state IT infrastructure

What this book covers

Chapter 1, Leadership, Will, and Mindset, offers insights into the importance of the leadership, will and mindset in setting up the organization's strategy and vision for success. This chapter also explores the significance of leadership with a few real-world examples and how it shapes their future.

Chapter 2, A Primer on the Cloud, provides an overview of the fundamental cloud concepts, including its essential characteristics. This chapter also explores cloud adoption across multiple industries, the myths of cloud adoption, and driving business agility with the cloud.

Chapter 3, Enterprise Challenges with Cloud Adoption, explores the challenges and complexities that enterprises face with cloud adoption and the techniques to navigate them. It further explores how enterprises can identify the right workloads for cloud transformation, cloud best practices, and dealing with cloud financial models.

Chapter 4, Building the Foundations for a Modern Enterprise, offers insights into organizational change management, cloud maturity assessment frameworks, establishing a cloud center of excellence, and building a cloud foundation that is based on open standards.

Chapter 5, An Enterprise Journey to Cloud Transformation, provides an overview of the multi-dimensional value-complexity matrix, various enterprise cloud transformation journeys, cloud migration strategies, and innovating with emerging technologies in the cloud.

Chapter 6, Building an Open and Nimble Cloud Framework, focuses on defining a cloud adoption framework, hybrid cloud design patterns, blueprints for hybrid cloud and multi-cloud architectures, security architectures, and cloud-native anti-patterns.

Chapter 7, Hybrid Cloud Use Cases, explores the cloud transformation journeys of enterprises that have embraced the cloud to drive business objectives

Chapter 8, Architecting a Cloud-Ready Enterprise, offers insights into an opinionated framework that can serve as a blueprint for architecting a provider-agnostic cloud framework and how organizations can choose the right cloud strategy.

Chapter 9, Facets of Digital Transformation, provides an overview of the core facets of digital transformation, including building a security-first cloud architecture, modernizing infrastructure, application modernization, data modernization, and optimizing and scaling cloud infrastructure to maximize cloud value realization.

Chapter 10, Leading and Innovating with the Cloud, explores the strategies organizations can leverage to lead and innovate in the cloud, including setting up innovation centers of excellence and innovating responsibly with emerging technologies.

Chapter 11, ESG and Sustainability, explores the value enterprises can gain from ESG and sustainability goals and initiatives, how to build a sustainability program, and how to leverage the cloud as an enabler for an organization's ESG objectives.

Get in touch

Feedback from our readers is always welcome.

General feedback: If you have questions about any aspect of this book, email us at `customercare@packtpub.com` and mention the book title in the subject of your message.

Errata: Although we have taken every care to ensure the accuracy of our content, mistakes do happen. If you have found a mistake in this book, we would be grateful if you would report this to us. Please visit `www.packtpub.com/support/errata` and fill in the form.

Piracy: If you come across any illegal copies of our works in any form on the internet, we would be grateful if you would provide us with the location address or website name. Please contact us at `copyright@packt.com` with a link to the material.

If you are interested in becoming an author: If there is a topic that you have expertise in and you are interested in either writing or contributing to a book, please visit `authors.packtpub.com`.

Share your thoughts

Once you've read *Enterprise-Grade Hybrid and Multi-Cloud Strategies*, we'd love to hear your thoughts! Scan the QR code below to go straight to the Amazon review page for this book and share your feedback.

`https://packt.link/r/1804615110`

Your review is important to us and the tech community and will help us make sure we're delivering excellent quality content.

Download a free PDF copy of this book

Thanks for purchasing this book!

Do you like to read on the go but are unable to carry your print books everywhere?

Is your eBook purchase not compatible with the device of your choice?

Don't worry, now with every Packt book you get a DRM-free PDF version of that book at no cost.

Read anywhere, any place, on any device. Search, copy, and paste code from your favorite technical books directly into your application.

The perks don't stop there, you can get exclusive access to discounts, newsletters, and great free content in your inbox daily

Follow these simple steps to get the benefits:

1. Scan the QR code or visit the link below

https://packt.link/free-ebook/9781804615119

2. Submit your proof of purchase
3. That's it! We'll send your free PDF and other benefits to your email directly

Part 1:
Challenges with Cloud
Adoption at an Enterprise Scale

In this part, we will explore and understand the challenges as enterprises embark on a digital transformation with the cloud, and the importance of leadership vision, will, and mindset. We will also review the fundamental elements of cloud computing and how organizations can leverage the cloud to drive business agility. Finally, we will explore the various challenges and complexities that enterprises face with cloud transformation and the strategies to address them.

This part includes the following chapters:

- *Chapter 1, Leadership, Will, and Mindset*
- *Chapter 2, A Primer on the Cloud*
- *Chapter 3, Enterprise Challenges with Cloud Adoption*

Leadership, Will, and Mindset

In a book on cloud computing, you might find it unusual to encounter an entire chapter dedicated to leadership, will, and mindset. As technology continues to evolve exponentially, enterprises often find themselves in a dilemma; some fall behind the innovation curve due to fear of failure, whereas others start chasing every new trend. This is a direct reflection of the lack of vision and leadership. Before we dive deeper into the world of cloud computing, the purpose of this chapter is to recognize the crucial role of leadership, will, and mindset for a successful digital transformation.

In today's digital world, an organization's business agility to react to market demands is directly proportional to its digital maturity and capability. In modern enterprise architecture parlance, IT has evolved into a core pillar of business innovation from just being a traditional cost center. At the heart of every successful digital transformation, leadership, will, and mindset are indispensable. Strong visionary leaders set the vision and strategic direction, shape an organizational culture for innovation, and advocate for enterprise digital transformation to tap into an organization's full potential for growth and competitiveness.

Digital transformation has become a critical factor in the rapidly evolving technology landscape to drive innovation. It is not merely an option or a trend; rather, it has become a necessity for enterprises to survive, thrive, and remain competitive. Digital transformation involves the integration of digital technologies into all aspects of an organization, fundamentally changing how it operates and delivers value to customers. However, successful digital transformation requires more than just adopting new technologies. The one common attribute among all successful organizations is their ability to innovate and create value for their consumers. Why are some organizations more successful than others, where innovation is almost always natural and does not require external motivation? The answer lies in strong leadership, will, and mindset that can guide, inspire, and cultivate a sustainable culture of innovation. Innovative leaders unleash digital transformation in enterprises by developing a clear vision, fostering an environment for experimentation, promoting customer centricity, and empowering teams to collaborate. In this chapter, we will explore the crucial role of leadership, will, and mindset in setting the pace and tone for an enterprise's digital transformation. We will also delve into the following:

- How innovation is NOT just a choice for enterprises in the modern age to sustain and thrive in a competitive landscape

- The exponential evolution of digital trends across various industries

- Establishing a process for innovation through the innovation continuum

- The tale of two enterprises – Kodak and Fujifilm and how leadership, will, and mindset shaped their destiny

- How can enterprise leaders lead a strategic and sustainable digital transformation?

Let's try to understand why innovation is not a choice but a necessity through the following case study.

The Blockbuster case study

In the fall of 1985, David Cook founded Blockbuster, which would later emerge as a home for not just video/DVD movie rentals but also as a social space for local movie buffs to meet and socialize. Within the next few years, backed by its success, Blockbuster expanded its operations internationally and became a popular household name. Soon after, Viacom acquired Blockbuster and took it public in 1999. At its peak, Blockbuster had over 9000 stores worldwide and boasted a revenue of USD 5.9 million [1]. Buoyed by the momentum and consumer demand, Blockbuster cemented its position and business model and leveraged its almost monopolized market advantage to penalize loyal consumers for late returns; this is evidenced by the fact that, in the year 2000, roughly 16% of Blockbuster's revenue came from late fees. By the turn of the century, with the exponential growth of technology, customer preferences and demands were evolving rapidly. Rather than walking into a physical store to rent DVDs, consumers fancied the idea of browsing DVDs on the web and having them delivered to their doorsteps at a palatable subscription fee minus the late fee that Blockbuster was infamous for. Capitalizing on digital disruption and changing customer demands, several new players emerged in the video rental space, such as Netflix and RedBox, offering newer channels such as DVD-by-mail and online streaming services. Despite the shift in consumer demand, digital disruption, and mounting competition, Blockbuster did little to change its strategy and refused to adapt to changing market trends. Ironically, in the year 2000, Blockbuster turned down an offer to acquire Netflix for USD 50 million, which subsequently led to Blockbuster filing for bankruptcy within the decade [2].

The primary factors attributed to the downfall of Blockbuster are the following:

- **Failure to embrace the digital disruption**: Blockbuster was comfortable with the existing business model and failed to recognize the shift in industry trends and customer needs and preferences, leading them to dismiss the potential of online rentals and streaming services, which ultimately disrupted the traditional brick-and-mortar video rental model. The company was too slow to adapt to the emerging trends such as online subscription and streaming services, whereas competitors such as Netflix were already capitalizing on digital technologies to offer convenience and accessibility to consumers, causing a dent in Blockbuster's market share.

- **Failure to create customer value**: Blockbuster misplaced its focus on topline revenue rather than creating consumer value. The company failed to generate consumer value while heavily relying on maximizing profits and revenue by charging loyal customers late fees. It also failed to assess the significant consumer value that could be generated by adopting modern digital trends. Competitors such as Netflix offered greater convenience, broader content libraries, personalized recommendations, and subscription models that resonated with consumers. Blockbuster struggled to match the offerings and value propositions offered by its competitors.

- **Poor strategic decisions**: Blockbuster made several strategic missteps that further exacerbated its decline. For instance, the company passed on an opportunity to acquire Netflix in its early stages, underestimating the potential of the emerging business model. Blockbuster also pursued late-entry initiatives such as DVD kiosks and online streaming, but these efforts failed to regain lost ground.

There have been several technological innovations that transformed the world forever, from the invention of paper to penicillin and electricity. However, the inventions of the last century, such as airplanes (1903), television (1927), VCRs (1965), personal computers (1971), cellular phones (1973), the internet (1983), the World Wide Web (1989), portable GPS (1990), Google Search (1997), Facebook (2004), YouTube (2005), the iPhone (2007), and Android (2008), have democratized technology advancements to the masses.

Another technological advancement that is fundamentally altering the way businesses innovate is artificial intelligence (AI). In 1950, Alan Turing, in his seminal paper titled *Computing Machinery and Intelligence*, opened with a thought-provoking question, "*Can machines think?*" [3]. Since then, AI has undergone rapid evolution and has matured into a disruptive technology that is having a profound impact on almost every industry. AI is powering creative applications, including autonomous vehicles, robotic surgery, fraud detection, and generative AI that creates new art, to name a few.

If we map these disruptive technologies against the time it took for them to penetrate the market, technological advancements in recent times, such as personal computers, the internet, mobiles, social media, and digital payments, only needed a quarter of the time to permeate the market compared to the innovations of previous generations [4]. In fact, modern technology disruptions are only growing exponentially, forcing enterprises across industries to keep up or lag behind [5]. It is important to note that the modern technology innovations of the digital era (highlighted area in the chart below) have exponentially penetrated the world market:

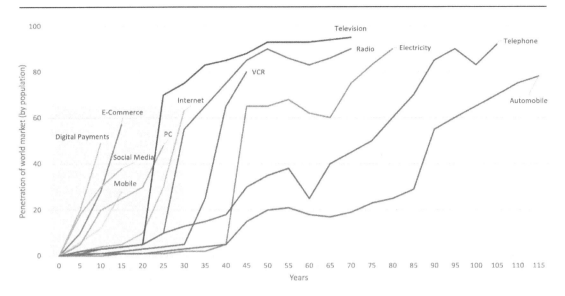

Figure 1.1 – Technological innovations and the time taken to penetrate the world market

Let's compare two revolutionary technological advancements - the automobile and mobile phones. The invention of the automobile disrupted the way we travel, and the invention of mobile phones transformed not just how people communicate but also how modern-day businesses are conducted. Since its invention in the late 19th century, it took the automobile industry over six decades to penetrate the market and become established, versus the advent of mobile phones, which only took a decade. Modern-day technologies evolve at a rapid pace, and it is crucial for organizations to stay relevant.

For mobile device manufacturers, it wasn't easy to stay abreast of the fast-paced technological advancements and the exponential disruption in communication technology at the turn of every decade: analog cellular (1G), digital cellular (2G), mobile broadband (3G), native IP networks (4G), and new radio (5G); traditional providers, such as Nokia and Motorola, who once commanded significant market share, were phased out by new entrants such as Samsung and Apple [6].

Innovation is NOT optional

Many long-standing enterprises find it difficult to generate organic growth, with younger companies outperforming established players. To put this in context, the average tenure of an S&P 500 company has been declining as the speed of digital disruption is accelerating [7]. In the late 1970s, the average age of an S&P 500 was 35 years, and this number is predicted to further decline to just 12 years by 2027.

Organizations that have stood the test of time amidst digital disruption have adopted strategies that evolve continuously to help them withstand more fluid or uncertain market times. It doesn't take much for a new entrant or a startup to come up with an idea that disrupts an entire industry. Let's look at a few companies that veered off traditional methods and revolutionized their respective industries:

- **Airbnb**, founded in 2008, is one of the largest accommodation platforms that disrupted the hospitality industry. While traditional hospitality companies owned, maintained, and operated properties, Airbnb revolutionized the tourism industry by serving as an online marketplace for short-term homestays and holiday experiences.

- **Uber**, founded in 2009, is the largest ride-sharing company that disrupted the car rental and leasing industry. While traditional car rental companies owned and leased cars to customers, Uber changed the dynamic by offering ride-shares through just a mobile app.

- **Netflix**, founded in 1997, started as a DVD rental business and is now the largest streaming platform that has transformed the way consumers rent and watch movies and TV shows. While Netflix does produce its own movies and TV shows, it primarily leases movies and TV shows that can be streamed on its platform.

- **Amazon**, founded in 1994 as an online marketplace for books, is the largest online retailer by simply serving as a marketplace platform connecting buyers and sellers, revolutionizing the retail industry, whereas traditional retailers have to own and operate a physical brick-and-mortar store and manage inventory. Since then, Amazon transformed itself into a conglomerate and expanded into several industries.

- **Spotify**, founded in 2006, is the largest music streaming service but doesn't own any music. Instead, it licenses music from record labels and lets subscribers stream it for a fee.

- **Robinhood**, founded in 2013, disrupted the financial services industry by offering commission-free trades of stocks and exchange-traded funds and cryptocurrencies, which was never thought possible before. Robinhood democratized trading through a simple mobile app.

- **Teladoc**, founded in 2002, is one of the largest telehealth companies that disrupted the healthcare industry by leveraging mobile technology to connect patients and doctors virtually anytime outside of a healthcare facility. Unlike traditional healthcare providers, Teladoc doesn't employ doctors or have its healthcare facilities.

- **Pillpack**, founded in 2013, disrupted the pharmaceutical industry that was traditionally dominated by retail players that operated in a physical space, filling prescriptions for patients. Pillpack ideated and implemented the concept of consolidating multiple pill prescriptions and delivering it to customers' doorsteps.

- **Chime**, founded in 2012, is a challenger bank that offers banking services exclusively through online and mobile, disrupting the banking industry by offering fee-free banking, early paydays, no fee, and no credit check credit cards, forcing traditional players to respond.

- **Rent the Runway**, founded in 2009, is a clothing rental company that disrupted the designer clothing industry by allowing customers to rent, subscribe, or buy designer clothes through their online platform. This business model addressed a major consumer concern of overspending and having to own apparel such as event garments, wedding dresses, and ski apparel, which are infrequently used.

One commonality across all these companies is that business disruption is almost always led by modern digital technology. Let us explore how enterprises can innovate and move up the digital frontier.

The innovation continuum

Contrary to the belief that innovation happens in a siloed, vacuum environment, it is actually a systemic and continual process. Innovation requires not only the generation of new ideas but also the implementation and sustained adoption of those ideas. This often involves overcoming significant barriers and challenges, such as resistance to change, regulatory hurdles, or technical limitations. It also requires a systematic approach to identifying and addressing customer needs, understanding market trends, and leveraging available resources and expertise.

Leaders must strive to create a culture and a systematic approach to a culture of innovation. An innovation continuum is critical for enterprises to thrive and grow in today's competitive landscape. The process of innovation is a set of strategic steps where an organization can take creative approaches to realize its vision, goals, and objectives within a timeline [8]. The following diagram illustrates the stages of the innovation continuum:

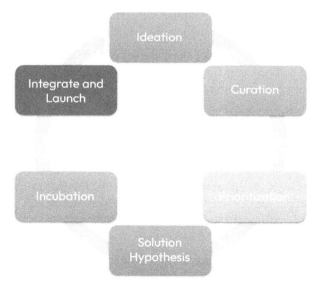

Figure 1.2 – The innovation continuum

Let's take a look at each of the stages shown in the preceding diagram:

1. **Ideation**: This is the initial stage of the innovation process, where new ideas are sourced and generated through brainstorming, market research, customer feedback, or other sources. The goal is to identify potential areas for innovation and generate a variety of ideas that can be explored further.

2. **Curation**: Once a promising idea has been identified, the next step is to curate and develop a concept around the ideas that can be tested and ratified. This can involve the following:

   - Stakeholder surveys (internal or external) to identify problem areas in different forms

   - Explore and identify solutions that are available both internally and commercially

   - Identify the stakeholders of the product in consideration

   - Build out MVPs (minimum viable product) prototypes or a proof-of-concept

   - Determine the viability of the idea across multiple dimensions, such as financial, technological, legal, and security dimensions, and its measurable potential impact

   Ideas that pass curation move onto the prioritization phase, and the ones that don't are moved to the back burner.

3. **Prioritization**: This is an important step where curated ideas get prioritized based on a variety of factors, including customer or market demands, technology, competitive intel, and applicability to core business capability vs. exploratory considerations. Some popular methods that enterprises can leverage are McKinsey's three horizons model, a portfolio of initiatives, a strategic control map, and a consumer decision journey [9]. Each of these methods caters to different kinds of prioritization factors that influence decision-making.

4. **Solution hypothesis**: At this stage, the concept is tested and evaluated to determine its feasibility, usability, and market potential. This can involve assessing product viability, business value, opportunity cost, customer or stakeholder value, and return on investment.

5. **Incubation and development**: Once the concept is deemed feasible and viable, the next step is to develop and implement the technology incrementally. This may involve further building out the MVP, designing the product, building the software, securing sponsorship, leadership oversight, and funding, and developing the infrastructure needed to support the innovation.

6. **Integrate, launch, and scale**: Once the technology has been developed, the next step is to integrate, launch, and scale to reach a wider audience. This may involve marketing and promotion, building partnerships, incremental releases, or expanding the product's capabilities to meet the evolving needs of the market.

As every enterprise is unique, leaders in enterprises can choose the appropriate innovation strategy that best fits their vision and objectives. However, it is crucial to create a culture of innovation and put in place a process that drives it. Several modern enterprises have created and funded R&D departments and innovation labs with a primary focus on industry research, technology research, and viability assessment. Leadership sponsorship is key to ensuring innovation centers do not operate in a silo and are embedded into the organizational structure. Let us explore the tales of two enterprises and how leadership played a crucial role in leading the digital disruption and the need to constantly innovate.

Two tales of leadership, will, and mindset

In 1880, George Eastman, in partnership with Henry A. Strong, founded the Eastman Dry Plate Company with the purpose of selling dry plates for cameras. Within the decade, the company introduced a new film roll process, filed multiple patents, and revolutionized the photography industry by democratizing photographic film products to virtually everyone. By 1888, the company introduced a portable box camera that came with a film roll of 100 exposures, and in 1892, what would eventually become a common household name (Kodak), then known as the Eastman Kodak Company was born.

For much of the 20th century, Kodak dominated the photographic industry and became one of the world's leading manufacturers of photographic film and cameras. In the early years, Kodak expanded rapidly and was able to keep competitors at bay via a combination of innovation, acquisitions, and exclusive contracts. The company was able to successfully navigate the great depression, both World War I and II, and expanded into producing cameras and films for the movie industry, cameras for surveillance satellites, and NASA space missions. From the 1930s until the 1970s, Kodak reigned supreme and enjoyed a monopoly in the photographic films and cameras business. The company's business model remained unchanged, with R&D focused solely on photographic films and cameras, as the company enjoyed an enviable market share.

In 1934, 6,000 miles across the planet, from the land of the rising sun, a photography and imaging company was established with the objective of producing photographic films. The company entered a market that was already dominated by Kodak in the US. However, Fujifilm enjoyed a supreme market position in camera films in Japan. During the same period when Kodak was still reigning supreme, holding its grip primarily focused on photographic films and cameras, Fujifilm started diversifying, producing films for photography, motion pictures, and X-rays, and after World War II, it further diversified into medical technology in fields such as X-ray diagnosis, electronic imaging, and magnetic materials.

In the 1980s, Fujifilm entered the US market with lower-priced film and photographic supplies, threatening Kodak's position in the market. Soon enough, Fujifilm made strong headways and took significant market share from Kodak by opening manufacturing plants in the US, employing strategies such as aggressive marketing and price cuts. This started a price war and started eating into Kodak's profits, reducing shareholder value. This was exacerbated by Fujifilm winning the bid for the official film of the 1984 Olympics in Los Angeles, giving the company a strong foothold in the world market. This period also saw Fujilfim innovating continuously in other markets. For instance, the invention of **computed radiography** (**CR**) revolutionized the medical equipment industry and solved major challenges regarding increased radiation exposure to both technicians and patients, which was conventionally attributed to traditional radiography.

By the dawn of the 21st century, the new millennium witnessed the exponential growth of digital technology. Demand for digital cameras caused a swift decline in photographic films, requiring a change in strategy to cater to new market demands. In the early 2000s, Fujifilm also faced increasing competition from modern digital photographic companies.

In response to this challenge, Fujifilm focused on business transformation and embarked on a digital transformation journey. The company invested heavily in new technologies, such as digital imaging and healthcare, and began to diversify its product portfolio. Under the leadership of Shigetaka Komori (2003–2021), Fujifilm underwent a bold structural reform and strategically acquired companies in chemical, healthcare, and electronics to diversify and complement Fujifilm's business model. He was instrumental in overseeing Fujifilm through the decline of the photo film industry and transforming it into a healthcare, medical, and office equipment maker. Under Komori's leadership, the company looked at the fields to which its expertise in chemical technology could be adapted and started acquiring companies that would complement its business. They moved into digital X-rays and endoscopes, gaining a 70% world market share of tac film, an essential component of all LCD screens. Another area the company pursued was cosmetics, and it launched an anti-aging skincare line in 2007, which helped expand Fujifilm cosmetics worldwide. As a result of these efforts, Fujifilm has been able to successfully transition to the digital age and maintain its position as a leading global conglomerate.

Kodak's response to the digital challenge of the 21st century was quite different. With Antonio M. Perez at the helm, Kodak, in 2005, began outsourcing development and manufacturing, which were originally done in-house, and divesting its digital camera manufacturing and operations. By 2007, Kodak succumbed to competitive pressures, exited the film camera market entirely, and started investing heavily in a potential high-margin printer ink business. This was a departure from the razor and blades business model that was a cornerstone of Kodak's business strategy. However, Kodak eventually exited the inkjet market owing to pressures from dominant players such as Hewlett-Packard. Kodak was removed from the S&P 500 in 2010 and, with declining profits, ultimately filed for bankruptcy in 2012. Since the bankruptcy, Kodak has been trying to diversify into other markets, such as pharmaceutical materials and digital printing products and services, with mixed outcomes.

To understand how deep Kodak's denial of the upcoming digital disruption was, in the 1980s, Kodak conducted extensive research on technology advancements and the potential of digital photography to take over film technology. The results showed that digital technology was poised to disrupt Kodak's bread-and-butter film business. The good news was that the change would be gradual, giving Kodak the opportunity to adapt and transition. Kodak did little to prepare for this despite the results of the study. To put this into perspective, under the leadership of George Eastman, Kodak took the technology disruptions head on: first, when they let go of the lucrative dry-plate business to move to film roll technology, and second, when they adopted color photo films despite having a dominant position with black and white film technology [10].

In perspective, Kodak's failure can be attributed to its oversight of capitalizing on the digital disruption opportunity, its over-reliance on brand marketing, banking on acquisitions for expansion into newer territories, and, more importantly, the failure to embrace an innovation continuum for several decades at the turn of the century, at a time when it was most needed. On the contrary, Fujifilm capitalized on the digital revolution opportunity and continued innovating ahead of the market and diversifying into other markets where its chemical expertise was complimentary, leading the digital transformation [11].

The primary factors in Fujifilm's successful digital transformation were the following:

- **Innovation continuum**: Fujifilm had a long history of research and development, and it continued to invest heavily in new technologies. This unwavering focus on innovation allowed Fujifilm to stay ahead of the competition, gain market share in new territories, and develop new products and services that met the needs of its customers.

- **Visionary leadership**: Fujifilm has been led by a strong and visionary leadership team that has been able to guide the company through the digital transformation process.

- **Employee engagement**: Fujifilm has been able to successfully engage its employees in the digital transformation process. This has been achieved through a number of initiatives, such as employee training and development programs and employee feedback mechanisms.

- **Customer focus**: Fujifilm's unwavering focus on customers has been a key factor in its success in the digital transformation process. The company has been able to understand the needs of its customers and develop products and services that meet those needs.

- **Financial resources**: Fujifilm leveraged its financial resources to invest in the digital transformation process. This has allowed the company to invest in new technologies, hire top talent, and develop new products and services.

- **A commitment to sustainability**: Fujifilm has a long history of environmental stewardship, and it has continued to invest in sustainable technologies and practices. This commitment to sustainability has helped Fujifilm to reduce its environmental impact and improve its bottom line.

In the next section, we will investigate how enterprises can lead digital transformation.

Leading the digital transformation of enterprise

Leadership is the cornerstone and an indispensable element for a successful digital transformation within any organization. Whether the aim is to perform incremental digitization, enter new markets, or launch new products, leadership involvement is quintessential. Leading digital transformation involves creating a vision for how technology can be leveraged to drive innovation, improve efficiency, and enhance customer experiences. Good leaders empower their teams to break through roadblocks, paint the big picture, and keep the teams strategically aligned toward organizational growth, value creation, and competitiveness. Using modern technology as an instrument for business growth continues to be the foundation of every enterprise's business strategy. However, the evolution of modern technology is exponential, and enterprises need to stay nimble and agile in order to adapt and execute a successful digital transformation.

Cloud technology has become a synonymous term for **digital** in enterprise digital transformation. According to the KPMG technology survey, 80% of organizations said their cloud-enabled transformations have been successful [*12*]. However, only one-third realized substantial **return on investment (ROI)** from their cloud investments. Cloud was positioned as a driver toward enterprise IT cost savings, but two-thirds of organizations still couldn't realize a substantial ROI, which is counterintuitive.

Figure 1.3 – The enterprise digital transformation pillars

Let's explore the core pillars and the key constituents in leading and executing a successful digital transformation of an enterprise:

- **Vision and strategy**: A well-defined strategy and vision serve as foundational guiding principles for digital transformation. They provide a sense of purpose, ensure alignment, foster stakeholder engagement, enable adaptability, and facilitate the measurement of progress. By establishing a strong strategy and vision, organizations can drive their digital transformation efforts with clarity, focus, and purpose, increasing the likelihood of achieving their desired outcomes. A lack of strategy and vision is one of the most common reasons why digital transformation initiatives fail. As with any large transformative initiative, it takes a village to march towards the North Star. Leadership, will, and mindset are crucial to the success of any digital transformation initiative. It is imperative for leaders who are responsible for digital transformation to establish a clear vision, lay out a strategic roadmap, secure partnerships across business stakeholders, and, more importantly, ensure the vision is clearly communicated to everyone within the organization. Without a clear understanding of what the organization wants to achieve with digital transformation and how it plans to get there, teams end up working on siloed objectives instead of working towards the larger objective, resulting in fractured digital transformation.

Lack of strategy and vision in a digital transformation can be a huge challenge for enterprises seeking to leverage technology to drive organic growth, improve efficiency, and stay competitive. Digital transformation is not just about implementing modern technologies; it also requires a clear strategy and vision from leaders on how these technologies will be integrated within an enterprise to achieve specific business goals. There are several reasons why enterprises may lack a clear strategy and vision when embarking on a digital transformation journey, including a lack of time or resources to develop a comprehensive plan, a lack of consensus among senior leaders about the organization's strategy, and a lack of will to undertake digital transformation. Irrespective of this, a lack of strategy and vision can have a devastating impact on an organization's digital transformation efforts, leading to wasted time, money, and resources, derailing the entire transformation effort.

Some of the key constituents in defining a strategy and vision for a digital transformation are the following:

- **Clarity of purpose**: Clarity of vision and strategy provides a clear direction and purpose for a successful digital transformation. They define the goals, objectives, and desired outcomes of the digital transformation journey. A well-defined strategy and vision help align stakeholders and employees around a common understanding of why the transformation is necessary and what it aims to achieve.

- **Alignment of efforts**: Having a clear digital strategy ensures that all initiatives and activities related to digital transformation are aligned with the overall strategic objectives of the organization. They guide decision-making, resource allocation, and priority-setting, enabling a co-ordinated and cohesive approach. This alignment maximizes the impact of digital initiatives and avoids fragmentation or conflicting efforts.

- **Future orientation**: Defining a digital strategy enables enterprises to focus on the future state of the organization and its desired position in the digital landscape by taking into account emerging technologies, market trends, and customer expectations to drive innovation and prepare the organization for long-term success. By envisioning the future, organizations can proactively shape their digital transformation efforts and stay ahead of the competition.

- **Stakeholder engagement**: Digital leaders must engage stakeholders across the organization to create a shared understanding of the digital transformation journey. This helps provide a compelling narrative that inspires and motivates employees, customers, partners, and investors. Clear communication of the strategy and vision fosters trust, encourages participation, and generates support and commitment from stakeholders.

- **Focus and prioritization**: Digital transformation often involves a multitude of opportunities as well as challenges. Having a clear strategy and vision enables organizations to prioritize initiatives and investments based on their alignment with the overall objectives. More importantly it helps in filtering out distractions, avoiding the *shiny object* syndrome, and ensuring that resources are directed towards the most impactful digital initiatives.

- **Manage resistance to change**: Digital transformation often requires significant changes in terms of processes, technologies, and organizational culture. A well-defined digital strategy provides a framework for change management, guiding the organization through the transition. It helps communicate the rationale for change, manage resistance, and create a sense of urgency and purpose among employees.

- **Adaptability and agility**: A digital strategy framework must strive to provide a strategic roadmap while allowing for flexibility and adaptability by setting overarching goals while also leaving room for experimentation, learning, and adjustment along the way. This agility enables organizations to respond to market dynamics, emerging technologies, and customer needs, ensuring digital transformation remains relevant and effective.

- **Basis for measurement**: As the saying goes, "*If you cannot measure it*", you cannot improve *it*; a well-defined digital strategy provides a basis for measuring the progress and success of digital transformation. Establishing **Key Performance Indicators** (**KPIs**) and milestones helps track the effectiveness and impact of digital initiatives and data-driven decision-making, as well as promote accountability and transparency and demonstrate value. Regular evaluation that is compared to the strategy and vision allows organizations to correct their course, celebrate successes, and identify areas for improvement.

- **Business–IT alignment**: The success of an organization's digital transformation hinges on the ability of leadership to effectively integrate its business strategy and goals with its IT capabilities and resources. The lack of alignment between business and IT is a common problem in many organizations and can lead to siloed thinking, duplication of effort, missed opportunities, inefficient processes, resistance to change, and a reduction in an organization's business agility. Digital transformation requires a clear alignment between business objectives and IT capabilities. When business and IT strategies are aligned, it ensures that technology investments and initiatives directly contribute to achieving the organization's goals and helps prioritize IT initiatives that have the greatest impact on business outcomes, improving overall strategic decision-making.

The following are the key constituents enterprise leaders must facilitate to ensure business-IT alignment:

- **Collaboration and communication**: It is quintessential for IT and business to communicate and collaborate to achieve the larger enterprise vision. Business–IT alignment fosters effective collaboration and communication between business and IT stakeholders. It breaks down silos and encourages cross-functional teamwork, enabling a shared understanding of goals, requirements, and challenges. This collaboration enhances the overall project delivery and fosters a culture of innovation and continuous improvement.

- **Seamless integration**: Digital transformation often involves implementing new technologies, systems, and processes across the organization. Business–IT alignment ensures a smooth integration of these digital solutions into the existing business infrastructure and, more importantly, allows for efficient collaboration between business stakeholders and IT teams, minimizing disruptions and maximizing the benefits of technology implementation.

- **Business agility**: Alignment between business and IT enables organizations to be more agile and responsive to changing market conditions and customer needs. When IT teams understand the business priorities and can quickly adapt technology solutions to support evolving requirements, the organization can capitalize on new opportunities and address challenges more effectively.

- **Customer experience**: Customer centricity is a fundamental aspect of any digital transformation. Business–IT alignment helps organizations better understand customer expectations and enables the development and implementation of digital solutions that enhance the overall customer experience. By aligning IT capabilities with business goals, organizations can leverage technology to deliver personalized, seamless, and value-added experiences to their customers.

- **Efficient resource allocation**: Business–IT alignment ensures that technology investments are aligned with business priorities and objectives. It helps to optimize resource allocation, ensuring that IT investments are focused on initiatives that have the highest impact on business performance. This prevents unnecessary spending on technology projects that do not align with the organization's strategic goals. For example, it prevents IT teams from developing solutions that do not align with business needs or business teams from investing in point solutions or technologies that are not aligned with the company's strategic goals.

- **Effective change management**: Digital transformation often requires significant changes in business processes, roles, and workflows. Business–IT alignment facilitates effective change management by ensuring that business stakeholders are engaged and involved in the digital transformation journey. When both business and IT teams work together, it promotes a shared understanding of the transformation goals and helps to address resistance to change.

- **Innovation and competitive advantage**: Business–IT alignment fosters a collaborative environment where innovation can thrive. It encourages the exploration and adoption of emerging technologies that can give the organization a competitive edge. By aligning business and IT strategies, organizations can identify innovative opportunities and leverage technology to drive differentiation and create new business models.

- **Scalability and future readiness**: Digital transformation is an ongoing journey, and organizations need to be prepared for future changes and advancements in technology. Business–IT alignment ensures that technology decisions are made with scalability and future readiness in mind. It enables organizations to adapt and evolve their technology infrastructure to meet future demands and capitalize on emerging opportunities.

- **Stakeholder satisfaction**: When business and IT teams work together cohesively, it improves stakeholder satisfaction. Customers, employees, and other stakeholders benefit from seamless digital experiences, efficient processes, and innovative solutions. Business–IT alignment helps with meeting and exceeding expectations, resulting in higher satisfaction and loyalty.

- **Capitalize on opportunities**: A lack of alignment between business and IT can result in missed opportunities. For example, if a business team is not aware of the latest technological advances, it may miss an opportunity to leverage these technologies to improve its operations or gain a competitive advantage, and IT teams may overlook opportunities that can offer a significant business edge.

- **Risk mitigation and security**: Digital transformation brings new risks and challenges, such as cybersecurity threats and data privacy concerns. Business–IT alignment ensures that security and risk management are integrated into the digital transformation initiatives from the outset. By aligning business requirements with IT security measures, organizations can proactively mitigate risks and protect valuable assets.

Overall, business–IT alignment is critical for digital transformation because it enables organizations to effectively leverage technology to achieve their strategic objectives. It promotes collaboration, agility, customer centricity, efficient resource allocation, and innovation, ultimately leading to improved business performance and a competitive advantage in the digital age. This may involve establishing cross-functional teams, developing shared goals and metrics, and investing in training and development to improve understanding between business and IT.

- **Customer focus**: Digital transformation is an ongoing journey and provides an opportunity for businesses to innovate and create new value for customers. Adaptability and responsiveness to customer needs are crucial to maintaining relevancy and staying ahead of the competition. However, without a customer focus, businesses may prioritize internal efficiency or technology-driven initiatives that are not targeted toward customer-driven innovation. This can limit the ability to identify and seize opportunities for disruptive or transformative solutions that truly address customer pain points and deliver meaningful value. Digital transformation that lacks customer focus can have several negative consequences, including missed customer expectations, a loss of competitive edge, disconnected customer experiences, and negative brand perception. The following are some key areas enterprises must focus on to ensure organizational digital initiatives are customer-centric:

  - **Meeting customer demands**: Digital transformation is driven by changing customer expectations and behaviors. Customers today expect seamless and personalized experiences across multiple channels, faster response times, and easy access to information and services. By putting the customer at the center of digital transformation efforts, businesses can better meet these expectations and enhance customer satisfaction.

  - **Customer experience**: Digital transformation provides opportunities to optimize and improve the customer experience. By leveraging digital technologies, companies can streamline processes, automate tasks, and provide self-service options, resulting in faster and more efficient interactions with customers. A customer-focused approach ensures that digital initiatives are designed with the end-user in mind, leading to a more intuitive and enjoyable customer experience.

- **Customer loyalty and retention**: A customer-centric digital transformation strategy helps build customer loyalty and encourages repeat business. By understanding customer needs, preferences, and pain points, businesses can tailor their digital offerings and experiences to create value for customers. This leads to increased customer satisfaction, loyalty, and advocacy, ultimately driving higher customer retention rates.

- **Competitive edge**: In today's digital landscape, customer experience has become a key differentiator among competitors. By prioritizing customer focus in digital transformation efforts, businesses can gain a competitive edge. By delivering superior digital experiences, companies can attract new customers, retain existing ones, and differentiate themselves in the market.

- **Driving innovation and agility**: A customer-centric approach in digital transformation encourages innovation and agility. By actively seeking customer feedback and leveraging data and insights, businesses can identify new opportunities, develop innovative products and services, and quickly adapt to changing customer needs and market dynamics.

- **New revenue streams**: A customer-focused digital transformation strategy can help businesses identify new revenue streams. By understanding customer needs and preferences, businesses can uncover opportunities to develop and offer additional products, services, or experiences that meet those needs. This opens up avenues for revenue growth and expansion into new markets.

- **Mitigate the threat of business disruption**: By prioritizing customer focus, businesses can mitigate the risk of losing customers to disruptive competitors. Understanding customer preferences and anticipating their future needs allows companies to proactively innovate and adapt their digital strategies. By embracing digital transformation and providing customer-centric experiences, businesses can safeguard against disruption and maintain a competitive advantage.

- **Employee engagement**: Customer focus extends beyond external interactions; it also includes fostering a customer-centric culture internally. When employees understand the importance of customer satisfaction and feel empowered to contribute to improving the customer experience, they become more engaged and motivated. Engaged employees are more likely to deliver exceptional customer service and contribute to the success of digital transformation initiatives.

Unwavering customer focus is an essential ingredient in driving digital transformation, as it helps enterprises align their efforts with customer expectations, enhance consumer experiences, drive loyalty, gain a competitive edge, foster innovation, and make data-driven decisions. By putting the customer at the center of digital transformation initiatives, enterprises can create sustainable business success in the digital era.

- **Organizational culture**: As Henry Ford famously said, "*Vision without execution is just hallucination.*" Enterprise digital transformation is a journey, and visionary leaders need to build the right organization with the right culture and mindset to get it right. Leadership plays a crucial role in driving and sustaining an innovative culture. Leaders need to demonstrate their commitment to innovation through actions and should actively support and participate in innovation initiatives, allocate resources, and provide a safe environment for experimentation and risk-taking. Leadership support sets the tone for the entire organization and sends a powerful message about the importance of innovation.

Creating a culture of innovation requires a supportive environment that encourages and nurtures creative thinking, experimentation, and continuous improvement. While the specific structure can vary depending on the organization's size, industry, and goals, here are some key elements to consider when building an organization for a culture of innovation:

- **Foster a learning mindset**: Cultivating a mindset where employees are encouraged to continuously learn, explore, and seek new ideas or opportunities is essential to organizational growth. Leaders must ensure access to learning and development opportunities, both internally and externally, to help employees develop the skills and knowledge needed for innovation, enable a blameless culture, and encourage employees to take calculated risks.

- **Cross-functional collaboration**: Breaking down silos and promoting cross-functional collaboration is crucial for a successful digital transformation, as it fosters the cross-pollination of best practices and lessons learned from earlier initiatives without having to reinvent the wheel and also prevents resource wastage. Encouraging employees from different departments and backgrounds to collaborate, share ideas, and work together on innovation projects, establishing mechanisms for seamless communication and knowledge-sharing, such as innovation workshops, showcase days, brainstorming sessions, and digital collaboration tools, will ensure an agile organization.

- **Empower and involve employees**: Empowering employees with the autonomy to explore new ideas, make decisions, and experiment with different approaches can accelerate innovation within an enterprise. Involving employees in decision-making processes, soliciting inputs, and creating channels for sharing ideas and suggestions, thus recognizing and rewarding employees for their innovative contributions, will reinforce the value an organization has placed on innovation.

- **Resources and support**: Allocate resources, both financial and non-financial, to support innovation initiatives. This includes providing dedicated time, budgets, and access to the tools and technologies necessary for innovation. Create an infrastructure that supports innovation, such as innovation labs, prototyping facilities, or collaborative spaces where employees can collaborate, experiment, and test new ideas.

- **Encourage external engagement**: Fostering connections with external partners, such as leaders in technology, startups, universities, or industry experts, will help broaden a team's perspective and understand market trends. External engagements such as collaborating on innovation projects, participating in industry events, and engaging in knowledge exchange promote fresh perspectives, access to new ideas and technologies, and opportunities for the cross-pollination of knowledge.

- **Feedback loop**: Implementing feedback loops and mechanisms for collecting and acting upon ideas and suggestions from employees can create a culture where employees feel comfortable sharing their thoughts and feedback and contributing to the innovation process. Leaders must strive to regularly evaluate and respond to employee feedback to demonstrate that their input is valued and taken seriously.

- **Continuous improvement**: Building a culture of innovation should be construed as an ongoing process within the organization, where approaches, strategies, and initiatives are continuously assessed and refined. Soliciting feedback from employees and stakeholders helps identify areas for improvement and encourages a mindset of continuous improvement and adaptability as you strive to create a thriving culture of innovation.

- **Measure everything**: Measuring the progress and impact of digital transformation is essential to assess the effectiveness of initiatives and ensure they are aligned with larger organizational goals. The inability to measure the impact and progress of digital transformation initiatives can have several downsides, including a lack of visibility into any effectiveness, the inability to identify bottlenecks, diluted accountability, and missed opportunities and lessons. While digital transformation can be complex and multifaceted, here are some approaches commonly used to measure digital transformation:

  - **Digital maturity assessments**: Often, the first step in a digital transformation strategy is to assess the current state of the enterprise across multiple dimensions, including organizational maturity, digital adoption rates, customer metrics, and IT maturity. Conducting assessments periodically helps enterprise leaders evaluate the organization's current digital capabilities, compare them to industry benchmarks and the competitive landscape, and provide an opportunity to improve incrementally. We will discuss maturity assessments in more detail in *Chapter 8*.

  - **Digital adoption rates**: Although we have explored the importance of Business and IT alignment, equally critical is the measurement of the level of user adoption and usage of digital technologies. Measuring adoption rates will ensure that IT organizations don't chase the next shiny object or spend time on innovations that can lead to tech debt. This can include tracking metrics such as the number of active users on digital platforms, the percentage of employees trained in digital skills, and the utilization rates of digital tools and systems.

  - **Customer experience metrics**: Every digital transformation effort must put the user right and center. For instance, the **objective and key results** (**OKRs**) must be defined according to **critical user journey** (**CUJ**) outcomes that can be measured qualitatively and quantitatively. Assessing the impact of digital transformation on customer experience provides a great insight into the effectiveness of the initiative. This can include monitoring metrics such as customer satisfaction scores, **net promoter score** (**NPS**), customer feedback and reviews, customer retention rates, and customer lifetime value.

  - **Employee engagement and enablement**: For successful digital transformation initiatives, leaders must ensure teams are involved and are committed to the objective, as employee engagement is critical. Measuring the level of employee engagement and their ability to embrace digital transformation provides leadership insights into skill gaps and the motivations of the teams. This can be assessed through surveys, feedback sessions, and metrics such as employee satisfaction scores, employee retention rates, employee contributions to thought leadership, and participation in digital upskilling programs.

- **Innovation and agility metrics**: Assessing an organization's ability to innovate and adapt to changes in the digital landscape is an essential performance indicator of an organization's business agility. This can involve metrics such as the number of new digital initiatives or projects launched, the time taken to bring new digital products or services to market, the success rate of digital innovation initiatives, and the level of agility in responding to market trends and customer needs.

- **Financial performance**: Monitoring financial indicators to gauge the impact of initiatives can serve as a powerful tool to sustain and embark on the continuous journey of digital transformation. This can also help stakeholders with clear insights into how budgets are spent, yielding value. This can include metrics such as revenue growth, profitability, ROI from digital initiatives, and **total cost of ownership** (**TCO**) savings from process optimization or automation. Mature organizations will often tie in financial value metrics for every digital transformation initiative.

- **Environmental, social, and governance** (**ESG**): ESG considerations are increasingly becoming critical in the context of digital transformation. Enterprise leaders play a vital role in shaping and guiding digital transformation efforts to ensure that digital transformation is pursued in a responsible, inclusive, and sustainable manner, taking into account environmental impact, social implications, ethical governance, stakeholder expectations, risk management, and long-term value creation. By integrating ESG principles into digital transformation strategies, organizations can drive positive change, mitigate risks, and enhance their overall impact on society and the environment. Let's explore some considerations for enterprises as it pertains to responsible digital innovation. However, we will delve into how ESG impacts enterprise innovation in greater detail in *Chapter 11*.

  - **Environmental sustainability**: Digital transformation can have both positive and negative environmental impacts. On the positive side, it offers opportunities for organizations to leverage modern digital technologies to optimize resource consumption, reduce energy usage, and promote sustainable practices. However, digital transformation also brings challenges such as increased electronic waste, energy consumption (by data centers), and carbon emissions. Incorporating ESG principles into the core of digital transformation ensures that initiatives prioritize environmental sustainability by minimizing negative impacts and maximizing positive contributions.

  - **Social impact and inclusion**: Digital transformation has the potential to drive positive social impact by promoting inclusivity, accessibility, and equality. ESG considerations ensure that digital transformation initiatives address social challenges and contribute to societal well-being. For example, organizations can leverage technology to enhance access to education, healthcare, and financial services for underserved communities. ESG also encourages ethical considerations such as data privacy, security, and the responsible use of emerging technologies, such as artificial intelligence, to avoid bias and discrimination.

- **Ethical governance and accountability**: ESG principles emphasize the importance of ethical governance and accountability in digital transformation. Organizations need to establish robust governance frameworks to ensure the responsible use of technology, protect stakeholders' data privacy, and mitigate the risks associated with emerging technologies. ESG provides a lens to assess the governance practices, transparency, and accountability of organizations in their digital transformation efforts.

- **Long-term value creation**: Digital transformation is not just about short-term gains; it should focus on creating long-term value for all stakeholders. ESG considerations provide a framework to evaluate the broader impacts of digital transformation beyond financial metrics. By considering environmental and social aspects alongside governance, organizations can align their digital transformation initiatives with sustainable business practices and generate long-term value that goes beyond immediate financial returns.

- **Stakeholder expectations and reputation**: Stakeholders, including customers, employees, investors, and regulators, increasingly expect organizations to demonstrate commitment to ESG principles. Failure to address ESG considerations in digital transformation can result in reputational damage, impact on consumer brands, and regulatory scrutiny. Embracing ESG principles as part of digital transformation efforts helps build trust and loyalty among stakeholders, enhancing the organization's reputation and long-term sustainability.

- **Investor and financial considerations**: ESG has gained significant attention from investors and financial institutions, and many investors now prioritize companies that demonstrate strong ESG performance and consider it a key factor in their investment decisions. Incorporating ESG principles into digital transformation can enhance the organization's appeal to investors, attract sustainable investment, and improve access to capital.

- **Regulatory compliance**: ESG considerations are increasingly embedded in regulatory frameworks. Governments and regulatory bodies worldwide are implementing stricter regulations related to environmental impact, data privacy, cybersecurity, and the ethical use of technology. By integrating ESG principles into digital transformation, organizations can ensure compliance with existing and upcoming regulations, reducing legal and reputational risks.

- **Reputation and brand equity**: Organizations that prioritize ESG in their digital transformation efforts can enhance their reputation and build strong brand equity. They are viewed as responsible corporate citizens, committed to environmental stewardship, social impact, and ethical practices. This positive reputation can enhance customer loyalty, attract new customers, and differentiate the organization from competitors in a crowded marketplace.

Summary

In this chapter, we explored how having a strong vision acts as a foundational element for a successful digital transformation within enterprises.

As was evident from the Blockbuster case study, fostering innovation within the organization and enabling business agility through technology is extremely crucial to thrive and become sustainable in the competitive digital landscape. It is also important for organizations to define and implement an inclusive process of digital transformation and an innovation continuum to ensure continuous improvement.

We also discussed the various aspects of how enterprises can lead digital transformation, such as setting the strategy and vision, ensuring business–IT alignment, unwavering customer centricity, cultivating a culture of innovation, measure everything, and focus on sustainability. We also explored the leadership, will, and mindset of two enterprises with very similar business models, Kodak and Fujifilm, and how Fujifilm evolved into a multinational conglomerate that is still going strong even after almost nine decades.

In the next chapter, we will explore the various cloud paradigms and how enterprises can leverage cloud technology as a vehicle to lead and drive digital transformation.

Further reading

The references used in this chapter as well as some additional resources are listed as follows:

1. `https://www.forbes.com/sites/gregsatell/2014/09/05/a-look-back-at-why-blockbuster-really-failed-and-why-it-didnt-have-to/?sh=3ccdbf711d64`

2. `https://en.wikipedia.org/wiki/Blockbuster_(retailer)`

3. `https://redirect.cs.umbc.edu/courses/471/papers/turing.pdf`

4. `Lead and Disrupt, How to solve the innovator's dilemma - by Charles A. O'Reily III and Michael L. Tushman`

5. *Representative data collected from the following sources*:

    • `https://www.insiderintelligence.com/content/proximity-mobile-pay-on-rise-worldwide`

    • `https://ourworldindata.org/rise-of-social-media`

    • `https://www.statista.com/outlook/dmo/ecommerce/worldwide#users`

6. `https://www.visualcapitalist.com/cp/how-mobile-phone-market-has-evolved-since-1993/`

7. https://www.mckinsey.com/~/media/McKinsey/Industries/Electric%20
    Power%20and%20Natural%20Gas/Our%20Insights/Traditional%20
    company%20new%20businesses%20The%20pairing%20that%20can%20
    ensure%20an%20incumbents%20survival/Traditional-company-new-
    businesses-VF.pdf

8. https://www.mckinsey.com/capabilities/strategy-and-corporate-
    finance/our-insights/enduring-ideas-the-three-horizons-of-growth

9. https://hbr.org/2017/09/what-your-innovation-process-should-
    look-like

10. https://www.forbes.com/sites/chunkamui/2012/01/18/how-kodak-
    failed/?sh=780e309d6f27

11. https://d3.harvard.edu/platform-rctom/submission/fujifilm-
    surviving-the-digital-revolution-in-photography-through-
    diversification-into-cosmetics/#:~:text=%5B2%5D%20Fujifilm%2C%20
    on%20the,%2C%20you%20heard%20right%2C%20cosmetics

12. https://advisory.kpmg.us/content/dam/advisory/en/pdfs/2023/
    digital-core.pdf

2
A Primer on the Cloud

Just under two decades ago, the only way every company on the planet could deliver IT services to support their business was to build their own data centers. The data centers offered a centralized facility to host applications, store data, process them, and offer essential IT services to support the business.

However, the concept of cloud isn't new. In the modern world, all of us are used to the general concept of the *cloud*. Until the late 19th century, every household had to generate their own power from firewood and source water from wells on their property. With the invention of electricity and the evolution of communities and towns, utility companies have transformed the way households receive power and water. This proved both convenient and sustainable, as households no longer needed to erect their own wells, produce energy, and, more importantly, maintain them. They also offered a turnkey solution with metering and chargeback, which allowed consumers to pay only for what they use without having to worry about installing, running, and maintaining the ecosystem, thus saving huge efforts and costs.

Until the 1970s, when minicomputers were introduced, most organizations couldn't afford to host their own IT infrastructure, or mainframes. Only large organizations and government agencies owned a mainframe. Everyone else was leasing compute power on a central mainframe system most commonly known as timesharing. Even today, for most organizations, IT is a major cost center, meaning the cost of IT has to be budgeted and is a necessary expense to keep up with business demands. Cloud computing has evolved from just being an infrastructure deployment platform to revolutionizing the way businesses innovate and transform. It has democratized IT for businesses of all sizes to compete more effectively in the digital age. Leveraging cloud computing, startups are able to innovate and deliver capabilities faster than ever, and even disrupt the traditional enterprises in their respective industries.

In this chapter, we will discuss the fundamental concepts of cloud computing with a particular focus on the following topics:

- Essential characteristics of the cloud
- Driving business agility with cloud

- Cloud adoption in different industries

- Adopting hybrid cloud

- Myths of cloud adoption

Essential characteristics of the cloud

The **National Institute of Science and Technology (NIST)** defines cloud computing as follows:

Cloud computing is a model for enabling ubiquitous, convenient, on-demand network access to a shared pool of configurable computing resources (e.g., networks, servers, storage, applications, and services) that can be rapidly provisioned and released with minimal management effort or service provider interaction.

The cloud model is composed of five essential characteristics, three service models, and four deployment models:

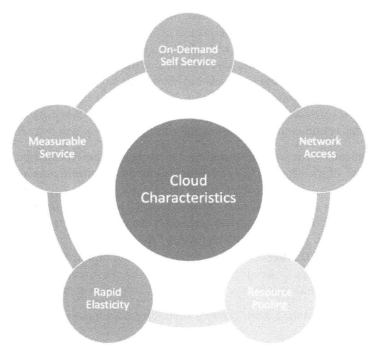

Figure 2.1 – Five essential characteristics of the cloud

In order for a system to be recognized as a cloud, it should have these five essential characteristics:

1. **On-demand self-service**: A consumer must be able to automatically provision computing resources such as compute capacity, storage, and network as needed without having to interact with a human service provider.

2. **Broad network access**: All service capabilities are accessible over the internet or network via standard networking protocols and can be consumed by a variety of client devices, such as workstations, mobile phones, tablets, and laptops.

3. **Resource pooling**: The cloud provider pools computing resources to serve multiple consumers using a multi-tenant model, where the underlying resources are shared, assigned, and re-assigned dynamically based on demand. The consumer of the cloud typically doesn't have the knowledge or control of where and how the computing resources are hosted.

4. **Rapid elasticity**: A cloud provider offers capabilities that can be seamlessly provisioned or de-provisioned based on user demands while also being able to scale resources rapidly up and down. To a cloud consumer, the capacity would appear limitless and elastic.

5. **Measured service**: Cloud systems leverage the concept of quotas, metering, and chargebacks to automatically control and optimize the usage of cloud resources. This allows both the cloud provider and consumer to transparently control, monitor, measure, and report the resource consumption or usage based on the nature of the service offered.

Service models

Broadly speaking, there are three primary service models through which cloud capabilities are delivered:

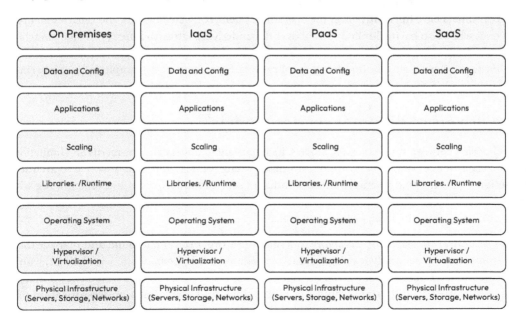

Figure 2.2 – Cloud service models

Let's briefly review the service models:

- **Software as a Service (SaaS)**: In a SaaS model, the consumer of the application or service is granted the ability to use the applications hosted on a cloud provider's infrastructure. The cloud provider assumes the responsibility of owning, managing, and operating the entire infrastructure encompassing the network, servers, and storage required to serve the application. The consumers can typically consume or access the application via a web browser or mobile device. Notably, consumers of a SaaS offering are relieved of the responsibility of developing, managing, and governing the application infrastructure while having limited customization or application configuration capabilities. Notable examples of SaaS offerings include Google Workspace (Gmail, Google Meet, etc.), Salesforce, Workday, and Dropbox.

- **Platform as a Service (PaaS)**: A PaaS service model provides a ready-to-use development and deployment platform that enables consumers to quickly build and deploy cloud-native applications without having to worry about the underlying infrastructure needs. A PaaS offering offers a complete cloud-based environment that includes everything a development team would need to write, build, test, deploy, and scale applications while the cloud provider manages the underlying hardware and software infrastructure. A PaaS consumer would have control over the deployed applications, binaries, and configuration settings for the application-hosting environment. Some examples of PaaS offerings include AWS Lambda, Google App Engine, Azure Cosmos DB, and Mulesoft.

- **Infrastructure as a Service (IaaS)**: An IaaS service model offers foundational infrastructure capabilities such as compute, storage, and network that enable consumers to run any software or application virtually. At a fundamental level, an IaaS platform acts as a hosted infrastructure where the cloud provider manages the underlying physical hardware infrastructure and consumers have full control over the operating system, software libraries, and binaries that run on it while also having limited control over the underlying infrastructure components, such as virtual networks and protocols. An IaaS service model allows users to provision and scale the basic infrastructure required to run applications. Some common examples of IaaS offerings include AWS EC2, Google Compute Engine, and Azure Virtual Machines.

Value drivers of different service models

While choosing between various service models, it's important to understand the merits and limitations of each. The three service models are not mutually exclusive. It is common practice to architect and design a solution that leverages a mix of different service models, oftentimes integrating with existing traditional IT on-premises systems. An important consideration should also be based on an organization's IT maturity level, skillset, and scale.

It could be entirely possible for *Company A*, a mature IT organization, to build and manage their own e-commerce by primarily leveraging IaaS capabilities, while *Company B*, with lean IT, would find an e-commerce SaaS solution to be the right fit. In this case, Company A would need a mature IT organization, expending significant time, effort, skills, and operational prowess for want of a higher level of control. Company B would sacrifice control over faster time to market and SLA-driven managed service offerings:

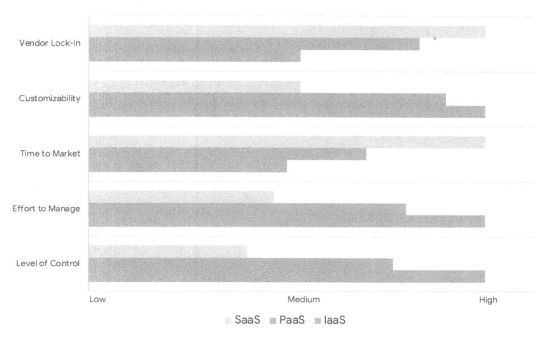

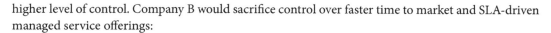

Table 2.3 – Cloud deployment models and value differentiators

There are also more evolved service models that are purpose-built for certain business functions. These are generally categorized as **Everything as a Service** (**XaaS**). Some of the more common ones are as follows:

1. **Containers as a Service** (**CaaS**): CaaS offers a cloud-based platform where consumers can bring their own containers and runtime and run on a managed platform. The cloud provider manages the underlying hardware, virtualization, and operating system layers. Some examples of CaaS include **Google Kubernetes Engine** (**GKE**), **Azure Kubernetes Service** (**AKS**), and Amazon **Elastic Kubernetes Service** (**EKS**).

2. **Unified Communications as a Service** (**UCaaS**): UCaaS offers a cloud-based platform for delivering a wide range of communication and collaboration services, including voice, video, messaging, and presence, on a subscription basis. Some examples of UCaaS providers include RingCentral, Zoom, 8x8, and Vonage.

3. **Identity as a Service** (**IdaaS**): IdaaS offers a cloud-based identity management infrastructure on a subscription basis, enabling businesses to manage user authentication, authorization, and access control across their applications and systems. Some examples of IDaaS providers include Okta, Azure AD, Google Identity, and Ping.

4. **Functions as a Service (FaaS):** FaaS provides a serverless platform that enables developers to code, build, and deploy microservices and serverless applications without having to manage their own infrastructure. Some examples of FaaS include AWS Lambda, Google Cloud Functions, and Azure Functions.

5. **Contact Center as a Service (CCaaS):** CCaaS is a subscription-based contact center service that includes inbound and outbound voice calls, email, chat, social media, and messaging services. Some examples of CCaaS include Genesys, NICE, Talkdesk, and Five9.

6. **Knowledge as a Service (KaaS):** KaaS provides a cloud-based platform for capturing, storing, and sharing knowledge and information across an organization. Some examples of KaaS include Bloomfire, Thought Industries, and WittyParrot.

While there are several cloud service models with certain specialized offerings, an enterprise would typically have several of these service models to serve a specific purpose while also allowing interoperability.

Cloud deployment models

As we have explored the various cloud service models, let's review some of the cloud deployment models. The choice of a cloud deployment model is one of the fundamental decisions for organizations in the digital transformation process, as it eventually dictates the cloud roadmap and capabilities that an organization can envision.

1. **Private cloud:** In this model, cloud infrastructure is provisioned for exclusive use by a single organization comprising multiple consumers (e.g., business units). It may be owned, managed, and operated by the organization, a third party, or some combination of them, and it may exist on or off premises.

   There are three different modes through which a private cloud can be offered—hosted, managed, and virtual:

   • **Hosted private cloud:** In this model, organizations will have full control over their cloud environments as the physical cloud servers are hosted within their own facility or data centers. Typically, a private cloud vendor offers the cloud stack constructs, including virtualization, security, networking, and storage, necessary to build a private cloud. However, the organization's IT staff would be required to deploy, operate, and manage. This would be best suited for organizations that require dedicated physical cloud servers, data residency, or sovereignty requirements and have IT staff with the right skill sets to manage and operate the cloud stack. Some examples of a hosted private cloud are OpenStack and Apache CloudStack.

   • **Managed private cloud:** This is very similar to a hosted private cloud, except the cloud servers are managed by a service provider. Typically, a managed private cloud provider would host, manage, and operate the cloud servers on behalf of the organization. This greatly simplifies things for organizations, as it eliminates the need for a physical data center space, the associated costs, and the day-to-day operations and management. Although the organization would still have greater control over its cloud environment, most management needs must be routed through the service provider. Some examples of a managed private cloud are Rackspace, NTT, and Sungard.

- **Virtual private cloud**: Although the name states private cloud, this is a private environment within a public cloud. More commonly known as a VPC, it is an isolated tenancy within a multi-tenant cloud. In this model, a public cloud provider typically manages the physical data center, the server infrastructure, networking, and security. An organization subscribing to a virtual private cloud will have full control over its own VPC but not the underlying physical infrastructure. Examples of cloud providers offering VPCs are Google Cloud, AWS, Microsoft Azure, and Oracle Cloud.

2. **Community cloud**: A community cloud is a specialized cloud computing environment that is typically shared by a group of organizations with similar goals and requirements. It can be owned and operated by either the organization or a third-party service provider. A community cloud can be a good fit for organizations that share common purposes, objectives, governance, and regulatory requirements. This could be having access to or sharing data, services, or compliance needs. An example of a community cloud would be a dedicated cloud infrastructure specific to government agencies, more commonly referred to as GovCloud (or Cloud for Government), where several departments might need access to a shared set of data and services governed under strict regulatory compliance requirements such as FedRAMP, CMMC, and ITAR.

   Some of the other common community clouds are purpose-built for hosting services for specific industries where industry regulations are warranted—HIPAA for healthcare, FINRA and PCI-DSS for financial services, etc.

   There are also community clouds built for universities and colleges where educational institutions can take advantage of a common set of services that can be shared and leveraged.

3. **Public cloud**: A public cloud is the most common type of cloud infrastructure provisioned for use by virtually anyone with an internet connection. A public cloud is owned, managed, and operated by a service provider while offering services to the consumers over the network. By definition, a public cloud infrastructure is hosted in one or more locations while allowing consumers to subscribe and use. The cloud provider owns and manages the data center, server infrastructure, and software stack required to access its services and offers its resources to be consumed through the internet, typically through a subscription. A public cloud is a multi-tenant model where many subscribers can lease cloud services.

   Some popular public cloud providers are **Amazon Web Services** (**AWS**), Google Cloud, Salesforce, and Workday.

4. **Hybrid cloud**: A hybrid cloud integrates traditional on-premises IT with one or more public clouds, which allows organizations to move workloads seamlessly. A hybrid cloud enables organizations to experience the best of both worlds—retaining legacy applications and data on-premises due to compliance, data sovereignty, or data residency regulations while leveraging public cloud capabilities to build and deliver modern applications and value-added services.

A hybrid cloud infrastructure is a composition of one or more public clouds with on-premises infrastructure that allows seamless application and data portability across environments. As enterprises innovate and modernize on the cloud while also leveraging existing investments in traditional on-premises infrastructure, applications, systems, and software, a hybrid cloud has become a defacto for the vast majority of enterprises, as it offers greater flexibility to choose the best environment for each of their workloads or move the workloads between clouds as their needs change.

A hybrid cloud also requires careful planning in terms of design and foundational architecture, as it would be key to successful execution. Some of the high-value use cases that a hybrid cloud enables are as follows:

- **Cloud bursting**: Cloud bursting is the ability to burst the application or service traffic to the cloud either due to seasonal demands or to handle a sudden spike. In a steady state, applications would serve traffic from on-premises data centers but can seamlessly divert traffic spikes to the cloud.

- **Disaster recovery (DR) in the cloud**: In a traditional on-premises data center, building out a DR environment is often expensive, as it is rarely used, but it still needs to be sized in parity with the production with the associated operational overhead. A cloud environment can support an on-demand DR through elastic scaling.

- **Geo redundancy and high availability (HA)**: A hybrid cloud can enable high availability and geo-redundancy for on-premises applications that are mission-critical, dramatically improving the SLAs.

- **Dev-test in the cloud**: With a well-architected hybrid cloud foundation, organizations can start spinning up multiple development and test environments, shut them down when not in use, and tear them down when no longer needed. This also allows organizations to run multiple release cycles in parallel.

- **Chartering new territories**: Oftentimes, enterprises have a need to test new waters and experiment with new technology, and they would like to *fail fast and fail cheaply*. The cloud can serve as a test bed and launchpad until a steady state is established.

Regardless of the cloud deployment model, it is important for enterprises to envision a long-term cloud strategy that would set the course for a successful business transformation through technology. In the next section, we will explore how cloud computing can help drive business agility.

Driving business agility with cloud

One of the primary ways cloud technology impacted the modern enterprise is by aiding business agility. With soaring consumer demands and ever-changing market dynamics, businesses across every industry had to lead innovation, rapidly scale, and go to market quicker to thrive.

The following are seven cloud principles that help drive business agility:

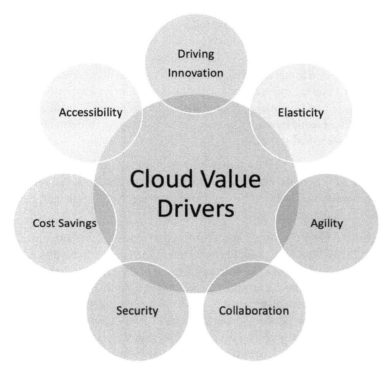

Figure 2.4 – Cloud value drivers

Let's briefly review the seven foundational value drivers of business agility of the cloud:

1. **Innovation**: Innovation has been a huge value driver of cloud adoption within enterprises. Cloud has given a clear edge to organizations as they can now explore unknown territories and experiment with new and emerging technologies without having to spend a fortune in terms of time, costs, and effort building expensive on-premises IT infrastructure. This has allowed businesses to fail fast and deliver new products and services faster.

    IKEA is a Swedish multinational conglomerate based in the Netherlands that designs and sells ready-to-assemble furniture, kitchen appliances, decorations, home accessories, and various other goods and home services. Leveraging bleeding-edge cloud technology, IKEA was able to successfully innovate and deliver immersive customer experiences [1]. With the COVID-19 pandemic affecting societies and communities at large, shoppers were looking for unique and different ways to shop and have their items delivered. IKEA transformed the way customers shopped by offering creative and immersive experiences such as AI-powered recommendations, chatbots for simpler yet effective customer service, and 3D visualization design tools to picture furniture in photo-realistic rooms.

2. **Elasticity**: The first thing everyone thinks of when talking about the cloud is its inherent capability to scale. This is in direct contrast to traditional IT where enterprises had to always size for the high watermark—the expected peak load. Capacity planning in traditional on-premises setups is a major challenge, especially when application demands are seasonal or unpredictable. Undersizing results in application downtime, causing poor user experience, and oversizing results in unnecessarily high CapEx (unused hardware and software) and OpEx (upgrades, power, cooling, and maintenance). The cloud alleviates capacity planning concerns by providing on-demand capacity that can be scaled both up and down based on application demands, enabling businesses to quickly respond to changes in demand, such as seasonal fluctuations or unexpected spikes.

    Netflix is a leading internet television network with over 230 million subscribers across 190+ countries. From a DVD rental company to what it is today, Netflix was a pioneer in leveraging the cloud to innovate and scale. As demand kept growing, Netflix relied on cloud elasticity to keep up with the demand [2].

3. **Business agility**: A key value driver that enables enterprises to have a significant competitive edge is the ability to be nimble, quickly experiment, deliver services, and respond faster to keep ahead of market demands. An intrinsic benefit of the cloud is that it offers enterprises on-demand access to modern cutting-edge technology. For instance, with a cloud strategy, organizations can gain immediate access to modern chipsets, software platforms, applications, and value-added services, allowing experimentation at low risk without breaking the bank. This would have traditionally required a ton of due diligence, proof-of-concepts, evaluation, and procurement cycles, which are prone to higher costs and risks.

    The COVID-19 pandemic impacted every industry and business on a global scale. Many retailers were forced to close the doors and several others just went out of business. Target started digital transformation several years before the pandemic. This allowed Target to swiftly respond to new health and compliance regulations, keeping their stores open while also keeping their associates safe [3]. Target was able to quickly roll out several changes such as plexiglass shields at check lanes, dedicated shopping hours for vulnerable guests, quantity limits on high-demand items, etc. across all their stores within a matter of days. More importantly, they could offer newer and safer ways of shopping for customers via their digital channels, such as Drive Up and Target Wallets. On the question of how the cloud is powering business agility, Brian Cornell, the CEO of Target, in the *Masters of Scale* podcast said, "*No one knows what will happen, but by putting my team first, I am putting the customer first – and serving the larger community.*"

4. **Collaboration**: Cloud technology has transformed the way teams and organizations collaborate in new and innovative ways, enabling real-time communication, document sharing, video conferencing, and project management from anywhere. As more and more enterprises adopt a hybrid and remote working culture, teams are spread out geographically. Global teams working on a project can leverage cloud-based collaboration tools such as Google Workspace or Microsoft Teams to work together seamlessly, regardless of their location or time zone. This allows teams to collaborate effectively, improve communication, and speed up decision-making.

Pinterest is a leading social media platform that allows users to share and discover visual content, such as images and videos. With over 450+ million monthly active users, Pinterest leveraged cloud technology to support its growing user base and handle vast quantities of data generated by its users.

GitHub is an internet hosting service for software development and version control. It has transformed the way developers write and share code and documents and collaborate with fellow developers. GitHub also functions as a social networking platform for developers to openly network, collaborate on projects, and promote their work *[4]*.

5. **Security**: Cloud providers typically have robust security measures, such as encryption, firewalls, and access controls. With a defense-in-depth security strategy, cloud providers often have multiple layers of security built into their infrastructure, including physical security, network security, and application security. Cloud-based applications and services are generally more secure than traditional data center-hosted applications in many ways. For instance, most reputable cloud service providers operate on a defense-in-depth security strategy and have built specialized capabilities to secure the overall cloud environment.

    There are several types of security threats that organizations have to protect themselves against every single day, ranging from targeted DDoS attacks to software and hardware vulnerabilities to ransomware. In 2017, Google's Project Zero team discovered serious security flaws caused by *speculative execution*, a technique used by most modern processors (CPUs) to optimize performance. Popularly referred to as Spectre and Meltdown, this impacted virtually every single machine. Following the discovery of this vulnerability and a solution, Google was immediately able to patch millions of servers within their cloud infrastructure through live migration to protect customer applications and data.

    Today's modern internet-facing applications are at constant risk of **distributed denial of service (DDoS)** attacks, where rogue agents initiate large volumes of HTTP requests to an application from a variety of IPs that might seem legitimate. Unsuspecting applications tend to respond to this sudden spike by scaling constantly, and are eventually taken down after running out of resources. These kinds of attacks typically require security not just for the application but the entire IT stack, from intelligent firewalls to available network bandwidth—more commonly referred to as the **defense-in-depth** security strategy. In June of 2022, a customer application deployed on Google Cloud was the target of the largest-ever layer 7 DDoS attack *[5]*. The attack started with 10,000 **requests per second (RPS)** and peaked at 46 million RPS within the next few minutes. Leveraging the defense-in-depth security-first cloud architecture, the attack was mitigated and blocked at the network edge. Thanks to the massive network bandwidth and security controls such as Cloud Armor, customers' services stayed online and continued serving.

6. **Cost**: An important value driver for cloud adoption is cost savings. Cloud computing can help businesses save costs by eliminating the need to invest in expensive hardware and software. Additionally, cloud-based services are often billed on a pay-as-you-go basis, allowing businesses to only pay for usage. However, it is important for IT leaders to consider the realization of cost savings from a **total cost of ownership (TCO)** and business value perspective. Although cloud

comes with a promise of overall cost savings, ironically, runaway cloud costs are one of the primary reasons for failed cloud initiatives. Rushed migrations, lack of direction and clarity on cloud objectives, and poor architectural design are some of the common pitfalls [6]. However, organizations can realize potential cost savings by taking advantage of native cloud features such as elastic scaling, Serverless, automation, and Cloud FinOps best practices.

7. **Accessibility**: Another key value of the cloud is that it allows employees, associates, and partners to gain access to business applications and data from virtually anywhere at any time. With a hybrid work culture and global teams with a follow-the-sun model, organizations have an increasing need to provide employees and partners with the right tools, applications, and services to ensure productivity and responsiveness to customer needs. For instance, a mobile workforce can use cloud-based APIs, applications, and services to access tools and data from any device anywhere at any time. For users with disabilities, the cloud can also enable assistive technology solutions such as voice recognition, text-to-speech APIs, screen readers, closed captioning, or real-time transcription.

In the next section, let's explore how cloud adoption has impacted different industries.

Cloud adoption in different industries

The following is true, according to McAfee's *Cloud Adoption and Risk Report*:

- 87% of companies experienced business acceleration from leveraging cloud services
- 52% of organizations realized better security in the cloud than in traditional on-premises IT environments [7]

According to a 2021 report by O'Reilly, organizations across industry verticals continue to accelerate cloud adoption [8].

Let's explore the impact of cloud adoption in some key industry verticals.

Retail

The retail industry has been at the forefront of Cloud adoption, as retailers seek to take advantage of cutting-edge cloud technology to meet ever-increasing consumer demands [9].

The cloud has led retail innovation by optimizing supply chains, transforming stores as micro fulfillment centers, enabling new shopping experiences such as **buy online, pick up in store** (**BOPIS**) and curbside pickups, managing omnichannel inventory levels, and creating AI-infused shopping experiences to augmented/virtual reality. Let's look at some areas where retailers are innovating and leading the digital transformation with the cloud.

The store of the future

Transforming shopping experiences for consumers is adding a significant competitive edge for retailers, and it is imperative for retailers to capture the market share. Several retailers are reimagining the creation of the **modern store** or the **store of the future**, leveraging modern cloud technologies infused with AI that focus on providing rich shopping experiences, improving customer engagement, increasing the lifetime value of consumers, and enhancing brand loyalty.

Point of sale (POS)

Cloud-based POS systems have become increasingly popular as they allow retailers to manage store transactions more efficiently and enable real-time insights into sales data. Modern cloud-based POS enables retailers to efficiently manage inventory, personalize the customer shopping experience, and track customer behaviors, which was not possible with traditional POS.

E-commerce to omni-commerce

As more and more shoppers take to online shopping for the convenience it offers, e-commerce sales in the US reached over a trillion dollars in 2022.

As omnichannel commerce takes center stage and the lines are blurred between in-store and online shopping channels, it is extremely important for retailers to meet consumer demands wherever they are. Traditional monolith e-commerce solutions are no longer effective at meeting these demands, and retailers have a need to adopt cloud-based e-commerce platforms to offer omnichannel personalized shopping experiences for consumers. Omni-commerce focuses on providing customers with a seamless shopping experience across all channels, including online, in-store, mobile, or voice, resulting in a better-personalized shopping experience regardless of where and how they shop. Hence, it's important for retailers to integrate different channels, follow customers' journeys, and manage inventory effectively.

Customer data platform

As consumer privacy measures are tightened across the world (GDPR in the EU, for instance) and third-party data and cookies are becoming less reliable, it is crucial for retailers to build a solid data foundation with a primary focus on enriching their first-party data while still offering personalized experience to customers. Harnessing the power of data from various sources, a well-defined CDP strategy can help predict trends and customer sentiment, enhance marketing ROAS, build brand loyalty, and increase customer lifetime value.

Supply chain demand planning and forecasting

The exponential growth of omni-commerce has forced retailers to quickly adapt and respond to consumer demands. Consumers expect accurate real-time inventory availability, delivery commitments, end-to-end order tracking transparency, and visibility as orders are fulfilled. Antiquated and manual supply chain systems are struggling to meet these demands. Modern supply chain systems infused with AI/ML are dramatically improving autonomous planning and decision-making, preventing stockouts and markdowns.

Associate productivity

Ensuring the productivity of associates, especially in the store, is key to providing a better customer experience. Automating mundane day-to-day tasks and operations such as shelf stocking, order picking, checking out, scheduling, and task management can greatly improve associate productivity, letting store associates focus on servicing customers. Technology can help store associates simplify shelf stocking, ensuring there are no stockouts and that the right products are in the right places. Self-service and contactless checkouts, assisted order picking, rewards-based task management, tasks scheduled based on priorities, and associate experience levels are increasing store associate productivity levels tremendously, improving sales and customer satisfaction. Back office and online customer service associates can greatly benefit from guidance on the next best decision, live recommendations through AI-powered conversational chatbots, and modern contact center solutions. With cloud-based collaboration tools, associates in corporate and IT can improve their quality of work and efficiency and devote more time to creative problem solving and innovation.

Other areas of innovation

Some other areas where retailers are innovating with modern cloud-native tech and AI include the following:

- **Edge computing**: Gone are the days when the batch processing of sales and inventory data was a norm. Retailers are actively innovating with processing data at the edge to accelerate and improve customer experiences.

- **Shrink reduction**: With thin margins and intensive competition, shrink reduction is critical to a retailer's topline. Technologies such as intelligent POS video analytics with exception-based reporting and edge computing can generate real-time alerts to prevent and reduce retail shrinkage.

- **Internet of Things** (**IoT**): IoT is rapidly transforming retail with inventory management, fraud detection, product tampering, targeted marketing campaigns in store, and operational efficiency. With the exponential increase in the number of devices, sensors and gateways, and network traffic, cloud technologies can help efficiently manage.

- **Blockchain and retail consortium**: Blockchain is a distributed ledger technology that can be used to create secure, transparent, and tamper-resistant transactions. This can help retailers build transparent and secure loyalty programs, manage customer data and transactions for regulatory compliance, protect customers from counterfeit goods by providing product authenticity and product tracing, and facilitate secure and instant payment between buyers and sellers.

- **Augmented reality (AR) and virtual reality (VR)**: AR and VR are emerging technologies that are revolutionizing the retail industry by helping customers visualize products in their homes or businesses, create immersive shopping experiences, and engage and interact with products, resulting in a better conversion rate. Cloud computing provides much-needed modern scalable and resilient infrastructure to render complex AR/VR experiences, store and deliver large quantities of data for 3D models, textures, and videos, and reduce the complexity for IT to develop and deploy AR/VR solutions.

- **Applied AI/ML**: The AI/ML revolution has had a major impact on the retail industry and finds application in every sphere of retail. Retailers are embedding AI/ML capabilities across lines of businesses from effectively targeted marketing to improve ROAS, automate customer service, implement dynamic pricing based on local and macroeconomic factors, personalize product recommendations, optimize inventory, and detect fraud. Cloud technology offers a scalable infrastructure to train and deploy AI/ML models and store and manage large datasets, tools, and services to rapidly test and iterate, making it a great fit to power innovation.

As is evident from the data, retail has been at the forefront of digital transformation and leading innovation at scale.

Healthcare and life sciences

Healthcare is another vertical experiencing a paradigm shift in digital transformation, leading to improved patient care and outcomes. Offering continuous patient care, empowering caregivers to make informed data-driven clinical decisions, and accelerating drug development, modern cloud and AI technologies have transformed healthcare and life sciences. Let's go over some areas where the healthcare and life sciences industry is innovating.

Connected health

Connected health refers to the use of wearable technologies that connect patients with healthcare providers to monitor patients' health remotely and facilitate communication. Cloud technology enables **remote patient monitoring (RPM)** programs that allow healthcare providers to monitor patients' health outside of traditional clinical settings. This has proven especially beneficial for patients with chronic conditions or patients living in remote areas with limited access to healthcare.

Telehealth and virtual care

Telehealth has become increasingly popular in recent years. Cloud-based telehealth platforms allow providers to connect with patients through secure real-time video and audio communications. This means that patients can receive medical care from anywhere at any time without having to travel to a physical healthcare facility, receive virtual consultations, and refill prescriptions. Cloud-based telehealth platforms can also be used to provide virtual consultations and prescription refills and to monitor patient health remotely. This enables healthcare providers to scale services on-demand based on patient volume while also securely managing patient data and integrating with backend **electronic health records** (**EHR**) *[10].*

Drug adherence

Drug adherence is the extent to which a patient follows the medical prescription. It has been a hard challenge to solve. Failure to adhere to a medication regimen or overuse can lead to poor patient health outcomes, increased healthcare costs, and reduced quality of life for patients. A cloud-based solution lets healthcare providers track patients' vital signs and medication usage through RPM, send medication reminders, offer education and support about medications, and provide community support. Cloud-based communication tools also enable secure patient-provider communication in real time to help support patients with drug adherence.

Genomic data processing

Genomic data processing is extremely complex and compute-intensive, requiring large amounts of data storage and processing power, which can be expensive and time-consuming to manage on-premises. With large, sensitive, and growing genomic datasets, cloud technology has revolutionized the way genomic data is stored, processed, and analyzed. It also helps overcome scalability, availability, and data security challenges by offering a scalable, secure, and cost-effective platform for genomic data processing. More importantly, cloud-based platforms facilitate collaborative research to help researchers in various regions collaborate, analyze, and share results.

Drug development

Speed and scale are critical to faster drug discovery and development, which involve massive amounts of data wrangling and analysis from clinical research and trials. This typically requires **high-performance computing** (**HPC**) that can burst for short intervals spanning long periods. Cloud computing has transformed drug development processes by enabling health sciences to accelerate discovery and drug development. Modern HPC resources enable faster analysis of large datasets, reducing timelines and costs with regard to drug development. Cloud-based AI/ML platforms and tools offer the ability to do predictive modeling, anomaly detection, and identification of potential drug targets. Virtual clinical trials can significantly reduce clinical trial costs and timeframes by collecting data from a diverse patient population.

Banking, financial services, and insurance

The BFSI industry is undergoing a significant transformation with the adoption of cloud technology, enabling organizations to enhance customer experience and operational efficiency. From open banking, fraud detection, risk management, streamlining regulatory reporting, and improving operational efficiency, cloud technology helps financial services innovate and scale. Let's take a look at some high-value use cases in the banking and financial services industry to understand how a digital transformation is taking place.

Digital banking

Open banking is revolutionizing the financial services industry by making it easier for consumers to compare products and services and find the best deals. This allows financial service providers to access customer data held by financial institutions to develop new and innovative products and services for better customer experience. Some popular open banking applications include **personal financial management** (**PFM**) tools that help consumers budget and track spending, transparent credit scoring tools that help consumers with lines of credit, convenient payment options, and tools to help consumers find better deals. Cloud-based solutions help financial institutions support open banking by providing consumers with a secure and scalable platform, real-time access to financial data, and innovative ways to interact with consumers, such as virtual assistants and chatbots.

Fraud detection and prevention

Financial fraud is a major challenge for businesses of all sizes. According to the **Association of Certified Fraud Examiners** (**ACFE**), "*Occupational fraud is likely the costliest and most common form of financial crime in the world. This is bigger than healthcare fraud, tax evasion, money laundering and identity theft.*" The ACFE estimates that a typical organization loses 5% of its annual revenue to fraud. Cloud computing can help businesses detect and prevent financial fraud in a variety of ways, including analyzing transactions in real time to help identify and stop suspicious transactions, leveraging machine learning to analyze and identify outlier patterns to proactively detect fraud, and analyzing massive datasets to detect trends in order to develop more effective fraud prevention strategies.

Regulatory reporting

Regulatory agencies across the world rely on the timely and accurate filing of financial reports by financial institutions. This is a critical activity for financial organizations with changing regulations that require a concerted effort from multiple organizations, including finance, legal, and IT. Traditional manual processes often tend to be time-consuming, expensive, and risk-prone. Cloud-based solutions offer technology-enabled data management, data governance, data aggregation between disparate lines of business and third-party organizations, and real-time and transparent insights for stakeholders. They can also automate and streamline repeatable business processes, resulting in quick, agile, and robust regulatory reporting.

Risk management

Financial institutions require complex risk assessments to keep up with market movements and stay compliant. Formal risk modeling valuations that leverage methodologies such as Monte Carlo require a significant amount of compute power. Traditional methods involve building a virtual server farm to meet extensive infrastructure demands and operations, and this can be cost-prohibitive. Cloud providers offer HPC grids and scalable infrastructure in real time on demand to perform timely risk evaluations and simulations such as **value at risk** (**VaR**) in an efficient and cost-effective way.

Claims processing and underwriting

Claims handling, processing, and underwriting are critical for insurance companies. These processes can be complex and time-consuming, but it is important to ensure that policyholders are treated fairly and that the claims are processed promptly. There are a number of factors that can affect the claims processing time, including the complexity of the claim, the availability of documentation, and the workload of the claims department. Cloud technology helps insurers automate tasks such as data entry and document processing to free up claim adjusters to focus on claim investigation and negotiation, improving accuracy and efficiency and creating a better customer experience. Augmented with AI/ML, cloud technology makes it possible for organizations to analyze large quantities of data to detect patterns and anomalies to prevent fraud, prioritize claims triage and automate claims processing, and predict trends with future claims to help develop effective underwriting strategies.

Telecommunications

The telecommunications industry is undergoing a period of rapid digital transformation driven by several factors, including the rise of new technologies such as 5G, **multi-access edge computing (MEC)**, network slicing for offering customized services to consumers, quantum computing, UcaaS, and exponential consumer demand. Digital transformation is critical for telecom companies to stay competitive and relevant. Let's look at some areas where the telecom industry is transforming and innovating with the cloud.

Network function virtualization (NFV)

Digital transformation in telecom involves virtualizing network functions such as routing, switching, and firewalls. This is critical to scaling and reducing the costs associated with proprietary hardware and improving scalability, flexibility, and agility. Cloud technology has enabled telecom companies to more easily deploy and deliver new network functions and services.

Telecom network intelligence

Telecom **network intelligence (NI)** is a technology that leverages data analytics to gain insights into network performance and behavior in real time. NI solutions typically collect data from a variety of different sources such as network devices, mobile applications, and user activity streams. Leveraging cloud technologies, vast quantities of data can be analyzed using machine learning algorithms to identify network patterns and trends, identify and resolve network issues quickly, optimize network traffic to improve performance, predict network capacity, and prevent threats or network attacks This results in improved customer experience.

Internet of Things (IoT)

Telecom companies are leveraging IoT to create new revenue streams and provide value-added and personalized services to customers. This involves using sensors and other devices to collect data and provide insights into customer behavior and preferences. IoT also enables new business models, helping several industries that could not exist before, such as smart city solutions, connected car services, smart metering, and energy optimization.

Cloud-based contact centers

Telecom companies are leveraging cloud technology to provide contact center solutions that enable businesses to provide customer services through multiple channels such as voice, chat, email, and social media. This enables businesses to offer omnichannel customer service.

Radio access network (RAN)

The RAN is the part of a telecom network that connects mobile devices to the core network, allowing users to access voice chats, data, and other services. Traditionally, the RAN has been deployed using proprietary hardware and software, which can be expensive and inflexible. With the emergence of cloud technologies, Telecom companies are exploring the possibility of moving their RAN functionalities to the cloud. This helps centralize the management of their networks, improve the efficiency of their network infrastructures, and reduce costs.

Unified communications (UC)

Cloud-based UC solutions are becoming increasingly popular in the business world due to their flexibility, scalability, and cost-effectiveness. Cloud-based UC solutions allow telecom companies to provide customers with a complete suite of communication and collaboration tools, such as voice chatting, video calls, messaging, and conferencing, all delivered from the cloud. This improves customer experience and allows companies to offer new revenue-generating services.

Government

With the rise of digital technology, several government agencies across the world are moving toward providing digital services to citizens, such as online application forms, e-payments, and digital signatures. The digitalization of government services makes it easier and faster for citizens to access government services, reducing wait times and operating costs and minimizing the need for in-person interactions.

Government agencies are increasingly using cloud computing to reduce costs, improve efficiency, and increase flexibility. By using cloud services, agencies can access software, data storage, and computing power as needed without investing in expensive infrastructure. Cloud computing also allows government agencies to collaborate more easily with each other and with external partners. Even modest initiatives to digitize government processes or services are typically governed by a lot of regulatory guidelines and restrictions. Several public cloud providers offer a dedicated GovCloud that complies with various security, regulatory, and compliance statutes, such as data security through layered encryption, data privacy, data retention, data sovereignty, audit tracking, and compliance with several government regulations across the world, such as FedRAMP, FISMA, PII and HIPAA, CJIR, MeitY, and NISC. For instance, the **US General Services Administration (GSA)** has developed a cloud-based program called FedRAMP that provides a standardized approach to security assessment, authorization, and continuous monitoring of cloud products and services. By providing a common platform for cloud security, FedRAMP has helped government agencies to collaborate more effectively and share data securely. Let's go over some areas where government agencies are transforming and innovating with the cloud.

Citizen services

Government agencies are leveraging cloud computing to improve citizen services in a number of ways, including providing online services such as online applications, tax filing, permit applications, and license renewals, making it easier and more convenient for citizens to interact with the government.

Public health agencies can leverage big data analytics, predictive analytics, and cloud computing to monitor emerging trends, such as public health threats, and provide effective interventions. The city of Los Angeles developed the **MyLA311** system to allow citizens to easily report service requests for garbage, graffiti, and other cleanup issues [11]. The city leveraged cloud-based technologies to streamline the process and monitor field crew progress. This has improved the quality of life for citizens by providing quick responses to service-related questions and more efficient waste-removal operations.

Public health services

Government agencies are required to constantly fight public health concerns that are both endemic and pandemic. Endemic concerns such as obesity, tobacco use, mental health, pollution, and substance abuse need to be addressed methodically, while pandemic situations such as COVID-19 call for a rapid response.

For instance, government agencies have been fighting the opioid crisis for decades. Leveraging modern AI/ML technology, the **Oklahoma Department of Mental Health & Substance Abuse Services (ODMHSAS)** developed a cloud-based opioid response solution to identify trends in their earliest stages and implement effective community responses at a zip code level, as well as broaden its scope to include survey data from more than 500 school districts. This helped it drive prevention and intervention strategies that brought officials and communities together in the fight against the opioid crisis [12].

Similarly, during the COVID-19 pandemic, the Commonwealth of Massachusetts leveraged the cloud to rapidly develop a centralized system to help citizens register, prioritize, and schedule appointments for constituents [13]. This helped with the efficiency of distributing vaccines statewide efficiently and helped residents notify proactively on assigned appointments and on the basis of their geographic proximity.

Food and safety

Public health and food safety regulatory agencies across the world are responsible for ensuring that domestic, exported, and imported meat, poultry, and processed egg products are safe, wholesome, and correctly labeled and packaged. This is a tedious process as it involves massive amounts of data that needs to be collected, consolidated, and analyzed. The adoption of the cloud has provided agencies with access to real-time data and improved the efficiency and accuracy of their operations.

As an example, the **US Department of Agriculture (USDA)** leverages cloud computing to improve efficiency in its food safety inspection process. The USDA has developed a cloud-based system called the **Public Health Information System (PHIS)**, which allows inspectors to access real-time data and conduct inspections remotely *[14]*. The PHIS has improved the efficiency of the inspection process, reducing the time and resources required for inspections and increasing the accuracy of inspection data.

Space research

The emergence of cloud and allied technological innovations in the AI/ML space has been very helpful for space research agencies to advance space research rapidly. Space research generates huge amounts of data, such as satellite imagery, space observations, and climate models. Complex simulations and calculations require HPC that is computationally intense.

For instance, the US **National Aeronautics and Space Administration (NASA)** is using cloud computing to leverage advanced technologies. NASA is using cloud services to process and analyze large volumes of data from satellites, telescopes, and other instruments. This data analysis has led to new discoveries and insights, such as the discovery of new exoplanets and the mapping of global climate patterns.

Digital marketplace

Government procurement and supplier tendering is a complex process that can be time-consuming and expensive due to the challenges around cost, quality, sustainability, competition, various local and federal regulations, and the need for fairness and transparency. Cloud technology has eased the process and enabled government agencies to ensure transparency through data access in real-time and the streamlining of business processes.

The United Kingdom's government has built a multi-cloud computing platform popularly known as G-Cloud to improve public services and reduce costs *[15]*. G-Cloud acts as a digital marketplace, providing a framework for government agencies to procure cloud services from approved suppliers. It has helped the government plan their expenditure across departments in the cost of IT procurement better and has enabled government agencies to deliver more efficient and effective services to citizens.

Education

Government agencies are using cloud computing to promote education in various ways that weren't possible earlier. One of the most common ways is through the development of cloud-based platforms that provide access to educational resources, such as online courses, digital textbooks, and multimedia content.

An example of this is the Indian government using cloud computing to improve access to education. The government of India has developed a cloud-based platform called the **National Digital Library of India (NDLI)**, which provides free access to digital resources, such as books, journals, and multimedia content, to students and researchers across India *[16]*. The NDLI has improved access to educational resources, especially in remote and underprivileged areas of the country.

The Australian government is using cloud computing to provide access to digital textbooks and other educational resources for students. The government has developed a cloud-based platform called the **Digital Education Revolution** that provides students with access to digital textbooks, online courses, and other resources *[17]*. The Digital Education Revolution has improved access to educational resources, especially in remote and underprivileged areas of the country.

Defense

Government agencies in the defense sector are increasingly using modern clouds, cybersecurity, robotics, and AI/ML to innovate and improve defense capabilities and operational efficiencies. Defense departments across the world are innovating with cloud-based solutions, from cybersecurity to collaborative work environments where multiple agencies can seamlessly collaborate, predictive analysis, and cost-effective virtual training and simulation.

The U.S. **Department of Defense (DoD)** has developed an enterprise cloud platform strategy that spans SaaS, PaaS, IaaS, and various service models, including multi-cloud and hybrid-cloud—DEOS, Cloud One, DISA Stratus, and JWCC *[18]*. DoD has created a DoD Cloud Strategy to align with the larger DoD cyber strategy, strengthening the security and resilience of the networks and systems that contribute to the department's military advantage *[19]*.

As is clearly evident from data across industry verticals, the cloud has evolved rapidly from just being yet another deployment platform to a powerhouse of innovation and business transformation. In the next section, we will explore how enterprises can adopt a hybrid cloud, some common strategies for doing so, and the drawbacks to adoption.

Adopting a hybrid cloud

A hybrid cloud is the future of IT across enterprises, as it offers the best of both worlds—the scale, resilience, and innovation of public clouds coupled with the control and security of private or on-premises clouds. As we briefly explored earlier, there are several high-value use cases that a hybrid cloud offers enterprises, such as cloud bursting, geo-redundancy, fallback DR, and a sandbox for innovation. In this section, we will explore hybrid cloud adoption and what constitutes a hybrid cloud.

The market share for hybrid clouds has been growing rapidly in recent years, as more and more enterprises look to take advantage of the benefits offered by combining public cloud capabilities with their existing on-premises or private cloud environments. Some critical factors contributing to the growth of hybrid cloud adoption include the need for data sovereignty, compliance, cost optimization, agility, and scalability.

Although cloud infrastructure's benefits are clear, it is still impractical—at least in the near term—for enterprises with on-premises IT estate and legacy mission-critical applications to migrate to a modern cloud deployment model.

According to a survey report by Data Bridge, the hybrid cloud market was valued at 47.67 billion USD in 2021 and is expected to reach 135.98 billion USD by 2029 with a CAGR of 14% [20].

Public cloud providers are responding to this by offering tools, platforms, and solutions that can span multiple deployment models. While there isn't a standard that all providers adhere to for building a hybrid cloud, it will be prudent for organizations embarking on a cloud journey to evaluate hybrid cloud capabilities, support models, and business-specific needs.

Although there are several core services that support a hybrid cloud architecture that is common across established public cloud vendors, such as network interconnects, data transfer services, identity services, and cloud management, we will review some specialized services across AWS, Google, and Azure.

AWS offers a hybrid cloud model that supports AWS on and off-premises via services such as AWS Outposts, AWS Wavelength, and AWS Snow Family. This enables customers to extend the public AWS cloud capabilities to where it's needed—at an on-premises data center, a co-location facility, or even an edge location [21]. This is a good fit for customers who are already on AWS or plan to adopt an AWS-centric cloud strategy.

- **AWS Outposts**: AWS Outposts brings the AWS cloud infrastructure and services to a customer's on-premises data center, hosting, or co-location facility and extends the cloud services to support local computational needs

- **AWS Wavelength**: AWS Wavelength extends AWS infrastructure to the edge, making it easier to develop and deliver high-performance applications that can leverage the capabilities of 5G networks

- **AWS Snow Family**: The AWS Snow family of services offers cloud computing capabilities at remote sites and locations where reliable or consistent network connectivity is not practical

Google Cloud Platform (GCP) offers hybrid and multi-cloud solutions that give organizations the ability to run applications anywhere through services such as Anthos, global load balancers, and Traffic Director [22]. Anthos offers several tools to modernize applications in place:

- **Anthos for VMs**: You can modernize VM-based workloads with the power of Kubernetes

- **Anthos Multicloud**: Anthos Multicloud API enables provisioning and management of **Google Kubernetes Engine** (GKE) clusters on AWS and Azure

- **Anthos on Bare Metal**: You can deploy Anthos on bare metal servers without the need for a type 1 hypervisor, enabling new scenarios such as deploying at edge locations

- **Serverless**: Cloud Run for Anthos is a flexible serverless development platform that supports the deployment of workloads to Anthos clusters and is a fully supported Knative offering and open source project that supports serverless workloads on Kubernetes

Microsoft Azure, through its Azure Stack offering, enables organizations to extend Azure services and capabilities to an environment of choice—from data centers to edge locations and remote offices—to help build, deploy, and run hybrid and edge computing apps consistently across the IT ecosystem [23]:

- **Azure Stack Edge**: An Azure-managed appliance that can run computing workloads at the edge
- **Azure Stack HCI**: A hyper-converged solution from Azure to modernize with a modern infrastructure stack managed by Azure
- **Azure Stack Hub**: Private cloud with cloud-native apps and Azure services that can be run in both connected and disconnected mode

Oracle Cloud is a hybrid cloud offering where organizations can leverage public cloud services on-premises, including Oracle IaaS, PaaS, and SaaS offerings *[24]*:

- **Oracle Exadata Cloud@Customer**: A hyper-converged infrastructure that can be run within a customer's on-premises data center and delivers Oracle's flagship database HCI, Exadata
- **Oracle Dedicated Region Cloud@Customer**: A complete OCI cloud region that offers OCI public cloud services within a private data center
- **Oracle Roving Edge Infrastructure**: **Ruggedized Oracle Roving Edge Devices** (**Oracle REDs**) that deliver computing and storage services at the edge of networks and in disconnected locations, allowing faster processing close to the data source

As we can see, different public cloud providers have unique approaches when it comes to offering hybrid cloud services. It is also important to understand the various private cloud platforms that exist, such as RedHat OpenShift, OpenStack, HPE Helion, Rackspace, VMware Cloud Foundation, Cloud Foundry, Cisco UCS, and Dell EMC.

What is and isn't a hybrid cloud?

As we look at hybrid cloud adoption, it's important to understand what is and isn't a hybrid cloud model.

An organization using multiple public clouds or multiple private clouds doesn't constitute a hybrid deployment. Isolated deployments of private cloud components that don't interact or integrate with a public cloud don't fit into the definition of a hybrid cloud model. A key criterion for a hybrid cloud model is the composition of one or more public clouds with an on-premises private cloud environment, integration of applications, APIs, or services, and management of the components as a single system.

Challenges in adopting a hybrid cloud

Although a hybrid cloud enables enterprises to have the best of both worlds, there are several challenges that organizations must be aware of before choosing a cloud strategy:

- **Consistency of platform**: Hybrid cloud environments can be complex to design, deploy, and manage. IT teams may need to integrate multiple cloud providers and on-premises systems, which can increase complexity and introduce potential points of failure.

- **Integration**: Integrating applications and data across multiple environments can be a challenge. Some applications may not be compatible with certain cloud environments, and data may need to be transformed or migrated to work in the hybrid cloud.

- **Data management**: Hybrid cloud environments can create data management challenges, as data may need to be moved and synchronized across multiple systems. This can be time-consuming and may introduce the risk of data loss or corruption.

- **Security**: Security is everyone's business and more so in hybrid cloud environments, as sensitive data and applications may be spread across multiple locations and infrastructures. It can be difficult to ensure consistent security policies and controls across different environments.

- **Governance**: Hybrid cloud deployments can make it difficult to enforce consistent governance policies and processes. Organizations need to ensure that their governance framework is designed to work in a hybrid cloud environment.

- **Vendor lock-in**: Organizations may run the risk of being locked into specific cloud providers, technology stacks, or vendors, making it difficult to switch providers or move workloads between environments. This quickly amplifies with HCI options, as there is a significant investment in the hardware stack.

- **Performance**: Hybrid cloud environments can introduce latency and performance issues, particularly if not well architected, as data will have to be transferred between environments. Organizations need to ensure that their hybrid cloud environment is designed to meet their performance requirements. This can also result in higher costs due to network egress.

- **Change management**: Changes to one part of the hybrid cloud environment can have unintended consequences in other parts of the environment. Organizations need to ensure that they have effective change management processes in place to minimize the risk of disruption.

Myths of cloud adoption

There are several myths surrounding cloud adoption that can sometimes hold organizations back from fully embracing cloud technologies. In this section, let's explore some common myths and the truths behind them.

Myth 1 – the cloud is a one-size-fits-all solution approach

The myth of the cloud being a one-size-fits-all is just that-a myth. Cloud computing is a complex and nuanced field, and there is no single solution that will work for every organization. However, it is important to understand that cloud computing is a broad spectrum that encompasses a wide variety of different applications, solutions, and services. It is relatively easy to get started with the cloud. However, it is tricky to get it right. The best cloud solution for a particular organization will depend on a variety of factors, including the organization's specific needs, budget, and security requirements.

Building differentiated solutions for specific business needs in cloud is key. Here are some of the factors to consider when building differentiated solutions by leveraging the cloud:

- Focus on industry vertical and market demands
- Identify the USP of the organization and business objectives
- Research cloud service providers
- Focus on innovation to support the customer base
- Security and compliance requirements

Myth 2 – the cloud creates a vendor dependency and lock-in

The myth that cloud computing creates vendor lock-in is based on the idea that once you move your data and applications to the cloud, you are unable to easily switch to another provider or even on-premises. Cloud computing is built on a wide range of open source technologies and standards. In fact, many of the core components of cloud computing, such as virtualization, containerization, and orchestration, were developed as open source projects. A few examples include OpenStack, Kubernetes, Docker, **Cloud Native Computing Foundation** (**CNCF**), **Open Container Initiative** (**OCI**), **kernel-based virtual machines** (**KVMs**), Linux, OpenAPI, Istio, Terraform, Prometheus, etc.

While it could be argued that organizations leveraging value-added services (managed services or proprietary services) of a cloud provider leads to vendor dependency, the same can be argued for traditional on-premises IT. However, with a competitive landscape and an increased demand for open source, cloud providers are increasingly offering value-added services that have parity with open source to enable portability. In reality, legacy tech investments and monoliths within an enterprise contribute to a high percentage of vendor lock-in and tech debt.

Organizations embarking on a cloud journey should also have an open platform strategy that facilitates portability. Some factors to consider include the following:

- Defining a portable application architecture (choice of cloud-native architecture, programming languages, frameworks, libraries, processes)
- Application containerization that leverages OCI or CNCF
- APIs (ensuring applications are service-enabled)
- Configuration management tools to support platform-independent deployments
- DevSecOps (choice of development platform, tools for monitoring)
- Scalability, geo-redundancy

Myth 3 – the cloud is more expensive than traditional on-premises

This myth stems from a few basic assumptions and misconceptions:

- **Blind lift and shift and overprovisioning**: Cloud technology brings a paradigm shift in IT architecture, with an objective to address the shortcomings of traditional IT, such as capacity planning, scaling on-demand, containerization, breaking down monoliths to microservices, change management, operational resiliency, etc. However, when organizations first embark on a cloud journey, failure to rethink and transform IT architecture is a key impediment that can result in failed cloud adoptions that are eventually attributed to costs.

   A common pitfall is for organizations to migrate their traditional on-premises applications or services as-is to the cloud either to avoid risks and efforts, resist change, or a combination of factors. Although this could be a viable solution in the short term for compelling reasons such as data center exits, contractual obligations, software or hardware licensing renewals, etc., this is more often cost-prone and detrimental in the long run. Blind lift and shift can lead to overprovisioning of resources, unnecessary complexity, higher costs, and less security.

- **Evaluating costs without considering cloud-native operations**: Cloud-native architecture offers modern tools and operational controls to help enterprises realize the full potential of the cloud. These include scaling on-demand, automating infrastructure using IaC, optimizing costs for sustained or committed usage, and implementing serverless infrastructure and native administrative and operational controls to help reap cost benefits.

Oftentimes, organizations expect to keep their IT processes and operations intact when migrating to the cloud. The following are some common pitfalls that can not only incur costs but also lost business value:

- **Capacity planning**: Unless there is strong business backing, there is little reason to right-size workloads in the cloud. Organizations following traditional capacity planning (or *sizing for high watermark*) in the cloud may fail to realize potential cost savings.

- **Automation**: Fundamental to cloud principles is the ability to automate everything. For instance, by leveraging IaC automations, organizations can save time, effort, and money, as mundane operations are offloaded from IT personnel. This can have the added benefit of saving costs arising out of human errors.

- **Re-architecting even with lift and shift**: Lifting and shifting traditional on-premises applications or services is one of the easiest in terms of effort, complexity, and risk. However, it may not be the most efficient. It would be prudent for IT leaders to think of components within the application ecosystem that can be quickly ported to take advantage of cloud-native tooling and operations to realize better value. We will explore this in a lot more detail in the *Pathways to Cloud Adoption* chapter.

- **Admin and SRE**: Traditional IT operations are often built around legacy systems, existing skill sets, and access to technology. The cloud aims to democratize administrative and SRE practices that companies of all sizes can take full advantage of. Organizations must strive to leverage continuous integration and continuous delivery practices and cloud-native operations automation to save costs.

- **Cost optimization and FinOps**: Cost optimization has been a critical value driver for cloud adoption. Most cloud providers offer cost optimization tooling and FinOps best practices to help gain more value out of cloud investments. Organizations must actively look for opportunities such as leveraging billing discounts for commitments, sustained usage, and reservations that can result in significant cost savings.

- **Failure to estimate the total cost of ownership and cost of business value**: Another common impediment to cloud adoption is the failure to measure the total cost of ownership and the business value of the cloud initiative. This is especially crucial for the first cloud initiative for businesses to understand the true cost and value. Sidestepping this could prove detrimental to the digital transformation journey and would risk missing out on the big picture.

  A TCO and business value analysis will help businesses to do the following:

  - Identify and quantify all associated costs with a specific cloud initiative and helps organizations make informed decisions before embarking on a cloud journey

  - Help compare available options, as it may otherwise be difficult to compare them directly

  - Identify hidden costs that may be associated with products, services, maintenance, and human resources

Organizations would also find it a crucial consideration to do a value realization exercise after the cloud migration to validate the actual business value realized. Oftentimes, a strategic business partner can help estimate the TCO and business value.

Myth 4 – the cloud is less secure than traditional on-premises

Another common myth is that a solution hosted on a public cloud is less secure than hosting within an on-premises data center. We recognize the fact that bad actors exist on the internet and there are security risks associated with any IT deployment model—cloud computing is not an exception. There are also new attack vectors that clouds—especially public clouds—are exposed to. However, cloud computing offers a number of security advantages over traditional on-premises that organizations can benefit from:

- **Security and compliance expertise**: Cloud providers have a wealth of experience with regard to security and compliance, with teams of security experts constantly working to improve the security of the cloud infrastructure. Cloud providers have a lot at stake if the overall security of the cloud platform is compromised. Any security breach could leave customer records exposed and could lead to a loss of customer trust and a significant economic loss for the cloud provider.

- **Secure infrastructure**: Cloud providers have a defense-in-depth security strategy and have significant investments in the security of the cloud infrastructure. Their data centers are typically located in secure facilities, and they use the latest security technologies. This includes things such as firewalls, intrusion detection systems, and data encryption.

- **Redundancy**: Cloud providers have multiple layers of redundancy in place. This means that even if one part of their infrastructure fails, your data will still be safe. For example, if one data center goes down, your data will be automatically replicated to another data center.

- **Monitoring**: Cloud providers have teams of security experts who constantly monitor their infrastructure 24/7 for any security threats or suspicious activity. This means that they can quickly identify and respond to security threats.

- **Compliance**: Cloud providers offer a range of industry regulatory and compliance attestations to help with deploying sensitive data and application workloads. This means that customers can be confident in the data that is being stored and processed within a cloud environment. For example, GovCloud with FedRAMP attestation, HIPAA attestations for healthcare workloads, PCI DSS compliance for payment processing, SOC for financial and operational compliance, etc.

Traditionally, public cloud providers offered a *shared responsibility* security framework and model to secure cloud computing environments. The shared responsibility model clearly defines the responsibilities of a cloud provider and a customer. Typically, cloud providers are responsible for the security of the underlying infrastructure, while customers are responsible for securing the applications and data. A more modern approach to cloud security is the *shared fate* model, which emphasizes the importance of collaboration between cloud providers and customers. Under this model, both the cloud provider and the customer are responsible for the security of the entire cloud environment and for identifying and mitigating security risks.

Myth 5 – the cloud is a panacea

Yet another assumption and a common myth is that, due to the elasticity and scalability of the cloud, the cloud is a panacea for ill-defined architectures. Although cloud technology aims to address some core challenges surrounding traditional on-premises IT, it still requires careful planning, assessment, and management.

Cloud computing can deliver several instantaneous benefits to applications, including high availability, elastic scaling, and faster time to market. However, it is critical to understand the nature of the workload, integration, security, performance, and compatibility needs before a cloud deployment choice is made.

For instance, poor application design (applications that are not designed for scale or fault tolerance) can become even more problematic when migrating as-is to cloud environments, as the inefficiencies can quickly manifest into increased complexity. Even in situations where a quick migration is warranted, enterprises should carefully consider approaches such as refactoring or optimizing the application design before migration.

Similarly, inefficient or poorly optimized code can lead to resource sprawl, higher costs, and performance degradation in cloud environments, as the resources required to run the application may be greater than necessary. While modern cloud platforms can offer powerful compute resources, this cannot make up for inefficient or poorly optimized code, and organizations will end up with a *throw more hardware at it* syndrome as a short-term measure. Enterprises would greatly benefit from fixing the smoking gun.

Also, some legacy applications just aren't compatible with modern cloud environments. This can pose a significant challenge for enterprises, as it may require significant effort, investment, and time to update or replace these applications, especially if they are mission-critical and core to the business. Enterprises can employ various strategies such as rehosting leveraging cloud options (e.g. Bare Metal, VMware Cloud, containers) for VM-based workloads as an intermediary step before rearchitecting the app stack.

To fully leverage the value and benefits that the cloud brings, enterprises require a paradigm shift and a methodical approach, as one size doesn't fit all and the cloud isn't a magic bullet.

Summary

In this chapter, we have discussed the different cloud deployment and service models and how enterprises can take advantage of the cloud as a platform to advance their digital transformation efforts. We also explored how cloud infrastructures are adopted across different industries and what impacts they have had on various verticals, the value drivers of the cloud, how enterprises can adopt a hybrid cloud strategy, and the myths that surround cloud computing.

Regardless of the cloud paradigm, the success of a cloud transformation is purely dependent on an organization's vision and the ability to craft a cloud strategy that complements it. For several large enterprises, leveraging a hybrid cloud strategy can be a welcome move, as it allows enterprises to take advantage of modern cloud computing platforms to solve business challenges while also leveraging existing investments in traditional on-premises setups.

In the next chapter, we will discuss the various challenges of enterprise cloud adoption and strategies to address them.

Further readings

The references used in this chapter as well as some additional resources are listed as follows:

1. `https://cloud.google.com/blog/topics/customers/how-ikea-is-creating-a-more-affordable-accessible-and-sustainable-future`
2. `https://about.netflix.com/en/news/completing-the-netflix-cloud-migration`

3. https://d3.harvard.edu/platform-digit/submission/covid-a-massive-distraction-or-an-opportunity-to-capture-online-market-share-for-target/

4. https://resources.github.com/devops/github-enterprise-ebook/

5. https://cloud.google.com/blog/products/identity-security/how-google-cloud-blocked-largest-layer-7-ddos-attack-at-46-million-rps

6. https://www.gartner.com/smarterwithgartner/6-ways-cloud-migration-costs-go-off-the-rails

7. https://www.businesswire.com/news/home/20190617005945/en/New-McAfee-Report-Finds-Eighty-Seven-Percent-Companies

8. https://ae.oreilly.com/l/1009792/2023-05-30/gykj/1009792/1685463216GOlmcbeM/The_Cloud_in_2021_Adoption_Continues.pdf

9. https://www.census.gov/retail/index.html

10. https://www.ncbi.nlm.nih.gov/pmc/articles/PMC3615826/

11. http://www.itadynamics.com/media/Microsoft-Dynamics-City-of-Los-Angeles-Bureau-of-Sanitation-Wastewater-Solid-Waste-Stormwater.pdf

12. https://cloud.google.com/blog/topics/public-sector/how-state-oklahoma-using-data-fight-opioid-epidemic

13. https://cloud.google.com/customers/commonwealth-ma

14. https://www.fsis.usda.gov/sites/default/files/media_file/documents/phis-industry-user-guide.pdf

15. https://www.gov.uk/guidance/g-cloud-suppliers-guide

16. https://ndl.iitkgp.ac.in

17. https://www.anao.gov.au/work/performance-audit/digital-education-revolution-program-national-secondary-schools-computer-fund

18. https://www.cloud.mil

19. https://media.defense.gov/2019/Feb/04/2002085866/-1/-1/1/DOD-CLOUD-STRATEGY.PDF

20. https://www.databridgemarketresearch.com/reports/global-hybrid-cloud-market

21. https://pages.awscloud.com/hybrid-cloud-outposts.html

22. https://cloud.google.com/anthos

23. https://azure.microsoft.com/en-us/solutions/hybrid-cloud-app/#products

24. https://www.oracle.com/cloud/hybrid-cloud/#rc30p0

Enterprise Challenges with Cloud Adoption

One of the common challenges that enterprises face with digital transformation and the adoption of cloud technologies is its ability to balance existing traditional on-premises IT ecosystems with the cloud. In a traditional enterprise, any adoption of new technology still had to rely on IT to deliver the business capability. For instance, a finance department looking to overhaul its ERP can choose ERP software or a vendor, but it still has to work with its IT department to deliver the infrastructure, platform, security, and integrations to have it fully functional. Modern cloud technologies have reduced the friction and dependency between businesses and IT. For instance, a sales organization can procure and operate a CRM SaaS solution almost instantly to address its business demands without the dependency of IT. Of course, an IT organization will still have to manage the application integration, data integration, and security complexities. The following figure illustrates how a typical enterprise IT ecosystem will look like:

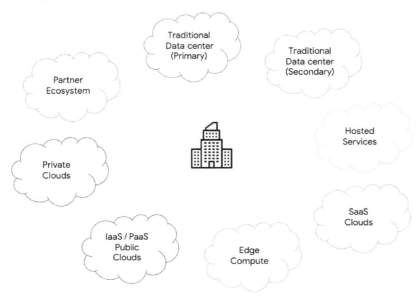

Figure 3.1 – A typical enterprise IT ecosystem

In this chapter, we will explore the challenges and complexities that enterprises face with digital transformation and some strategies for addressing them. Specifically, we will discuss and address the following:

- Where do we start digital transformation given the complexities surrounding the enterprise IT ecosystem?

- Choosing the right cloud strategy through an e-commerce application modernization example

- How to identify the right workloads for cloud transformation and various strategies

- Best practices in hybrid cloud and multi-cloud adoption

- How can enterprises deal with new financial models—specifically moving from CapEx to OpEx

Where do we start? Complexities of an enterprise IT ecosystem

Today's enterprise IT ecosystem spans beyond the boundaries of the physical enterprise. With organic growth and contributing business demands, enterprise IT management has become a challenge to administer and manage. Owing to market dynamics and growing customer demands, enterprises have grown beyond the perimeters of traditional data centers and have forayed into hosting services, SaaS clouds, edge computing (i.e. micro data centers), private clouds, public clouds, and integration with partner ecosystems. Although these initiatives have augmented business capabilities, there are natural challenges with data sprawl, data redundancy, anti-patterns arising from myriad application architectures, integration, vendor management, data security, privacy, and compliance. Let's review some of the complexities surrounding enterprise IT.

Tech debt

Technical debt or tech debt refers to the accumulated consequences of suboptimal decisions, compromises, and shortcuts made over time in the development and maintenance of software systems. It represents the cost an enterprise incurs over time trading off high maintenance for expeditious solution delivery. Tech debt is prevalent in several enterprises and can arise from various factors, such as time constraints, budget limitations, changing business priorities, a lack of technical expertise, inadequate planning, and evolving technology landscapes. Development teams may choose quick and dirty solutions to meet immediate deadlines or cut corners due to resource limitations, which can result in accumulating tech debt.

Tech debt can manifest in different forms:

- **Architectural debt**: Sub-optimal system design and architecture decisions
- **Code debt**: Complex, convoluted, and poorly documented codebases
- **Data debt**: Redundant copies of data also commonly referred to as data sprawl or data silos
- **Software debt**: Outdated and unsupported software, redundant software capabilities
- **Legacy debt**: Legacy systems that require substantial maintenance and rework
- **Hardware debt**: Accumulated investments in hardware stack; hyper-converged infrastructure requiring specialized consultants and support

Accumulated tech debt can have significant repercussions for enterprises as it can slow down development, hamper productivity, increase maintenance costs, and introduce higher risks of system failures, bugs, and security vulnerabilities. It can impede innovation and hinder the enterprise's ability to adapt to changing market demands.

Business units creating their IT marts

As consumer and market demands grow exponentially, enterprises are constantly challenged to meet business demands to stay competitive. As the primary driver for businesses is to stay abreast of market demands, lines of business leaders often opt for solutions that offer faster time to market, ease of management, low administrative overhead, and dependency on IT. With the emergence of **Software as a Service** (**SaaS**) business models, business units can invest in solutions that quickly address business demands. For instance, a sales team can leverage its budget and invest in a modern CRM platform to improve customer retention, offer better customer service, increase sales forecasting accuracy, and gain insights into customer behavior. Although this might help meet a specific business need in the short term, this may quickly result in siloed solutions and the proliferation of diverse technologies, platforms, and architectures within the enterprise IT ecosystem across the enterprise, leading to application integration, data integration, and security complexities. Enterprises must have a well-defined business strategy and a complementing IT strategy to deliver sustainable long-term business goals without increased IT complexity and maintenance burden.

Proprietary private clouds

Cloud technologies are fundamentally built on open source technologies. However, with more and more cloud vendors building proprietary wrappers in an effort to deliver differentiated product offerings on top of open source, it is prudent for enterprises to carefully evaluate merits and demerits with proper planning, design, and management. This effect is exacerbated in private cloud offerings where it often requires large upfront investments in infrastructure, hardware, software, development methodologies, and consulting efforts. The use of proprietary technologies limits flexibility and leads to vendor lock-in. In a private cloud, resource allocation and optimization are crucial to ensuring the efficient utilization of available infrastructure. Balancing workloads, managing virtual machine placement, and optimizing resource allocation based on demand can be complex tasks that require continuous monitoring and fine-tuning. Other primary considerations for enterprises when choosing a private cloud deployment model are data sovereignty and compliance needs. Since private clouds store sensitive enterprise data and applications, it necessitates robust security measures, managing access controls, data encryption, and protecting against threats that can become complex. Compliance with industry-specific regulations such as HIPAA or GDPR adds another layer of complexity, requiring careful configuration and auditing of security controls. Another common challenge with building and managing private clouds is the ability to offer **service-level agreements** (**SLAs**), monitoring, capacity planning, and chargeback mechanisms, that require robust service management processes and tools.

Data sprawl and integration

Another very common challenge with digital transformation is data sprawl across the enterprise. Data sprawl refers to the uncontrolled growth and dispersion of data across an enterprise, presenting a host of complexities. Data sprawl can make it difficult to locate and access relevant data when needed. It becomes challenging to search and discover data across multiple systems and repositories, leading to inefficiencies and delays in data-driven decision-making processes. It becomes challenging to establish and enforce consistent data governance policies, maintain data quality and security, and comply with regulations. Managing data across multiple systems and locations leads to increased storage and infrastructure costs, while data integration and interoperability suffer due to inconsistent formats and silos. Discovering and accessing relevant data becomes difficult, impacting decision-making processes and ensuring data backup and recovery becomes more complex. To address these complexities, robust data governance frameworks, integration strategies, and technologies must be implemented alongside data classification, metadata management, and regular audits to mitigate the challenges of data sprawl.

Security

Security challenges are a critical consideration in the process of digital transformation within enterprises, as organizations adopt new technologies and embrace digital initiatives. As the enterprise IT ecosystem begins to span across on-premises infrastructure, public clouds, edge computing, third-party integrations, and IoT, it leads to complex and dynamic IT environments with increased attack surfaces. Securing this intricate ecosystem requires continuous monitoring, threat detection, and vulnerability management. Ensuring data protection and privacy becomes critical, particularly with evolving regulations such as GDPR or CCPA, and enterprises must develop and implement robust security measures, including encryption, access controls, and data lifecycle management.

Choosing the right cloud strategy

Enterprises have unique business demands, and it is crucial to assess, evaluate, and plan the right cloud strategy. With a wide variety of cloud deployment models and cloud hyperscalers, enterprises must carefully assess their business objectives, identify workload suitability, and evaluate vendor capabilities and support/security measures before embarking on a cloud journey. One primary challenge for enterprises is deciding where to start the cloud journey. One business problem can be addressed through a variety of solutions. The choice of solution depends primarily on the current capabilities, skill set, compelling events, IT maturity, and availability of resources within an enterprise.

Example

Let's consider an example of a retail enterprise embarking on a digital transformation journey to build a modern omnichannel e-commerce platform. A traditional monolith e-commerce application architecture is shown:

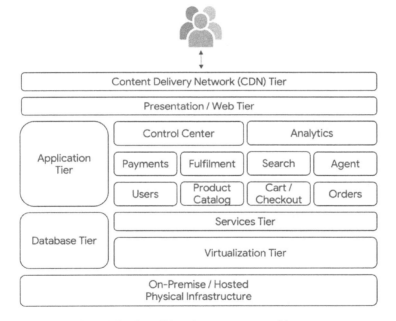

Figure 3.2 – A traditional e-commerce architecture

From a business requirement perspective, the retailer can define business objectives along with the associated key results and metrics:

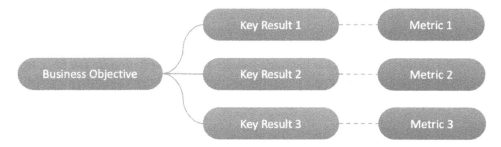

Figure 3.3 – Objectives and key results (OKR)

The following is an example of how OKRs can be envisioned and defined for e-commerce modernization.

- **Objective**: The goal is to enhance e-commerce platform efficiency and offer an omnichannel user experience to meet, serve, and support the demands of modern-day shoppers.

- **Key results**: The outcomes are to address e-commerce modernization objectives such as platform efficiency, offer an omnichannel user experience, and meet new consumer expectations. The following are some key results that can directly impact the overall objective:

  - **Modern user experience**: An intuitive and easy-to-navigate interface provides a seamless user experience across different devices and screen sizes, including web, mobile app, mobile web, and voice assistants.

  - **Mobile experience**: With the increasing use of smartphones, tablets, smart devices, and wearables, it's crucial for an e-commerce platform to be fully optimized for mobile devices to cater to the growing number of mobile shoppers.

  - **Robust product catalog management**: Enable efficient management of product information, including detailed descriptions, multiple product images, pricing, stock availability, and variations.

  - **B2C, B2B, B2B2C capabilities**: This is the ability to support consumers, business-to-business commerce, and direct-to-consumer selling.

  - **Secure and reliable payment processing**: Support various payment methods, including credit/debit cards, digital wallets, and integration with open banking ecosystems to offer personalized flexible payment and financing options such as **buy now, pay later** (**BNPL**) and other online payment systems.

  - **Efficient order management**: Enable seamless cross-channel order processing, including order placement, tracking, and fulfillment. Integrate with inventory management systems to provide accurate stock information.

- **Integration with third-party services**: Integrating with external services such as shipping providers, analytics tools, CRM systems, supply chains, marketing automation platforms, and enterprise backend systems is essential for efficient operations and data analysis.

- **Robust search and filtering capabilities**: A powerful search function and advanced filtering options help customers quickly find the products they are looking for, enhancing user experience and driving conversions.

- **Scalability and performance**: Build in the capability to handle high volumes of traffic and transactions without significant performance degradation while also accommodating future growth and spikes in demand such as seasonal or flash sales.

- **Cross-channel personalization**: Offering a seamless shopping experience across multiple channels, such as websites, mobile apps, social media, and physical stores, allows customers to interact with the brand through their preferred channels and supports personalized promotions, emails, and dynamic product recommendations.

- **Embedded AI**: Support a wide array of capabilities leveraging modern AI solutions, such as personalized shopping experiences, product recommendations, virtual assistants to offer 24/7 support, intelligent product discovery, fraud detection and prevention, visual and voice search capabilities, dynamic pricing, and promotions.

- **Security and compliance**: Guard against malware attacks such as ransomware, DDoS attacks, financial frauds, intelligent scraping bots, phishing, **cross-site scripting** (**XSS**), and **man-in-the-middle** (**MITM**) attacks. The platform should also support various regulatory and compliance statutes such as PCI, PII, GDPR, COPPA, and ADA.

From a technology perspective, this problem statement and objective can be addressed in a variety of ways. Let's explore a few options along with the pros and cons of each approach.

Option 1: Building an e-commerce platform using SaaS

SaaS e-commerce platforms have become increasingly popular due to their convenience, speed to market, and cost-effectiveness. SaaS e-commerce platforms are an attractive option for businesses looking for a cost-effective, scalable, and hassle-free solution to establishing and managing their online stores. However, it is essential for enterprises to evaluate the pros and cons of leveraging a SaaS-based e-commerce platform.

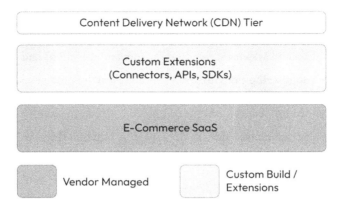

Figure 3.4 – SaaS-based e-commerce architecture

The following are some advantages of the SaaS approach:

- **Faster time to market**: SaaS platforms offer a user-friendly interface and provide pre-built templates and themes, making it easy for businesses to quickly set up and launch their online stores.

- **Cost-effective**: SaaS platforms offer a subscription-based pricing model, allowing businesses to pay on demand instead of making a large upfront investment. This can be particularly beneficial for small and medium-sized businesses or organizations with limited IT resources and budgets, as it can help them avoid costs associated with hosting, security, and maintenance.

- **Scalability**: SaaS platforms are designed to scale effortlessly as the business grows. The SaaS service provider assumes the responsibility to scale the infrastructure and resources needed to handle increased traffic, transactions, and product catalogs without requiring significant changes to the underlying architecture.

- **Security and compliance**: SaaS providers typically invest heavily in security measures to protect their platforms and customer data by implementing industry-standard security protocols, conducting regular security audits, and ensuring compliance with various data protection regulations. SaaS platforms provide robust security measures, including data encryption, regular backups, and compliance with industry standards such as PCI. Platform providers usually handle security updates and ensure the platform is protected against vulnerabilities.

- **Reduced IT burden**: With a SaaS e-commerce platform, enterprises can offload the infrastructure management and technical complexities to the service provider. This frees up internal IT teams to focus on more strategic tasks and core business activities rather than routine maintenance and updates.

- **Feature enhancements**: SaaS platforms generally offer frequent updates and new feature releases, ensuring that the e-commerce store remains up to date with the latest technologies and trends. These updates can help businesses stay competitive in the market.

- **Operations and maintenance**: Since SaaS platforms are operated and maintained by the service provider, this can be a great fit for small and medium businesses and lean IT organizations where enterprises can devote their efforts to other business priorities.

- **Data analytics and insights**: SaaS e-commerce platforms include built-in analytics and reporting features that provide valuable insights into business performance. Organizations can track key metrics, analyze customer behavior, and make data-driven decisions to optimize e-commerce operations and drive growth.

With the aforementioned advantages, enterprises must be aware of there are some shortcomings:

- **Limited customization**: SaaS platforms may have limitations compared to self-hosted solutions when it comes to customization options. While they provide templates and themes that can be customized to some extent, businesses will typically have restrictions on modifying the underlying code or implementing highly specific design and functionality requirements.

- **Vendor dependency**: Since the e-commerce platform is hosted and managed by a provider, businesses are reliant on the platform's uptime, performance, and support. If the platform experiences technical issues or downtime, it may impact the availability and functionality of the online store.

- **Differentiated services**: A SaaS-based solution can also become a hurdle to implementing unique differentiated services, e.g., embedding AI-based solutions, third-party search/product discovery offerings, etc.

- **Data ownership and migration challenges**: When using a SaaS platform, the data is stored on the provider's servers. This can raise concerns about data ownership and portability if you decide to switch platforms in the future. Enterprises may also face challenges in migrating your data and customizations to a different system.

- **Limited integration and control**: With a SaaS platform, you have limited control over the backend infrastructure and server configurations. This can be a disadvantage for businesses with specific hosting requirements or those needing advanced customization and integration with external or existing enterprise backend systems.

- **Long-term operational costs**: While the subscription-based pricing model can be cost-effective for many businesses, it can become a long-term expense. Over time, as enterprise needs grow, businesses will have to leverage various add-on services to build capabilities, and the cumulative subscription costs may exceed the cost of building and maintaining a self-hosted e-commerce solution.

Option 2: Building an e-commerce platform based on headless commerce

Another big trend in developing an e-commerce solution is headless composable commerce based on the **Microservices-based, API-first, Cloud-native, and Headless (MACH)** architecture. In a headless composable commerce architecture, the content management capabilities are decoupled from the presentation layer or the frontend of an e-commerce application. A headless composable commerce enables developers to compose and combine content from multiple sources, including external APIs, microservices, or other content repositories, allowing for greater flexibility in content aggregation and integration across various systems. A headless commerce provides a user-friendly interface for content creators and editors to create, manage, and organize content including features such as content editing, version control, content workflows, and user permissions. With a headless CMS, the frontend is decoupled from the backend, allowing developers the flexibility to choose the most appropriate frontend technology or framework (such as React, Angular, or Vue.js) to build the presentation layer. This separation of concerns between the content management and presentation layers enables independent development and faster iteration cycles.

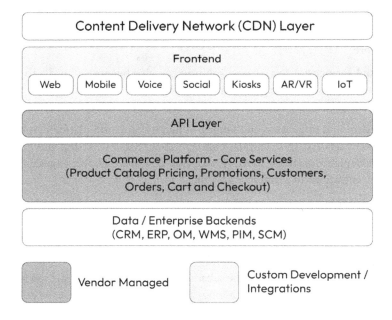

Figure 3.5 – Headless commerce architecture

Let's review some advantages of choosing a headless commerce platform for enterprises:

- **Engaging customer experience**: A headless composable commerce allows enterprises to choose the most suitable frontend framework or technology for the e-commerce platform, which enables the creation of highly customized and engaging user interfaces that uniquely align with specific business requirements.

- **Seamless omni-channel experiences**: With a headless commerce architecture, content can be easily distributed to various channels, such as websites, mobile apps, voice assistants, or IoT devices to enable businesses to provide a consistent and personalized experience across multiple user touchpoints.

- **Future-proofing and scalability**: Headless architectures are inherently more adaptable to technological advancements. Businesses can easily adopt new frontend frameworks or technologies, upgrade existing components, and integrate with emerging technologies without disrupting the CMS backend. This scalability helps businesses stay relevant and agile in a rapidly evolving e-commerce landscape.

- **Faster time-to-market**: With the decoupled nature of composable headless architecture, the frontend user experience can proceed independently of the backend, allowing for parallel development and reducing time to market for new features, updates, or redesigns.

- **A/B testing and experimentation**: With a headless composable commerce, enterprises can easily conduct A/B tests and experiment with different front-end experiences. This enables data-driven decision-making, user engagement optimization, and improved conversion rates.

- **Easier integrations**: Headless composable commerce platforms generally offer well-documented APIs, making it easier to integrate with enterprise backend systems, third-party services, external systems, and microservices. This enables businesses to seamlessly leverage specialized services for payments, inventory management, analytics, or marketing automation, expanding the functionality of their e-commerce platform.

The disadvantages of choosing a headless commerce platform for enterprises are as follows:

- **Development complexity**: Implementing a headless composable commerce requires a higher level of technical expertise compared to traditional monolithic commerce solutions. Developers need to handle the integration and synchronization of the frontend with the backend, which can increase development complexity and time. Since the frontends and backends are developed separately, it requires additional development effort to build and maintain, which may lead to increased costs, especially if enterprises lack the necessary IT resources or expertise.

- **Dependence on APIs and backend stability**: The performance and reliability of the backend and its APIs become critical to ensuring smooth content delivery and overall platform functionality. Any issues with the backend or API disruptions can directly impact the user experience and require immediate resolution.

- **Limited out-of-the-box features**: Compared to traditional e-commerce platforms, headless composable commerce solutions may offer fewer out-of-the-box features and functionalities, as the focus is primarily on custom frontend and backend development rather than integrated e-commerce features. This requires enterprises to invest additional development effort to build or integrate specific e-commerce functionalities.

- **Increased system complexity**: A headless composable commerce introduces additional components and integrations, which can increase the overall system complexity. Managing and maintaining multiple technologies, APIs, and services requires careful coordination and ongoing monitoring. This complexity can be alleviated by leveraging a vendor-managed stack.

- **Operational costs**: A headless commerce platform requires enterprises to invest significantly in building the IT muscle, skill set, development, and operational resources. It is expensive to implement and most commonly suited to enterprises with large, technically savvy commerce teams.

As with any architectural design decision, before choosing the headless commerce approach, it is essential to carefully evaluate its advantages and disadvantages.

Option 3: Building a cloud-native e-commerce platform

Developing a microservices-based e-commerce system can be a perfect solution for enterprises seeking full flexibility, granular control, and the delivery of unique customer experiences via e-commerce. In this model, a traditional e-commerce application stack is broken down into smaller, loosely coupled services that can be developed, deployed, and scaled independently. This involves identifying the core functional components; defining service boundaries; designing APIs; choosing the right technology stack and deployment platform; implementing service discovery and orchestration; ensuring data consistencies, CI/CD practices, and deployment; and scaling automation. It is important to note that developing a microservices-based e-commerce platform requires careful planning, coordination, and expertise. The following is a representation of a typical e-commerce application based on cloud-native architecture:

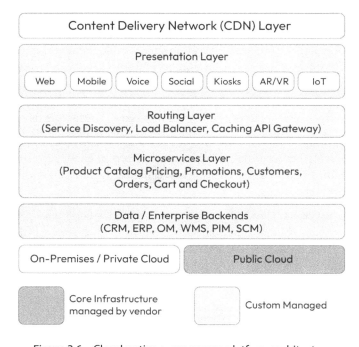

Figure 3.6 – Cloud-native e-commerce platform architecture

It will be prudent for enterprises to assess and understand the merits and demerits of this approach. Let's review some of the advantages:

- **Scalability and flexibility**: Microservices allow for the independent scaling of different components based on demand. This flexibility enables efficient resource utilization and the ability to handle high traffic during peak seasons and flash sales and also accommodate future growth.

- **Faster time to market through modular development**: Microservices promote modular development, allowing teams to work independently on different services. This speeds up development cycles and enables the use of different technologies and frameworks that best suit the requirements of each microservice.

- **Rapid innovation and deployment**: Microservices-based architecture facilitates faster deployment cycles and enables teams to innovate and release new features or updates independently. This agility allows businesses to respond quickly to market trends and customer needs.

- **Technology diversity**: With microservices, IT teams have the freedom to choose different technologies and programming languages for each functional service. This allows teams to leverage the strengths of specific technologies and frameworks, enabling optimal performance and productivity.

- **Improved fault isolation and recovery**: Microservices offer better fault isolation, meaning that the failure of a single service will not impact the entire system. This isolation allows for easier troubleshooting, faster recovery, and improved overall system stability.

The following are some of the disadvantages of this approach:

- **Increased complexity**: Managing a distributed system of microservices introduces additional complexity compared to a monolithic architecture. Challenges such as inter-service communication, data consistency, and transaction management need to be carefully addressed.

- **Operational overhead**: Maintaining and managing multiple microservices requires additional operational efforts. Tasks such as deployment, monitoring, and orchestration can become more complex and require robust DevOps practices.

- **Architectural consistencies**: Microservices rely heavily on inter-service communication, which can introduce network latency and impact overall system performance. Proper design and efficient communication patterns are essential to mitigating this challenge.

- **Data integrity**: Maintaining data consistency across multiple microservices can be complex, especially when dealing with transactions or shared data. Techniques such as event sourcing or distributed transactions may be required to ensure data integrity.

- **IT skills and resources**: Developing and managing microservices requires specialized skills and expertise. It may be challenging to find and retain talent with experience in building and maintaining distributed systems.

- **Service orchestration and integration**: Coordinating and orchestrating multiple microservices can be challenging. Implementing service discovery and API gateways and ensuring seamless integration between services require additional planning and implementation effort.

The following table shows a side-by-side comparison of the various criteria of different approaches:

Criteria	Traditional e-commerce (packaged apps)	SaaS-based e-commerce	Headless commerce	Microservices-based e-commerce
Scalability	Limited	High	High	High
Upfront investments	$$$	$	$$	$$
Flexibility	High	Low	Medium	High
Time to market	Slow	Medium	Fast	Fast
IT skills needed	Advanced	Basic	Intermediate	Advanced
IT resources required	High	Low	Medium	High
Vendor dependency	Low	High	High	Low
Built-in security and compliance	Medium	High	Medium	Low
HW/SW licensing and support	High	N/A	N/A	Medium (on-premises) N/A (public cloud)
Operational expenses	$	$$$	$$	$$
Integration support	High	Medium	Medium	High
Out-of-the-box analytics	Limited	Medium	Medium	Custom
Ongoing maintenance	High	Low	High	High

Table 3.1 – Comparison of different e-commerce architectural approaches

It will be prudent for IT organizations to carefully assess the capabilities, consider the tradeoffs, evaluate against the business priorities, and choose the right strategy.

Identifying the right workloads for cloud transformation

One of the primary challenges for enterprises is identifying the right workloads for cloud transformation, as business challenges are unique in every enterprise context. The one-size-fits-all approach doesn't work even for enterprises within the same industry vertical or with similar business models and revenue, and it is critical for enterprise leaders to have a clear vision and strategy for an enterprise-wide cloud transformation journey. There are several cloud transformation strategies that enterprises can choose based on unique business needs and compelling events, including big bang migration, data center exit, lift and shift, building net new initiatives, or augmenting applications with cloud-native capabilities. We will review these cloud journeys in greater detail in *Chapter 5, An Enterprise Journey to Cloud Transformation*. In this section, let's explore the challenges with some of the enterprise cloud transformations.

Big bang migration

A big bang cloud migration is an approach where an entire enterprise's infrastructure, applications, and data are migrated to the cloud in a single, coordinated effort. The objective of a big bang migration is to rapidly migrate and achieve a smooth and uninterrupted transition of all enterprise systems and applications to the cloud within a defined timeframe, minimizing downtime and ensuring minimal impact on business operations. It involves moving all systems and workloads from on-premises or hosted data centers to a cloud-based infrastructure. The transition to the cloud occurs over a relatively short time frame, often with planned downtime to execute the migration process. It typically involves a comprehensive analysis and planning phase to ensure all dependencies, security requirements, and compliance considerations are addressed prior to the migration.

An organization might choose a big bang cloud migration approach based on specific circumstances and requirements such as data center consolidation, legacy system modernization, global business expansions, mergers, divestitures, or acquisitions. While big bang migration can offer benefits in certain scenarios, it requires careful planning, resource allocation, and risk management. Enterprises should thoroughly assess their readiness, evaluate dependencies, conduct proper testing, and develop robust contingency plans to mitigate potential risks to ensure a successful migration.

Some challenges associated with a big bang migration approach are as follows:

- **Scale and complexity**: Big bang migrations involve migrating the entire enterprise infrastructure and applications in one go. This can be highly complex, especially for large organizations with numerous interconnected systems and dependencies. The scale of the migration requires meticulous planning, coordination, and execution to ensure a smooth transition.

- **Downtime and disruption**: Big bang migrations often require temporary downtime during the migration process. This can result in disruptions to business operations, including online services, customer support, and internal workflows. Minimizing downtime and ensuring a seamless transition is critical to avoiding potential revenue loss and negative customer experiences.

- **Migration risks**: With a big bang migration, the risk of failure is higher compared to phased or incremental migration approaches. Issues arising during the migration process can impact the entire enterprise simultaneously, leading to widespread disruptions. Robust contingency plans, thorough testing, and fallback strategies are crucial to mitigating migration risks.

- **Data and application dependencies**: Many enterprise systems and applications have intricate dependencies on each other. A big bang migration can potentially disrupt these dependencies and lead to unforeseen issues. Identifying and addressing dependencies prior to the migration is crucial to ensuring a successful transition and avoiding potential data inconsistencies or application failures.

- **Resource and budget management**: Big bang migrations warrant significant resources, both in terms of personnel and budget. An organization must ensure the allocation of sufficient resources for planning, migration, testing, and post-migration support. Adequate budget allocation and resource planning are essential to preventing delays, bottlenecks, and budget overruns.

- **Limited fallback options**: In a big bang migration, rolling back to the previous environment or infrastructure may be challenging due to the scale and complexity of the migration. This highlights the importance of thorough testing, validation, and fallback plans before executing the migration.

- **Change management**: Enterprise-wide migrations impact the entire organization, and change management becomes critical to ensuring user adoption and minimizing resistance. Adequate communication, training, and support are necessary to help users transition to the new cloud environment and ensure they can effectively utilize the new tools and services.

- **Software IP and licensing**: Many traditional enterprise systems and applications are based on legacy COTS and packaged applications. Certain proprietary software deployments may contain contractual language on target deployment platforms and location constraints that can be impediments to cloud migration. Depending on the choice of the destination cloud platform, the migration of these applications and systems can trigger licensing and supportability constraints. Hence, it is critical to involve various internal and external stakeholders and vendors to assess and plan the migration.

- **Specialized legacy and HCI**: Traditional large organizations typically have enterprise applications and systems that are legacy, obsolete, out-of-support software stacks and **hyper-converged infrastructure** (HCI) for specialized workloads and business functions. Organizations can choose from several methods that are available to migrate these systems, including retiring (systems that are no longer needed), re-hosting (redeploying applications with zero code change), co-locating (hosting systems, especially specialized hardware adjacent to target cloud infrastructure), re-platforming (migrating to cloud-based runtime with minimal changes), refactoring (restructuring and optimizing existing application code), or emulating (virtualizing applications on an emulator to mimic legacy behavior) based on specific business objectives and needs. Thorough assessment and planning is critical to ensuring these are captured and accounted for ahead of the migration.

- **Networking and security**: Another common challenge enterprises face while performing a big bang migration is the move from traditional hierarchical IP networking to flat cloud-native **software-defined networking (SDN)**. Although cloud networks are customizable and several major providers offer capabilities such as BYOIP and support for collocating components such as hardware load balancers and firewalls, a comprehensive migration strategy must be clearly defined and planned. Cloud-native SDN also introduces new security considerations as enterprise data traverses outside the network perimeter. Enterprises must carefully plan and implement security measures to protect data, such as encryption, access controls, and network segmentation, leveraging the defense in depth security architecture and controls offered by cloud providers.

Data center exit

Another common digital transformation journey several enterprises choose is exiting out of existing data centers. While a big bang migration is focused on completely pivoting all on-premises systems and applications to a public cloud, typically in a short timeframe, a data center exit can have several unique enterprise objectives. Some primary motivations for enterprises choosing to exit data centers include cost optimization, leveraging cloud economies of scale, reducing hosting expenses, scalability, focusing resources on core business, innovating with technological advancements, and simply avoiding compelling events such as hardware and tech refreshes. Depending on the business motivation and objective, a data center exit strategy must be carefully assessed and planned. For instance, an organization might choose to exit a data center and migrate to cloud-based infrastructure to avoid an impending hardware and tech refresh. Migrating from a data center to the cloud can present several challenges for enterprises. The following are some key considerations:

- **Legacy systems and applications**: Enterprises often have legacy systems and applications that are tightly integrated with several other applications, services, and data center infrastructure. These systems may have dependencies on specific hardware or software configurations, making it difficult to migrate them directly to the cloud. Modernizing or rearchitecting these legacy applications to be cloud-compatible can be time-consuming and complex. A clear migration assessment and planning exercise must be developed to capture the current landscape and targeted future state. We will take a detailed look at some migration patterns and blueprints and how to build a cloud migration assessment plan in *Chapter 6, Building an Open and Nimble Cloud Framework*.

- **Data transfer**: Moving large volumes of data from the data center to the cloud can be challenging, especially over the wire, as the available network bandwidth may be limited and can even become cost-prohibitive. The time it takes to transfer data over the network and the associated costs can impact the migration timeline and budget. Enterprises need to carefully plan and optimize the data transfer process to minimize disruption. Most public cloud providers offer an affordable offline bulk data transfer/migration service that can facilitate data migration from on-premises or hosted data centers through physical storage devices. Careful consideration must be placed on data encryption to prevent sensitive data loss.

- **Application compatibility**: Not all applications are designed to run in a cloud environment. Some applications may require modifications, refactoring, or even complete rewrites to be cloud-native and take advantage of cloud efficiencies and automation capabilities. An application compatibility plan must be established as part of the cloud migration assessment, along with potential options, to ensure successful migration and business continuity.

- **Security and compliance**: Public cloud providers operated on *shared responsibility* and *shared fate* models. It is crucial for organizations to gain a clear understanding of the security paradigms offered by the cloud provider. Shared responsibility models work on the premises that the security responsibilities for each layer are well defined, where **cloud service providers (CSPs)** and customers are responsible for securing their respective tiers. However, in the shared fate model, the CSPs play a significantly more active role in securing the cloud environment. For instance, CSPs that support shared fate offer secure-by-default jumpstart configurations and meet compliance obligations, security blueprints, risk protections programs, and policy intelligence tools by taking a partnership approach to securing the customer tenant. It is important to understand that the cloud security measures and practices may differ from those in the data center, necessitating a thorough understanding of the shared security responsibilities between the enterprise and the cloud provider. Ensuring data privacy, access controls, and encryption during transit and at rest is critical. We will dive deeper into cloud security frameworks and best practices in *Chapter 9, Facets of Digital Transformation*.

- **Vendor lock-in**: Enterprises must carefully consider the potential vendor lock-in risks when choosing a cloud provider. Migrating applications and data to a specific cloud provider's platform may limit the ability to switch providers easily in the future. Developing an open cloud-friendly strategy or a multi-cloud strategy that distributes workloads across different cloud providers can mitigate the risk of vendor lock-in and also provide increased flexibility.

- **Network connectivity**: Establishing reliable and high-performance network connectivity between the enterprise's on-premises infrastructure and the cloud environment is crucial, especially for enterprises choosing a hybrid cloud or multi-cloud approach. Depending on the geographical location of data centers and cloud regions, network latency and connectivity concerns may arise. Network architecture plans should be defined as part of the migration plans to implement appropriate network configurations to help optimize network performance. Several connectivity options exist, including dedicated connectivity to establish direct MPLS connectivity from a data center to the cloud, partner-driven connectivity to establish an MPLS connectivity to the cloud through an ISP, cross-connects for enterprises that already have a data center co-located with the cloud provider, and IPSEC VPNs to connect to cloud services securely over public internet.

- **Skill gap**: Migrating to the cloud requires a specialized skill set that may be different from traditional data center operations. Enterprises may need to upskill their IT staff, work with partners, or hire cloud experts to understand cloud technologies, management tools, and best practices. Ensuring the workforce has the necessary skills to manage and optimize the cloud environment is essential for a successful migration.

- **FinOps and cost management**: While the cloud offers potential cost savings, enterprises need to carefully manage and optimize cloud costs. Without proper monitoring and governance, cloud expenses can quickly escalate. A common pitfall that several organizations make while embarking on a cloud transformation is *sizing for high watermark* (this refers to the practice of planning for and configuring servers with anticipated peak capacity upfront) as you would do with traditional data centers, without taking advantage of the cloud elasticity and pay-for-use model. Understanding pricing models, optimizing resource utilization, and implementing cost control measures are crucial to avoiding unexpected cost overruns. It will be prudent for mature organizations to have a FinOps practice for ongoing cost management and governance.

- **Cloud operations**: The operational processes and procedures used in the data center may not align with those required in the cloud environment. Enterprises need to adapt their operational practices to manage and monitor cloud resources effectively. This includes configuring auto-scaling, implementing monitoring and alerting, managing cloud-native services, and ensuring proper governance and compliance.

- **Disaster recovery (DR) in the cloud**: Another specialized use case for enterprises is setting up a new disaster recovery instance in the cloud to build resilience for production environments on-premises or exit out of a DR data center to optimize costs. Enterprises must carefully plan application and environment parity between on-premises production and DR in the cloud for seamless disaster recovery. We will discuss this journey in more detail in *Chapter 5*.

Lift and shift applications to the cloud

A lift and shift strategy, also known as a *rehost* or a *lift and drop* strategy, refers to migrating applications and systems from an on-premises data center to the cloud environment with minimal or no modifications. In most cases, a lift and shift strategy is often the first step in a multi-phased migration approach. In this approach, the goal is to quickly move the existing infrastructure, applications, and data to the cloud platform while preserving their functionality and architecture. The lift and shift strategy is chosen when the primary objective is to achieve cloud benefits such as scalability, cost optimization, minimal disruption to business operations, preservation of existing investments in application and software licenses, and flexibility for phased application modernization by gradually refactoring or rearchitecting. We will dive deeper into lift and shift as a cloud transformation journey in *Chapter 5*. While the lift and shift strategy can provide a relatively faster path to migrating applications to the cloud, it also presents certain challenges and limitations for enterprises:

- **Inability to leverage cloud-native optimizations**: Lift and shift migrations often prioritize speed and simplicity over taking full advantage of cloud-native capabilities. As a result, enterprises may miss out on opportunities to optimize their applications to achieve better performance, scalability, and cost efficiency in the short term. However, with a well-defined application modernization roadmap, enterprises can use the lift and shift approach as a great landing zone for a phased transformation. For instance, a lift and shift migration will enable teams to better understand the cloud platform, provide quick wins and confidence to stakeholders, and upskill IT teams for cloud-native application modernization.

- **Application interdependencies**: Enterprise mission-critical applications typically have several complex interdependencies with core infrastructure, libraries, databases, and other systems in the on-premises environment. Application dependencies can pose challenges when migrating the application, requiring careful evaluation of alternative cloud-native solutions to ensure proper functionality in the cloud environment. A clear migration plan must be defined for associated infrastructure requirements and environment considerations, along with peripheral applications and services, to ensure business continuity.

- **Data transfer and cutover**: Large-scale data transfers from the on-premises environment to the cloud can be time-consuming, impacting the overall migration timeline. Additionally, enterprises must plan for one-time bulk data transfers, incremental data transfers over the wire, and a cutover strategy to minimize the disruption and downtime of applications under consideration during the migration process.

- **Performance and scalability**: Applications lifted and shifted to the cloud may not automatically benefit from the full potential of the cloud's inherent scale and elasticity. Several application monoliths are traditionally developed with the intention to scale vertically. Without architectural modifications or optimizations, some of these applications may not achieve the desired performance improvements or the ability to scale horizontally based on workload demands. Enterprises can leverage cloud-native elasticity, scale, and performance benefits by rearchitecting, refactoring, or rewriting applications.

- **Limited cost optimization**: While cost savings are one of the primary motivations for cloud migration, the lift and shift strategy may not fully optimize costs. Applications lifted and shifted to the cloud may not fully leverage the cloud's ability to optimize resource utilization. Without proper assessment and optimization, enterprises may end up over-provisioning resources or underutilizing the available cloud resources, resulting in increased costs or suboptimal performance. Proper monitoring and optimization efforts are necessary to realizing cost savings in the long run.

- **Operational challenges**: The operational processes and tools used in the on-premises environment may not align seamlessly with the cloud environment. Enterprises need to adapt their operational practices to effectively manage and monitor cloud resources, including implementing cloud-specific monitoring, management, and governance processes.

- **Licensing and support**: The lift and shift strategy may not account for software licensing models or pricing structures that differ between the on-premises environment and the cloud. Enterprises will need to review and optimize licensing arrangements and consider potential cost implications to avoid unexpected expenses or non-compliance. It is also critical for enterprises to ensure that infrastructure and environment baselines are supported while migrating to the cloud. Certain application vendors may also prescribe a recommended or supported cloud provider or platform in order to gain continued enterprise support.

- **Fault tolerance**: Applications migrated using the lift and shift strategy may not inherently benefit from the cloud's built-in resilience and fault tolerance features. Enterprises should assess and implement appropriate mechanisms for backup, disaster recovery, and fault tolerance to ensure high availability and business continuity in the cloud.

- **Security and compliance**: Lift and shift migrations must address security and compliance requirements specific to the cloud environment. This includes ensuring data protection, access controls, identity and access management, and compliance with relevant regulations. Enterprises need to assess the security capabilities of the cloud provider, implement identity syncs and single sign-on for seamless business operations, and implement necessary measures to secure the migrated applications and data.

- **Change management and user adoption**: Migrating applications to the cloud requires change management efforts to ensure smooth user adoption. Users and stakeholders need to be informed about the migration process, trained on any changes or new functionalities, and provided with support during the transition to minimize disruptions and maximize user satisfaction.

Hybrid cloud strategy

A **hybrid cloud strategy** is an approach where enterprises have the ability to combine the use of both public and private clouds or on-premises environments to meet their unique business requirements. In a hybrid cloud setup, organizations maintain some of their applications, data, and infrastructure on premises or in a private cloud while leveraging public cloud services for specialized workloads and use cases. This strategy allows enterprises to get the best of both worlds and create a flexible and scalable IT environment in the public cloud as an extension of their private or on-premises IT infrastructure. As we explored the various cloud paradigms in *Chapter 2, A Primer on the Cloud*, according to the NIST definition, "*a hybrid cloud is a composition of two or more distinct cloud infrastructures that remain unique entities but are bound together by standardized or proprietary technology that enables data and application portability*." The key phrases here are "*bound together*" and "*enabling data and application portability*". This means a hybrid cloud environment must enable users to interface with both private cloud and public cloud services as a unified entity managed by a common set of tools. An organization simply operating in multiple public clouds, private clouds, and on-premises traditional servers without unifying or portability capabilities doesn't constitute a hybrid cloud architecture. With a well-defined hybrid cloud strategy, enterprises can leverage specialized capabilities such as flexibility in application placements and deployments across public and private clouds; optimize costs by choosing cost-effective deployment modes, efficient data integration, implement robust disaster recovery and business continuity solutions; implement cloud bursting for seasonal demands; avoid vendor lock-ins and unified management. Organizations can reap all these benefits via careful planning, architectural design, and ongoing management. We will review some of the challenges that enterprises face when implementing a seamless hybrid cloud strategy:

- **Architectural complexity**: Hybrid cloud environments introduce additional complexity compared to siloed on-premises and cloud deployments. Integrating and managing resources across one or more cloud platforms, on-premises infrastructure, and data centers can be challenging and requires careful planning and architectural design. If done right, this can serve as a robust foundation and launchpad for enterprises to deliver modern business capabilities faster.

- **Interoperability**: Hybrid cloud architectures can introduce interoperability challenges and ensuring seamless data integration and interoperability between public and private cloud environments can be complex. Enterprises need to establish efficient data movement mechanisms, implement appropriate integration solutions, and maintain data consistency and security across different platforms.

- **Operational complexity**: Managing hybrid cloud deployments requires effective operational processes and tools. Enterprises will have to establish operational frameworks, automate management tasks, and ensure consistent monitoring and performance management across both on-premises and cloud environments. This complexity can increase the operational burden and require additional investments in SRE practices, management tools, and expertise.

- **Governance and compliance**: Establishing unified governance policies and ensuring consistency across on-premises and public cloud platforms can be challenging for enterprises. Organizations need to define and enforce policies for resource provisioning, access controls, data management, and compliance monitoring across both public and private cloud environments.

- **Legacy system integration**: Integrating legacy systems with the hybrid cloud environment can present challenges due to differences in architecture, protocols, or compatibility. Enterprises may need to invest in modernization efforts, application refactoring, or implementing integration solutions to seamlessly connect legacy systems with cloud resources.

- **Data sovereignty**: In hybrid cloud deployments, enterprises need to consider data sovereignty and residency regulations that govern where certain types of data can be stored and processed. Ensuring compliance with these regulations can be challenging when data is distributed across public and private cloud environments.

- **Data backup and recovery**: Implementing consistent data backup and recovery mechanisms across hybrid cloud environments can be challenging. Enterprises need to ensure that critical data is appropriately backed up and can be recovered in the event of data loss or system failures, considering different backup and recovery options available in both public and private clouds.

- **Performance variability**: Hybrid cloud deployments may experience performance variability due to factors such as network latency, data center regions, data transfer speeds, and variations in the performance of different cloud platforms. Ensuring consistent and predictable performance across hybrid environments requires careful architectural design and network optimization.

- **Skill set and expertise**: Hybrid cloud deployments require specialized skills and knowledge for architecting, designing, and effectively managing consistency and resource optimization across public and private cloud platforms. Enterprises may face challenges in finding and retaining IT professionals with the right expertise in cloud architecture, integration, security, and hybrid cloud management.

- **Migration and integration**: Migrating existing applications and systems to a hybrid cloud environment and integrating them with the new infrastructure can be complex and time-consuming. Enterprises need to carefully plan and execute migration strategies, ensure compatibility between different environments, and minimize disruptions to business operations.

- **Vendor management**: Working with multiple providers requires effective vendor management practices. Enterprises need to establish relationships with multiple vendors, manage SLAs, and ensure consistent support and communication channels. Coordinating and resolving issues across different vendors can add complexity to the management process.

- **Security and compliance**: Implementing security and compliance controls can increase complexity in hybrid cloud deployments. Enterprises must ensure consistent security controls and access management across public and private infrastructures, maintain consistent data protection standards, and comply with industry-specific regulations. Addressing security risks, such as data breaches or unauthorized access, requires a well-defined security architecture and strategy.

- **Organizational culture**: Embracing a hybrid cloud requires a cultural shift and changes in the way IT teams operate, especially when embracing modern cloud-native technologies and operations. Enterprises may face challenges in managing change, educating staff, and fostering collaboration between teams that manage different cloud environments. Building a culture that embraces cloud technologies and encourages collaboration is crucial for success.

A hybrid cloud strategy presents a strategic opportunity for enterprises to seamlessly integrate and manage a combination of on-premises infrastructure, private cloud services, and public cloud resources. Let's explore a multi-cloud strategy for enterprises with multiple public clouds.

Multi-cloud strategy

Several enterprises adopt a **multi-cloud strategy** where an organization leverages multiple public clouds in conjunction with a traditional on-premises infrastructure to take advantage of the unique capabilities that each deployment platform offers. A good multi-cloud strategy for enterprises involves leveraging multiple cloud providers to meet their specific business needs. It allows organizations to avoid vendor lock-in, achieve higher availability, optimize costs, and gain access to a broader range of services and capabilities. For instance, an organization may choose to subscribe to Google Cloud, Microsoft Azure, and Amazon Web Services public cloud platforms to realize the unique value offerings from each platform.

A successful multi-cloud strategy involves defining clear objectives; evaluating cloud providers based on the strength of offerings, pricing models, geographic presence, reliability, security features, compliance capabilities, business interests (conflict of business), and customer support; identifying workload placements; architecting for interoperability; FinOps; and establishing consistent governance controls. To reap the full potential of the multi-cloud strategy, such as flexibility and distinctive benefits, it is essential for enterprises to consider the unique requirements and constraints of the organization, understand business demands, and continually adapt the strategy to maximize the benefits of utilizing multiple cloud providers. Although a multi-cloud strategy offers unique benefits, enterprises must address some key challenges:

- **Management complexity**: Managing multiple cloud providers introduces complexity, as each cloud provider has its own set of tools, interfaces, and management consoles. Enterprises must invest in specialized skills and tools to efficiently manage cross-cloud resources, deployments, and configurations across different clouds.

- **Vendor dependency**: While multi-cloud aims to avoid vendor lock-in, enterprises must carefully plan and architect their applications to ensure portability. Avoiding dependencies on proprietary services and APIs is crucial to maintaining flexibility and preventing challenges when transitioning between providers.

- **Consistent service experience**: While deploying applications across multiple clouds, providing a consistent user experience can be challenging, since each provider may have different performance characteristics, service levels, regional presences, and availability zones. Ensuring consistent service quality and uptime across all clouds requires careful planning and monitoring. Although efforts are being made to standardize cloud services and APIs, there is still a lack of uniformity among different providers. This can lead to compatibility issues, making it difficult to integrate and manage services consistently across multiple clouds.

- **Vendor management**: Managing relationships with multiple cloud vendors requires dedicated resources and effective vendor management practices. Enterprises need to establish strong relationships, negotiate contracts, and ensure clear communication and alignment of goals with each provider.

- **Interoperability and integration**: Ensuring seamless interoperability and integration between different cloud platforms can be a challenge, and enterprises will need to invest in robust integration solutions, utilize industry standards, and adopt compatible architectures to enable smooth data and application flow across clouds. Managing data across multiple cloud providers requires a well-defined data management and governance strategy.

- **Security controls**: Implementing consistent security measures and compliance controls across multiple clouds can be complex. Each provider has its own prescriptive security frameworks, and enterprises must ensure a unified and robust security posture across all clouds. Monitoring, threat detection, and incident response can become more challenging in a distributed environment.

- **FinOps**: While a multi-cloud strategy can offer cost optimization opportunities, managing costs effectively across different providers can be challenging. Enterprises must implement a consistent and robust FinOps practice to gain visibility into usage, spending, and resource optimization across all clouds. Choosing the right pricing models, leveraging cost management tools, and monitoring usage are crucial.

- **Upskill and reskill**: Adopting a multi-cloud strategy requires specialized skills and training for IT teams. Each cloud provider has its own unique features and management interfaces, necessitating a deep understanding of each platform. Enterprises must invest in training programs to ensure proficiency in multiple clouds for their IT staff. Constant upskilling and re-skilling of IT teams is crucial to a successful multi-cloud strategy.

- **Network management**: Multi-cloud environments often require interconnectivity between different cloud platforms and on-premises infrastructure. This can result in significantly high network management efforts and costs, especially those associated with bandwidth and egress. Ensuring low latency, high bandwidth, and reliable network connectivity is essential to offering consistent a user experience. Enterprises must evaluate network architecture and establish robust connections to optimize performance.

- **SLAs and support**: Managing SLAs and support across multiple cloud providers can be complex and organizations must understand the service guarantees, support channels, and escalation processes of each provider to ensure consistent and reliable service levels across all clouds.

- **Data migration and transfer**: Transferring data between multiple cloud providers can be complex and time-consuming, especially when dealing with large volumes of data. Ensuring efficient data migration processes, minimizing downtime, and maintaining data integrity can pose challenges during the transition.

- **Performance optimization**: Enterprises need to consider factors such as data locality, network latency, and workload distribution to ensure optimal performance across all clouds, as optimizing performance in multi-cloud environments can be tricky. Balancing resource allocation and workload placement can pose complexities with multiple providers.

- **Workload monitoring**: Monitoring and troubleshooting applications and infrastructure spread across multiple clouds can be challenging. Organizations should implement a unified monitoring and troubleshooting approach to gain visibility into the multi-cloud environment in order to quickly identify and resolve issues.

As enterprises embark on cloud transformation, it often requires adopting multiple strategies for multiple workloads with different business priorities. However, it is crucial to have a detailed assessment of the workloads and to consider the challenges, tradeoffs, and long-term vision for a successful digital transformation. After the right strategy is identified, it is important to choose the right cloud provider that meets all dimensions. In the next section, we will explore the critical factors to consider while choosing a cloud provider.

Choosing the right cloud provider

Choosing the right cloud provider for enterprise use cases can often be a challenge, especially for organizations with hybrid cloud and multi-cloud strategies, as it forms the foundation for enterprise digital transformation. Choosing the right cloud provider requires careful evaluation and consideration of multiple dimensions, depending on current and future business demands. It is crucial to assess the reliability, long-term focus, and capability of a CSP, as we entrust it with mission-critical applications and data.

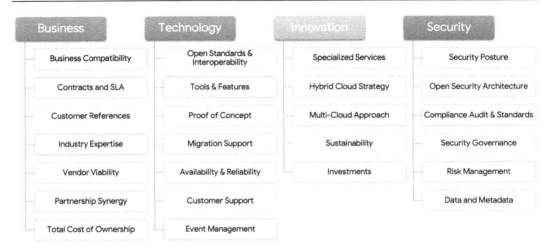

Figure 3.7 – Factors to consider when choosing a cloud provider

Let's review some critical factors that enterprises must assess and evaluate before embarking on a cloud journey. Note that several of these factors also apply when choosing a private cloud.

Business aspects

The first pillar to consider is the constructive value, collaboration, and compatibility of the cloud provider with the enterprise business model. This is often a crucial factor, as it can have impacts on aspects such as supporting long-term visions, industry expertise, and compliance. For instance, choosing a cloud provider with a competing business model can sometimes be detrimental to an organization's business interests and goals, especially when sensitive data is stored and served. This pillar covers aspects such as business compatibility, SLAs, industry, and technology leadership.

- **Business compatibility**: The first step in choosing a CSP is to clearly define an organization's business and functional requirements, goals, and priorities and create an assessment map against a CSP's capabilities. As part of this critical step, enterprises must also consider business compatibility with a CSP to ensure there would be no conflict of business interests.

- **Contracts and SLAs**: A crucial next step for enterprise sourcing and procurement teams is to carefully review the enterprise contracts, commercials, and SLAs along with details pertaining to data security, data privacy, **intellectual property** (**IP**) rights, data processing, use of third-party vendors to offer capabilities (if any), termination and dispute resolution processes, pricing and payment terms, liability, and indemnification.

- **Customer references**: A key criterion in evaluating CSP maturity and reliability is researching customer references and feedback that align with the enterprise's industry and technology maturity. Organizations can also work with technology research and advisory companies such as IDC, Gartner, and Forrester to gain insights. Seeking customer references, connecting with industry peers, attending conferences, or leveraging online communities to gather real-world experiences and recommendations can help enterprises make informed decisions.

- **Industry expertise**: Enterprises must also consider the industry expertise and specialization of the cloud providers in addition to pure technical capabilities. Some CSPs may offer specialized solutions or services tailored to certain industries, such as retail, healthcare, manufacturing, finance, telecom, etc., which can augment the industry expertise capabilities of the enterprise. Choosing providers that have a strong understanding of the industry requirements can be hugely helpful.

- **Vendor viability**: It will be prudent for organizations to assess the reputation, financial stability, and long-term viability of cloud providers, considering factors such as their market presence, customer base, financial reports, and strategic partnerships.

- **Partnership synergy**: In addition to native cloud provider services, partner offerings often provide extended capabilities, custom solutions, and jumpstarts for enterprises. This can also be hugely beneficial for enterprises where there are existing solutions and partnerships in traditional on-premises infrastructure. It's essential for enterprises to understand a CSP's partnership with different vendors, accreditation, technical capabilities, and certifications. An ideal service provider can easily fit into the enterprise's larger ecosystem. In addition to marketplace offerings, enterprises must also consider the **system integrator (SI)** and **managed service provider (MSP)** partnerships of a cloud provider.

- **Total cost of ownership**: Enterprises must evaluate the various pricing models offered by cloud providers and understand how they align with budget and usage patterns. Organizations will also benefit from **total cost of ownership (TCO)** and **return on investment (ROI)** evaluations by considering factors such as pay-as-you-go, flexible commitments, spot instances, sustained use discounts, and pricing tiers. Ensuring a transparent pricing structure, provider cost management tools, and FinOps practices to optimize cloud spend is crucial.

Technology aspects

The next important pillar of consideration when choosing a cloud provider is technology. This refers to the cloud provider's tech capabilities, which can simplify the cloud transformation while also fostering innovation. This includes aspects such as adherence to open standards, easing migrations with tools, processes tailored to industry verticals, and customer support:

- **Open standards and interoperability**: Vendor lock-in can often be a serious concern for enterprises, either by contract or proprietary technologies. Organizations must assess potential vendor lock-in risks associated with each cloud provider. The cloud is fundamentally built on open source technologies and enterprises must evaluate the level of standardization, use of open standards, and compatibility of services that cloud providers use to build their managed offerings, as well as the availability of migration tools and support to avoid and mitigate vendor lock-in.

- **Tools and features**: Assess services and offerings provided by different cloud providers. Consider factors such as compute instances, storage options, databases, networking capabilities, security features, machine learning tools, managed service offerings, and developer services to determine alignment with business requirements.

- **Proof of concepts**: Consider conducting a proof of concept or pilot project with shortlisted cloud providers. This allows enterprises to evaluate the provider's services, performance, support, and compatibility with applications and workload requirements before committing to a long-term partnership.

- **Migration tooling and support**: Migrating existing workloads to the public cloud—especially those with a lot of data—is complex, time-consuming, and risky. But with the right planning, organizations can rapidly establish the right practices to accelerate migrations, lower risk, and succeed in the cloud. Mature cloud providers offer several jumpstart templates, migration frameworks, and toolsets customized for legacy application migration, application refactoring, and data modernization, which can prove helpful for enterprises.

- **Availability and reliability**: The performance, reliability, and availability of cloud providers are foundational and crucial to the success of cloud transformation for enterprises. Consider factors such as uptime guarantees, availability zones, network connectivity, and latency requirements.

- **Customer support**: Evaluate the level of support and customer service offered by the cloud providers. It's important to understand their support channels, response times, and escalation processes and also consider factors such as documentation, community support, forums, skill availability, and training resources available to assist in onboarding and troubleshooting.

- **Event management**: Enterprises may also consider specialized event management support offered by CSPs specific to business needs. For instance, CSPs may provide capacity planning and advanced reservation support for retailers during peak seasons such as Black Friday sales, dedicated support mechanisms for open enrollment periods for healthcare, etc.

Innovation aspects

Innovation and digital disruption represent the highest level of cloud maturity for any enterprise. A cloud provider's leadership in innovation, contribution to open communities, and technological expertise can all be extremely critical factors in helping lead innovation. For instance, the provider's expertise can be cross-pollinated through early access programs, operational research programs, and workshops across the enterprise's innovation centers, which can accelerate the innovation process. This important pillar covers aspects of creative services, access to emerging technologies, open standards support, and sustainability.

- **Specialized services**: One of the primary motivators for enterprises with cloud transformation is innovation. Enterprises must consider unique and specialized service offerings provided by CSPs that can augment, benefit, and offer impetus to enterprise objectives and goals. For instance, enterprises may offer differentiated services to their customers by leveraging specialized AI offerings.

- **Hybrid cloud support**: Even if a hybrid cloud is not an initial consideration, it will be prudent for enterprises to ensure that the cloud provider offers a robust portfolio of hybrid cloud solutions, products, and services that can seamlessly help enterprises shuttle workloads between cloud and on-premises infrastructure. Hybrid cloud support can save time, effort, and resources for enterprises, and it can support a **Build Once, Deploy Anywhere (BODA)** architecture.

- **Multi-cloud approach**: If the multi-cloud approach is a core part of an enterprise cloud strategy, organizations must ensure CSP support for open standards and frameworks, as application and data portability is key. As more and more cloud providers continue to standardize and build offerings that are based on open architecture, it is still an evolving space.

- **Sustainability**: ESG and sustainability goals are key characteristics of a mature and modern enterprise. With double materiality and ESG considerations being crucial to long-term success, enterprises will find it prudent to work with CSPs that share common objectives on sustainability goals and mitigating carbon footprints, for example.

- **Investments**: One of the primary objectives of cloud transformation is continuous innovation and keeping up with change. This requires continued investments in modern technologies to meet and exceed consumer demands. Enterprises may assess a CSP's historical, current, and future commitments to R&D, innovation, and technology investments, which can directly benefit the vision of an enterprise.

Security aspects

Security is fundamental and is often an afterthought when choosing a cloud provider. It is important to ensure that the security aspects of the cloud provider are consistent with the enterprise security blueprints. Security aspects span beyond the basic compliance requirements, and it will be prudent to consider factors such as the foundational security posture, adherence to open security standards, integration with on-premises and third-party security tools, defense-in-depth security, and risk management:

- **Security posture**: Security is everyone's business and it is relevant in the cloud transformation journey more than ever. Enterprises must carefully evaluate the security posture, frameworks, and policies offered by CSPs. This can include physical data center security and security posture on shared responsibilities vs. shared fate. Enterprises must assess the resilience of the cloud provider, with particular attention paid to regional capabilities/historical figures on uptime.

- **Open security architecture**: As enterprises embark on cloud transformation, it is prudent to envision an open security architecture that can seamlessly support multiple deployment targets. **Open security architecture (OSA)** refers to a framework or methodology that provides a structured approach for designing, implementing, and managing security solutions within an organization. Choosing a cloud provider that supports OSA promotes the use of open standards, best practices, and collaboration to develop robust and effective security architectures.

- **Compliance audit**: When choosing a cloud provider, enterprises must consider the implications of federal, state, and industry regulations. CSPs often have a published set of compliance, attestations, and certifications by service and region that can help enterprises confidently deploy solutions and comply with various reporting and regulatory obligations.

- **Security governance**: Enterprises must ensure that the chosen CSP offers comprehensive security policies and procedures for controlling access to provider and customer systems. A cloud governance framework done right can help manage risks, enhance data security, and enable seamless cloud operations for an enterprise.

- **Risk management**: Risk management in cloud computing involves identifying, assessing, and mitigating the potential risks associated with using cloud services. Enterprises must evaluate data security, data privacy, data governance, network, and shared infrastructure risks and develop mitigation strategies. This can also involve evaluating CSP capabilities to offer threat intel, cyber threat detection, attack vector detection, and monitoring. Enterprise security must also perform periodical penetration and vulnerability testing outside of meeting regulatory compliances such as SOC.

- **Data security and privacy**: Enterprises must ensure there is a comprehensive security infrastructure and access control policies offered by CSPs for all levels and types of cloud services. It is important to evaluate the data management, data residency, data backup, replication, retention, and geofencing security policies and procedures of the CSP to ensure the integrity of enterprise and customer data.

Dealing with financials

As enterprises embark on their first cloud transformation journey, there is often a huge debate on whether the cloud is actually as financially viable and beneficial as it promises to be, as there is a paradigm shift in financing. Traditional on-premises IT investments typically incur upfront **capital expenditures** (**CapEx**) that are expected to be utilized over multiple years, continue to benefit the business in the future, and eventually pay for themselves. **Operating expenditures** (**OpEx**) are incurred via the day-to-day operations of a business and generally include services and maintenance. With the exponential evolution of technology and rapidly changing business demands, the lifetime of CapEx investments has become uncertain, outdated, or even obsolete before they have paid for themselves. Another inherent downside of a traditional CapEx investment is that an organization may end up paying for excess capacity the business does not require in the future or end up in the painstaking and expensive process of adding capacity. As cloud subscription fees are typically OpEx, IT leaders in some traditional enterprises may face challenges in persuading their finance counterparts on the cost-value equation since it involves a fundamental change to how traditional IT investments are amortized and depreciated. As we explored in *Chapter 2, A Primer on the Cloud*, cloud transformation requires a cultural shift across the organization, and enterprise leaders must put in place value assessment frameworks capturing TCO, ROI, and business value; FinOps practices to optimize OpEx; and value realization programs to measure and demonstrate value. When it comes to dealing with the shift from CapEx to OpEx in the context of cloud computing, enterprises can employ several strategies:

- **Financial planning**: Enterprises should carefully analyze the financials along with long-term goals to determine the most appropriate allocation of resources between CapEx and OpEx. This involves considering factors such as cash flow, tax implications, cost predictability, and the overall financial impact on the organization.

- **FinOps and cost management**: Implementing FinOps and robust cloud cost management practices is crucial to optimizing OpEx in the cloud. This includes monitoring and analyzing cloud usage, implementing cost control measures, leveraging automation for resource provisioning and de-provisioning, and regularly reviewing and optimizing cloud resource utilization to minimize unnecessary expenses.

- **Strategic workload placement**: Enterprises should analyze workloads and determine which applications are better suited for the cloud in terms of cost savings, innovation value, and operational benefits. By strategically building or migrating specific workloads to the cloud, organizations can optimize OpEx by taking advantage of the cloud's scalability, flexibility, and pay-per-use model.

- **Leverage flexible pricing models**: Cloud providers offer various pricing models, such as pay-as-you-go, reserved instances, sustained use discounts, and spot instances. Enterprises should carefully evaluate these options and choose the pricing model that aligns with their workload patterns, cost predictability, and budget requirements. Selecting the right pricing model can help manage OpEx effectively.

- **Total cost of ownership (TCO) analysis**: Conducting a comprehensive TCO analysis helps enterprises compare the costs of deploying and managing applications in the cloud versus on-premises infrastructure. This analysis takes into account factors such as hardware, software licensing, maintenance, personnel, and infrastructure costs and provides insights into the financial implications of adopting a cloud-based OpEx model. This can also help IT leaders build business value justification.

- **Vendor negotiations**: Enterprises can often negotiate commitment contracts and SLAs with cloud providers to optimize costs and ensure flexibility. Negotiating discounts, favorable pricing terms, and flexible agreements based on workload fluctuations can help manage OpEx effectively.

- **Cloud governance**: Establishing governance frameworks and implementing monitoring and tracking mechanisms enable organizations to gain visibility into cloud usage and spending. This allows them to identify areas of cost optimization, enforce cost control policies and alerts, and ensure compliance with budgetary constraints.

- **Hybrid and multi-cloud strategies**: Enterprises can adopt hybrid or multi-cloud strategies to achieve a balance between CapEx and OpEx. By utilizing a mix of on-premises infrastructure, private clouds, and public clouds, organizations can optimize costs and leverage the benefits of different cost models based on specific workload requirements.

- **Continuous Optimization**: Cloud costs and pricing models are subject to change, requiring enterprises to regularly review and optimize cloud spending. This involves conducting periodic cost assessments, analyzing usage patterns, identifying areas for optimization, and making adjustments to ensure ongoing cost efficiency.

By implementing some of these strategies, enterprises can effectively manage the transition from CapEx to OpEx in the cloud, optimize cloud spending, and align with financial models and the operational benefits offered by cloud computing.

Summary

In this chapter, we explored the various challenges that enterprises face with cloud adoption and digital transformation. Enterprises embarking on cloud adoption journeys encounter a spectrum of challenges that demand strategic planning and thoughtful implementation. Navigating these hurdles ensures that cloud adoption becomes a transformative force for innovation and efficiency rather than a source of unexpected complications.

We also discussed how enterprises can identify and choose the right cloud strategy to modernize IT—through the example of a retailer's e-commerce application—while also exploring the various cloud transformation strategies. In addition, we discussed the various aspects that enterprises must assess and evaluate while choosing a cloud provider.

Finally, we discussed how to handle the new financial models introduced by the cloud and realize financial viability and value through cloud adoption.

In the next chapter, we will explore the core constituents required to build a robust cloud foundation, as enterprises embark on a cloud transformation journey.

Part 2: Succeeding with Hybrid Cloud and Multi-Cloud

In this part, we will learn about the strategies and techniques that enterprises can leverage to build the foundations of a modern IT enterprise. As every enterprise is unique, so are the digital transformation journeys. We will explore the various cloud journeys that enterprises can leverage to digitally transform their business. In addition, we will learn some proven strategies that organizations can employ to build an open and agile framework for cloud transformation. Finally, we will delve into some real-world examples of enterprises that have digitally disrupted their respective industries.

This part includes the following chapters:

- *Chapter 4, Building the Foundations for a Modern Enterprise*
- *Chapter 5, An Enterprise Journey to Cloud Transformation*
- *Chapter 6, Building an Open and Nimble Cloud Framework*
- *Chapter 7, Hybrid Cloud Use Cases*

4

Building the Foundations for a Modern Enterprise

In the previous chapter, we discussed the challenges that enterprises face in leading a digital transformation. As an enterprise IT leader, it is important to ensure the right foundation is laid for a successful cloud transformation journey. This chapter aims to lay out some foundational frameworks that can help enterprises navigate the complexities and embrace change effectively. In today's hypercompetitive business landscape, organizations strive to achieve and sustain success amid evolving market dynamics and technological advancements. To navigate this complex terrain, enterprises require a comprehensive approach – one that encompasses the interplay between people, processes, and technology. Managing change is vital for enterprises to thrive and allows organizations to adapt to changing market trends, innovate with change, engage employees, mitigate risks, and achieve a competitive advantage. As we navigate this chapter on building the foundations of a modern cloud-ready enterprise, we will explore various strategies, tools, and frameworks that will help enterprise leaders manage, embrace, and lead digital disruption in their respective industries.

In this chapter, we will cover the following topics:

- Tools and frameworks that help enterprises manage change

- Enterprise cloud adoption strategies and cloud maturity assessment frameworks

- Establishing a **cloud center of excellence** (CCoE)

- Building the foundations for a cloud-first enterprise with a startup mindset, product thinking, and platform engineering

- Customer-centric design thinking through **critical user journeys** (CUJs)

- Building a cloud foundation on open source and open standards

Leavitt's diamond for change management

Every transformation initiative introduces change and digital transformation at the enterprise scale exacerbates it. One of the hardest challenges enterprise leaders face with digital transformation is managing change across people, processes, and technology. Well-thought-out change management is crucial to digital transformation as it mitigates resistance by preparing employees, streamlining operations, and fostering innovation through technology for upcoming changes. Effective change management ensures that everyone within the organization works toward a common vision.

In 1965, **Harold J.Leavitt**, a professor of organizational behavior and psychology at Stanford University, developed an integrated model for organizational change management known as **Leavitt's system model**, also referred to as **Leavitt's diamond** *[1]*. It was proposed by Leavitt as a way to understand the interrelationships between four key components within an organization – structure, people, technology, and tasks.

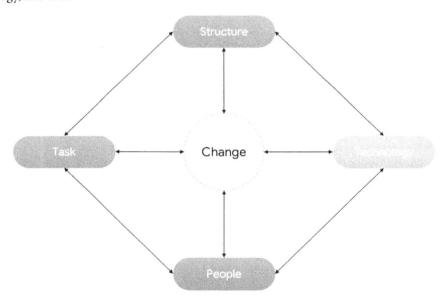

Figure 4.1 – A representation of Leavitt's diamond change management

Let's take a closer look:

- **Structure**: Organizational structure refers to the formal arrangement of roles, responsibilities, and reporting relationships within an organization, encompassing aspects such as organizational charts, roles, and responsibilities. In today's enterprises, the structure has evolved to accommodate changes such as flatter hierarchies, matrix organizations, and agile teams. This structure influences communication, decision-making, and coordination, and plays a vital role in supporting collaboration, innovation, and flexibility.

- **People**: The people component emphasizes the significance of employees in organizational effectiveness to effectively embrace and manage change. Today's enterprises focus on employee engagement, talent management, diversity, and inclusion initiatives. With the growing importance of remote and flexible work arrangements, managing virtual teams and fostering a positive organizational culture are key considerations. Supporting employees' well-being, continuous learning, and professional development is crucial to ensure that employees participate in the decision-making process as change agents while influencing high-performance objectives.

- **Technology**: Technology has become an integral aspect of modern enterprises and encompasses the tools, systems, and processes that are used within the organization to help people accomplish tasks and achieve objectives. It includes both hardware and software tools, systems, and digital platforms. As enterprises leverage emerging technologies such as **artificial intelligence** (**AI**), big data, cloud computing, and automation to enhance efficiency, decision-making, and customer experience, the adoption and effective utilization of technology are vital to drive innovation, competitiveness, and operational excellence.

- **Tasks**: Task management encompasses the specific activities, processes, and workflows that individuals and teams undertake to accomplish organizational goals. Today's enterprises often focus on process optimization, workflow automation, and agile methodologies. Streamlining processes, identifying bottlenecks, and implementing lean practices are key to improving efficiency, quality, and customer satisfaction. The rise of digital transformation has led to tasks being reimagined and redesigned so that they align with digital capabilities and customer expectations.

Leavitt's diamond emphasizes that these four components are interconnected and influence one another. Changes or modifications in one component can have ripple effects on the other components. For example, implementing new technology may require adjustments to the organizational structure, changes in job tasks, and training for employees. The model suggests that organizations should strive for a balanced alignment among the four components to achieve optimal performance and effectiveness. By considering the interdependencies and interactions among structure, people, technology, and tasks, organizations can identify areas for improvement, manage change effectively, and enhance overall organizational performance. Even today, Leavitt's diamond continues to be a valuable framework for enterprises analyzing organizational systems and identifying opportunities for improvement, including organizational behavior, management, and systems thinking.

Applying Leavitt's diamond in today's enterprises involves considering the interdependencies and interactions among these four components. This highlights the need for alignment and integration to achieve organizational effectiveness. Here are some examples of how Leavitt's diamond applies in contemporary enterprises:

- **Organizational change**: When implementing changes, such as adopting new technologies, reorganizing teams, or introducing new processes, enterprises must assess the impact on all four components of the diamond. This ensures that the change aligns with the organizational structure, engages and supports employees, leverages appropriate technologies, and optimizes tasks to achieve desired outcomes.

- **Digital transformation**: Digital transformation initiatives require enterprises to evaluate and align all components of the diamond. This involves considering the organizational structure in terms of its support for digital capabilities, reskilling or upskilling employees to leverage new technologies, integrating appropriate digital tools and platforms, and redefining tasks and processes to leverage digital advantages.

- **Agile and cross-functional teams**: Enterprises adopting agile methodologies need to consider the interactions between structure, people, technology, and tasks. Organizations must ensure the appropriate structure is in place to support collaboration and decision-making, select team members with diverse skills and expertise, provide them with suitable technology tools and platforms, and define tasks and workflows to enable agility and iterative development.

- **Change management**: Applying change management principles involves addressing all four components of the diamond. This includes effective communication and stakeholder engagement (people), assessing the impact of the change on organizational structure, roles and reporting lines, providing the necessary training and support for technology adoption, and redefining tasks and processes to align with the change.

Leavitt's diamond provides a change management framework and a holistic approach to managing change within an organization. As every enterprise is unique, Leavitt's diamond can offer insights into a company's critical success factors across the four components – structure, tasks, people, and technology. In the next section, we will explore the three pillars of the golden triangle that builds on top of Leavitt's diamond.

The golden triangle

In a dynamic business environment, enterprises face the daunting challenge of achieving and sustaining success. To tackle this challenge, a holistic approach is necessary – one that integrates people, processes, and technology into a seamless framework. **People-process-technology** (PPT), also known as **the golden triangle**, is another hugely popular and important organizational management framework that enterprises must leverage to ensure seamless functioning amidst change. PPT builds on top of Leavitt's diamond and underscores the critical role of people, processes, and technology, emphasizing the interconnectedness and mutual reliance of these three elements in achieving organizational success. It recognizes that each pillar is essential and interconnected, requiring careful attention and integration. By focusing on nurturing and empowering people, optimizing processes, and leveraging technology, an organization can enhance its effectiveness, efficiency, and innovation capabilities. The PPT framework serves as a roadmap for enterprises to build a solid foundation and can pave the way for sustainable growth, improved customer satisfaction, and increased profitability.

People – the foundation of organizational success

The people pillar is the cornerstone of the golden triangle and recognizes the importance of human capital to an organization. It also underscores the need for strategic human resource management, talent development, and a supportive work culture that values individuals, fostering a symbiotic relationship between the organization and its most valuable resource. Let's take a closer look:

- **Human capital**: Human capital, comprising the skills, knowledge, and capabilities of individuals, is integral to innovation, problem-solving, and creativity, which are essential components of successful digital transformations. A skilled workforce not only enables the implementation of digital solutions but also fosters a culture of agility and resilience, allowing organizations to thrive amid technological disruptions. The strategic investment in human capital serves as a linchpin for unlocking the transformative power of digital technologies and ensuring the long-term success and sustainability of organizations.

- **Organizational culture and leadership**: Organizational culture and leadership play pivotal roles in the success of digital transformation initiatives while also addressing resistance to change, which is a common challenge during digital transformation. In the context of digital transformation, where technologies continually evolve, a positive and adaptive organizational culture provides the fertile ground necessary for embracing change and innovation. Leadership, both at the executive and middle-management levels, is crucial in setting the tone for the organization's digital journey.

- **Talent acquisition, development, and retention**: As enterprises embark on digital transformation, talent management becomes extremely crucial to ensure that the organization has the right people with the necessary skills, thereby equipping them to stay relevant and retaining top talent to create a stable and committed workforce. In a three-pronged approach – talent acquisition, development, and retention – talent acquisition strategies should focus on bringing in individuals from diverse backgrounds who not only have technical skills but also bring new perspectives and demonstrate innovative thinking and a forward-looking mindset. On the other hand, a talent development strategy must focus on providing continuous learning opportunities, career development, cultivating adaptability, and the willingness to embrace change. Finally, a positive and inclusive work culture with opportunities for professional growth, rewards, and recognition can foster appreciation and increase talent retention.

Processes – streamlining operations and enhancing efficiency

As the saying goes, embracing new technologies with old processes will only yield a very expensive old process. As organizations build a foundation for the modern digital enterprise, it is extremely important to identify and recognize the opportunities to replace old processes with modern best practices to realize a higher return on investment. Here are a few key areas of process improvement that enterprises can embrace:

- **Operational excellence and continuous improvement**: Streamlining and optimizing processes improves efficiency. Consistent outcomes eliminate waste and enhance resource utilization. A strong operational foundation allows organizations to focus on innovation as day-to-day operations run smoothly, leaving room for creative thinking. Implementing the lean and Six Sigma methodologies enables organizations to identify and eliminate process bottlenecks and variations. Continuous improvement helps organizations not only to enhance current operations but also to remain adaptive to changing trends. Together, operational excellence and continuous improvement empower organizations to consistently deliver high-quality products or services, meet customer expectations, and stay competitive.

- **Workflow and collaboration**: Embracing digital transformation empowers organizations to respond swiftly to changing market trends and customer expectations. However, this requires a paradigm shift in development, operational, and process controls. Enterprises will have to adopt agile methodologies to foster a culture of continuous improvement, with a focus on delivering tangible incremental value with regular feedback loops enabling teams to adapt and refine strategies throughout the project life cycle. It is also essential to cultivate cross-functional collaboration between business and IT teams to break down silos, for a holistic understanding of the organization's goals and customer needs.

- **Quality assurance and risk management**: The integration of new technologies, changes in processes, and evolving regulatory landscapes introduce various risks, such as cybersecurity threats, data breaches, and operational disruptions. With the exponential evolution and adoption of technological advancements, ensuring the quality of digital solutions is paramount for meeting customer expectations and gaining customer trust while also achieving business objectives. Quality assurance practices involve rigorous testing, validation, and verification of digital processes and technologies to guarantee their functionality, reliability, and security. This not only enhances the overall user experience but also contributes to the credibility and trustworthiness of the organization. Simultaneously, proactive risk management and adherence to regulatory and legal compliance are crucial in identifying, assessing, and mitigating uncertainties and building stakeholder trust.

Technology – enabling innovation and competitive advantage

Technology is the catalyst that fosters innovation and drives digital transformation. It empowers organizations to reimagine traditional processes, enhance efficiency, and create new business models. Continual adoption of emerging technologies is at the crux of digital transformation for enterprises to innovate and secure their position as the digital disruption leader:

- **Emerging technologies and automation**: Emerging technologies offer transformative capabilities that help redefine traditional business models and enable organizations to harness the power of technology to enhance customer experiences, as well as drive operational efficiencies. By embracing automation and emerging technologies, organizations can unlock new levels of agility, scalability, and competitiveness, positioning themselves at the forefront of industry evolution and ensuring long-term success with digital transformation.

- **Data transformation**: Organizations can strategically leverage data transformation as a linchpin for successful digital transformation initiatives. In the modern digital landscape, data is an invaluable asset to every enterprise and it is crucial to harness its full potential. Data transformation involves the comprehensive process of collecting, cleaning, organizing, and analyzing data to derive actionable insights. Data-driven insights enable organizations to understand customer behavior, anticipate market trends, tailor marketing strategies, and optimize supply chain management for enhanced efficiency.

Enterprise cloud maturity assessment

Building a solid foundation for a modern cloud-ready enterprise is crucial to ensure successful digital transformation. A cloud-readiness assessment is an indispensable first step to understanding where an organization stands in the maturity curve and devising appropriate strategies that align with business objectives. As every enterprise is unique, a maturity assessment can be a helpful tool to not just assess the current state but also serve as a guiding post for futuristic transformation goals. A cloud maturity assessment is an important tool and can help enterprises improve cloud adoption and usage. Several kinds of maturity assessments focus on specific functions, such as cloud readiness, security, and service maturity. The best cloud maturity model for an enterprise will depend on the specific needs and goals of the organization. However, all of the models can provide valuable insights into an organization's cloud maturity level and help develop a roadmap for improvement.

Cloud Adoption Maturity Model (CAMM)

The CAMM is an opinionated framework that helps enterprises assess and measure their cloud adoption maturity. By evaluating their present cloud maturity, organizations can gain valuable insights to drive their efforts toward attaining a transformative maturity level. Drawing upon my experience working with several enterprises across diverse industry sectors, this CAMM framework is an adaptation of several industry-leading frameworks tailored to align with the requirements of enterprises. The CAMM model is composed of six levels of maturity across different dimensions and is uniquely tied back to the golden triangle, to help manage change:

- **Baseline**: At this level, enterprises predominantly operate in traditional on-premises or hosted environments with legacy systems and monolithic application stacks. There are no major cloud initiatives at departmental or organizational levels, and no plans to migrate or adopt cloud computing yet.

- **Explore**: Enterprises at this maturity level are at an investigational stage. Any cloud service adoption and usage is typically exploratory and minimal with isolated proof-of-concepts not involving executive sponsorships.

- **Ad hoc**: Organizations at this level are embarking on cloud computing either as a private or public cloud deployment. Most of the cloud usage is departmental and is driven by specific business requirements to add modern capabilities that IT isn't able to deliver either concerning speed or capability constraints. At this level, there is no enterprise-wide cloud adoption and it's mostly spearheaded by LOB leadership.

- **Define**: At this level, enterprises start to adopt cloud computing as a standard across the enterprise, but the usage of the cloud is still tactical and restricted due to a lack of established governance policies, best practices, and controls. At this stage, cloud access is typically centralized, making it tougher for teams to access, explore, and innovate. There is some level of executive sponsorship at the organizational level.

- **Orchestrate**: Organizations at this maturity level have a well-defined cloud strategy and have implemented processes and controls to manage and monitor the cloud environments efficiently. There is a seamless integration of on-premises, public clouds, and private clouds with a unified set of DevOps practices, automation, processes, controls, and tools. At this level, enterprises typically have defined governance policies, processes, and tools to enable teams to lead change and deliver advanced capabilities in the cloud faster than ever before. At this stage, cloud access is decentralized, with individual teams taking ownership and accountability.

- **Transform**: Organizations at this level are continuously optimizing cloud environments to improve performance, resiliency, security, and cost-efficiency. At this stage, digital transformation sets in, and enterprise workloads are highly flexible, secure, portable, and can be developed and hosted on different platforms. Enterprises at this maturity level typically lead the digital disruption and are considered leaders in their respective industries.

The following figure depicts the levels of enterprise cloud adoption and maturity:

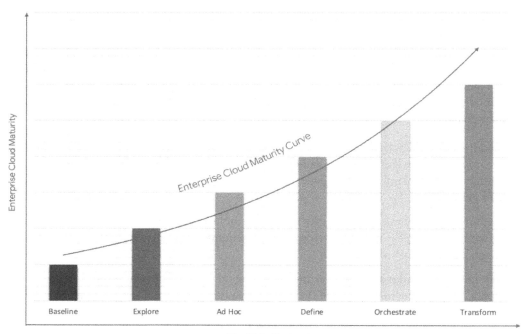

Figure 4.2 – Enterprise cloud adoption and maturity levels

The CAMM framework is a valuable tool for enterprises of all sizes and helps measure an organization's current maturity level and improve cloud adoption and usage. It is fairly easy to use and can be customized to meet the specific needs of an organization. By leveraging the CAMM framework, organizations can realize some great benefits, such as assessing an organization's cloud maturity level, identifying areas of improvement with cloud usage and adoption, ensuring the organization's cloud strategy is secure and compliant, assessing the organization's cloud governance capabilities, alignment with long term business objectives, and being able to develop a roadmap for cloud maturity improvement.

An enterprise's cloud maturity is generally measured across different dimensions of the golden triangle or the PPT framework. A typical assessment involves measuring an organization's maturity score in each of the dimensions, with the cumulative score indicating the overall maturity score. This is often the first step for enterprises to measure, track, and improve overall cloud maturity. As every enterprise is unique, an organization can consider fewer or more dimensions to adapt across each of the three pillars. Let's review the maturity levels and how they're assessed across these dimensions in detail.

The people pillar

The people pillar involves dimensions that span organizational skill development, hiring, strategic partnerships, and team collaboration. This section provides a guide on how organizations can leverage the CAMM framework to self-assess cloud adoption maturity.

Organization skill development

Organizational skill development involves the intentional and systematic efforts made by an organization to enhance the skills, competencies, and capabilities of its workforce. As technology, industry trends, and job requirements evolve, ongoing organizational skill development becomes crucial for maintaining a skilled, motivated, and resilient workforce:

- **Ad hoc**: No formal training goals, certifications, or targets have been established.
- **Explore**: Training, certifications, and hands-on exercises must be specifically requested
- **Define**: On-demand and instructor-led training is offered, and formal certifications are actively supported and promoted
- **Orchestrate**: In addition to formal training and on-demand learning, cross-organizational knowledge sharing, personalized development plans, and role-based certification guidance are promoted and rewarded
- **Transform**: Organizations promote external knowledge sharing, tech talks, industry leadership, hackathons, and merit incentives for upskilling

Hiring process

This dimension refers to the strategic steps that organizations take to attract and hire a workforce that is not only proficient in cloud and digital technologies but also passionate about driving innovation and contributing to the organization's digital transformation journey:

- **Ad hoc**: Candidates need no prior cloud experience
- **Explore**: Certain job positions require prior cloud experience
- **Define**: The most relevant jobs require candidates to have prior cloud experience
- **Orchestrate**: Relevant job roles are redefined, mandating that people upskill as a foundation for building a cloud-first organization
- **Transform**: All job postings require cloud experience, with a goal of enterprise digital transformation

Partners

The partner dimension defines the organization's ability to leverage strategic partnerships with vendors and partners that would help advance and catapult its IT maturity and lead the industry with technology disruption:

- **Ad hoc**: Third parties are relied upon to deliver cloud capabilities. Partners own and maintain cloud tenancy
- **Explore**: Third parties deliver most of the cloud capabilities
- **Define**: Partners offer specialized knowledge or skills to deliver modern cloud capabilities
- **Orchestrate**: Partners are engaged with in-house IT to deliver cloud capabilities, with an eye toward upskilling
- **Transform**: Third parties are predominantly used for staff augmentation and advisories

Team composition

The team composition dimension refers to the ability of IT teams to effectively collaborate with cross-functional teams and share their expertise and learnings so that they can contribute to a common business objective:

- **Ad hoc**: Teams work independently of each other, siloed by function based on on-premises role definitions
- **Explore**: The organization has pockets of cloud expertise with informal cross-functional collaboration
- **Define**: Formal cross-functional collaboration with CCoE providing foundational support
- **Orchestrate**: Teams leverage CCoE-defined standards, templates, and patterns with cross-functional collaboration common across the organization

- **Transform**: Fully autonomous and self-sustaining teams with expertise across technology and process domains

The process pillar

The process pillar involves dimensions such as leadership, executive sponsorship, measurement of KPIs, and budget allocation. This section explains how organizations can leverage the CAMM framework to self-assess cloud adoption maturity.

Leadership and sponsorship

This dimension helps assess the leadership involvement and executive sponsorship within the organization as it embarks on cloud transformation. This is an important dimension that sets the tone for an organization's success with digital transformation:

- **Ad hoc**: No executive sponsorship for cloud initiatives

- **Explore**: Sponsorship from LOB heads or senior management

- **Define**: Sponsorship from one or more C-level executives

- **Orchestrate**: Comprehensive C-level sponsorship for cloud adoption and migration

- **Transform**: Executive sponsorship sets the tone and pace for enterprise-wide cloud-first adoption, R&D, and innovation

Measure

As the saying goes, *that which cannot be measured cannot be improved*. Measurement is a key dimension that helps assess and guide how organizations measure success and outcomes from a cloud initiative:

- **Ad hoc**: No defined success criteria for cloud initiatives

- **Explore**: Proof of concepts and **minimum viable product** (**MVP**) efforts guide enterprise foray and serve as pseudo-measures

- **Define**: Successful outcomes are measured by deploying production workloads to the cloud and realizing business value

- **Orchestrate**: Success criteria are measured as a function of scaling production workloads, operating core services integrated with mission-critical enterprise applications

- **Transform**: Success criteria are measured based on business value creation through transformational initiatives and innovation

Budget

This dimension helps assess how an organization funds and allocates financial resources for cloud initiatives that directly influence and impact business value:

- **Ad hoc**: No explicit funding for cloud initiatives or enterprises allocate cloud budgets purely based on projected cost savings

- **Explore**: Department-level budgets allocated for specific cloud projects

- **Define**: Dedicated budgets for specific initiatives and some cloud-based R&D

- **Orchestrate**: Budgets allocated for cloud-first initiatives with a reduced focus on on-premises investments

- **Transform**: Implicit budget allocation for cloud initiatives to realize business value and on-premises investments only where justified

The technology pillar

The technology pillar encompasses dimensions such as IT architecture, automation capabilities, IT operations, security, data management, and emerging technologies such as AI and ML. This section outlines how organizations can leverage the CAMM framework to self-assess cloud adoption maturity in the technology pillar.

Architecture

The architecture dimension assesses the extent of an organization's IT maturity concerning how it leverages modern cloud-native architectures for IT initiatives:

- **Ad hoc**: Predominantly on-premises monolithic applications with a wide range of technology stacks, typically provisioned for anticipated peaks.

- **Explore**: Most workloads are deployed in long-running VMs. There's limited experimentation with containers and microservices. Container-based workloads in the cloud offer scalability benefits.

- **Define**: Production workloads are deployed on containers or serverless compute with some workloads still on short-lived VMs, leveraging autoscaling for some workloads

- **Orchestrate**: The majority of applications are on microservices-based architecture. Regular use of short-lived VMs, containers, or function-based compute results in autoscaling being leveraged based on application metrics.

- **Transform**: There's a broad use of resilient, scalable, and consistently secure architecture blueprints. Here, you can leverage containers, serverless functions, and optimized VMs with consistent use of cloud-native tooling across deployment topologies – on-premises or the cloud.

Automation capabilities

Automation is a critical capability that helps streamline operations, eliminate errors, improve time to market, and realize cost savings. This dimension is extremely crucial for organizations embarking on cloud transformation and helps assess the automation maturity of an enterprise:

- **Ad hoc**: Manual or no provisioning of cloud services

- **Explore**: Cloud services are provisioned through scripting, but no formal organization-wide process and standards exist

- **Define**: Cloud services provisioning is automated but not leveraged consistently across projects

- **Orchestrate**: Most project teams leverage **Infrastructure as Code** (**IaC**) tools to automate cloud services provisioning

- **Transform**: A consistent set of IaC tools and processes are used enterprise-wide, as prescribed by the CCoE

Operations

The operations dimension assesses the ability of the IT organization to embrace modern DevOps practices such as IaC, CI/CD, and SRE practices:

- **Ad Hoc**: Projects employ traditional code, build, test, and deploy practices. No CI/CD processes are in place. Applications are updated in place.

- **Explore**: Lack of consistent SRE practices and limited use of CI/CD tools and processes. New releases are delivered through rolling updates, which require a maintenance window.

- **Define**: Many project teams leverage CI/CD and SRE practices. New releases are deployed alongside the current version with a manual cutover and fallback mechanisms.

- **Orchestrate**: Organization-wide usage of SRE best practices and project-based CI/CD. Modern SRE practices such as canary or blue-green deployments are leveraged with an any-time deployment strategy.

- **Transform**: There are standardized and consistent SRE and CI/CD tools across the enterprise. New releases are transparent and incremental releases are done multiple times a day, with no manual intervention.

Security

The security dimension helps assess an organization's security measures in the cloud and its ability to stay abreast of modern security threats:

- **Ad hoc**: Manual user or system account provisioning with inconsistent identity policies. Infrastructure security primarily relies upon network firewalls. SysAdmins manage access controls manually based on ad hoc requests.

- **Explore**: Centralized organizational IDP with a common set of identity, audit, and access policies with manual interventions. Network-based security is enhanced by user identity context verification. Access controls are regularly reviewed but separate for on-premises and cloud.

- **Define**: Common IDP standards are established across on-premises and cloud infrastructure, with org-wide identity, audit, and access control policies. Here, you can introduce 2FA or MFA with periodical access policies and control reviews.

- **Orchestrate**: Federated identity management and auto synchronization across on-premises and the cloud with SSO and mandating 2FA/MFA requirements for all users. Automated risk-based workflows control access management with a lesser reliance on network-based security controls. Access policies and controls are reviewed and certified regularly, with issues remediated proactively.

- **Transform**: This is a single source of user and service identity that has fully centralized and automated identity and access control policies. MFA and SSO are established enterprise standards with just-in-time privileges for access management and real-time alerts. There are also fully integrated and automated risk-based access privilege reviews with little to no reliance on network-based security and access managed on user identity, context, and devices.

Data management

The data management dimension helps assess an organization's data maturity as the data spreads across on-premises and cloud infrastructure:

- **Ad hoc**: Data sprawl with data management is decentralized with little to no organizational awareness of where data is stored. There's no manual data classification. Backups are maintained locally or cross-site.

- **Explore**: Departments hold data and documentation of schema, sensitivity, and data access policies. Policies exist to prevent unauthorized data access. Data backups are automated for critical applications on network-attached devices.

- **Define**: Data inventory exists, with manually curated data classifications and sensitivity. There's a centralized set of policies and controls with limited monitoring. Data backups are automated for most applications on the cloud with manual interventions.

- **Orchestrate**: Organizations have a comprehensive understanding of data location, lineage, redundancy, classification, and sensitivity. Data exfiltration risk is mitigated by preventive, detective, and corrective policies and controls. Data backups are fully automated with immutable copies for faster recovery.

- **Transform**: Automated data and metadata catalogs, a business-friendly glossary, data quality metrics, data lineage tracking, automated backup and recovery testing, and data redundancy with immutable copies. It provides fully automated preventive controls, proactive monitoring, anomaly detection, audits, and alerts.

AI/ML

The AI/ML dimension describes the ability of an organization to embrace modern AI/ML capabilities to advance business objectives and lead digital disruption:

- **Ad hoc**: AI/ML is not an organizational focus.

- **Explore**: The organization is still in assessment mode. There are no formal organization-wide standards, with departments building prototypes to solve interesting problems.

- **Define**: CCoE establishes an AI vision with systematic blueprints and guidance. Organizations move from proofs-of-concept to productionizing some AI workloads

- **Orchestrate**: The Organization advocates AI/ML to be embedded in applications and creates an AI practice to explore, research, and modernize.

- **Transform**: AI is part of the organizational DNA, with several applications leveraging AI capabilities to transform how business is conducted. The organization starts to lead this disruption.

It is important to note that the dimensions we discussed under the CAMM framework are some core dimensions and are not exhaustive. As every enterprise is unique, organizations must strive to define dimensions and attributes across the people, processes, and technology pillars while also ensuring they keep them updated. A periodical assessment of the cloud's maturity is essential to measure the current state while also establishing the target goals.

Google's Cloud Adoption Framework (CAF)

There are several different variants of cloud readiness assessment frameworks that exist. One of my personal favorites is **Google's** CAF as it builds on the golden triangle rubric of people, processes, and technology *[2]*. This is a generic framework that enterprises can leverage to assess their cloud maturity and build toward a cloud-first organization. The framework prescribes four realms across three phases that help measure and improve an organization's cloud readiness. This is an opinionated framework that advocates that, while building a cloud-first organization, organizations must excel across four realms.

The four realms

CAF defines four realms – learn, lead, scale, and secure – that help assess and measure an organization's cloud readiness and adoption maturity:

- **Learn**: This pillar describes the extent and the caliber of an organization's learning and upskilling programs made available and the ability of the organization to continuously learn, upskill, and reskill. This realm also helps organizations understand the quality of learning initiatives offered and the ability to partner with third-party vendors and partners to advance their business objectives through the cloud.

- **Lead**: This pillar helps assess the top-down commitment of leadership sponsorship and mandates for a cloud transformation, and the bottom-up momentum from cross-functional teams to lead cloud adoption initiatives toward a common business objective.

- **Scale**: This pillar describes the organization's ability to leverage cloud-native architecture, managed services, and serverless offerings to abstract away infrastructure that enables seamless scalability while reducing operational overhead.

- **Secure**: This pillar describes the ability of organizations to secure and protect applications and services in the cloud from unauthorized and unsolicited access by leveraging a defense-in-depth security model.

The three phases

CAF also defines three phases of cloud maturity for organizations – tactical, strategic, and transformational:

- **Tactical**: In the tactical maturity phase, organizations typically have pointed objectives to deploy individual cloud workloads without a larger plan or strategy for future expansion. In this phase, the primary objectives are to realize cost reduction for specific systems and applications through cloud migration. While this approach may yield quick wins and short-term benefits, it lacks the necessary foundation for scalability and innovation.

Figure 4.3 – PPT alignment in the tactical maturity phase

- **Strategic**: In the strategic maturity stage, organizations are guided by a comprehensive vision that encompasses multiple workloads. These workloads are meticulously architected and designed with a keen focus on future demands and scalability. In this phase, organizations embark on a journey of transformation, actively involving both people and processes in the equation. IT teams demonstrate remarkable efficiency and effectiveness, enhancing the business value derived from leveraging the cloud for business operations.

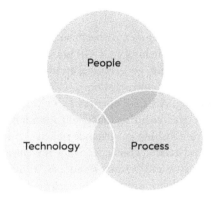

Figure 4.4 – PPT alignment in the strategic maturity phase

- **Transformational**: In the transformational maturity stage, organizations have well-established, smooth-running cloud operations and focus on integrating data and insights gained from their cloud experience. Organizations leverage the cloud as a strategic platform to reduce operational overhead, allowing teams to focus on innovation and business transformation. This technological shift is further supported by the transformation of people and processes. In the strategic maturity phase, IT has evolved from a cost center to a strategic business partner.

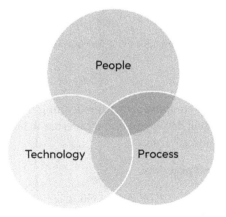

Figure 4.5 – PPT alignment in the transformational maturity phase

CAF serves as a good example of how organizations can leverage a framework to assess, measure, and improve their cloud adoption and maturity. However, as organizations build the foundations for a cloud transformation, the framework can act as a good starting point and can be customized and evolved to suit specific needs. In the next section, we will review how enterprises can set up and establish a CCoE to advance digital disruption.

CCoE

As cloud adoption continues to grow, building a CCoE becomes an indispensable initiative for enterprises seeking to thrive in the digital era. Establishing a CCOE is a crucial step for enterprises embracing cloud computing. By providing leadership, governance, architectural guidance, skill development, cost optimization strategies, and fostering collaboration, a CCoE empowers organizations to leverage the full potential of cloud computing. A CCoE ensures that cloud initiatives are aligned with the organization's overall business objectives, ensuring that cloud adoption supports the company's vision, mission, and long-term goals. By establishing governance policies, guidelines, and controls, a CCoE enables enterprises to manage cloud-related risks effectively. It ensures compliance with regulatory requirements, data protection, security, and privacy standards. More importantly, a CCoE fosters a culture of knowledge sharing and collaboration among various stakeholders, including IT teams, developers, operations, and business units that promotes cross-functional expertise and accelerates the adoption of cloud technologies.

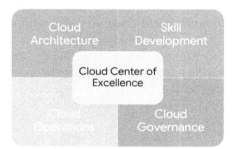

Figure 4.6 – CCoE framework

Key components of a CCoE

The CCoE focuses on four primary components – from defining cloud architecture blueprints and best practices and enabling cloud skill development and expertise to implementing cloud operational best practices and establishing cloud governance:

- **Cloud architecture and best practices**:
  - **Architecture framework**: The CCoE defines cloud architecture frameworks and reference architectures that provide guidelines for designing and deploying cloud solutions. These frameworks must consider scalability, availability, security, and performance to ensure the successful implementation of cloud-based applications and infrastructure.

- **Best practices**: The CCoE identifies and promotes best practices for various aspects of cloud adoption, including cloud migration strategies, application development methodologies, infrastructure management, and security protocols. It fosters continuous improvement and encourages the adoption of industry-recognized standards and frameworks.

- **Skill development**:

  - **Cloud training programs**: The CCoE develops and delivers training programs to educate employees on cloud computing concepts, technologies, and services. It offers certifications, workshops, and learning resources to enhance cloud knowledge and skills across the organization.

  - **Skill assessment and development**: The CCoE conducts skill assessments to identify skill gaps and areas of improvement. It collaborates with HR and training teams to develop targeted skill development plans and provides resources for employees to upskill in areas such as cloud architecture, security, DevOps, data analytics, and advanced skills such as AI/ML.

- **Cloud operations**:

  - **Cost optimization strategies**: The CCoE implements cost optimization strategies to manage cloud spending effectively. It leverages tools for monitoring resource utilization, identifies cost-saving opportunities such as rightsizing instances, reserved instances, and spot instances, and establishes policies for budget allocation and tracking.

  - **Financial governance**: The CCoE develops financial governance frameworks to ensure financial accountability and control in cloud spending. It establishes processes for cost allocation, budget management, and chargeback mechanisms for internal departments or projects utilizing cloud resources.

- **Cloud governance**:

  - **Leadership sponsorship**: A successful CCoE requires strong executive sponsorship to drive cloud adoption and ensure alignment with business goals. Senior leaders must serve as executive sponsors to provide guidance, support decision-making, and advocate for the benefits of the cloud across the organization.

  - **Governance framework**: One of the primary responsibilities of the CCoE is to establish enterprise-wide governance policies, standards, and controls to manage cloud-related risks. It defines roles and responsibilities, establishes decision-making processes, and ensures compliance with regulatory requirements and industry best practices.

As organizations navigate the complexities of the cloud landscape, a CCoE serves as a strategic driving force behind a well-orchestrated and successful cloud adoption and digital transformation. A CCoE sets up an organization for long-term success and innovation in the cloud while also minimizing risks.

Building the foundations for a cloud-ready enterprise

Digital transformation involves reinventing IT processes and technology teams operating within an enterprise as new technologies, such as cloud computing, continually evolve. In a traditional IT environment, typical **software development life cycle** (**SDLC**) practices such as waterfall methodology proved sufficient with isolated teams of development, testing, security, and operations. However, with rapidly evolving business demands and technologies such as cloud computing, technology organizations face demanding speed to market and IT agility to thrive in a competitive landscape and require a fundamental cultural shift in software engineering practices. DevSecOps is key to successful IT management in modern enterprises and it clearly illustrates the tight interdependency between development, security, and operations. As we discussed the crucial role the golden triangle plays in digital transformation, it is important to understand the paradigm shifts that enterprises will need to adopt in all three aspects of people, processes, and technology. Let's review some of the best practices that enterprises can leverage to build a solid foundation for a cloud-ready organization.

The startup mindset

While it may not be always feasible or desirable for enterprises to replicate all aspects of startup culture, adopting a startup mindset can provide organizations with the agility, innovation, and customer-centricity needed to thrive in a rapidly changing business environment. It allows enterprises to embrace change, take calculated risks, and seize opportunities for growth and transformation. Startups often disrupt established industries by introducing new business models, products, and services. They tend to prioritize understanding customer needs and delivering value, operate in a fast-paced environment, appeal to top talent, and prioritize learning and experimentation. Enterprises that operate with a startup mindset can proactively identify and capitalize on emerging opportunities, gaining a competitive edge over their more traditional counterparts. To operate with a startup mindset, enterprises can take several steps to inculcate the culture across the organization:

- **Entrepreneurial approach**: Encouraging employees to think like entrepreneurs will promote autonomy, ownership, and willingness to take risks. Creating an environment that supports rapid experimentation, fail-fast, and learning from failures can have a huge positive impact on digital transformation.

- **Customer-centricity**: Every initiative or project must place a strong emphasis on understanding customer needs and preferences. Implementing customer feedback loops, conducting user research, and involving customers in the product development process will ensure alignment with business and market demands.

- **Flat organizational structure**: Reducing hierarchical structures and fostering a more flat organizational hierarchy promotes open communication and quick decision-making, and it also empowers employees to contribute their ideas and expertise.

- **Streamlining processes**: What most organizations fail to do when embracing new technologies is look at existing processes that could go away. New methods or functions are often hindered owing to the pressures of existing processes that were developed for a different problem statement. Identifying and eliminating bureaucratic processes that slow down decision-making, simplifying approval workflows, and empowering employees to make autonomous decisions within predefined boundaries can have a magnified impact on associate productivity and operational efficiency.

- **Agile project management**: Implementing agile project management methodologies such as Scrum, Kanban, Lean Development, Crystal, or Extreme Programming to promote flexibility, adaptability, and incremental progress can result in shorter development cycles, frequent feedback loops, and the ability to pivot quickly.

- **Incremental value delivery**: Traditionally, enterprise applications are delivered as an all-or-nothing package. A startup mindset will increase bias toward action and outcomes to deliver incremental value and minimum viable products faster and rapidly incorporating feedback.

Everything is a product

In traditional IT, organizations tend to focus on technology infrastructure, maintenance, providing technology services, and meeting internal stakeholders' requirements, prioritizing technical requirements and constraints over user needs. More importantly, IT operates in a silo without a deep understanding of how the technology aligns with broader business goals with the primary objective of maintaining and supporting existing systems rather than proactively seeking ways to improve them. In contrast, product thinking places a stronger emphasis on user-centricity, delivering value to end users or customers. It helps organizations embrace product ownership by defining the product vision, prioritizing features, and ensuring alignment with business goals and user needs. It prioritizes understanding user needs, designing intuitive user experiences, and continuously improving the product based on user feedback. Here are some key principles enterprises can leverage to inculcate product thinking in digital transformation:

- **Product vision**: The *everything is a product* mindset enables establishing a clear product vision and identifying the desired outcomes, benefits, and values that cloud transformation should deliver that align with overall business objectives.

- **User-centricity**: The primary objective of product thinking is user-centric design, prioritizing the needs and requirements of the end users when designing and developing cloud-based solutions. Product thinking facilitates a deeper understanding of user personas, conducting user research, and gathering feedback to ensure that the solutions align with user expectations and provide a seamless experience.

- **Product ownership and value delivery**: Enterprises should designate product owners or product managers who will be responsible for driving cloud transformation initiatives. Product owners must have a deep understanding of both the business and technical aspects and act as advocates for the customer and stakeholders, identifying the highest-value areas for cloud adoption and prioritizing them based on their potential impact and feasibility. This helps organizations focus on delivering incremental value early and frequently, addressing critical business needs and pain points.

- **MVPs**: In digital native cloud transformations, it is not always feasible to predict and plan, especially when organizations innovate at scale. Product thinking emphasizes the concept of building and delivering MVPs to validate assumptions, test hypotheses, and gather feedback early in the cloud transformation process. This approach allows for faster learning, reduces waste, and ensures that resources are focused on delivering value.

- **Ideate, iterate, and innovate**: Adopting an iterative and agile methodology to build and improve cloud services promotes a culture of continuous improvement and experimentation throughout the cloud transformation journey. This encourages teams to experiment with different cloud services, architectures, and technologies to identify the most effective solutions for the enterprise's specific needs. This involves breaking down the cloud solution into smaller, manageable increments and continuously iterating and refining based on user feedback and changing business needs.

Platform as a product

With the product thinking approach, enterprises can start designing, architecting, and developing great products. However, it all boils down to how fast these products are delivered. In a dynamic business landscape, speed to market is key to staying competitive and gaining market share. DevOps unified the SDLC by integrating development and operations, gaining process scalability, and trading off complexity. With the *You built it, You run it* mindset, developer complexity has become ever so exponential as more products get rolled out with more modern technologies and tools, especially in the cloud-native era. For instance, in methodologies such as twelve-factor apps and the cloud-native fifteen-factor, developers had to learn how to code, build, test, release, deploy, operate, monitor, and master the plethora of tools that support each facet of the DevOps life cycle. Several organizations, such as Spotify, Netflix, and Uber, have developed extensive capabilities to overcome this challenge by developing a *platform* that can help automate the SDLC, giving rise to the modern trend of *platform engineering*. In Gartner's hype cycle for agile and DevOps, platform engineering is seen as a natural evolution in the cloud-native landscape.

According to www.platformengineering.org, *"Platform engineering is the discipline of designing and building toolchains and workflows that enable self-service capabilities for software engineering organizations in the cloud-native era."* [3]

The Internal Developer Platform (IDP)

Platform engineers often build a platform that can service the most common and operational necessities of the entire SDLC, preventing the need to reinvent the wheel. This is more commonly referred to as the IDP. Why is this called IDP? Each IDP is expected to be unique for every enterprise based on the technology choices, architecture patterns, security controls, and blueprints. In a traditional IT system, a legacy role called *SysAdmin* existed, typically the gatekeeper who manages the operations of an application or software. Developers typically develop software applications and *throw it over the fence* to the SysAdmins to deploy and operate, resulting in poor experiences for both.

The goal of platform engineering is to develop and maintain an IDP that abstracts away the underlying complexities of operating and managing the software and infrastructure layers. As with the *everything is a product* approach, an IDP must be seen as a product whose consumers or stakeholders are product teams. The primary objectives of an IDP are to provide a self-service platform that allows technology teams to interact and self-serve infrastructure needed to run their applications, normalize the technology stack by gluing together the toolchain required to ship products, reduce the variability, and automate infrastructure delivery:

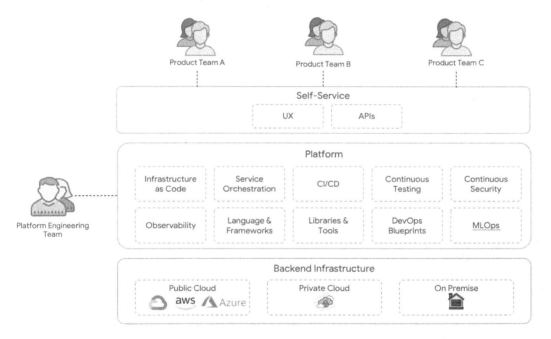

Figure 4.7 – Layers and interactions of an IDP

The IDP defines three distinct layers – backend infrastructure, platform, and self-service – that abstract the underlying infrastructure to simplify and democratize access:

- **Backend infrastructure layer:** This is the most fundamental layer that the platform engineering team will support. This involves platform and vendor selection, the decision to support hybrid or multi-cloud architectures, creating a matrix of approved, authorized, and supported services in the dimensions of security, compliance, and enterprise objectives, and managing maintenance, scale, and FinOps associated with the chosen platforms. Platform engineering also needs to periodically review, release, vet, and enable new technologies and features as they're made available by cloud vendors.

- **Platform layer**: This is the core abstraction layer that aids with normalizing the DevSecOps functions, irrespective of the underlying infrastructure of choice. The objective of this layer is to automate and simplify the management of infrastructure and prescribe best practices to enable product teams to implement solutions faster without having to reinvent the wheel as it pertains to DevSecOps. For instance, this layer would provide an opinionated view for product teams in the choice of software architecture frameworks, service orchestration, CI/CD pipelines, security controls, and observability.

- **Self-service layer**: The self-service layer is the primary interface for product teams as they embark on cloud initiatives. An ideal self-service layer would offer the user experience and APIs to help various product teams across the enterprise to provision sandboxes, test beds for R&D, or even production-grade environments. Through a common platform approach, product teams can deliver solutions that can seamlessly interact with other products while rapidly developing and iterating, resulting in operational efficiency and speed to market.

A focus on CUJs

In agile development methodologies, user stories are fundamental components that several organizations leverage for software development and user experience design. User stories are typically scoped to fit within a single development iteration or sprint, which helps break down larger features or functionalities into smaller, manageable units of work, and primarily guides the development team in implementing specific features or functionalities. On the other hand, CUJs take a much broader perspective and provide an end-to-end view of a user's journey. They encompass multiple user stories and capture the complete end-to-end user experience across different touchpoints and interactions. But why are CUJs important? In product thinking, enterprises need to think beyond products, features, and user stories as CUJs cut across product and feature boundaries, help teams focus on the entire user journey, and reduce friction to provide a seamless experience for end users. Users do not care about the product, feature, or technology that lets them accomplish a task and are instead interested in the seamless experience it offers.

For example, consider the following CUJ for an e-commerce chatbot service.

As an online shopper, I want the ability to inquire about product recommendations through an interactive interface without having to navigate the website extensively.

There are three primary parts to any CUJ – a user, a goal, and a role:

- **User**: Before defining a CUJ, it is important to understand the persona or user who will interact with the service

- **Goal**: This defines what the user is trying to achieve

- **Role**: Attributes that influence the user journey

In our example, the user is an online shopper on the e-commerce website, with their goal being inquiring about product recommendations and their role being to interact through an interface without having to navigate the website. From a CUJ perspective, this can traverse multiple product areas and components, such as the frontend, chatbot APIs, product catalog service, recommendations engine, cart, and checkout. Components in a CUJ can either be directly or indirectly involved, but they are crucial to consider to ensure a successful user experience. In this case, the product catalog, cart, and checkout services are existing services but have to consider the additional API request volume that the chatbot service would generate. After a CUJ has been defined, we must go through some key steps that help categorize, prioritize, evaluate, and measure the CUJs:

1. **CUJ categorization**: Once the CUJs have been defined, the next step is to categorize the CUJs to offer a seamless user experience. One way to categorize a CUJ is to understand the frequency of the CUJs. This helps product teams focus attention on CUJs based on the frequency of user interaction. Although all CUJs are critical in delivering a seamless user experience, the frequency categorization can help product teams deliver incremental business value.

2. **CUJ evaluation**: CUJ evaluation is the next key step where the product teams can conduct extensive user research and hypothesis testing, validate assumptions through walkthroughs, and more. The goal of a CUJ evaluation is to identify and uncover issues to prioritize based on user needs and feedback.

- **CUJ prioritization**: The next step is CUJ prioritization. A few different strategies exist, such as targeting top issues that users report or targeting an area with high-frequency usage that's part of a cohesive CUJ path.

- **CUJ observability**: The final step in a CUJ is defining the metrics to help identify, measure, and improve the service behavior. Product teams should identify the behaviors of the service to observe – referred to as the **service-level indicators** (**SLIs**) – set time targets for service response – commonly referred to as the **service-level objectives** (**SLOs**) – and configure alerts based on the service's health. This is a key step to ensure the success of a CUJ and can also serve as a feedback loop for further improvement.

Adopting a CUJ approach to application and product development enhances the ability of organizations to put the customer and the user at the center to offer a seamless customer experience.

Embracing open source in the cloud

The cloud is fundamentally built and powered by **open source software** (**OSS**) and open standards. Some popular OSS that forms the foundations of cloud platforms includes Linux, KVM, Kubernetes, Docker, Nginx, PostgreSQL, Git, Jenkins, Apache Kafka, TensorFlow, and open standards such as HTTP, TCP/IP, REST, SSL/TLS, ANSI, XML, JDBC, AMQP, SAML, JSON, MQTT, and others. Increasingly, most cloud service providers are either part of or contribute to open source software and open standards such as CNCF, OASIS, and CSA. If the cloud is built on open source, should enterprises build their applications on open source software? The simple answer is yes. There are several compelling reasons, such as cost efficiency, flexibility, vendor neutrality, vibrant community support, and interoperability, why enterprises should consider building an IT foundation on the cloud based on open source software and standards. However, in the context of an enterprise use case, the choice is not always easy. While there are huge advantages in leveraging open source technologies, with the two primary motivators being upfront cost savings owing to license or subscription fee avoidance and preventing vendor lock-in, there are some considerations that enterprises must be aware of, such as costs associated with OSS customization, implementation and maintenance, reliance on community support, availability of skilled resources, and scalability, security, and performance requirements.

There is always a raging debate between the choice of *building your own* versus *buying off-the-shelf* solutions. Neither approach is better or worse, so long as enterprises are self-aware of their strengths and their decisions are aligned with the overall vision. *Understanding the enterprise DNA is key*. In my capacity as an enterprise architect, I have had a Fortune 100 retail enterprise that prefers **commercial off-the-shelf (COTS)** and managed service offerings that enable their lean IT to spend more time and focus on addressing business needs while offloading software maintenance, support, feature rollouts, security, and compliance. This perfectly fits within their organization's DNA. On the other end of the spectrum, another Fortune 100 enterprise strongly favors building from scratch and leveraging open source software. While this strategy allowed them the flexibility to tailor, customize, and build capabilities that fit their needs, they needed significant investments in IT and maintenance.

As we discussed in the previous chapter, enterprises must aim to mitigate vendor lock-in risks but in most cases cannot avoid it completely. Striking the right balance between when to build versus buy is crucial to digital transformation success. This must also resonate when enterprises choose a cloud provider. Building software and applications that support open standards is more crucial than the choice of open versus closed software as it would aid in interoperability. For instance, organization A can choose a COTS B2B software to send and receive purchase orders and invoices with their suppliers, while organization B favors building a B2B software using open source technologies. The key consideration here is ensuring an open standard such as EDI is leveraged. In cloud parlance, here are some factors that enterprises could consider to navigate vendor neutrality and interoperability benefits:

- **Common platform for portability**: Instead of building directly on a vendor platform or service fabric, enterprises can reap long-term benefits by building a common platform foundation based on open source and open standards that can run anywhere. This can be a great hybrid cloud and multi-cloud strategy for enterprises to run applications and services on any target platform or infrastructure.

- **Cloud provider choice**: Enterprises can avoid vendor lock-in by choosing a cloud provider that invests and adopts open source and open standards. For instance, leveraging a managed service offering from a cloud provider in itself does not constitute a lock-in, so long as the service is built on unforked open source software and based on open standards. Leveraging this, an enterprise can build a seamless exit strategy.

- **Cloud-agnostic architecture**: Designing infrastructure, applications, and services based on open standards such as IaC, microservices, and open APIs can enable seamless portability and interoperability and aid with vendor neutrality.

Embracing open source and open standards is a natural design choice as enterprises embark on a cloud transformation journey as the cloud foundation is built on open source. It enables key capabilities for organizations, including application portability and interoperability, while also mitigating vendor lock-in.

Summary

In this chapter, we discussed how to build a solid foundation for a cloud-first enterprise, as well as how to embrace and manage change across the people, processes, and technology functions within the organization. We reviewed the cloud adoption maturity model and the maturity assessment framework that can be tailored to assess, measure, and improve an enterprise's cloud maturity. We also explored how to envision and establish a CCoE that acts as a central entity within the organization to advise and advocate cloud architecture and operational best practices to ensure success with cloud adoption and mitigate risks.

Then, we discussed how enterprises can build a robust foundation for cloud transformation by embracing a startup mindset, product thinking, and platform engineering. We also established how design thinking, by leveraging frameworks such as CUJs, can help organizations innovate with a custom-centric design. Finally, we explored the benefits of developing a cloud strategy based on open source and open standards.

In the next chapter, we will explore the various cloud transformation journeys and strategies that enterprises can leverage to modernize IT and innovate.

Further reading

The references used in this chapter as well as some additional resources are listed as follows:

1. `https://cio-wiki.org/wiki/Leavitt%27s_Alignment_Model`

2. `https://services.google.com/fh/files/misc/google_cloud_adoption_framework_whitepaper.pdf`

3. `https://platformengineering.org/blog/what-is-platform-engineering#:~:text=Platform%20engineering%20is%20the%20discipline,in%20the%20cloud%2Dnative%20era`

5

An Enterprise Journey to Cloud Transformation

Cloud computing has proven to be an engine for digital transformation for enterprises across multiple dimensions, fueled by the desire to innovate and compete. As we explored in *Chapter 4, Building the Foundations for a Modern Enterprise*, cloud transformation can deliver numerous benefits for enterprises, including enhanced flexibility, reliability, improved operational resilience, lower IT costs, and drive innovation. However, the journey to the cloud is not a one-size-fits-all process, as each enterprise embarks on a unique voyage, influenced by its specific goals, challenges, and organizational culture. An enterprise's journey to the cloud is a highly individualized process that's influenced by a multitude of factors, such as the existing IT landscape, industry regulations, organizational culture, timing, and market demands. The cloud journey is also dependent on the maturity level of the enterprise. Based on specific business objectives and maturity levels, some enterprises may prioritize cost reduction and seek to migrate their infrastructure to the cloud to achieve operational efficiency, while others may focus on leveraging the cloud's scalability and flexibility to drive innovation and lead digital disruption. In this chapter, we will explore the various cloud journeys for enterprises, including the following:

- Picking the right cloud initiatives using the multi-dimensional value-complexity matrix
- Various enterprise cloud transformation journeys
- Strategies while migrating workloads to the cloud
- Hybrid cloud strategies
- Innovating in the cloud through emerging technologies

Picking the right cloud initiatives using the multi-dimensional value-complexity matrix

In the previous chapter, we discussed the various strategies that organizations can employ to build the foundations for a modern cloud-ready enterprise and the cloud-readiness assessment framework to assess cloud maturity. One of the most critical steps in a cloud journey for enterprises is choosing the right workloads for the cloud. There are several different strategies that organizations can leverage to migrate or build applications in the cloud. However, it is critical to pick the right workloads – especially if it is the organization's first foray into the cloud – to ensure the success of the digital transformation. In this section, we will explore the multi-dimensional value matrix that enterprises can leverage as a tool to help pick the right workloads for a cloud journey. In a traditional approach, organizations typically use the value-complexity matrix, which measures the value-to-complexity ratio, to assess the right workloads. The multi-dimensional value-complexity matrix methodology allows for a more comprehensive approach where the value and complexity are evaluated across multiple dimensions. The value-complexity matrix in *Figure 5.1* shows various projects plotted against the perceived value and complexity with the bubble size representing the **net present value** (**NPV**) of the project:

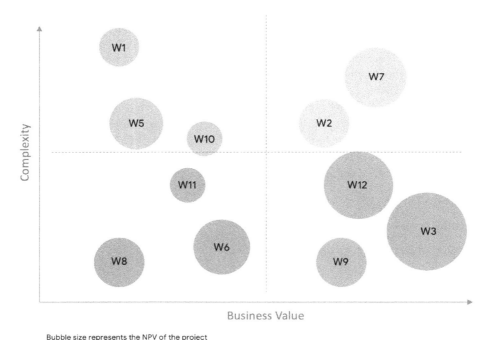

Bubble size represents the NPV of the project

Figure 5.1 – Value complexity matrix

Mapping out the complexity factors on the Y-axis and the business value elements on the X-axis while having a bubble size representing the NPV of an initiative or a project yields a holistic view of which initiatives are best suited for the cloud. At every enterprise maturity level, DNA and perceived business value are unique, and it is crucial to build out a value-complexity matrix to pick the right workloads for the right business value yield. For instance, multi-dimensional factors, such as the business criticality of the workload, interdependencies with other enterprise systems, security considerations, data sovereignty, licensing, effort required to migrate or implement, and cost, can all dictate the complexity of a particular initiative or workload. Similarly, value realized through innovation, speed to market, total cost of ownership, foray into newer markets, enhanced performance, and improved customer **satisfaction and sustainability** (based on the **ESG** framework) score pronounces the business value benefits. We will cover ESG and sustainability in more detail in *Chapter 11, ESG and Sustainability*. Finally, it may prove prudent for enterprises to evaluate the NPV of the cloud initiatives for business value realization that can be attributed to them.

Let's review the complexity and business value factors and how enterprises can score these elements.

Complexity factors

Complexity factors define the complexity and risks involved with any cloud initiative. These factors could include things such as application architecture complexity, interdependencies with upstream or downstream systems, time, effort, and cost complexity. As every cloud initiative within an enterprise context can be unique, organizations can tailor these complexity factors. However, the following are some complexity factors to consider:

- **Business criticality**: This represents the process of evaluating and classifying workloads or applications based on their business impact. This can be influenced by various attributes of an application, such as its revenue generation impact, business continuity, customer impact, **recovery time objective** (**RTO**), **recovery point objective** (**RPO**), and risk profile. Based on these attributes, an application, initiative, or workload can be categorized as mission-critical, vital, important, or ancillary. It is important to factor in the business criticality of an application as any disruptions or downtimes can be detrimental to business.

- **Interdependencies**: Application interdependencies form another critical complexity factor and are more often misunderstood in cloud migrations, either due to organic growth over time or lack of documentation. A mission-critical application can have tens or even hundreds of integrations from both upstream and downstream systems, which can increase the nature of their complexity. It is critical to understand and score the interdependencies of an application and categorize them accordingly.

- **Security**: Another critical factor to consider in a cloud transformation is the security posture of an application. This can range from data security, network security, access controls, and web application firewalls. Security considerations for internal-facing applications can be uniquely different from their external-facing counterparts.

- **Data sovereignty**: Data sovereignty has become increasingly significant due to the widespread collection and processing of data, concerns over privacy and security, and the need to comply with various data protection regulations. Ensuring compliance with applicable data protection laws and understanding the legal implications of data residency is crucial to maintaining the data sovereignty of applications. This is an important complexity factor to consider to maintain application integrity and compliance.

- **Licensing and support**: Another key complexity that is especially associated with cloud lift and shift migrations is the licensing and support considerations of the application or software in consideration. Certain applications and software vendors have authorized and supported cloud platforms in which they would sustain support. It is also crucial for enterprises to explore alternative strategies, such as application refactoring, marketplace availability, and others.

- **Effort**: The most important consideration in cloud transformations is the effort that is required to implement or migrate a solution to the cloud. Enterprises embarking on their first cloud initiatives must ensure the workloads are not extremely mission-critical and require significant efforts.

- **Governance and operations**: Governance and operational considerations, such as application uptime, availability, SLAs, SLOs, network architecture, and monitoring and release management, are crucial to ensure that disruptions to critical applications are kept to an absolute minimum. It is also an important consideration that operations and governance of applications in a cloud environment can significantly differ from traditional on-premise setups.

Having reviewed the complexity factors, let's review the business value factors.

Business value factors

Business value factors define the perceived value that organizations can realize from cloud initiatives. These factors can include an organization's speed to innovate, delivering modern capabilities, time to market, performance improvements, and reduction in total cost of ownership, to name a few. Here are some business value factors to consider:

- **Innovation**: Measuring the value of innovation is critical but can also be challenging since the value of innovation is not easily quantifiable and often involves qualitative and long-term outcomes. However, enterprises can leverage several key indicators and metrics to assess the value of innovation efforts, such as increased profitability, customer feedback and satisfaction, patents and intellectual property filings, social impact scores, and market share.

- **Total cost of ownership** (TCO): Another critical metric to assess the potential business value of cloud initiatives is the TCO. A comprehensive TCO and ROI assessment can set the direction for picking the right workloads or projects.

- **Application performance**: Performance considerations such as application scalability, resilience, performance, accessibility, and usability can directly impact business value. For instance, a retailer e-commerce website is a classic example and a solid measure of customer experience as the performance and usability of the website can result in improved conversions, as well as the scalability of the site, both of which are equally crucial during seasonal peaks.

- **Customer satisfaction**: Customer satisfaction scores are another crucial element in evaluating the business value and impact of a cloud initiative. This can include incremental improvements in customer service, ease of access, contact center automations, loyalty programs, immersive experiences, personalized service or product recommendations, a seamless omnichannel experience, and more. The CSAT scores of an identified workload can dictate the business value of the initiative.

- **Environmental, social, and governance** (**ESG**): ESG scores for cloud initiatives can be measured using a combination of qualitative and quantitative metrics. To measure ESG scores, enterprises can create customized frameworks or adopt existing ESG rating methodologies provided by specialized rating agencies. These methodologies typically use a combination of data from public disclosures, reports, and independent assessments. For instance, environmental impact can be measured by the energy-efficient technologies powered by renewable energy sources, the carbon footprint of an application, and green certifications by recognized agencies. Likewise, social considerations can be measured by data privacy and security standards such as GDPR adherence, labor practices, supply chain responsibility, and accessibility. Similarly, governance metrics such as data governance, transparency, and compliance with ethical standards and regulations can directly impact the ESG score and deliver business value.

It is important to understand that these are directional business value factors and organizations must carefully choose and tailor them based on the business context. Now that we have reviewed the various business value factors, let's see how to define and assess NPV for the chosen cloud initiatives.

NPV

Financial viability is crucial to every initiative and it also applies to cloud transformations. A common gripe across enterprises is the failure to assess and evaluate the financial viability which can be detrimental to digital transformation efforts. Calculating the NPV of cloud initiatives involves estimating the expected cash flows associated with the initiative over its lifetime and discounting them back to their present value using an appropriate discount rate. This involves estimating the cash flows, determining the NPV, and performing sensitivity analysis. It's important to consider both the initial investment (for example, migration costs and setup costs) and the ongoing operational costs (for example, subscription fees and maintenance costs) in the cash flow estimation. NPV assessment is beyond the scope of this book. In the value-complexity matrix, the bubble size represents the NPV of a cloud workload or initiative. A bigger bubble represents a better NPV score and negative NPVs should be ignored as they are not financially viable. For negative NPV initiatives, alternative strategies must be considered.

Once the complexity and business value factors have been identified, enterprises can leverage a scoring framework to score each of the factors for each identified workload or initiative. The cumulative score constitutes the overall complexity and business value of the workload. Typically, organizations with a **cloud center of excellence** (CCoE) practice own and define a framework and guidance for cloud initiatives to ensure consistency of scoring across the enterprise. Here are some questions that can help assess the complexity and business value of the workloads under consideration:

Sl. no.	Assessment topic	Impact area
1	Is there an impending hardware refresh required for the application infrastructure?	TCO/ROI
2	Is the cost of running the application significantly lower in the cloud versus on-premises?	TCO/ROI
3	Would the application benefit from cloud-native scale, availability, resilience, and disaster recovery?	Performance
4	Would the application benefit from cloud-native services that significantly boost performance?	Performance
5	What is the business criticality of the application?	Business criticality
6	Is the application external (customer) facing or internal (corporate) facing?	Business criticality
7	How many integrations/dependencies does this application have?	Interdependencies
8	Does this application have clear, up-to-date documentation on architecture?	Effort
9	What are the operational requirements (SLAs, SLOs) of this workload?	Governance
10	Are there any legal, regulatory, or compliance requirements for this workload?	Security, data sovereignty
11	What are the latency sensitivities of this application?	Governance, business criticality
12	Is the application portable? Can this application benefit from running on a cloud-native platform?	Effort
13	Is the application data governed by data residency or other privacy regulations?	Data sovereignty
14	Does the application have licensing and support requirements (COTS application, legacy, open source)?	Licensing and support
15	Can the application benefit from rehosting, replatforming, repurchasing, or refactoring?	Effort
16	Are there time sensitivities to application migration (license renewals, data center exits, contractual obligations, and so on)?	Licensing and support, effort, interdependencies
17	Are there specific hardware dependencies for the application?	Interdependencies
18	Does the IT team have the required skills and resources to migrate?	Effort

Table 5.1 – Cloud workload complexity and business value assessment

Once the complexity and business value factors have been assessed, the dimensions must be scored individually to arrive at a cumulative score for both complexity and business value. It is important to adopt a weighted scoring mechanism for the various complexity and business value dimensions as not all dimensions are equal. For instance, in a specific business context, the security complexity factor might warrant a higher weightage, while a TCO business value dimension might demand a relatively lower weightage.

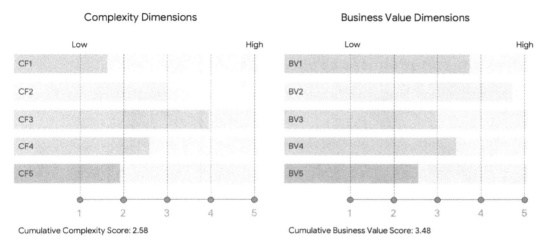

Figure 5.2 – Scoring complexity and business value dimensions

Leveraging this framework, enterprises can choose the right workloads that would yield the best business value through cloud transformation. It is important to weigh in on the value and complexity of a workload before migration. For instance, it can seem like a no-brainer decision to just pick the workloads from the fourth quadrant (high-value, low-complexity) as the first workload for cloud migration. However, this workload could be extremely mission-critical, and risks associated with migration, cutover, and timelines can outweigh the business value. On the contrary, moving an application that is ancillary and infrequently used will prove difficult to substantiate the value. It is crucial to get some early wins, especially with the first cloud transformation journey; hence, the rule of thumb is to pick a workload that is vital to the business and offers significant business value, a positive NPV, and relatively low complexity.

In the next section, we will explore the various cloud journeys enterprises can consider and the pros and cons of each approach.

Enterprise cloud transformation journeys

Every enterprise's journey to the cloud is unique and guided by specific business objectives. An enterprise cloud journey can be as diverse as the organization itself. The uniqueness of each journey is influenced by factors such as technological objectives, industry-specific challenges, cultural readiness, and the desire to innovate. Broadly, there are three primary cloud transformation journeys:

- Modernize on-premises applications
- Optimize on-premises data center
- Born in the cloud

Let's embark on these cloud transformation journeys and explore them.

Modernizing on-premises applications

This is the most common cloud journey as most enterprises have traditional data centers with IT estate encompassing legacy systems and applications. Established organizations choose a cloud journey to modernize existing applications to improve agility, scalability, and cost efficiency. Enterprises can adopt multiple strategies to modernize the on-premises IT landscape, depending on the established business objectives. Let's consider some scenarios.

Data center exit

The data center exit cloud journey is a strategic decision for enterprises seeking to optimize their operations, modernize applications, reduce costs, and improve scalability. By transitioning from on-premises data centers to the cloud, organizations can take advantage of faster deployment of applications, elastic resource allocation, and improved disaster recovery capabilities. Several enterprises choose data center exit as a strategy to migrate off traditional data centers and modernize on the cloud. This can stem from a myriad of reasons, such as an organization's objective to focus on business functions and get out of the data center business, the cost-prohibitive nature of data center operations, an impending major hardware refresh, and data center lease renewals in the case of hosted solutions, acquisitions, divestiture, and more. Irrespective of the rationale, enterprises can leverage the opportunity to modernize applications on the cloud. A successful data center exit cloud journey involves careful planning and execution. Enterprises must assess their current infrastructure and applications to determine the best migration approach while considering the balance between time, effort, and complexity – whether it's rehosting, collocating, refactoring, or repurchasing. This allows organizations to reap the benefits of the cloud, such as scalability, flexibility, cost optimization, and access to cutting-edge technologies. Although the journey may present challenges, careful planning, adherence to best practices, and collaboration with cloud providers can help businesses successfully navigate a data center exit. By embracing the cloud, enterprises position themselves to thrive in a rapidly changing digital landscape and remain adaptable to future innovations. The following are some considerations regarding data center exits:

- **Pros**: A data center exit enables an organization to restructure and reimagine the IT landscape and lay the foundation for innovation
- **Cons**: Typical data center exits can be elaborate and complex, thereby requiring careful assessment, planning, and collaboration

A data center exit is often a strategic and bold choice for enterprises that also demonstrates leadership commitment and vision for the future. More importantly, it allows organizations to focus on their core business instead of owning and running an IT data center.

Lift and shift applications

The lift and shift applications to the cloud journey is a valuable strategy for enterprises looking to rapidly embrace cloud computing while minimizing disruption. By migrating applications as-is to the cloud, enterprises can experience immediate benefits, such as scalability, cost-efficiency, and improved accessibility. A lift and shift migration strategy involves moving workloads from on-premises data centers to the cloud with minimal changes. In this approach, the application's underlying architecture, code base, and functionality remain largely unchanged. The goal is to quickly transition applications to the cloud without the need for extensive re-architecting or refactoring, thereby reducing migration complexities and downtime. By moving applications as-is to the cloud, enterprises can realize immediate benefits such as improved accessibility, scalability, and reduced maintenance costs. This migration strategy acts as a stepping stone toward more comprehensive cloud adoption and offers a quicker return on investment compared to other migration methods. The following are the pros and cons of the lift and shift approach:

- **Pros**: A lift and shift strategy offers enterprises the ability to quickly move applications to the cloud with very minimal changes

- **Cons**: A lift and shift strategy does not take full advantage of cloud-native capabilities and can result in sub-optimal value realization

Often considered the quick and dirty approach to the cloud, a lift and shift strategy allows organizations to rapidly migrate to the cloud and take advantage of cloud capabilities while also allowing for a phased transformation.

Upgrading to SaaS

The upgrading to SaaS cloud journey represents a transformative shift for enterprises, empowering them with flexible, scalable, and cost-efficient software solutions. By embracing SaaS, organizations can focus on core business activities while leaving software updates, maintenance, and security in the capable hands of cloud service providers. Enterprises may choose this strategy for want of business transformation due to the inability of existing applications to handle growth or innovation, delivering new capabilities, and lack of an existing application roadmap. Upgrading to SaaS involves transitioning from traditional, on-premises software installations to web-based, subscription-based solutions, enabling organizations to leverage a diverse range of cloud-native applications. While SaaS adoption offers numerous benefits, it is essential to craft strategies around data migration, integration, and governance. The following are some considerations when organizations upgrade applications to SaaS:

- **Pros**: Embracing SaaS can offer several immediate benefits, such as scaling based on user demands, built-in business continuity plans, reduced maintenance efforts, access to modern technologies, and improved accessibility and collaboration

- **Cons**: SaaS can enforce restricted customization with enterprises having to devise clear strategies around application integration, data access, and migration

Aside from the benefits it offers, upgrading to SaaS can also prove hugely advantageous for organizations with lean IT.

Re-architecting on the cloud

Another common strategy that enterprises can leverage to modernize applications is re-architecting the application on the cloud. Re-architecting applications on the cloud is a strategic move that empowers organizations to harness the full potential of cloud platforms. This is a comprehensive process that goes beyond simple lift and shift migrations and involves breaking down monolithic applications into smaller, modular microservices that can be independently deployed and managed. By adopting cloud-native practices, organizations can optimize performance, enhance scalability, and streamline operations. The following are some pros and cons of re-architecting applications on the cloud:

- **Pros**: Re-architected applications can enable dynamic scaling, resilience, resource efficiency, cost savings, and innovation

- **Cons**: Re-architecting applications requires a deep understanding of application architecture, dependencies, and IT skills, as well as significant time and resources

Besides the pros and cons, re-architecting applications can let enterprises start with a clean slate and reimagine applications for the future.

Optimizing on-premises data centers

As enterprises increasingly adopt cloud computing to gain agility, scalability, and cost-efficiency, optimizing existing on-premises data centers can be a crucial element. Being able to integrate on-premises infrastructure with cloud services allows organizations to leverage the benefits of both worlds while minimizing disruptions to ongoing operations. On-premises data centers have been the backbone of enterprise IT infrastructure for decades, providing control, privacy, and direct access to data. They serve as the foundation for mission-critical applications, ensuring low-latency operations, and adhering to specific regulatory and compliance requirements. However, on-premises environments are typically unoptimized to handle the scale, flexibility, and tech advancements at the scale of the cloud. Enterprises can leverage several strategies to optimize on-premises data centers. Let's take a look.

Building a private cloud

Building a private cloud involves strategically transforming traditional on-premises data centers into a dynamic and self-service-oriented cloud environment. This encompasses modernizing infrastructure through virtualization and software-defined technologies, enabling the automated provisioning and management of resources. A private cloud journey presents a transformative opportunity for enterprises to strike a balance between realizing the benefits of cloud computing within their data center while maintaining control and flexibility, co-existing with legacy applications, and aligning with data residency or compliance needs. By embarking on this journey, organizations can modernize their IT infrastructure, optimize resource utilization, and foster agility in deploying applications. The following are the pros and cons:

- **Pros**: A private cloud offers enterprises the flexibility to tailor cloud environments for specific needs that are optimized for performance, provides full control over data sovereignty, and offers predictable performance.

- **Cons**: Building a private cloud typically requires higher initial costs, which can be cost-prohibitive for some organizations, limit scalability compared to public cloud hyperscalers, and introduce maintenance complexity

By offering dedicated resources within a secure and isolated environment, a private cloud enables businesses to host and manage sensitive data and critical applications while adhering to stringent regulatory requirements. This level of control and customization ensures that organizations can tailor the private cloud environment to their specific needs, optimizing performance and meeting unique business demands.

Hybrid cloud adoption

Another approach in on-premises optimization is building cloud capabilities on-premises, to build out a hybrid cloud strategy. Several public cloud providers offer services that can help enterprises build public cloud capabilities within their data centers. This is a niche area that can be hugely beneficial to some enterprises where the nearest access to a public cloud data center just isn't viable due to latency-sensitive applications on-premises and data residency requirements. This can be a great approach for enterprises that have an established public cloud strategy and are seeking a hybrid cloud option to address the gaps. The primary advantage of this model is that it mimics the same public cloud architecture that can seamlessly extend to on-premises applications. Some service providers offer this as a fully managed offering while others can be self-managed. This can also help address some niche cloud use cases for enterprises, such as cloud bursting. Some examples include AWS Outposts, Google Anthos, Azure Stack, and Oracle Cloud@Customer. The following are some considerations for a hybrid cloud approach:

- **Pros**: The public cloud meets you where you are with super low latencies, it addresses data residency constraints, and it has same the architecture as the public cloud

- **Cons**: High upfront investments; in the case of fully managed services, there could be longer contractual obligations, and not all services in the public cloud are fully featured or available

A hybrid cloud approach allows seamless integration between on-premises and cloud environments, offering the ability to leverage the benefits of both worlds, and is often a sought-after strategy for enterprises with significant on-premises investments.

Born in the cloud

Born in the cloud refers to businesses and organizations that are conceived and established with a cloud-native mindset, leveraging cloud computing as the foundation for their operations from inception. Unlike traditional enterprises, which migrate to the cloud later in their life cycle, born in the cloud entities harness the full potential of cloud computing from day one. To be *born in the cloud* means to establish an organization with a fundamental reliance on cloud-based technologies for its infrastructure, applications, and services.

Being born in the cloud offers several advantages to organizations to innovate and disrupt traditional industry counterparts:

- **Agility**: For organizations without the burden of traditional IT and legacy applications, being born in the cloud helps them rapidly develop, test, and deploy new applications and features. This allows the business to respond quickly to market changes, customer demands, and emerging trends, fostering a culture of continuous innovation.

- **Resource efficiency**: Born in the cloud organizations can avoid the upfront capital expenses associated with building an on-premises infrastructure. With a cloud-first model, they only pay for the resources they consume, reducing financial risks and allowing for efficient allocation of resources.

- **Global reach**: Cloud platforms innately provide a global network of data centers, enabling born in the cloud entities to reach customers and users around the world without the need for extensive global physical infrastructure. This global presence supports rapid expansion and market penetration.

- **Lean IT**: By outsourcing infrastructure management to cloud providers, born in the cloud organizations tend to focus their resources and expertise on their core competencies and business differentiation.

- **Technology innovation**: Cloud providers offer a plethora of advanced technologies and services, such as artificial intelligence, machine learning, big data analytics, and **Internet of Things** (**IoT**) capabilities. This allows born-in-the-cloud organizations to rapidly experiment, innovate, and readily integrate into their offerings.

- **Sustainability**: Born in the cloud entities often boast a smaller carbon footprint compared to traditional counterparts as they consume resources more efficiently and contribute less to electronic waste.

Born in the cloud is more than a technological approach. As technology continues to advance, it signifies not just a way of doing business but a pathway to redefining the very essence of what an organization can achieve in the dynamic landscape of the digital age.

Some examples of companies that exemplify the born-in-the-cloud approach include Slack, Twilio, Zoom, Stripe, and HashiCorp *[1] [2] [3]*.

Other unique transformation journeys

The following sections cover some unique cloud journeys that some enterprises leverage that are strongly influenced by the desire to innovate, disrupt the market, and lead an industry transformation.

Global expansion journey

Enterprises looking to expand operations globally or enter new markets may use the public cloud to establish themselves in different regions quickly. When expanding into new geographies, businesses have to comply with various local regulatory and compliance protocols. Public clouds provide a few major benefits for enterprises expanding into new markets:

- Building out a new data center and IT ecosystem in a new geography is extremely time-consuming; an established cloud provider offers a major advantage – ease of use and speed to market

- Cloud providers generally comply with various local and governmental regulations, which can be a huge advantage for enterprises to jumpstart and stay in compliance

- Enterprises with established public cloud strategies in one region can leverage the same infrastructure, architecture, network, security, and operating models.

Data cloud journey

As the saying goes *data is the new oil*, and leveraging the cloud for data needs is another unique journey for enterprises. An enterprise's innovation and digital transformation success is primarily dependent on how it harnesses the power of its first-party data with second and third-party data. A strong data foundation is key to activating modern use cases while leveraging artificial intelligence and machine learning. This empowers organizations to make data-driven decisions, gain insights, and deliver personalized experiences by unifying customer data and taking action on insights with artificial intelligence and automation in real time.

Green cloud journey

Aside from the technology and business motivations, environmentally conscious enterprises embark on a cloud transformation journey with a strong focus on sustainability measures such as minimizing e-waste and carbon footprint. Many hyperscalers have an increased focus on ESG due to operating cloud data centers on carbon-free energy and renewable energy sources, offering tools to visualize and report on carbon emissions from usage of cloud services, building smarter and energy-efficient data centers, and promoting sustainable supply chain practices. Enterprises with a focus on green cloud initiatives have the option to choose a cloud provider with a track record and commitment to sustainability. According to a World Economic Forum report, a transition to cloud computing between 2021 and 2024 should prevent at least 629 million metric tons of CO_2 from entering the atmosphere *[4]*. To put this into context, this is equivalent to the carbon sequestered by 4.1M acres of US forests preserved from conversion to cropland in 1 year.

Cloud journeys are unique and must be guided by the larger vision of the enterprise, which sets the tone for the cloud transformation. Now, let's explore the various cloud migration strategies that enterprises can leverage.

Cloud migration strategies

After carefully evaluating and understanding the IT landscape, the most crucial phase of cloud transformation for enterprises is embarking on a migration. Earlier in this chapter, we reviewed the value-complexity matrix, which can help you pick the right workloads for cloud migration. In this section, we will discuss the different cloud migration strategies that enterprises can leverage.

The 6 R's application migration strategies

In 2010, Gartner published the 5 Rs approach for migrating applications to the cloud – *Rehost, Refactor, Revise, Rebuild, and Replace [5]*. Since then, several other *R* migration strategies have been floated, such as AWS' 6 Rs, Citrix's 7 Rs, and Infosys' 8 Rs. However, the core objective is to provide guidance on the various strategies that organizations can leverage while migrating applications to the cloud. Over the years, the cloud migration strategies evolved into what we more commonly refer to as the 6 R's of application migration – Rehost, Replatform, Repurchase, Refactor, Retire, and Retain. It is crucial to understand that these migration strategies are not mutually exclusive. Most enterprises have application migrations that can be addressed through one or more of these migration strategies. It is important to evaluate the pros and cons of each that aligns with the overall business objective. For instance, an application can be either rehosted, refactored, or repurchased. Interestingly, an application can even have parts that can fall into one or more of the R's – parts of an application can be replatformed, while other parts can be rehosted. The decision depends on a variety of factors and is unique in every enterprise context. Let's review these cloud migration strategies.

Rehosting – also known as lift and shift

Rehosting, also more commonly referred to as **lift and shift**, is the most common migration approach. It's where applications and workloads are migrated from on-premises infrastructure to the cloud without the need to significantly modify the application. The majority of enterprises start their cloud transformation journey with a rehosting strategy as a quick way of testing cloud capabilities and realizing value. In this approach, the core architecture and functionality of the application remain largely unchanged to achieve a rapid migration while capitalizing on cloud benefits such as scalability, ease of management, and potential cost savings. There are a few different approaches that enterprises can choose to rehost applications on the cloud based on the application's type, complexity, and business objective.

Use the public cloud as an infrastructure platform – predominantly leveraging compute, storage, and networking – to lift and shift applications to the cloud. This could be a viable strategy where the application can run on cloud-native VMs. With this approach, the application architecture is predominantly unchanged except for minor changes to networking and OS. Organizations can benefit from rapid migration times, low migration efforts, cloud-native scalability, availability, backups, and down-the-stack maintenance offload. In this approach, enterprises still don't benefit from the full-scale cloud benefits as there is still a maintenance burden – OS/kernel patching in the case of a custom OS, application, libraries, and database maintenance.

Legacy applications that are simply unsuited to run on cloud infrastructure can benefit from emulators offered by public cloud providers or third-party solutions. This approach can be beneficial for enterprises where migration is warranted due to business demands such as data center exits, hardware refresh cycles, or contractual obligations. Largely used as an intermediate step toward a larger optimization journey, the emulation option offers a landing zone for legacy applications. Although the emulation is a great intermediate solution, there can be performance impacts on the application. Mainframe modernization to the cloud is an example of emulator-based migration.

Nested virtualization is another option that enterprises can leverage and can be a great fit for applications that cannot sustain any change to their architecture, including IP addresses, OS, kernels, and networking. Some legacy applications require static IPs and specific OS and kernel patch levels that are either harder to maintain on the cloud or just aren't plausible. In such cases, nested virtualization solutions on public clouds can be a great option as there are no modifications to application functionality and architecture. Hardware-assisted nested virtualization tends to be better than software-based solutions. However, applications can still have a performance impact.

As part of an application modernization, a variety of enterprise workloads are still based on VMware. As enterprises seek to leverage existing investments and migrate these workloads with very little change, creating and running VMware on public clouds can offer a seamless way to run workloads the same as they were run traditionally on-premises. Although this offers ease of migration, workloads still don't benefit from cloud-native capabilities such as horizontal scaling and TCO owing to VMware licensing and maintenance costs.

Another less common rehosting approach, albeit crucial in some instances such as a big bang data center exit, acquisition, or divestiture situations, is colocation. Colocating legacy hardware, applications, and hardware-based solutions such as load balancers, firewalls, and hyper-converged infrastructure can offer enterprises a novel way to leverage the best of both worlds as they try to optimize the cloud transformation journey. With the legacy stack physically adjacent to the cloud provider network and infrastructure, enterprises can benefit from lower latencies and gradual transformation.

In general, rehosting can offer several advantages for enterprises:

- **Speed**: Rehosting offers a straightforward migration path, making it a swift and efficient option. The absence of extensive code changes reduces the complexity and time required for migration.

- **Cloud benefits**: By rehosting, enterprises can quickly take advantage of cloud features such as scalability, high availability, automated backups, maintenance, and management. This allows organizations to enjoy cloud benefits without overhauling their application architecture.

- **Cost savings**: While not the most cost-efficient option in the long term, rehosting can yield initial cost savings by avoiding the need to redevelop or refactor applications. It can be a practical first step for organizations looking to migrate promptly and later optimize their cloud environment.

- **Risk mitigation**: Rehosting minimizes the risk associated with migrating critical applications as it preserves the existing functionality and reduces the chances of introducing new bugs or errors during migration.

Here are some disadvantages of rehosting:

- **Suboptimal cloud utilization**: Rehosted applications do not fully capitalize on cloud features and cloud-native capabilities, potentially leading to underutilization of cloud resources and a missed opportunity for cost optimization. For instance, applications that have been rehosted typically scale vertically, leading to overprovisioning of resources.

- **Limited agility and innovation**: While rehosting provides a quick migration, it might hinder the ability to leverage cloud-native features for agility and innovation. Organizations must leverage rehosting as an intermediate step and must refactor their applications later to unlock the full potential of the cloud.

- **Potential security gaps**: Rehosted applications might inherit security vulnerabilities or configurations from their original environment. Ensuring proper security measures and access controls in the cloud is crucial and can open up applications to cyber threats, which may result in them requiring additional security measures.

- **Lack of cost optimization**: While initial cost savings can be realized, organizations might not achieve the same level of cost optimization as cloud-native strategies. A careful analysis of the long-term cost implications is necessary.

While rehosting may not provide the same level of optimization and innovation as more transformative migration strategies, its importance lies in its ability to offer a quick and relatively low-risk path to cloud adoption. It allows organizations to start benefiting from the cloud's scalability, flexibility, and cost efficiency while preserving the existing application architecture.

Replatforming – also known as move and improve

Replatforming involves migrating applications to the cloud while making minimal code changes to capitalize on cloud-native features. Unlike the lift and shift approach, replatforming allows for targeted adjustments to application architecture, configurations, and integrations, to optimize the application's performance and efficiency in a cloud-native environment. Rather than just moving the application as-is to the cloud, the focus of replatforming involves migrating portions of the application stack to cloud-native services to better leverage the cloud capabilities and economies of scale. It's important to note that replatforming does not intend to change the core architecture of the application under consideration. For example, consider a packaged application with the following stack running on-premises:

Application	App1 (COTS)
Load Balancer	F5 (HW based LB)
Web/App Server	Apache / WebLogic
Operation System	RHEL
Virtualization	VMware ESXi
Caching	Redis
Database	Oracle
Storage	EMC

Figure 5.3 – A sample on-premises web application stack

While a rehosting migration would seek to deploy the stack as-is with modifications to an absolute minimum, a replatforming exercise entails a deeper investigation into the application's architecture, certification, and supportability. In the preceding example, a COTS application that is critical to the business functions of an enterprise might have a variety of certified and supported target platforms. Enterprises can realize potential long-term benefits such as lower TCO, improved performance, reduced licensing requirements, and lower administration and maintenance efforts, even with seemingly smaller replatforming efforts. For example, replatforming an application's virtualization stack from a commercial hypervisor to a cloud-native hypervisor such as KVM can have significantly positive impacts on the overall TCO, portability, availability, and maintainability of a given application.

In the preceding example, a replatformed application stack could look something like this:

Application	App1 (COTS)		Application	App1 (COTS)
Load Balancer	F5 (HW based LB)		Load Balancer	Cloud Load Balancer
Web/App Server	Apache / WebLogic		Web/App Server	Nginx / Tomcat
Operation System	RHEL		Operation System	CentOS
Virtualization	VMware ESXi		Virtualization	Cloud-Native KVM
Caching	Redis		Caching	Redis
Database	Oracle		Database	Managed DBaaS
Storage	EMC		Storage	Cloud Storage

Figure 5.4 – Application replatform from on-premises to the cloud

Replatforming offers several benefits:

- **Performance optimization**: Replatforming enables enterprises to fine-tune applications to take maximum advantage of cloud features and cloud-native capabilities, resulting in improved performance, responsiveness, and scalability.

- **Cost-efficiency**: By optimizing application performance and resource utilization to offload applications from the commercial stack, replatforming can lead to more efficient usage of built-in cloud features, thus reducing operational costs and TCO and avoiding potential wastage of resources.

- **Availability and scalability**: Replatformed applications are better equipped to handle dynamic workloads, automatically scaling resources up or down based on demand, thus ensuring optimal performance during peak periods. By leveraging cloud-native capabilities, replatformed applications can intrinsically offer better SLAs (think running multiple instances of the application behind a cloud load balancer, spreading application instances across multiple zones, and creating a disaster recovery environment), thus improving the availability of applications.

- **Easier management**: Cloud-native features such as auto-scaling, load balancing, patching, security tuning, and automated backups simplify mundane management tasks, freeing up IT resources and allowing teams to focus on business functions, innovation, and value-added activities.

- **Integration and innovation**: Replatforming allows enterprises to seamlessly integrate applications with a variety of cloud services, such as databases, analytics, and machine learning, enhancing functionality and enabling data-driven insights. For instance, replatformed applications are better equipped to augment capabilities improving speed to market.

Here are some challenges and considerations that enterprises must be aware of:

- **Application compatibility**: While replatforming minimizes code changes, it may still require significant adjustments to ensure compatibility with cloud environments and services, which might introduce complexity and potential issues. As discussed earlier, it is important to assess the application stack, compatibility, certifications, and supportability on target platforms. In commercial applications, organizations must also take into account the licensing and support constraints to ensure seamless business continuity.

- **Not an end state**: Although replatforming can be an attractive migration approach, it is important to understand that this may not be an end state. Consistent improvements and gradual changes (for example, possible refactoring considerations and envisioning microservices-based architecture) must be qualified and approached in phases.

- **Resource constraints**: Organizations must carefully assess the resources that are required for replatforming, including expertise in cloud technologies and the potential impact on project timelines. Building MVPs and a phased migration approach is key.

- **Data migration and integration**: Ensuring smooth data migration and integration with existing systems is crucial for maintaining data integrity and business continuity during the replatforming process.

- **Testing and validation**: Comprehensive testing and validation are essential to identify and address any performance or compatibility issues that may arise after replatforming.

Replatforming offers a good balance for enterprises between modernizing applications and minimizing disruptions. It provides organizations with an efficient path to cloud adoption, enabling them to leverage the advantages of cloud infrastructure while preserving compatibility with existing systems and minimizing risks.

Repurchasing – also known as drop and shop

Repurchase, more commonly referred to as the drop and shop migration strategy, involves replacing existing software applications with cloud-native alternatives. In this approach, businesses make a strategic decision to transition from on-premises or legacy systems to purpose-built cloud services that offer improved functionalities, scalability, and alignment with modern business needs. In contrast to the migration approaches we discussed earlier – rehosting and replatforming – where the tactical focus is on retaining the core application architecture, functions, and business process integrations while augmenting it with cloud-native capabilities, repurchase is a strategic migration strategy and decision. More often, a repurchase decision is made primarily by lines of business stakeholders as the business demands outgrow existing technology. For example, consider a traditional CRM solution that once excelled at capturing and managing customer information. However, as businesses evolve in the digital age and grapple with customer and market demands, traditional CRM software has fallen short of modern capabilities, such as providing omnichannel customer experience, customer 360 visibility, mobile access, targeted marketing, predictive analytics, forecasting, and integrations with emerging technologies such artificial intelligence, chatbots, and more, stunting the growth and innovation. Instead of rehosting or replatforming, a repurchase migration strategy embodies a strategic evolution of applications, positioning enterprises to leverage the full potential of cloud-native software solutions.

Repurchasing offers several strategic advantages to enterprises:

- **Access to cutting-edge functionality**: Cloud-native software solutions often come with advanced features, capabilities, and integrations that empower organizations with enhanced functionalities and better alignment with evolving business requirements.

- **Scalability and flexibility**: Repurchasing allows enterprises to leverage inherent cloud scalability, enabling them to adapt software capabilities to match varying workloads and demands in real time. A repurchase strategy also offers SLA-driven service capabilities with built-in high availability and disaster recovery.

- **Resource efficiency**: By repurchasing, organizations can free up valuable IT resources to focus on critical business functions rather than on mundane administration and maintenance. A repurchase decision also reduces and frees up the data center footprint.

- **Rapid deployment**: Cloud-native software solutions are designed for quick deployment, enabling organizations to reduce implementation timelines and accelerate time-to-market for new features or services.

- **Cost optimization**: While repurchasing may involve substantial initial and subscription costs, the long-term benefits can include reduced maintenance, operational, and support expenses, leading to overall total cost of ownership savings over time.

- **Vendor management**: Cloud-native solutions often come with managed services, alleviating the burden of software maintenance and updates and allowing businesses to focus on their core competencies.

Enterprises must also be aware of the following challenges and considerations:

- **Data migration and integration**: Transitioning to a new cloud software solution requires careful planning to ensure a seamless migration of data and integrations with existing systems. Application integration can be tricky and can involve additional software considerations, implementation efforts, and costs. Careful evaluation of these integrations and data egress can help mitigate this challenge.

- **Change management**: Repurchasing may necessitate a cultural shift within the organization – especially with business users as they adapt to new workflows and interfaces. Change management strategies are crucial to mitigate resistance and facilitate a smooth transition.

- **Vendor lock-in**: While repurchasing offers significant advantages, organizations must be cautious about potential vendor lock-in, where migrating away from a cloud service may be complex or costly.

- **Customization**: Some cloud-native solutions may offer limited customization options compared to custom-built on-premises applications. Organizations should evaluate the extent of customization needed against the capabilities of the chosen solution.

As technology continues to shape the future of business, repurchase or drop and shop represents a strategic option for organizations to rapidly transform and serves as a pathway for organizations to innovate, optimize, and thrive in the dynamic digital landscape.

Refactoring – also known as re-architecting

In the quest to harness the full potential of the cloud, enterprises often find themselves at a crossroads when it comes to legacy application modernization. Although several migration strategies exist, such as rehosting, repurchasing, and replatforming, re-architecting promises to unlock the benefits of the cloud while modernizing applications to meet evolving business needs. Typically, this strategy is adopted when organizations can benefit from a tailor-made solution that can uniquely differentiate it in the marketplace yielding high business value. Re-architecting is a paradigm shift where an application is rearchitected and rewritten to align with cloud-native principles to leverage full advantage of cloud capabilities. It also facilitates the addition of new features and improvements to make the application future-proof. When it comes to modernizing applications on the cloud, re-architecting truly embodies a complete transformation, helping enterprises reimagine how legacy applications can be rebuilt and operated in response to business demands. Re-architecting can also be a great strategy for enterprises that can invest the time and effort to entirely rewrite the application. However, it is important to ensure the application rewrite follows best practices such as adherence to open source, open standards, and portability. Enterprises should choose this strategy for mission-critical applications as this can warrant significant resources, effort, and time to ensure that the potential long-term benefits outweigh the investments. Re-architecting can also be a compelling choice of strategy in case of applications that are approaching end-of-life or heavily outdated. For example, an organization may consider re-architecting an aging or packaged e-commerce application to a microservices-based architecture to unlock capabilities such as elastic scalability to support seasonal spikes, improve customer experience, deliver modern capabilities such as personalized recommendations, digital assistants, and **augmented reality/virtual reality (AR/VR)** to enhance shopping experience, increase site resiliency, and improve overall efficiency in terms of both resource and costs.

Refactoring or re-architecting can provide a significant edge to enterprises:

- **Cloud-native optimization**: Rearchitected applications fully embrace the native capabilities and services offered by the cloud, leading to optimized performance, scalability, and resource utilization. Refactoring takes advantage of inherent cloud capabilities and achieves higher availability and resilience for applications, minimizing downtimes and ensuring business continuity.

- **Agility with microservices**: Re-architecting often involves adopting a microservices architecture, which enables independent development, testing, and deployment of smaller, focused components, thus enhancing agility and modular development and facilitating easier maintenance.

- **Cost efficiency**: By leveraging cloud economies of scale, re-architecting can lead to better cost management through efficient resource use and allocation. Cloud capabilities such as on-demand auto-scaling and pay-as-you-go pricing models enable organizations to optimize expenses by only paying for the resources they use.

- **Future-proof**: Re-architecting positions applications for future innovation, allowing for the rapid adoption of emerging technologies and capabilities as they evolve.

- **Vendor lock-in mitigation**: By re-architecting applications to adhere to open standards and best practices in the cloud, organizations can reduce the risk of vendor lock-in. This makes it easier to port, migrate, or integrate with other cloud providers in the future.

While there are numerous benefits to rewriting applications for the cloud, it is important to consider the challenges and address them:

- **The complexity of re-architecting**: Re-architecting is a complex and resource-intensive endeavor as it requires significant effort, time, expertise, and financial investment to analyze, design, develop, test, and deploy the new architecture. This is an important factor to consider, along with overall business objectives, before planning a re-architecture. It is also important to consider the cost of running parallel application infrastructure until the re-architecture is complete.

- **IT skills and effort**: Adopting cloud-native technologies and architectures requires development teams to acquire new skills and knowledge. This learning curve can slow down development initially and impact productivity. Organizations can leverage some tactical and strategic investments by engaging partners and system integrators while also upskilling internal IT.

- **Data migration and integrity**: Migrating data from legacy systems to the re-architected application can be complex and time-consuming. Ensuring data integrity, consistency, and compatibility between the old and new systems can pose challenges.

- **Potential over-engineering**: In the pursuit of cloud-native optimization, there's also a risk of over-engineering the application, leading to unnecessary complexity and features that may not align with actual business requirements.

- **Continuous maintenance and updates**: Cloud-native applications require continuous monitoring, maintenance, and updates to keep up with evolving cloud technologies, security vulnerabilities, and best practices. Enterprises can mitigate this challenge by adopting cloud-managed offerings while still aligning with open standards to strike a good balance between maintenance overhead and vendor lock-in.

- **Uncertain ROI and business impact**: The ROI of re-architecting may not always be immediate or guaranteed. Organizations need to carefully assess the potential business impact and long-term benefits against the upfront costs and effort. A strong business value assessment and value realization exercise can help mitigate these uncertainties.

Refactoring or re-architecting applications for the cloud represents a strategic move that goes beyond mere migration. It helps enterprises unlock the full potential of cloud computing and positions organizations for scalability, efficiency, and innovation in a rapidly evolving digital landscape.

Retiring – also known as sunset applications

Retiring applications is a targeted initiative that enterprises adopt to identify and retire legacy applications that are no longer in use or adding value to the business. In a typical enterprise setup, it is not uncommon to find application orphans or several versions of the same application within the application portfolio. Application retirement refers to the deliberate process of discontinuing the use and support of software applications. As businesses evolve, technologies advance, and user demands change, legacy applications can hinder growth, increase operational costs, and also create potential security vulnerabilities and threats. For instance, legacy applications that still require or run on older versions of OSs and protocols can be a weak link for enterprise IT security. With an increase in cyber-attacks such as ransomware, Petya and NotPetya, for example, exploited the SMBv1 protocol on older Windows servers to target and launch attacks *[6][7]*.

While retiring or sunsetting applications, enterprises must assess and prioritize application decommission based on user impacts and business value, plan and execute the data migration process meticulously to ensure valuable and sensitive data is preserved or transferred, engage the right stakeholders, and transition users as required.

Here are the core benefits of application retirement:

- **Cost savings**: Retiring applications eliminates maintenance, licensing, and support costs associated with legacy software, freeing up resources for more strategic initiatives.

- **Enhanced security**: Outdated applications are most vulnerable to security breaches. Retiring them reduces the attack vector surface and minimizes cybersecurity risks.

- **Simplified IT landscape**: A streamlined application portfolio simplifies IT management, making it easier to focus on maintaining and improving critical systems.

- **Operational efficiency**: With fewer applications to manage, IT teams can allocate resources more efficiently and respond more promptly to business needs.

- **User experience improvement**: Transitioning to modern applications often improves user experience, offering enhanced features, better performance, and a more intuitive interface.

Some considerations while retiring applications are as follows:

- **Data migration and preservation**: Transferring data from the retired applications to a new system while maintaining data integrity can be complex, especially if the data structure is incompatible.

- **User impact**: Users who are accustomed to the retired application may face a learning curve as they transition to new systems, potentially leading to resistance and reduced productivity. In some cases, it may be hard to assess and evaluate user impacts due to a lack of knowledge of the system, documentation, or usage. Careful assessment and planning can help mitigate user impact.

- **Integration with other systems**: Retiring an application may disrupt integrations with other software or services, requiring meticulous planning to ensure seamless business continuity.

- **Regulatory compliance**: If the application contains sensitive or regulated data, retiring it must adhere to data protection and compliance requirements.

Retiring applications is a strategic imperative that can help organizations optimize costs, improve agility, reduce technical debt, and enhance security. Regularly evaluating and decommissioning applications is an integral part of cloud strategy and governance and contributes to long-term success and sustainability.

Retaining

While the allure of the cloud is undeniable, retaining applications on-premises remains a valid strategy and choice for many enterprises and is driven by factors such as data sensitivity, technology, or regulatory constraints. As more and more organizations are adopting a hybrid cloud strategy, certain applications that may not benefit from cloud economies of scale or capabilities while still commanding low cost of ownership make a case for retaining them on-premises. Several factors influence the decision to retain applications on-premises, such as data sovereignty, complex legacy systems, and applications requiring low-latency communication between peripheral components, costs, and manageability.

Here are some of the benefits of a retention strategy:

- **Data sovereignty**: By retaining applications on-premises, organizations maintain complete control over their data and where it resides. This is especially important for enterprises in certain highly regulated industries, such as governmental, healthcare, and financial sectors, to stay in compliance with data protection regulations and data residency requirements.

- **Customization and control**: On-premises environments provide greater flexibility for customizing and tuning applications to specific business needs. Applications require specific infrastructure requirements where organizations have investments in fine-tuned hardware and hyper-converged infrastructure, software, and configurations to optimize performance.

- **Predictable costs**: Organizations can have better control over budgeting and forecasting as they can avoid potential fluctuations in cloud service costs. This is particularly beneficial for applications with stable workloads.

- **Data transfer or egress**: For applications that require large data transfers between on-premises systems, keeping them local can eliminate or reduce data transfer costs associated with cloud migrations.

- **Compliance and legal**: Industries with strict regulatory requirements or legal obligations may find it easier to maintain compliance by keeping applications and data on-premises, where they have more direct oversight and compliance with cyber insurance.

Some considerations and mitigation strategies while retaining applications on-premises are as follows:

- **Scalability and flexibility**: On-premises environments may require constant infrastructure alignments and capacity planning to support the scalability and compatibility needs. Organizations can mitigate this by carefully planning for future growth and investing in appropriate hardware and resources.

- **Maintenance and upgrades**: While retaining applications on-premises, organizations are responsible for the maintenance, updates, and patches of on-premises systems. Establishing robust IT management practices and regular monitoring is crucial to ensure system stability and security.

- **Expertise and skill set**: On-premises environments require in-house expertise in hardware and software management. Organizations may need to invest in training or hire specialized personnel to manage these systems effectively.

- **Disaster recovery and redundancy**: Cloud providers often offer built-in redundancy and disaster recovery options. Organizations retaining applications on-premises must plan and implement robust disaster recovery and backup strategies to ensure business continuity.

As we've reviewed, the various cloud migration strategies, advantages, and considerations that enterprises can leverage require meticulous assessment and planning to ensure a successful cloud transformation. Although various strategies exist, they are not mutually exclusive in an enterprise context and a variety of migration approaches can be leveraged simultaneously.

Hybrid cloud strategies

Traditionally, enterprises have significant investments within their on-premises or hosted data centers, which makes it harder to start from a clean slate. This also does not make financial sense in most cases. Embracing a hybrid cloud strategy aids an organization in taking advantage of the incremental benefits that cloud solutions offer while also tapping into the on-premises investments, offering the best of both worlds. With a hybrid cloud journey, enterprises can start to innovate in the cloud with a few low-hanging fruit use cases. Some strategies that enterprises can leverage in a hybrid cloud strategy are as follows:

- Dev-test in the cloud, production on-premises
- Disaster recovery in the cloud
- Cloud bursting

Let's explore these hybrid cloud strategies in a little more detail.

Dev-test in the cloud, production on-premises

The dev-test in the cloud, production on-premises approach epitomizes the fusion of cloud-based agility and on-premises control while addressing the diverse needs of modern software development in enterprises. This entails conducting development and testing phases of software projects in a cloud environment while deploying the production environment on-premises. It capitalizes on the advantages offered by both cloud and on-premises infrastructures, presenting a nuanced and balanced solution to the multifaceted challenges of software development. The objective of this strategy is to take full advantage of the pay-only-for-use model, where development and testing teams can create and operate multiple development and test instances on-demand, stop the environments when they're not in use, and tear them down when no longer required. This helps enterprises create multiple simultaneous release cycles and operate multiple streams of projects for canary, A/B, or blue-green deployments while innovating on iterations.

Development teams also benefit from experimenting with software or code on a variety of infrastructure and platform options available on the cloud, which can be highly challenging and cost-prohibitive to test and benchmark on-premises. For example, a software engineering team can write application software and deploy it on a variety of CPU and GPU compute families, OSs, and library combinations to benchmark and optimize for scale and performance. This can provide a solid reference for the production environment buildout on-premises. This also helps development teams have a jumpstart with development where infrastructure buildout on-premises can be time-consuming, especially for net new initiatives. Dev-test in the cloud can also help optimize costs, especially when there are multiple branch releases each requiring a dedicated environment. Another strategy is to only have the non-production instances running during working hours to optimize resource usage and costs. While this is a great hybrid-cloud strategy, it is critical to ensure cloud-native principles are followed with a focus on adopting microservices architecture, **Infrastructure as Code** (**IaC**), secure data management, automated testing, backups, and monitoring and analytics as they can seamlessly port between the cloud and on-premises.

Here are some key benefits of this approach:

- **Agile development**: Cloud platforms enable rapid provisioning of resources, empowering development teams to create, test, and iterate on software solutions quickly. The cloud's scalability and flexibility accelerate the development life cycle.

- **Cost efficiency:** The pay-as-you-go model of cloud computing minimizes upfront capital expenditure for development and testing while deploying production on-premises helps manage ongoing operational costs.

- **Resource optimization:** Cloud environments can dynamically scale to accommodate the fluctuating resource demands of development and testing, enhancing resource efficiency. Non-prod environments can be spun up, stopped, or torn down as needed to ensure resource optimization.

- **Experimentation**: The cloud's sandboxing capabilities provide an isolated environment for experimentation, reducing the risk of disrupting the production system during development and testing.

- **Global collaboration**: Cloud-based development fosters collaboration among geographically distributed teams, enabling seamless communication and knowledge sharing.

While this hybrid cloud strategy is great, it is crucial to consider and address the following challenges:

- **Hybrid cloud complexity**: Managing resources across two distinct environments introduces complexity in terms of configuration, deployment, and monitoring, requiring an organized approach to ensure consistency. Enterprises must ensure cloud-native principles are consistently adopted while architecting applications and solutions to mitigate the complexity.

- **Application compatibility**: Ensuring compatibility between cloud-based development and on-premises production environments requires meticulous design and rigorous testing.

- **Operational efficiency**: Effective coordination between development and operations becomes crucial to maintain consistent deployments and updates across cloud and on-premises environments. Automating infrastructure provisioning through IaC tools, development and deployment through CI/CD pipelines, and config management through tools such as Ansible and test automations can help mitigate this challenge and embrace the hybrid cloud effectively.

- **Data security**: Transferring sensitive data between cloud and on-premises environments demands robust encryption and compliance adherence to industry standards and regulations.

- **Network latency**: Real-time applications might experience latency challenges when communicating between cloud and on-premises systems, necessitating careful network optimization. Establishing dedicated network interconnects to cloud environments and routing critical network traffic through them can help mitigate this challenge.

Dev-test in the cloud and running production on-premises provides a safer entry point in the cloud for enterprises in a hybrid cloud journey while also delivering resource and cost optimization benefits, among others. Now, let's explore another low-risk hybrid cloud journey – running disaster recovery in the cloud.

Disaster recovery in the cloud

One of the ways cloud computing has revolutionized the way enterprises ensure data integrity and business continuity in the face of unforeseen disruptions is backup and disaster recovery in the cloud. Although many mission-critical applications and data have a disaster recovery strategy within enterprises, this can also be cost-prohibitive and effort-intensive to set up and manage for other applications that are still critical and vital to business continuity. The cloud offers a cost-effective way to create data backups in cold, warm, and even hot disaster recovery environments. Organizations can replicate critical data and applications in real time across multiple geographic regions, enabling seamless failover in the event of a disaster. This replication ensures that no single point of failure exists, significantly reducing the risk of data loss and downtime. Automated failover mechanisms play a pivotal role, swiftly redirecting traffic and workloads to the replicated resources, minimizing service disruption and maintaining a seamless user experience.

A typical enterprise IT estate consists of two data centers spread across geographies – one for production (primary) and another dedicated to disaster recovery (secondary). Secondary data centers are traditionally either self-managed or outsourced to an availability service provider. Irrespective of the model, operating and maintaining a secondary data center can incur high capital and operational expenditures. Another primary complexity in setting up a dedicated disaster recovery environment on-premises is the need to size them for peak capacity needs as their production counterparts. Ironically, this capacity stays idle the vast majority of the time. As the saying goes, undersized disaster recovery is as good as no disaster recovery – since an undersized disaster recovery environment would run with degraded performance, or worse, crash in response to peak traffic. In contrast, cloud-based solutions follow a pay-as-you-go model, reducing capital expenditure and allowing organizations to scale resources up or down only when needed. This allows for several unique combinations that are available for enterprises:

- **Leverage cloud storage for backups**: In this setup, the cloud is purely leveraged for application and data backups.

- **The cloud for cold disaster recovery**: Here, data and application-consistent backups are synchronized with no active running instances. In this model, the application RTOs are high enough to warm up instances.

- **The cloud for warm disaster recovery**: Here, applications and data are synchronized to the cloud and run on the bare minimum capacity that can be scaled up in the event of disaster recovery. The RTO needs of these kinds of applications are medium.

- **The cloud for active (hot) disaster recovery**: In this model, mission-critical applications can benefit from strict RPO and RTO objectives as the cloud environment behaves like an active disaster recovery instance where the on-premises traffic can be redirected to the cloud seamlessly with no downtime.

This flexibility not only optimizes costs but also eliminates the need to over-provision resources, making disaster recovery solutions more accessible to businesses of all sizes. This cost-efficiency, combined with simplified management and automated recovery processes, ensures that organizations can focus on their core operations while maintaining a robust disaster recovery posture.

Another key use case that the cloud unlocks is secure, immutable backups to prevent and guard against malicious cyber security attacks such as ransomware. Although setting up or having an established dedicated secondary data center on-premises can serve business continuity needs, enterprise security must put in additional controls at various levels – from network to disk to apps – and keep up with patching security vulnerabilities. Most modern cyber-attacks target the weak links within an organization and traverse laterally through networks. For instance, a malicious malware attack such as ransomware can originate anywhere within an IT network but can also encrypt data across the connected servers effectively, rendering the backups and disaster recovery in the secondary site unusable. Cloud storage backups are security-hardened at various tiers managed by the **cloud service provider** (**CSP**) and offer mechanisms to create secure immutable backups.

The benefits of cloud-based disaster recovery are manifold. Rapid recovery times ensure minimal downtime, reducing revenue loss and preserving customer trust. The pay-as-you-go cost model eliminates hefty upfront investments in physical infrastructure, transforming disaster recovery into an operational expense. Moreover, the cloud's vast network of data centers ensures geographic diversity and resilience, enhancing data integrity and availability. However, organizations must consider and address challenges proactively. Data security and compliance considerations demand robust encryption and adherence to industry regulations during data replication and failover processes. Network latency, particularly in hybrid cloud scenarios, can affect RTOs and RPOs, warranting a comprehensive understanding of the organization's specific needs when designing and implementing a cloud-based disaster recovery strategy.

Cloud bursting

Cloud bursting is a niche hybrid-cloud strategy that enterprises can leverage to optimize resource utilization, enhance performance, and manage costs effectively. Cloud bursting refers to the dynamic and seamless expansion of computing resources from a private or on-premises cloud environment to a public cloud when there is a surge in demand for computational power, storage, or other resources. This allows organizations to harness the capacity and scalability of the cloud to accommodate temporary spikes in workloads while maintaining their core operations within the on-premises infrastructure.

For cloud bursting to be successful, organizations maintain a baseline of resources both in the private (on-premises) environment as well as in the cloud. On-premises serves as a primary and caters to regular workload traffic and during periods of increased demands, such as seasonal spikes, the surplus traffic is dynamically shifted to the public cloud (co-primary). This shift is orchestrated through automated processes and predetermined triggers, ensuring a swift and efficient response to changing resource requirements. To facilitate cloud bursting, organizations establish connectivity between their private cloud and the chosen public cloud provider. This connection can be established using dedicated network links, **virtual private networks** (**VPNs**), or direct interconnections, ensuring secure and efficient data transfer between environments.

Cloud bursting can help unlock the following advantages:

- **Scalability**: Cloud bursting enables organizations to instantly and seamlessly scale resources to meet peak demands, ensuring optimal performance and user experience.

- **Cost efficiency**: By utilizing public cloud resources only when needed, organizations avoid over-provisioning on-premises hardware and resources, thus reducing infrastructure costs during periods of lower demand.

- **Business continuity**: Cloud bursting enhances business resilience by preventing service disruptions and ensuring uninterrupted access to critical applications and services. This can also serve as a primary in the cloud while planned or unplanned maintenance is warranted in on-premises infrastructure without disruption to business functions.

- **Improved performance**: The burst resources from the public cloud can significantly enhance application performance during high-traffic periods, improving response times and user satisfaction.

- **Resource optimization**: Organizations can maintain a leaner on-premises infrastructure while leveraging the elastic capacity of the public cloud when necessary.

Despite its advantages, cloud bursting presents certain challenges that require careful consideration:

- **Data transfer and latency**: Moving data between private and public clouds can introduce latency, potentially impacting performance and user experience. Maintaining two baselines and ensuring application and data synchronization across on-premises and the cloud can be complex and challenging.

- **Data security and compliance**: Ensuring data security and compliance during data transfer and processing across multiple environments is paramount.

- **Application compatibility**: Applications must be designed or modified to seamlessly transition between environments, accounting for potential differences in configurations and dependencies.

- **Network complexity**: Managing network connectivity and traffic between private and public clouds requires robust networking infrastructure, security controls, and careful monitoring.

- **Cost management**: While cloud bursting can optimize costs, proper monitoring and governance are essential to prevent unexpected expenses associated with bursted resources.

Now that we have reviewed the various hybrid cloud strategies, let's explore how enterprises can differentiate and innovate in the cloud.

Innovating in the cloud through emerging technologies

Aside from leveraging cloud computing as a pure infrastructure, deployment model, or an extension of a traditional data center, several enterprises envision cloud platforms as a vehicle for innovation. As digital trends evolve and modern technologies are primarily cloud-native, the cloud has become a change agent for enterprises to lead innovation both to transform business and IT. In this section, we will review some of the innovation-driven cloud journeys that enterprises can adopt.

IoT

The intersection of two groundbreaking technologies, IoT and cloud computing, has unleashed a paradigm shift in how devices, data, and services are interconnected and managed. IoT refers to the interconnected network of physical edge devices equipped with sensors, software, and connectivity capabilities. This advanced network allows these devices to gather, exchange, and communicate data, facilitating various applications. Cloud computing, on the other hand, provides a flexible, scalable, and accessible platform for storing, processing, and analyzing data. The fusion of IoT and cloud computing creates a powerful synergy, allowing organizations to seamlessly connect, manage, and glean insights from a myriad of IoT devices. IoT devices generate an astonishing amount of data, from smart thermostats and wearable fitness trackers to industrial sensors and autonomous vehicles. Cloud computing provides the ideal environment to process and analyze this data. By harnessing the computational power and storage capacity of the cloud, organizations can derive actionable insights from the torrents of IoT-generated data, enabling informed decision-making, predictive maintenance, and optimized resource allocation. For instance, in healthcare, IoT has enabled use cases such as smart wearable devices, which help with remote patient monitoring and rapid emergency response. In the manufacturing sector, IoT-enabled machinery can communicate with cloud systems to optimize production processes and minimize downtime. Similarly, in retail, IoT devices can help track real-time store inventory levels, analyze consumer behavior, and enhance personalized shopping experiences.

Artificial intelligence

Artificial intelligence finds application in every aspect of digital transformation and has enabled modern use cases from advanced data analytics, predictive analytics, **natural language processing** (**NLP**), and building autonomous systems to cybersecurity and threat detection. Multimodal generative AI capabilities are revolutionizing the way how organizations can leverage modern technologies to automate complex creative tasks and deliver personalized and dynamic net new user experiences. Cloud computing offers a modern, scalable, and cost-efficient infrastructure that supports the artificial intelligence life cycle, from massive data storage and processing to model development, training, and deployment. The synergy between cloud computing and artificial intelligence plays a crucial role in democratizing AI capabilities, making them accessible to organizations of all sizes and accelerating the pace of innovation. From on-demand access to modern chipsets, GPUs, and TPUs to pre-trained plug-and-play APIs, cloud computing platforms have become the de facto standard for artificial intelligence and machine learning applications. For instance, organizations can embed artificial intelligence capabilities practically across applications to enhance existing application functionality, improve user experiences, and harness the power of data.

Edge computing

Edge computing is an innovative deployment model where enterprises can deploy compute clusters at the edge – this can be stores, restaurants, hospitals, and so on – where data and signals emanating at the source (edge) from thousands or even millions of devices and sensors can be processed and acted upon instantaneously to create immersive customer experiences. Edge computing focuses on processing data closer to its source, minimizing latency and enhancing real-time responsiveness. Edge devices, such as IoT sensors and edge servers, process data locally, reducing the need for constant data transmission to centralized cloud servers. This opens up a wide array of possibilities for organizations to deploy fully featured applications at the edge. For instance, in retail, edge computing can enable modern shopping experiences such as in-store virtual try-ons, AR, VR, shrink reduction, shelf checking, and walk-out checkout experiences. Similarly, in logistics and supply chains, edge computing enables use cases such as real-time inventory tracking, pallet and product matching, product picking, and **automated guided vehicle** (**AGV**) navigation.

Blockchain

Blockchain is another example of an emerging technology that's born in the cloud. From **decentralized finance** (**DeFi**) to secure patient data management, blockchain has unlocked new business opportunities for enterprises across the board. In a world where cyber threats loom large, enterprises can leverage blockchain to safeguard sensitive information, protect against data breaches, and establish an irrefutable record of transactions. Blockchain's cryptographic principles create an immutable and tamper-proof ledger, ensuring that data remains secure and trustworthy. By eliminating the need for intermediaries and central authorities, blockchain reduces the risk of fraud and unauthorized access, instilling confidence in customers, partners, and stakeholders.

Blockchain's transparent and decentralized nature ensures that every transaction is recorded in a traceable and verifiable manner. This can unlock capabilities such as accounting transparency and independent transaction audits. The ability to track and verify the origin and journey of goods along the supply chain, for instance, enhances visibility and helps prevent counterfeiting, ultimately leading to more reliable and ethical business practices.

In the context of driving innovative digital journeys, as emerging technologies continue to evolve rapidly and change continuously, cloud computing has matured as a platform of innovation for enterprises large and small while enabling new business opportunities that drive positive business outcomes.

Summary

Every enterprise has a unique business model that calls for a unique cloud transformation journey. It is imperative to align the cloud journey with the business objectives. In this chapter, we explored the multi-dimensional value-complexity framework that organizations can leverage to identify and pick the right cloud initiatives that deliver the maximum business value. We discussed the various cloud transformation journeys and their merits and demerits. We also reviewed the different cloud migration strategies, including the 6 R's that enterprises can leverage as a structured framework to migrate and innovate in the cloud.

For enterprises with a traditional on-premises ecosystem, we explored the different hybrid cloud strategies and cloud transformation journeys that can yield incremental business value. Finally, we reviewed the modern use cases that organizations can use as a tool to drive innovation and digital disruption.

In the next chapter, we will learn how enterprises can jump-start digital transformation through a well-defined framework.

Further reading

To learn more about the topics that were covered in this chapter, take a look at the following references:

1. `https://investors.twilio.com/news/news-details/2023/Twilio-and-Google-Cloud-Expand-Partnership-to-Improve-Customer-Experience-with-AI/default.aspx`

2. `https://www.forbes.com/sites/amazonwebservices/2021/12/07/the-future-of-work-how-slack-is-reinventing-hybrid-collaboration-with-machine-learning/?sh=7d53ff353dce`

3. `https://explore.zoom.us/docs/doc/WhitePaper_CE2_2015.pdf`

4. `https://www.weforum.org/agenda/2021/09/the-next-big-cloud-competition-is-the-race-to-zero-emissions/`

5. `https://www.gartner.com/en/documents/1485116?_its=JTdCJTIydmlkJTIyJTNBJTIyYTk3NDg4ZjktN2VhMS00ZmM1LWJjMzUtYjU2YmVlNTA0MDVmJTIyJTJDJTIyc3RhdGUlMjIlM0ElMjJybHQl2BMTY5MTI2ODYyMX5sYW5kfjJfMTY0NjVfc2VvVxzlhY2IwMjk3ZDJmODkwNTZhOGEyMTc3ODg3MmZkOGM0JTIyJTJDJTIyc2l0ZUlkJTIyJTNBNDAxMzElN0Q%3D`

6. `https://nvd.nist.gov/vuln/detail/cve-2017-0144`

7. `https://www.malwarebytes.com/petya-and-notpetya`

6

Building an Open and Nimble Cloud Framework

As we explored the various cloud transformation journeys, the next crucial step is establishing a foundation that is open and nimble to support the current and future business demands. An open cloud framework is extremely critical to the success of digital transformation within an enterprise and is often an overlooked aspect when organizations embark on cloud journeys. For instance, an organization may start its cloud journey within an isolated line of business that continues to push the boundaries of digital innovation and transformation, which, over time, can lead to **cloud debt**. Cloud debt can stem from a lack of a standardized infrastructure or platform, a lack of established standards for integration, cloud anti-patterns, a lack of governance, and a lack of reuse.

Choosing the right technology stack and tooling is more important than the actual choice of a cloud provider and platform. Irrespective of whether an organization is establishing a single strategic cloud choice, a hybrid cloud strategy, or a multi-cloud strategy, building a robust technology stack foundation that is based on open standards is essential to future-proof and aid with portability. Establishing an open standards-based cloud framework requires careful assessment and planning across all tiers of the stack, including foundational infrastructure, platform, application, data, security, and governance. In this chapter, we will explore the strategies that enterprises can leverage to build a framework for cloud transformation, including the selection of a platform, technology, tools, and some of the anti-patterns in the cloud that enterprises must be wary of. This chapter focuses on the following key topics:

- Defining a cloud adoption framework that can offer a structured and methodical approach to cloud transformation
- Various hybrid cloud and multi-cloud deployment patterns
- Foundational network blueprints for hybrid and multi-cloud deployment architectures
- Security foundations for enterprises
- Designing a security-first cloud architecture
- Cloud-native anti-patterns

In the previous chapters, we explored various strategies that enterprises can employ to choose the right cloud provider and platform, assess maturity and capability, and carry out workload assessments and migration strategies. The next logical step in a cloud transformation journey is defining a **cloud adoption framework (CAF)**. The CAF offers a structured set of guidelines that helps organizations move to the cloud in a methodical and efficient manner. It also serves as a blueprint for planning, executing, and governing cloud adoption initiatives. Although a CAF can be defined in various degrees of granularity, the four core phases that define a cloud adoption framework include assessment, planning, deployment, and optimization.

Assess

The assessment phase serves as a diagnostic and planning step, helping organizations understand their current state and prepare for a move to a cloud environment. The assessment phase is followed by other phases that focus on deeper planning, actual cloud migration or deployment, and then ongoing management and optimization. The quality of work done in the assessment phase directly impacts the success of the entire cloud adoption journey. Key steps in an assessment phase are as follows:

- **Cloud maturity assessment**: This is a critical step, especially for organizations embarking on their first cloud initiative. As we discussed the various methods to evaluate and assess an organization's cloud maturity, this step helps assess organizational readiness across various dimensions, such as skillset, culture, and processes.

- **IT landscape assessment**: Evaluating the current IT landscape across infrastructure, application, data, security, and compliance footprints is the next key step in the assessment phase. In the case of cloud migrations, this helps develop the right cloud migration strategies, and in the case of net new cloud initiatives, it provides insights into leveraging existing best practices and architecture synergies.

- **Identify business objectives**: The next step in the assessment phase is identifying the top three business objectives that enterprises would realize through cloud transformation. Every cloud transformation objective is unique and can be guided by identified business objectives such as cost savings, innovation, agility, or speed to market.

- **Choosing cloud models**: In this step, enterprises decide on the most suitable cloud model – IaaS, PaaS, or SaaS – and the deployment model – public, private, hybrid, or multi-cloud – that best fits the organizational objectives.

- **Business case development**: Developing a business case starts early in the assessment phase, as it is crucial to the success of the cloud transformation. It starts with ensuring key stakeholder and leadership alignment, outlining key milestones and potential value realization. This would tie into the business value realization that happens post transformation.

- **Dependency analysis**: Dependency analysis offers insights into the business and technical dependencies, potential risks, and integration touchpoints.

- **Financial assessment**: Financial assessment helps define, budget, and allocate the financial resources for cloud initiatives and identify ongoing operation costs. In this step, enterprises perform cost-benefit and ROI analyses.

Plan

The plan phase is the next critical stage in the CAF, following the assessment phase. In the plan phase, organizations formalize the strategy, create detailed architecture and migration plans, and prepare for the implementation of the cloud environment. The plan phase provides the necessary blueprint for the subsequent phases in the cloud adoption framework, and helps minimize risks, ensuring the efficient use of resources, and sets the stage for successful cloud adoption. Here is a breakdown of the key activities typically involved in the plan phase:

- **Formalize cloud strategy**: In this step, enterprises create a detailed business case that outlines the scope, benefits, risks, and ROI. Organizations also establish key performance indicators to measure the success of the cloud adoption journey.

- **Technical plan**: Developing an architecture design, migration plan (in case of migration from on-premises to cloud), deployment plan (in case of born-in-the-cloud initiatives), and a security and compliance plan constitute this step. In this step, organizations develop the cloud architecture based on the findings and decisions made during the assessment phase. This includes setting up an **enterprise architecture review board** (**EARB**) (if one doesn't exist) to flesh out details of infrastructure design, network architecture, security architecture, integration design, and storage planning.

- **Resourcing**: Resourcing includes plans for human and financial resources. Training internal teams or identifying external partners to augment skill gaps, confirming budget allocation for cloud adoption processes, including migration and operational expenditures.

- **Application and platform services**: Another crucial step in the planning phase is the choice of application and platform components and services. The choice of various application and platform components can depend on the cloud transformation or migration strategy under consideration.

- **Cloud center of excellence** (**CCoE**): Enterprises embarking on strategic cloud transformation initiatives must consider establishing a centralized CCoE to govern, manage, guide, and influence the cloud transformation or adoption program.

- **Operational readiness**: This step in the planning phases helps establish a governance framework for cloud management, and identifies and defines an operational model that includes monitoring, alerting, incident management, SLAs, and SLOs.

- **Communication plan**: Establishing communication and change management plans are critical to the success of overall cloud transformation. Developing a communication plan is important to keep stakeholders informed and engaged during the cloud adoption process and prepare the organization for change in the technology, processes, and workflows that come with cloud transformation.

- **Roadmap creation**: In this step, organizations create a detailed timeline and roadmap, specifying what, how, and when various cloud components would be built or migrated, identifying dependencies, and creating contingency plans. The definition of the core success criteria and metrics is a key planning exercise to measure the success of the cloud initiative.

- **Validation**: Developing **proof of concepts (PoCs)**, **proof of value (PoV)**, **minimum viable products (MVPs)**, and benchmarking for complex migrations or new architectures is crucial to ensure the validation of a broader cloud transformation. This also helps organizations fail fast and develop fallback strategies.

Deploy

The deployment phase in a CAF is where the rubber meets the road. Following thorough assessment and planning, the deploy phase involves the actual deployment or migration of resources, applications, and data into the cloud environment. This phase is often the most resource-intensive and time-critical, requiring meticulous co-ordination among cross-functional teams, departments, and stakeholders. The following is a breakdown of the activities typically involved in the deploy phase:

- **Pre-migration checklist**: The first step in the deploy phase involves validation and the setting up of the target cloud infrastructure according to the architecture design. Some key activities include securing a full backup of critical data and configurations, and the verification of all dependency requirements are addressed, finalizing a cutover and rollback plan.

- **Cloud provisioning**: This step involves creating or allocating cloud resources per the architecture design, cloud tenancy setup, identity, and access policies, integration with the enterprise **identity provider (IDP)**, configuration of **single sign-on (SSO)**, baseline security, and compliance design activities.

- **Network design**: Network design is one of the most crucial elements in technical cloud architecture design, and getting it right can mean long-term success. Especially in the case of public cloud IaaS and PaaS deployments, organizations must focus on creating a robust network design that is extensible as well as efficient. Establishing dedicated **multi-protocol label switching (MPLS)** and **border gateway protocol (BGP)** network circuits to cloud provider networks and configuring VLANs, VPNs, and firewalls are some key steps in cloud network design.

- **Security architecture design**: Akin to network design, security architecture is paramount to cloud transformation success. With an ever-growing increase in cyber security incidents, securing cloud infrastructure using cloud-native tooling and adherence to existing security architecture blueprints is crucial.

- **Data migration**: For cloud transformations involving migrating applications or data to the public cloud, migrating data from on-premises to the cloud securely and efficiently is critical.

In this step, based on the nature of data, data volume, data sensitivities, organizations must carefully evaluate options such as over the network data transfer or data transfer appliances.

- **Application and platform services**: This stage involves creating and configuring application and platform services such as API interfaces, API gateways, Kubernetes clusters, web servers, load balancers, etc.

- **Testing**: In this step, basic functional testing, such as unit tests, integration testing, performance or load tests, user acceptance testing, and security testing, is conducted to ensure all core success criteria are met.

- **Dry runs**: This step involves performing dry runs and A/B tests to verify and validate that cloud deployment meets the defined criteria and objectives.

- **Governance**: In this stage, organizations implement logging and monitoring tools and create dashboards to capture and report application performance metrics, alerts for KPI tracking, and audit tracing for compliance reporting.

- **Operations transition**: Once the production roll out and cutover is complete, the operations are transitioned to the CloudOps team for ongoing maintenance and support, and the deploy phase culminates in a fully operational cloud environment that aligns with the organization's strategic goals.

Optimize

The optimize phase of the CAF aims to fine-tune cloud services and solutions to deliver better value to the business. After the initial cloud deployment, this phase ensures that operations are not only stable but also efficient and cost-effective. As opposed to the first three phases, the optimize phase is a continuous ongoing process with periodic reviews, adjustments, and the fine-tuning of the cloud environment and application footprints to consistently meet business objectives more efficiently. Some key steps in this phase include the following:

- **Governance and compliance**: As governance and compliance policies tend to change regularly based on industry regulations, security postures, and technological advancements, the periodic assessment of governance and compliance is a critical step to ensure the cloud services and applications meet the requisite standards. This is a core function of an organization's platform team.

- **FinOps**: Cost management is key to any cloud transformation, as subscription-based services can throw up surprises if not well managed. Regularly evaluating the application needs and consistently right-sizing environments, setting up budgets and alerts, leveraging cloud-native cost management tools to monitor and analyze costs, reviewing various cost-efficient levers, such as cloud commitments and sustained use discounts, and migrating to cloud-native frameworks (e.g., serverless) where possible constitute a strategic FinOps practice.

- **Site reliability engineering (SRE)**: This step consists of monitoring **key performance indicators (KPIs)** to measure cloud service effectiveness, log aggregation and analytics to trace and understand user behavior, **application performance monitoring** (APM), security patching, and ensuring high levels of availability and reliability. These factors are extremely critical to the success of any cloud transformation initiative.

- **Automating everything**: This is also considered part of SRE; the practice of automating everything is considered the highest maturity level of cloud transformation, as this can lead to repeatable and reliable systems owing to fewer human touchpoints and errors. Automating common tasks and workflows, such as infrastructure automation through **infrastructure as code** (IaC), the automation of configuration, application deployments, backups, automatic scaling, and tear-downs, are important constituents of this stage.

- **Business continuity**: In this step, organizations implement robust **business continuity plans** (BCPs) and data backups and test them regularly.

- **Identifying reuse**: Another key element in the optimize phase is the ability to identify patterns and architecture that can be reused across the enterprise. A consistent feedback loop must exist between cloud operations, CCoE, and EARB to identify architecture blueprints and apply best practices across the organization, preventing the need to reinvent the wheel.

Having understood the important phases and constituents of setting up a cloud adoption framework, let us explore how organizations can build the foundation for a hybrid cloud deployment.

Various hybrid cloud and multi-cloud deployment patterns

For most enterprises, the hybrid cloud deployment model offers the unique flexibility of a public cloud and the control of a private infrastructure. However, unifying a public cloud architecture with a traditional on-premises setup poses challenges primarily because of their inherently different operational, security, and governance frameworks. Since infrastructure, existing DevOps practices, skillsets, workloads, and processes are unique to every enterprise context, a hybrid cloud or multi-cloud deployment strategy must be adapted to specific needs. Hybrid cloud and multi-cloud terminologies are typically overloaded and used inconsistently. **Hybrid cloud** refers to a deployment strategy where an application or workload is deployed across on-premises and public clouds, interconnected through a common network, while **multi-cloud** refers to a deployment strategy where applications or workloads are deployed across multiple public clouds, with or without integrations to on-premises. In this section, we will review some common hybrid cloud deployment patterns.

Tiered hybrid cloud pattern

The tiered hybrid cloud deployment pattern involves the strategic allocation of workloads and applications across cloud and on-premises private computing environments based on their criticality, performance requirements, and security concerns. This pattern broadly classifies an application or workload into two tiers – **frontend** and **backend**. A frontend that is user-facing runs on modern technology stacks and fluctuates based on demand, whereas a backend is a traditional application or system that serves core business functions that are business critical and yet are harder to re-platform. In this pattern, a frontend takes advantage of flexible and modern public cloud infrastructure, whereas the backend is left as-is in an on-premises environment. This pattern allows organizations to exploit the advantages of each environment for specific sets of tasks, offering a balanced approach to cost, performance, and security.

Some key benefits of this pattern include the following:

- **Experimentation and innovation**: This pattern allows enterprises with significant investments on-premises to test, experiment, and innovate faster in the cloud while also retaining critical assets within their on-premises environment.

- **Scalability and resource optimization**: The tiered pattern allows enterprises to scale resources up or down based on demand in a public cloud environment while leveraging existing resources and optimizing on-premises backends. Applications can also be dynamically moved between different tiers, optimizing resource utilization and ensuring optimal performance.

- **Security and compliance**: Critical and sensitive applications can be safeguarded within the private cloud or on-premises, ensuring compliance with industry regulations, data residencies, and data protection standards. Less-sensitive workloads can be placed in the public cloud while maintaining appropriate security measures.

- **Cost optimization**: By strategically distributing workloads, organizations can optimize costs across a public cloud and on-premises. Critical backends that are too risky or time-consuming to rehost, replatform, or re-architect can continue to run on-premises or in private clouds to avoid potential data transfer costs, whereas frontends and application components can leverage the cost-effective scalability of public clouds.

- **Performance optimization**: Tiering workloads based on performance requirements ensures that applications receive the necessary resources to meet performance expectations. This prevents resource contention and latency issues that could arise in a one-size-fits-all cloud approach.

While there are several advantages to this pattern, organizations must be aware of the following challenges and considerations.

- **Complexity**: Managing multiple tiers across various public cloud environments can be complex, requiring specialized skills and tools. Splitting tiers across public clouds and on-premises cuts across heterogeneous deployment paradigms and, hence, requires a thorough understanding of the workload characteristics, architecture, data flow, and security requirements. Another key consideration is the choice of compatible technologies that can seamlessly operate across public clouds and on-premise environments.

- **Network latency**: As the tiers are split across public cloud and on-premises, it can introduce network latency, particularly for applications requiring real-time data processing. The meticulous planning of network architecture, interface design, and API gateways are crucial to mitigate this challenge.

- **Resource allocation**: Allocating resources to workloads running across public clouds and on-premises appropriately among tiers can be challenging, for instance, during peak demand or unexpected workloads. Careful design considerations, such as implementing mechanisms for monitoring resource utilization and dynamic resource allocation, are essential to mitigate this challenge.

Partitioned multi-cloud pattern

A partitioned multi-cloud pattern leverages a multi-cloud deployment strategy where applications are deployed across multiple cloud environments. This strategy offers enterprises the greatest level of flexibility to deploy workloads that are suited or can operate efficiently in the optimal cloud environment. There are two variants of this pattern:

- A workload is partitioned and distributed across multiple clouds, allowing application traffic to traverse seamlessly.

- Applications are deployed in cloud environments on a best-fit basis while maintaining portability.

Some key components in a partitioned multi-cloud pattern include the following:

- **Compute partition**: In this pattern, cloud environments are purely leveraged as an infrastructure deployment platform to support workload portability through adherence to open standards. For instance, services such as AWS EC2, Google Compute Engine, and Azure VMs can be selected based on specific computing needs for a service or application. The same can be extrapolated to hypervisor-level portability for VM-based live migrations that leverage Hyper-V, KVM, or VMware.

- **Container partition**: In this model, a common container orchestration platform is chosen across multiple clouds that can help deploy, port, or migrate applications seamlessly. For instance, services such as **Google Kubernetes Engine (GKE)**, AWS EKS, and **Azure Kubernetes Service (AKS)** can simplify the deployment of a Kubernetes cluster across multiple clouds, including on-premises as a way to develop and deploy modern cloud-native microservices-based applications.

- **Data storage partition**: Leveraging a common data storage architecture can help enterprises seamlessly extend a unified storage platform to enhance data durability, and redundancy, and optimize costs. For instance, AWS S3, Google Cloud Storage, and Oracle Object Storage can be leveraged using a common S3-based storage API.

- **Network partition**: A network partition is critical to a multi-cloud deployment architecture pattern. By leveraging software-defined networking, organizations can define virtual private clouds to fulfill distinct networking requirements while also enabling seamless inter-cloud communication through cross-connects. Several public cloud providers either natively support cross-connects or can be enabled through a cloud exchange service provider such as Equinix, Digital Realty, or CenturyLink.

A partitioned multi-cloud offers some unique benefits to enterprises, such as the following:

- **Best-of-breed approach**: Organizations have the ability to tap into specialized services from different cloud providers, maximizing capability and efficiency by having best-of-breed solutions.

- **Vendor independence**: Avoidance of vendor lock-in is a primary advantage for enterprises, as the partitioned approach mitigates the risk of vendor lock-in, making it easier to switch providers for individualized services as needed.

- **Resource optimization**: The optimal use of resources and specialized services offered by different cloud providers can often lead to better resource efficiency and financial outcomes compared to a one-size-fits-all approach.

- **Standardization**: A partitioned multi-cloud can enable the standardization of enterprise IT that can lead to the seamless adoption of modern technologies and open standards.

While this pattern offers several advantages, including flexibility and cost-effectiveness, it also comes with challenges that should not be overlooked.

- **Complexity**: Managing multiple cloud providers adds a layer of complexity in terms of administration, billing, and governance.

- **Data transfer and integration**: Transferring data between different cloud providers can incur costs and latency issues. Meticulous planning is essential to mitigate cross-cloud latency and egress costs.

- **Security strategy**: Defining and managing a unified security posture and compliance that can be uniformly applied across partitions can become challenging when dealing with multiple cloud providers.

- **Skillset and effort**: A diverse skillset is required to build, manage, and optimize services from different cloud platforms. The standardization of tech stacks and automation is essential to address this challenge.

Edge computing deployment pattern

In a hybrid edge computing deployment pattern, the primary objective is to share the computational load between a centralized cloud infrastructure and edge computing nodes located closer to the data source. This helps businesses create a flexible deployment pattern, where data can be processed locally at the edge or sent to a central server based on computational complexity, latency sensitivity, consumer experience, or other specific requirements. The typical applications of a hybrid edge compute deployment pattern include the following:

- **Internet of Things (IoT)** deployments include devices, sensors, and gateways that are deployed at the edge of the network in various settings such as retail stores, hospitals, manufacturing facilities and logistics. IoT deployments at the edge generate substantial volumes of data that are processed locally using the available computing power. Subsequently, the correlated and consolidated data are transmitted to a central cloud computing infrastructure for further processing and analysis.

- Kiosks, **point of sale** (**POS**) systems, and **next unit of computing** (**NUC**) can process data at the edge to enable extremely fast response times to improve consumer experience or be micro-batched before being sent to central cloud services. The typical applications of this use case can be found in restaurants and retail stores.

- The remote connectivity or areas lacking network availability guarantees can take advantage of this pattern to deliver business-critical services, for example, sea-faring vessels, agricultural farms, remotely deployed surveillance bots/devices that can synchronize data with a central cloud server on a periodic basis.

Some key benefits of this pattern are the following:

- **Low-latency applications**: Hybrid edge computing patterns reduce latency by enabling data processing closer to the source. This is particularly important in applications that require real-time analytics or control, such as autonomous vehicles or industrial automation systems.

- **Efficient bandwidth utilization**: By preprocessing data at the edge, only pertinent information needs to be sent to the centralized cloud, thereby saving bandwidth and reducing transmission costs.

- **Scalability**: This approach allows organizations to start small at the edge and scale upwards, incorporating more centralized cloud resources as needed.

- **Resource optimization**: The hybrid edge model allows tasks to be assigned to the most suitable processing unit, be it an edge node or a central cloud server, based on the resource requirements and constraints.

The challenges of this pattern include the following:

- **Technical complexity**: Managing a hybrid system is more complex than a purely centralized or edge-based model due to the need for dynamic task allocation, data synchronization, and network management.

- **Upfront costs**: The initial setup costs for edge infrastructure can be high. However, this may be offset by the long-term operational cost savings and the value delivered by the overall solution.

- **Security and compliance**: Hybrid models, due to their distributed nature, can present more security challenges that organizations need to actively manage. For instance, securing edge devices is extremely critical, as they can be easy targets for bad actors to gain access to corporate data and **Man-in-the-middle** (**MITM**) attacks.

Redundant hybrid deployment pattern

Redundant hybrid deployment refers to an architectural pattern where computational resources are strategically replicated across both cloud and data centers. In this pattern, redundancy is introduced at each level to ensure high availability and fault tolerance, enabling tasks and data to be processed in more than one location with synchronization mechanisms in place to maintain data consistency and integrity. Enterprises can leverage this pattern to enable three hybrid use cases:

- **Environment hybrid pattern**: Commonly referred to as a dev-test in the cloud, this refers to a model where an application's development and testing environments are spun up and torn down on-demand in a cloud-based environment while the production environment is built within private on-premises. This pattern might seem risky at the outset, as environment parity is hard to establish between a public cloud and traditional on-premises. However, this allows organizations to achieve functional equivalence across all environments instead of environment parity, necessitating a cloud-native deployment paradigm. This is also a low-risk pattern for enterprises embarking on a hybrid-cloud journey that will ensure familiarity with cloud concepts and move subsequent workloads with greater confidence. Some primary advantages of this pattern include the following:

  - On-demand and automated provisioning environments using IaC constructs can standardize entire environment provisioning, deploy code, perform tests, and tear down.

  - Development and testing environments are often used intermittently. Provisioning these in a cloud environment can help reduce costs by stopping environments that are not in use and provisioning only on demand. Cloud-based environments also enable multiple parallel release cycles for an application.

  - Leveraging managed services in the cloud that have technology equivalence (open source software) can help save time and resources to install, administer, patch, and manage these for multiple non-production environments.

  The following are some architectural considerations that enterprises must be aware of while using this pattern:

  - Ensuring a network topology allows and prevents communications across the environments. For instance, non-production environments might have a logical application and data network segregation, whereas production environment networks are isolated from lower environments.

  - To ensure application or workload portability and to abstract away the environment parity considerations, enterprises need to design and architect a common tool chain facilitating a microservices-based deployment approach that leverages containers and container orchestration platforms.

  - To account for the variations in infrastructure and resource availability between on-premises and cloud environments, it is important to select CI/CD tools that support hybrid cloud deployment models, offering flexibility, portability, and integration with existing systems.

Designing standardized workflows and implementing change management processes to track and manage changes in CI/CD pipelines, infrastructure, and applications is critical.

- Implement a single pane of glass governance model that helps establish holistic governance and compliance policies for CI/CD processes in hybrid cloud environments. From a monitoring and observability perspective, it is prudent to implement comprehensive monitoring and observability tools to track the health, performance, and security of CI/CD pipelines and deployed applications across both on-premises and cloud systems.

- The choice of caching, storage, messaging, and database services that have parity across on-premises and cloud managed services. For instance, an Apache Kafka topic could be a preferred messaging service for on-premises while Cloud Pub/Sub (GCP) or Amazon MSK (AWS) can be leveraged as managed services for the functional parity of a message broker.

- **Business continuity hybrid pattern**: In the business continuity hybrid pattern, production environments primarily run within an on-premises data center, whereas a **disaster recovery (DR)** environment is configured on a public cloud. Mission-critical applications and systems are typically configured in a way that makes them resilient during disasters. By replicating mission-critical systems in a public cloud, enterprises can avoid a single point of failure, minimize the risks that affect local infrastructure, and protect against unforeseen security threats. This pattern also serves as a low-risk foray into the cloud for enterprises. A key aspect of DR planning is to replicate and back up data to the public cloud periodically to minimize the **recovery point objective (RPO)** and maintain cloud (warm or hot) standby to minimize the **recovery time objective (RTO)**.

Leveraging the business continuity hybrid pattern offers a number of advantages:

- Public cloud providers typically have several cloud regions with redundant data centers, commonly referred to as **availability zones** or domains, which can natively offer uptime, availability, and resilient infrastructure architecture.

- With the elastic scale of a public cloud, data can be replicated and backed up to public clouds securely with immutable backups encrypted and protected using HSM.

- A disaster recovery environment configuration in a public cloud can prove substantially cheaper, especially when they are configured as warm or cold DRs, as stopped resources typically don't incur costs in a public cloud.

- A hot standby in a public cloud environment can be extended to serve traffic for different geographies and support creative strategies such as A/B tests, canary deployments, etc.

- This pattern enables and supports new business continuity plans for applications and workloads that are harder to achieve in a traditional on-premises environment owing to higher costs, efforts, and maintenance.

The following are some considerations while leveraging this pattern:

- A comprehensive **business continuity plan** (BCP) is required for every application to help configure the right DR strategy, RPO, and RTO objectives.

- Since data are transferred or exchanged between on-premises and clouds, a robust network topology must be established with redundant and fallback connections to ensure a seamless and secure data flow.

- Workload dependencies with other on-premise systems must be carefully evaluated to avoid bottlenecks due to traffic spikes – especially in a hot standby or active-active setup.

- Especially in an active-active configuration, bi-directional data synchronization between the on-premises and public cloud environments can expose the environments to a split-brain problem, causing conflicts, data inconsistencies, and even data loss or corruption. One of the common causes of a split-brain problem is incorrect or deficient network cluster configuration. Mitigation strategies, such as ensuring redundant networks, quorum checks, or dedicated master nodes, should be considered.

- Automating everything is critical, which can avoid single points of failure in the architecture, for instance, if one environment becomes unavailable, ensuring CI/CD processes are able to deploy new releases and apply configurations in a new environment.

- Periodic and willful failover testing is essential to ensure the BCP is stable, current, and fully functional.

- **Cloud bursting pattern**: One of the edge use cases that public cloud enables for enterprises is **cloud bursting**. The idea of the cloud bursting pattern is to leverage the on-premises or private cloud environment for a steady application load and burst to a public cloud during traffic spikes or when extra capacity is required. Typically, internet-facing applications that experience traffic fluctuations, batch jobs, or training AI/ML models can be good candidates for this pattern. In a traditional setup, this challenge is mitigated by overprovisioning on-premise resources. This approach can be cost-prohibitive. However, a key requirement for cloud bursting is ensuring application or workload portability and having a strategy to seamlessly distribute traffic across environments. Generally, for internet-facing applications, a global load balancer must be configured either in the on-premises environment or the public cloud that can intelligently track and route traffic appropriately.

The key benefits of this pattern are the following:

- Cloud bursting enables high resource utilization across on-premises and public cloud environments since enterprises no longer need to over-provision on-premises resources in anticipation of a spike.

- Capacity planning can be tedious, especially for organizations with unpredictable traffic spikes during flash sales or seasonality, and cloud bursting can ensure application availability and reliability to satisfy peak demands.

- Cloud bursting also allows organizations to creatively address challenges with on-premises (primary) application or resource maintenance, such as major upgrades, rolling updates, patching, or even hardware refresh cycles, without having to cause application downtime.

- This pattern can be leveraged to run batch jobs in a public cloud environment, which typically have to be queued within the on-premises environment for off-peak runs or when having to overprovision resources. This can also be extremely cost-effective when leveraging spot or pre-emptible VM instances.

- By leveraging this pattern, enterprises can also develop and build modern AI/ML-based applications and services by training ML models in the public cloud, as the data are readily available with on-demand CPU and GPU availability for model training.

Some considerations while adopting the cloud-bursting pattern include the following:

- A meshed network topology is essential to ensure there is seamless access to resources across on-premises and cloud environments.

- Careful consideration must be given when choosing a public cloud provider and region, along with the capabilities that can address the current and future needs of the application, for example, picking a cloud region that is geographically closer to the on-premises data center, establishing a low-latency MPLS connection and platform and managed services support, and having core infrastructure capabilities that can coexist with on-premises resources such as hybrid global load balancers.

- Meticulous planning is essential with respect to security, access controls, and policies to reduce the attack vector. For instance, all network traffic must be encrypted with traffic routed only over trusted channels such as VPN tunnels or dedicated MPLS circuits, establishing a common identity to securely authenticate across environment boundaries.

- Applications, especially internet-facing applications that react to traffic spikes, must follow modern cloud-native application architecture and best practices to achieve seamless workload portability. Stateful application components can be tricky to handle, especially during cloud bursting.

- DevOps and SRE practices must ensure the standardization of CI/CD processes, monitoring, observability, and governance.

Having reviewed the various cloud deployment patterns, their merits, and considerations, let's explore some of the foundational network topology blueprints for hybrid cloud and multi-cloud deployments.

Foundational network blueprints for hybrid and multi-cloud deployment architectures

Before embarking on the cloud transformation, securely and reliably connecting the enterprise's on-premises data center or private computing environment to the public cloud is crucial to any successful hybrid or multi-cloud deployment. As enterprises navigate the complexities of hybrid and multi-cloud deployments, a reliable, extensible, and secure network architecture becomes increasingly significant and acts as the backbone that supports high availability, performance optimization, enhanced security, and efficient scalability. Ultimately, a robust network architecture is not just an operational requirement but a strategic enabler that can significantly influence an organization's agility. As every enterprise cloud journey is unique, the chosen foundational architecture and network topology must meet the business demands. In this section, we will explore some foundational blueprints for enterprise hybrid and multi-cloud deployments.

Meshed hybrid cloud network topology

In this topology, connectivity is established between the on-premises private computing environment and a public cloud provider, either through a simple VPN tunnel configuration or a dedicated MPLS circuit. This is also commonly referred to as **meshed network topology**, as this establishes a flat network that can span multiple environments, allowing all systems and services to communicate seamlessly with each other. Fine-grained access controls are governed by routing rules and firewalls. This topology is best suited for tiered applications and cloud-bursting scenarios.

Figure 6.1 shows a typical meshed hybrid cloud network architecture, where the on-premises environment establishes a connection to a public cloud through a VPN (over public internet), a dedicated interconnect (MPLS), or a combination of those for failover and redundancy:

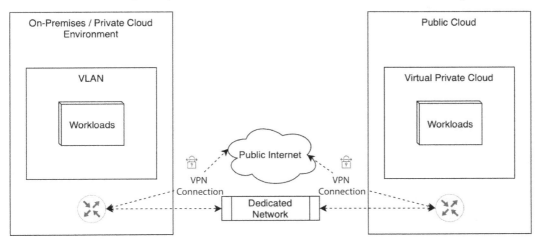

Figure 6.1 – Meshed hybrid cloud network topology

Multi-cloud network topology

Similar to a hybrid cloud network topology, a **multi-cloud network topology** involves at least two public cloud providers that interface with the on-premises private computing environment. Enterprises embarking on a multi-cloud strategy can establish dedicated MPLS network connectivity with each public cloud – preferably through a cloud exchange partner that can support multiple cloud networks while also enabling redundant VPN tunnels as failover and highly available network mesh. Meticulous network and security architecture planning is required in order to configure non-overlapping unique address ranges for each cloud, routing logic, egress management, network firewall, and security.

Slight variations of this architecture may include the following:

- Configuring and allowing only private access to cloud environments from an on-premises network.
- Establishing cross-connect to enable cloud-to-cloud data flow and communication – This topology is particularly useful for workload shuttling and cross-cloud analytics use cases.
- Setting up the common Layer 4 network firewall security.
- Configuring public egress only from on-premises VLAN environments.

As can be seen from *Figure 6.2*, a dedicated network is established preferably through a cloud exchange to connect to the chosen public cloud networks. Alternatively, a secure VPN connectivity is also established over the public internet for delay-independent connections or for network redundancy. It is also an important design to choose a cloud exchange provider that can support all the public clouds in consideration.

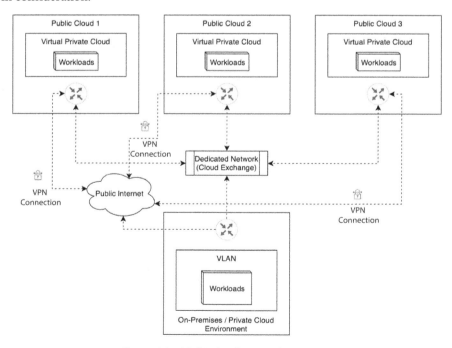

Figure 6.2 – Multi-cloud network topology

Gated egress hybrid cloud topology

The fundamental idea of a **gated egress network** topology is to expose only selected services and APIs from the on-premises environment to public cloud workloads. This topology prevents exposing the application VLAN, where an API gateway is deployed in a DMZ network zone that acts as a gatekeeper for network traffic. This topology is great for use cases where the traffic needs to be restricted only to certain services and workloads and to create a network perimeter in the on-premises environment. In this topology, on-premises workloads or services are disallowed to directly communicate with public clouds, and connections are always initiated from the public cloud through the on-premise DMZ.

Figure 6.3 shows a gated egress hybrid cloud network topology, where the connectivity to on-premises APIs is exposed via an API gateway to the choice public cloud network either via a dedicated network or through VPN over public internet:

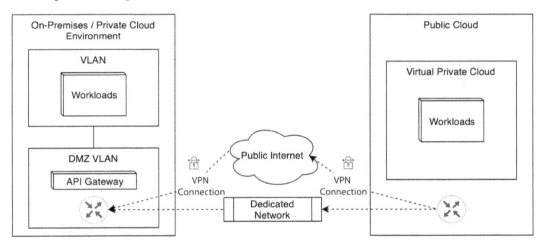

Figure 6.3 – Gated egress hybrid-cloud network topology

Gated ingress hybrid-cloud topology

Gated ingress topology is the exact opposite of the gated egress model, where public cloud resources and services are exposed via specific endpoints or APIs to on-premises environments. In this network topology, the resources and services hosted within the public cloud are typically configured to deny all traffic except the ones originating from trusted on-premises networks. This topology can be a great fit for edge hybrid scenarios where only specific endpoints are exposed to the outside world.

As can be seen in *Figure 6.4*, a gated ingress hybrid-cloud network topology helps expose the API service layer deployed in one or more public clouds, preferably through an API gateway to the on-premises environment, either via a dedicated network or through VPN over public internet:

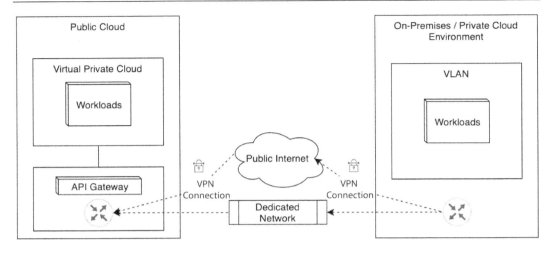

Figure 6.4 – Gated ingress hybrid-cloud network topology

Shared network topology

A **shared network architecture** allows for the creation of commonly used resources in a host project that can be shared with service projects. This topology can help network administrators have centralized control over network resources such as subnets, routes, and firewalls while also delegating certain administration responsibilities to service projects. It is important to note that the concept of shared networks differs based on the cloud provider.

Figure 6.5 depicts a shared cloud network topology that helps isolate and contain all network traffic ingressing or egressing from a public cloud through a dedicated VPC network, commonly referred to as the host VPC:

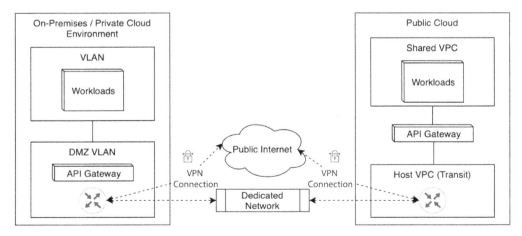

Figure 6.5 – Shared network topology

Private hybrid topology

In a **private hybrid network** topology, the resources within a public cloud environment are configured to be *private only* and disallowed to any internet traffic. For internet access, traffic from the public cloud is routed back to on-premise routers to serve the requests. Although this can be achieved using a NAT gateway (natively) within a public cloud, this can be extremely helpful for enterprises that operate within extremely sensitive security boundaries and would like granular control over egress traffic.

From *Figure 6.6*, we can see that all internet traffic from a public cloud network is disallowed, and connectivity to an on-premises environment is established through either a dedicated network or VPN. All internet-bound traffic from a public cloud environment is routed to on-premises:

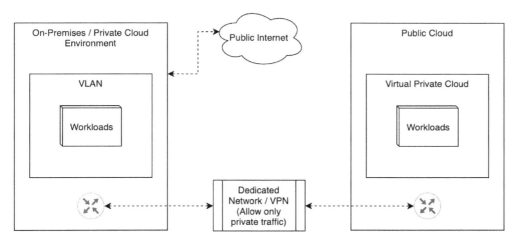

Figure 6.6 – Private hybrid-cloud network topology

Network peering topology

Network peering is yet another incredibly powerful network topology, where multiple cloud networks can be peered together in a mesh or a hub and bespoke architecture. Network peering allows public cloud resources across multiple networks and even across organization boundaries to communicate with each other. This can be an extremely powerful topology, where an enterprise that has multiple departments with isolated network boundaries can still communicate across networks while also maintaining dedicated control over their networks. A few other creative use cases that this network topology enables, include the following:

- Organizations can build and publish custom **software as a service** (**SaaS**) offerings privately via one virtual cloud network to another.

- Partners and service providers who happen to be on the same cloud provider network can privately communicate without having to traverse public networks.

- This architecture can also offer extremely low network latencies, as the traffic traverses over private internal network fabric and also offers high network security with relatively low network egress costs.

A sample network peering topology is described in *Figure 6.7*, where two virtual cloud networks are peered together to form a network mesh to allow traffic between services in VPC 1 and VPC 2 to communicate seamlessly over a private network without having to traverse external networks:

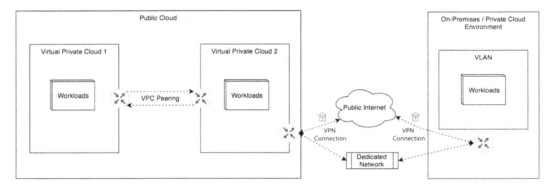

Figure 6.7 – Network peering topology

Edge network topology

The **edge network** topology is best suited for enterprises with edge computing and IoT needs. In this architecture, data from IoT sensors, devices, and edge computing devices, such as NUCs, are aggregated and processed at the edge using an edge gateway and are sent in real time or as micro batches to the public cloud for further processing, telemetry, or analysis.

The edge network topology, as shown in *Figure 6.8*, describes a typical edge site that houses edge devices, such as IoT sensors and NUCs, that connect locally to an IoT gateway through lightweight messaging protocols, such as **message queuing telemetry transport** (**MQTT**) and Zigbee or Z-Wave for local processing, consolidation, and correlation. The gateway device then interfaces with a public cloud network periodically or in real time for further processing and analysis.

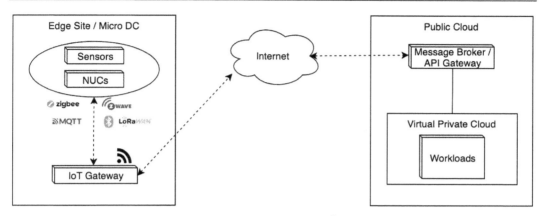

Figure 6.8 – Edge network topology

Having explored the various hybrid, multi-cloud, and edge network topologies and how organizations can establish a strong network foundation, let's now understand how to set up a solid security foundation for the cloud.

Security foundations for enterprises

Once the network foundation is laid out, the next most important foundational tier is security. Security is a broad topic and encompasses several layers of security. It is quintessential for enterprises embarking on a cloud journey – irrespective of native hybrid, multi-cloud, or full-on cloud methods – to ensure a robust security foundation at all layers. As the saying goes, security is everyone's business; it is even more relevant and pronounced in the cloud deployment model, as every aspect of cloud transformation – from application development, deployment, data storage, access, and compliance – has a core security dependence. Conventional security architecture in private on-premises environments differs intrinsically from public cloud security, as there is a shared responsibility model – , meaning that some aspects of security are managed and governed by the cloud provider while the rest are managed by the enterprise. Shared responsibility varies according to the cloud service provider used and the type of service offered. For instance, a SaaS provider owns the security that is responsible for a majority of the cloud stack, whereas an IaaS offering only manages security for the underlying physical hardware and up to the guest OS layer. In general, a shared responsibility model looks like the following image for various cloud deployment models, although some services have overlapping responsibilities for all practical purposes. For instance, a cloud infrastructure (IaaS) provider may claim responsibility for physical network management, whereas the software-defined network configuration is the customer's responsibility. *Figure 6.9* shows a cloud provider's typical shared responsibility model across multiple service areas:

Services	On-Premises	IaaS	PaaS	SaaS
Data	○	○	○	○
Applications	○	○	○	☐
Identity and Access	○	○	☐	☐
Network Security	○	○	☐	☐
Guest OS	○	○	☐	☐
Network	○	☐	☐	☐
Storage	○	☐	☐	☐
Virtualization	○	☐	☐	☐
Physical Infrastructure	○	☐	☐	☐
Data Center	○	☐	☐	☐

○ Customer Responsibility   ☐ Cloud Provider Responsibility

Figure 6.9 – Public cloud-shared responsibility model

Let us now explore the shared security models advocated by major cloud service providers, namely Amazon Web Services (AWS), Google Cloud Platform (GCP), and Microsoft Azure.

Shared security models of major CSPs

Amazon Web Services (AWS) defines the shared responsibility model as follows:

AWS claims responsibility for the "*Security of the Cloud*," whereas the customer is responsible for "*Security in the Cloud*."

AWS is responsible for protecting the infrastructure that runs all of the services offered in the AWS Cloud. This infrastructure is composed of the hardware, software, networking, and facilities that run AWS Cloud services.

Customer responsibility will be determined by the AWS Cloud services that a customer selects. This determines the amount of configuration work the customer must perform as part of their security responsibilities.

Figure 6.10 is adapted from the AWS documentation and shows the clear delineation of AWS and customer responsibilities [*1*]:

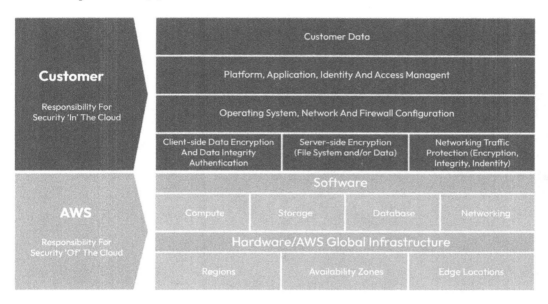

Figure 6.10 – AWS shared responsibility model

For instance, a pure IaaS offering requires customers to perform all of the necessary security configuration and management tasks, whereas a PaaS offering or an abstracted service will only require customers to secure the data assets on the platform. For a detailed understanding of the AWS shared responsibility model, refer to the *Further reading* section.

AWS also offers a comprehensive security reference architecture that aligns with the AWS security foundations [2]:

- **AWS CAF**: Provides guidance on best practices and approaches to building solutions on AWS.

- **AWS well-architected framework**: Focuses on cloud architects to help build a secure, resilient, and efficient AWS cloud environment.

Microsoft Azure supports the division of responsibility across the various services offered. Regardless of the type of deployment, the physical datacenter, network, and hosts are fully managed by Azure, whereas the data, endpoints, accounts, and access management are the customer's responsibility. *Figure 6.11* is adapted from Azure documentation that shows the Azure shared responsibility model [3]:

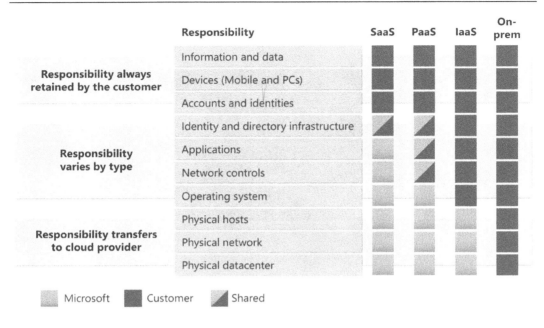

Figure 6.11 – Azure shared responsibility model

Microsoft Azure also offers an **Azure Security Benchmark Foundation** blueprint that helps build a secure and compliant Azure environment. Refer to the *Further readings* section at the end of this chapter for further details [4].

Google Cloud advocates for a **shared fate model** that supersedes the traditional cloud-shared responsibility model. The shared fate builds on the shared responsibility model but views cloud security as an ongoing partnership by offering clear, opinionated, transparent security controls, landing zones, security foundations blueprints, and best practices. *Figure 6.12* describes Google Cloud's shared fate model [5]:

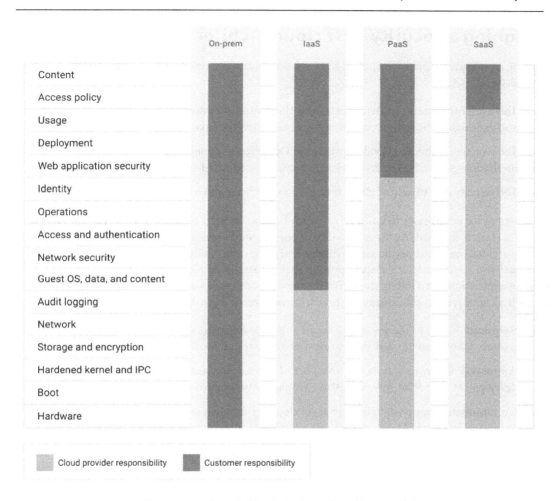

Figure 6.12 – Google Cloud platform shared fate model

Google Cloud offers an opinionated view of Google Cloud security best practices to help enterprises customize and adapt as needed. For further details on Google Cloud's shared fate model, refer to the *Further readings* section at the end of this chapter [6].

Let us now explore how to architect a security-first cloud foundation.

Designing a security-first cloud architecture

Securing cloud infrastructure is quite different from traditional on-premises environments due to some of the following:

- There are fundamental differences in how the cloud environments are provisioned, accessed, and exposed when compared to traditional on-premises environments that are locked in.

- The evolution of modern cloud-native DevSecOps practices democratized application development methodologies such as microservices, containers, and API-first.

- The velocity and variety of cloud services and offerings and how they are consumed.

It is essential for enterprises to build an in-depth defense security strategy to ensure every layer of the cloud stack is fortified. As the availability of public cloud services constantly evolves, enterprise security architecture must periodically evaluate and certify the public cloud services based on a host of security and compliance criteria and publish them internally as a guide for enterprise teams while building applications on a public cloud. For instance, cloud services and standards can be earmarked as required, approved, conditionally approved, alternative, or denied:

- **Required**: Refers to the pre-requisites of a specific deployment. For example, only private IP address ranges can be used for organization-wide resources.

- **Approved**: Refers to a fully approved list of services that can be used for cloud application development. This refers to services that have passed the required security and compliance controls.

- **Conditionally approved**: Refers to a set of cloud services that are approved with some qualifiers. For example, cloud object storage can be used only if restricted to private access.

- **Alternative**: Refers to an alternative solution – open source or existing third party – to be used in lieu of a managed service or offering. For example, the use of Terraform for infrastructure automation in lieu of a provider native solution.

- **Denied**: Refers to a set of services that are expected to not be used within the enterprise cloud deployment and do not have security clearance or are yet to be assessed.

Let us review some of the foundational security aspects and best practices.

Network security

At the foundational level, the security of the network is quintessential to prevent inbound network threats from the internet or external elements to resources deployed within the cloud environment. Optimizing the cloud network architecture is pivotal for cloud security. Some key elements for network security include the following:

- Securing traffic between on-premise networks and public clouds through dedicated MPLS connection or VPN tunnels.

- Segmenting and securing networks through VPCs and VPC network peering to reduce lateral network traffic movements.

- Implementing stateful and stateless firewalls to help control network traffic.

- Adopting a zero-trust network security architecture, where no entity within or outside of the cloud network is trusted by default, minimizing the risk of both internal and external threats.

- Employing endpoint security solutions to monitor and secure connected devices.

- Implementing **intrusion detection (IDS)** to monitor network traffic for anomalies and abnormal patterns that may indicate an ongoing attack and **intrusion prevention (IPS)** to identify deviations proactively from normal system behavior.

- Implementing packet detection through **next-gen firewall (NGFW)** solutions to ensure network security. NGFWs are an essential safeguard for enterprises, especially in heavily regulated industries, such as healthcare or finance. A typical NGFW also performs **deep packet inspection (DPI)** that goes beyond the traditional firewall approach, which only inspects the protocol header. An NGFW solution can help inspect and track all network traffic from Layer 2 to the application layer.

Identity and access management

Identity and access management (IAM) is a cornerstone of network security, especially in cloud environments where resources and services are distributed across various locations and accessed by numerous users. IAM serves as the gatekeeper for cloud resources and plays a crucial role in cloud security. IAM is the practice of granting access to the right cloud resources for the right individuals at the right access level. As cloud environments often feature a complex, fluctuating set of users, devices, applications, and services, the application of best practices in IAM becomes critically essential. Some best practices for IAM include the following:

- **Role-based access control (RBAC)**: RBAC is a critical element of IAM that restricts system access based on the roles within an organization. RBAC ensures that users have only the access required to perform their jobs, adhering to the principle of *least privilege*. By organizing users into roles based on their job responsibilities and only assigning access permissions to these roles instead of individual users, organizations can streamline the process of managing permissions, thereby reducing the risk of unauthorized or unnecessary access.

- **Identity management**: Managing identities in the cloud forms the foundation of IAM. While it is foundational, it is also important to manage the provisioning, securing, and deprovisioning of identities, users, roles, and groups within the cloud IAM. Leveraging either provider-native key management solutions to rotate keys, leveraging **hardware security module (HSM)**-based keys, or leveraging an existing on-premise key management solution can all be great strategies to secure credentials. Primarily, there are three kinds of identities:

- **Corporate identities**: These identify corporate employees, partners, and contractors that need access to corporate resources.

- **Service identities**: Also known commonly as service accounts, these identities help manage app-to-app or system-to-system interactions.

- **Customer identities**: These identify the end users or customers who interact with an application or system deployed on a cloud.

- **Identity federation and single sign-on**: SSO solutions can provide users with the convenience of a single set of credentials to access multiple services or platforms. When implemented securely, SSO reduces the number of passwords that users need to remember and manage, thereby reducing the potential for password-related security risks. Although most cloud providers offer an identity platform, in a typical enterprise context, an existing identity provider such as an active directory – commonly referred to as the IDP – can be leveraged without having to re-create the user organization in the cloud IDP. In this scenario, the cloud provider acts as a **service provider** (**SP**) and supports standard federation protocols such as SAML to enable SSO.

- **IAM lifecycle management**: IAM best practices also involve managing the entire lifecycle of identities. This includes the onboarding, provisioning, de-provisioning, and offboarding of user identities. Automated systems can help in streamlining this process, making sure that access is granted quickly when needed and revoked when no longer necessary, thereby minimizing the window of opportunity for unauthorized access.

- **Privileged access management**: Privileged accounts, such as network admin and security admin accounts, often have broad and powerful access, making them a prime target for attackers. **Privileged access management** (**PAM**) solutions help secure these sensitive accounts through various mechanisms, such as session isolation and monitoring, and they require justification for use. Implementing PAM becomes even more critical in cloud environments where administrative access can potentially impact multiple services and data stores.

- **Multi-factor authentication**: One of the primary tenets of IAM best practices is implementing MFA. The adoption of MFA offers an additional layer of security, establishing a strong security infrastructure to ensure regulated access to cloud resources. It is not enough to just enter a username and password; users may also have to enter a code sent to their phone or provide biometric verification. Implementing MFA decreases the likelihood of unauthorized access, even if passwords are compromised.

- **Just-in-time access**: While following the principle of least privilege, instead of granting permanent access, organizations can grant users just enough access for just enough time to carry out everyday activities and nothing more. This principle can reduce the significant risk involved with privileged access management to sensitive resources while also reducing the friction for users to get their jobs done.

- **Periodic audits and reviews**: The continuous monitoring and regular auditing of access controls and permissions can highlight potential issues before they become significant problems.

Regularly scheduled reviews of roles, permissions, and authentication policies help maintain a secure IAM posture. This also allows for adapting IAM policies to meet the evolving needs and structural changes within an organization.

Infrastructure security

Computing resources such as VMs, containers, serverlessness, and storage in public clouds form the foundational layer for application and data. Securing computing resources in a public cloud environment is crucial for ensuring the confidentiality, integrity, and availability of applications and data that run on top of it. Each of the infrastructure components, such as a VM, container, or storage, requires different types of security. While public cloud providers offer a shared responsibility or shared fate model, where the underlying physical infrastructure security is managed by the cloud vendor, organizations are still required to secure the upper stack infrastructure, such as the guest operating systems in VMs, RBAC for storage, and securing container registries for containers. The following are some best practices to consider when securing infrastructure in a public cloud:

- **Network security groups (NSGs) and firewalls**: NSGs and firewalls often serve as the first line of defense for infrastructure security by regulating inbound and outbound traffic to **network interface card** (**NICs**), **virtual machines** (**VMs**), and other networked resources. NSGs are composed of a list of security rules that allow or deny traffic based on factors such as source and destination IP address, port numbers, and the protocol used. They are highly scalable and can be associated with subnets, individual VMs, or even specific network interfaces, offering granular control over network traffic. Firewalls, on the other hand, can be either hardware-based or software-based and offer a more complex set of features, including deep packet inspection, intrusion detection systems, and application-layer filtering. Firewalls are often used in conjunction with NSGs for layered security, commonly referred to as a defense-in-depth security strategy.

- **Organization-wide policies**: As cloud usage constantly grows within an organization, it can quickly become difficult for security administrators to identify, detect, and remediate anti-patterns. For example, a VM instance in production is configured with a NIC that is associated with a public IP address or an object storage bucket configured as a public bucket that is exposed to the internet, and this could mean security threats. Organizations can leverage cloud-native capabilities, such as organization policies or service control policies, to control the best practice usage of cloud resources. In the preceding example, an organization-wide policy can be set up to block the creation of a public bucket across all projects.

- **Service accounts**: Service accounts are specialized identities that are used by applications, services, and automated tasks to interact with other resources in a public cloud. In a cloud environment, a service account is typically used to run processes that require restricted access to certain resources. For example, a service account might be used to run a script that routinely checks a database for new entries and then performs some action based on those entries. The permissions granted to this service account would be precisely defined to allow access only to the specific database and operations that the script requires. This is in line with the principle of least privilege, which dictates that accounts should have only the permissions they need to complete their tasks, minimizing the potential damage from accidental misconfigurations or malicious attacks. Service accounts can also be used in tandem with security policies to control access to cloud resources, offering fine-grained security control.

- **Patch management**: Patch management in a public cloud environment is a critical aspect of maintaining a secure and stable infrastructure. Leveraging cloud-native tools for inventory management, vulnerability scanning, and automated patching can help organizations maintain a robust security posture while also taking advantage of the scalability and flexibility that cloud environments offer. Cloud providers often offer built-in services for automating routine tasks, including patch management, allowing organizations to keep their systems up-to-date more easily with the latest security patches and feature updates. One of the critical steps in cloud patch management is to maintain an inventory of all assets. Knowing what instances, services, and software are running is crucial for identifying what needs to be patched. Cloud services often come with tagging features that make it easier to classify and manage resources. Once an inventory is established, organizations can use automated scanning tools to identify vulnerabilities that need patching. These scans can be scheduled to run at regular intervals and can trigger automated workflows to apply patches as they become available.

- **Container security**: As organizations continue to develop cloud-native applications, a paradigm shift is often necessary when it comes to container security. Although microservices-based architecture can offer extreme scale, flexibility, and agility for IT and business alike, it warrants a specialized set of security controls. Some best practices and considerations for container security include the following:

    - Leveraging a container-optimized OS that has a smaller OS footprint that is ideal and security-hardened for use with containers.

    - Using cloud-native tools, such as binary authorization, to certify and trust container images before deployment and regularly updating them with security patches.

    - Restricting container registry access to prevent unauthorized access to container images.

    - Using immutable images to prevent malicious deployments.

    - Implementing runtime security measures such as using tools to monitor malicious activity.

- **Encryption**: Encryption is critical to secure data both at rest and in transit. Most cloud providers offer turnkey solutions and tools to automatically encrypt and decrypt storage volumes, persistent disks, and network traffic. However, organizations can leverage customized on-premises key management solutions to manage encryption keys or use HSM key management solutions to further improve security posture.

- **Confidential computing environments**: Enterprises in highly regulated industries or processing sensitive data can leverage a confidential computing option offered by most public cloud providers. It involves the use of specialized hardware and firmware to protect the **data in**

use, where the data are decrypted for processing and are exposed to various risks, including unauthorized system access or potential hackers. Confidential computing, also commonly referred to as shielded VMs in GCP and the Nitro System in AWS, accomplished this through the use of specialized hardware – often referred to as **Trusted execution environments** (TEEs) or secure enclaves – that isolates and executes code in a secure portion of the processor. By safeguarding data throughout their lifecycle, confidential computing opens new possibilities for secure data analytics, privacy-preserving computations, and cross-organizational data sharing, among other applications.

- **Factory pattern**: Finally, automation is critical to security, as it prevents user error and allows for a **secure by default** operation in the cloud. By configuring a security blueprint through IaC automation tools, such as Terraform, which encompass predefined authentication, authorization, logging, monitoring, approved trusted images for VMs and containers (also known as golden images), and preventive and detective controls, enterprises can ensure security-first cloud transformation.

Application security

As enterprises migrate existing applications to the cloud or build net-new cloud-native applications, concerns about application security loom large. While cloud environments offer unparalleled scalability and flexibility and serve as a launchpad for innovation, they also introduce a set of unique security challenges, especially for applications. Effective application security in the cloud requires a blend of traditional practices tailored for on-premises software and new approaches that are unique to cloud environments. One of the foundational elements of application security in the cloud is secure design. This includes both the architecture of the application itself and how it interacts with other services within the cloud. Regardless of the application development strategy and framework chosen, such as a 12-factor app or 15-factor app, adopting a *secure-by-design* approach from the inception of the development process can minimize vulnerabilities. For instance, implementing microservices-based architecture can isolate failures and potential security breaches to a smaller surface area, thus limiting damage:

- **Application migration**: For applications that are migrated to a cloud – especially in lift-and-shift or move-and-improve scenarios, enforcing cloud-native best practices may not be possible or minimal. In such cases, enterprises can fortify application security by modernizing peripheral application components with cloud-native components; these include leveraging native cloud virtualization instead of hypervisor lift-and-shift, cloud-native load balancers augmented with **web application firewalls** (**WAF**) to prevent against SQL injection, code injection, and **cross-site scripting** (XSS), and secure computing environments such as confidential computing, hardened Oss, and kernel IPCs.

- **Cloud-native app development**: Enterprises embarking on refactoring or re-architecture application development strategies can leverage modern AppDev principles such as 12-factor or 15-factor methodologies to develop secure cloud-native applications [7]. This helps leverage declarative formats for application setup automation, ensure maximum portability regardless of deployment platform, build resilient, scalable applications, and minimize divergence between development and production. Let us briefly review the 15 factors of cloud-native application development:

- **Code base**: One code base tracked in revision control, with many deploys

- **Dependencies**: Explicitly declare and isolate dependencies

- **Configuration**: Store the config in the environment

- **Backing services**: Treat backing services as attached resources

- **Build, release, and run**: Strictly separate the build and run stages

- **Processes**: Execute the app as one or more stateless processes

- **Port binding**: Export services via port binding

- **Concurrency**: Scale-out via the process model

- **Disposability**: Maximize robustness with fast startup and graceful shutdown

- **Dev/prod parity**: Keep development, staging, and production as similar as possible

- **Logs**: Treat logs as event streams

- **Admin processes**: Run admin/management tasks as one-off processes

- **API-first**: Define service contracts

- **Telemetry**: Monitor process performance

- **Authentication**: Secure applications across the hardware, network, and software layers

- **API security**: In cloud environments, applications interact with other services and resources through APIs. Securing these APIs is crucial for the overall application security. This involves using secure methods for API calls, securing APIs behind an API gateway, leveraging modern authentication and authorization protocols, such as OpenID and OAuth, using **JSON web tokens** (**JWTs**) for internal API communications, and creating scopes for application API access are some best practices.

- **DevSecOps practices**: Integrating security into DevOps is critical to ensure a security-first architecture and is a recommended best practice, as DevSecOps aims to secure the application development process by integrating security early and throughout the **software development lifecycle** (**SDLC**). This is also more commonly referred to as **shift left**. For instance, as can be seen from *Figure 6.13*, security aspects are integrated early on and through the architecture planning phase, integrating **static application security testing** (**SAST**) to analyze and find source code vulnerabilities, software composition analysis, **dynamic analysis security testing** (**DAST**) to detect vulnerabilities in running applications, performing penetration testing, vulnerability tests, compliance validation, logging, auditing, security monitoring, threat intelligence, and compliance validation.

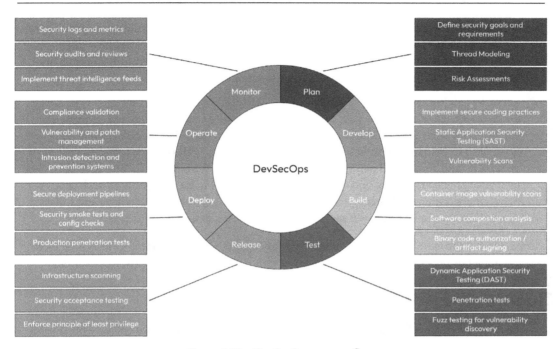

Figure 6.13 – DevSecOps process flow

- **API management**: By adding a proxy layer to cloud services, the API gateway serves as an abstraction or facade to secure backend APIs. API management platforms also help abstract away application code to enforce quotas and service levels through spike arrests, threat protection, data masking, and audit traffic.

- **Microservices**: While offering tremendous flexibility and scale, well-architected microservices-based architectures most importantly reduce the attack surface by containing the requests from laterally traversing the environment, and it is imperative to integrate security into the SDLC from code building, continuous integration, and deployment. For instance, leveraging container analysis vulnerability scan tools, securing artifact or container registry within a service perimeter, and using binary authorization to allow only trusted images to deploy can help secure the cloud environments in multiple tiers.

- **Service mesh**: A service mesh offers robust capabilities for managing complex, distributed, microservices-based applications. It operates on the principle of zero trust and does not simply rely on a network perimeter for security, requiring verification at each touchpoint. Employing best practices such as **mutual TLS (mTLS)**, fine-grained authorization, a centralized **certificate authority (CA)** for key and certificate management, continuous monitoring, sidecar and perimeter proxies for **policy enforcement points (PEPs)**, and configuration automation can help improve the overall security of a cloud-native application.

- **Vulnerability management**: Regular penetration testing and vulnerability assessments are indispensable for identifying potential security weaknesses. Cloud providers often offer tools for the continuous monitoring and scanning of applications to identify known vulnerabilities, and third-party solutions can offer even more comprehensive capabilities.

- **Serverless architectures**: Serverless architectures, while offering many benefits such as scalability and cost-efficiency, also come with a different set of security considerations and, in many ways, can be more secure than traditional server-based architectures. For instance, since there are no servers to manage, the attack surface associated with serverlessness is reduced. Due to its ephemeral and short-lived nature, serverlessness can limit the window for attack vectors, can be resilient to DDoS attacks, and can take advantage of built-in security features, such as RBAC, private networking, and encryption. By applying the principle of least privilege and isolating in a separate container, the blast radius of serverlessness can also be minimized.

Having reviewed the various considerations on how to design and architect for a security-first cloud environment, let us now explore some anti-patterns while developing cloud-native applications.

Cloud-native anti-patterns

As we have explored thus far, cloud-native architectures have revolutionized the way businesses reimagine IT and manage and deploy their software and services. It offers a range of benefits, such as scalability, flexibility, and cost-effectiveness. However, the cloud is not a panacea for all problems. In fact, with the benefits come challenges, and these challenges often manifest as anti-patterns – common practices that lead to unintended consequences and hinder the full potential of cloud-native solutions. Understanding these anti-patterns can help avoid the pitfalls and capitalize on the benefits of cloud computing. In this section, we will review some of the common cloud-native anti-patterns to watch for while embarking on a cloud transformation.

Monolith castles in the cloud

One of the common anti-patterns in cloud transformation is the lift and shift of monoliths to the cloud. Although there are certain exceptions to this anti-pattern, such as a contractual obligation or a data center exit scenario, where it is used as an intermediate stage before a cloud-native transformation, this is a more commonly used pattern across enterprises of all sizes. Monolithic architecture, while widely used in traditional software development, can present several downsides when applied to cloud environments. Since monolithic applications are designed to operate as a single unit, it can hinder scalability, slow down responsiveness, and prevent organizations from leveraging modern technologies:

- **Hindered scalability**: Monolithic applications are typically designed as single units, making it challenging to scale individual components independently. In cloud environments, the ability to scale resources dynamically to handle varying workloads is crucial. With a monolithic architecture, scaling requires scaling the entire application, even if only certain parts are experiencing increased demand. This can lead to inefficient resource utilization and higher costs.

- **Reduced agility**: Cloud-native applications are expected to be agile and responsive to changing requirements. Monolithic architectures can slow down development cycles since any changes or updates to the application requires extensive testing and co-ordination due to the interconnected nature of the components. This can hinder the rapid iteration and deployment that cloud-native development encourages.

- **Single point of failure**: Cloud-native architectures promote fault tolerance by isolating and replicating components and services for high availability. Monolithic applications, on the other hand, have a single point of failure. If a part of the monolith fails, the entire application might become unavailable, impacting user experience and business operations. Cloud environments offer opportunities to build resilient and highly available systems, which can be challenging with a monolithic architecture.

- **Technology innovation**: Cloud platforms provide a wide range of services and tools that can enhance application performance, innovation, security, and scalability. In a monolithic architecture, adopting new technologies or services to serve business demands can be complex due to the interdependencies within the application. This can prevent organizations from fully unleashing the capabilities of the cloud platform.

- **The perils of overprovisioning**: Monolithic applications often require static resource allocation to ensure the proper functioning of the entire stack. In cloud environments, resources can be allocated dynamically to match demand, improving resource utilization and cost-efficiency. Monolithic architectures often result in the overprovisioning or underutilization of resources, impacting operational costs.

Ignoring resource and cost optimization

Resource and cost optimization are key considerations and highlights of a cloud transformation. Ignoring cost optimizations in a cloud environment can have significant negative consequences for businesses, potentially leading to overspending, budgetary constraints, and inefficient resource utilization. This is one of the common anti-patterns for enterprises that leads to inefficient resource utilization in the cloud and diminished ROI on cloud initiatives:

- **Overprovisioning**: A common anti-pattern that most enterprises carry over from a traditional on-premises mindset is the over-provisioning of resources. Sizing for high watermarks or peak usage and allocating resources in anticipation is an anti-pattern for cloud-native architectures. Cloud resources are typically billed based on usage, and without monitoring and control, it is easy to overspend on services that are not being fully utilized. Ignoring cost optimizations can lead to ballooning expenses, impacting the overall financial health of the organization.

- **Inefficient resource utilization**: Without proper cost optimization strategies, organizations might provision more resources than necessary, resulting in underutilization. This wastes valuable computing power and increases costs without delivering proportional value to business.

- **Missed opportunities**: Most cloud providers offer various cost optimization and FinOps tools and features, such as auto-scaling, reserved instances, spot instances, and spend or commit-based discounts. Failure to take advantage of these opportunities can lead to missed opportunities to reduce costs while maintaining or improving service quality.

- **Diminished ROI**: Cloud investments are meant to provide a return on investment by delivering value through improved performance, scalability, and efficiency. Ignoring cost optimizations can erode the potential ROI, as the benefits of cloud services might be outweighed by unnecessary expenses.

- **Limited innovation**: Overspending on cloud resources can drain resources that could otherwise be invested in innovative projects and other strategic initiatives. Ignoring cost optimizations can hinder an organization's ability to allocate resources for business growth and technological advancement.

Undifferentiated heavy lifting

This anti-pattern occurs when organizations manage operational tasks, such as resource provisioning and maintenance, which could be automated through cloud services. This can lead to increased complexity, reduced agility, and operational overhead that distracts from core business goals. Undifferentiated heavy lifting encompasses the operational tasks that cloud users need to manage but that do not provide a competitive advantage or contribute directly to their core business objectives. These tasks include activities such as provisioning servers, managing databases, configuring networking, and ensuring security compliance. While essential for the smooth functioning of cloud resources, these tasks can divert valuable time and resources away from innovation and core business activities. Another variant of this anti-pattern is the overuse or over-reliance on open source or third-party tools and offerings instead of a simple cloud-native or provider-native offering. For example, deploying a PostgreSQL database on a compute VM instead of leveraging a managed database offering that supports PostgreSQL natively for fear of vendor lock-in. This could be a highly undifferentiated heavy lift for an enterprise because the underlying software – in this case, PostgreSQL – is a database standard and can easily be ported or migrated to a different deployment platform. Some key challenges with this anti-pattern include the following:

- **Resource drain**: Organizations often spend significant time and effort managing infrastructure-related tasks that do not directly differentiate their products or services in the market. This diverts resources from strategic initiatives and innovation, which is one of the key impediments of this anti-pattern.

- **Solution complexity**: Purely leveraging a cloud platform as yet another infrastructure or as a replacement to on-premises environments can overly complicate the solution. This can quickly become overwhelming to maintain and manage.

- **Time-to-market delays**: The time spent on undifferentiated heavy lifting can slow down development cycles and time-to-market for new features and services.

Bloated containers

Another common anti-pattern for enterprises building cloud-native applications is the challenge of **bloated containers**. A bloated container refers to a situation where the size of a container increases, which can lead to several challenges that can impact the efficiency, performance, and manageability of the application cluster. A container image size can increase due to various factors, such as inefficient dependency management, unused build artifacts, unnecessary layer caching, building an image with a full operating system as a base layer, and building images with large binaries, such as compiled executables or media files. Some key challenges with this anti-pattern include the following:

- **Inefficient resource consumption**: Bloated containers consume more CPU, memory, and storage resources. This can lead to inefficient resource utilization, resulting in higher costs and reduced overall cluster performance.

- **Scalability**: Containers that are too large can impact the ability of Kubernetes to efficiently scale applications. When scaling is based on resource utilization, larger containers might lead to inaccurate scaling decisions, resulting in the overprovisioning or underprovisioning of resources.

- **Slow startup times**: Larger containers typically take longer to start up, as they need to load more resources and dependencies. This can slow down deployment and scaling processes, affecting the responsiveness of your applications.

- **Increased attack surface**: Larger containers may contain unnecessary software or dependencies, increasing the potential attack surface and security risks. Unpatched or unnecessary software can make applications vulnerable to exploits and attacks.

- **Troubleshooting complexity**: Bloated containers can make troubleshooting and debugging more complex, as identifying performance bottlenecks, resource contention issues, or compatibility problems becomes harder when a container has numerous components and dependencies.

- **Network traffic**: Containers with excessive dependencies can generate more network traffic, affecting overall network performance and leading to congestion or latency issues.

- **Resource fragmentation**: Large containers might require more resources than are available on a single node. This could lead to resource fragmentation and under-utilization, as multiple smaller containers could have been scheduled on the same node.

- **Maintainability**: Managing large or complex containers becomes more challenging over time. Upgrading, patching, and maintaining such containers can be error-prone and time-consuming.

Mutable infrastructure

Mutable infrastructure refers to the practice of making changes directly to existing infrastructure components rather than replacing them with new ones. In the context of cloud computing, this involves modifying existing resources such as virtual machines, databases, and networking components rather than creating new instances from scratch, which can be an anti-pattern. Cloud-native architecture advocates for infrastructure components to be treated as immutable, which refers to the practice of creating new instances instead of modifying existing ones. Some of the challenges with mutable infrastructure in the cloud include the following:

- **Configuration drift**: Over time, with mutable infrastructure, configuration settings on different instances might deviate from their original state, leading to configuration drift. This can result in inconsistencies and difficulties in maintaining a predictable and stable environment.

- **Dependency management**: As incremental modifications to components are made in mutable infrastructure, the dependencies between those components can become complex and hard to manage. Ensuring that changes to one component don't inadvertently impact others requires careful consideration.

- **Rollback challenges**: In case of a failed update or a problem caused by a change, rolling back the changes can be more challenging in a mutable infrastructure setup. This requires that rollback mechanisms are well-defined and tested to minimize downtime and potential data loss.

- **Version control and tracking**: Managing changes to mutable infrastructure components can be challenging without proper version control and tracking mechanisms. Keeping track of changes, who made them, and why they were made is crucial for troubleshooting and auditing.

As organizations embark on a cloud transformation journey, anti-patterns can be detrimental to the optimal utilization of cloud value. Comprehending and recognizing these anti-patterns is crucial for organizations to avoid costly mistakes, maximize efficiency, and improve reliability while maximizing cloud benefits.

Summary

In this chapter, we focused on how organizations can build a robust, open, and agile foundation for a cloud-ready enterprise that can support current and future business demands. We explored the four stages of a cloud adoption framework, namely assess, plan, deploy, and optimize, and the key constituents in each stage that can provide a structured approach to a cloud transformation initiative. We also discussed, in detail, the various hybrid and multi-cloud deployment patterns that enterprises can adopt, with a particular focus on organizations that have a heavy on-premises IT footprint, acknowledging the challenges with cloud adoption.

As organizations navigate the complexities of hybrid and multi-cloud deployments, an extensible yet secure network architecture is extremely crucial to support the key considerations, such as high availability, optimized performance, and scale. With this in consideration, we reviewed some of the core foundational network architecture blueprints, their applicability, and their considerations. We also delved into how enterprises can architect security as a first-class citizen of their cloud environment with a focus on various security aspects such as identity and access management, infrastructure, and application security. Then, we explored the security models offered by major cloud service providers AWS, Azure, and Google Cloud.

Finally, we discussed the five cloud-native anti-patterns that are often a common pitfall for organizations that shift from on-premises to the cloud. In the next chapter, we will explore the cloud use cases of some major enterprises.

Further readings

The references used in this chapter as well as some additional resources are listed as follows:

1. AWS shared responsibility model: `https://aws.amazon.com/compliance/shared-responsibility-model/`

2. AWS security foundations: `https://docs.aws.amazon.com/prescriptive-guidance/latest/security-reference-architecture/foundations.html`

3. Azure shared responsibility model: `https://learn.microsoft.com/en-us/azure/security/fundamentals/shared-responsibility`

4. Azure security benchmark foundations: `https://learn.microsoft.com/en-us/azure/governance/blueprints/samples/azure-security-benchmark-foundation/`

5. Google Cloud shared fate model: `https://cloud.google.com/architecture/framework/security/shared-responsibility-shared-fate`

6. Google cloud enterprise foundations: `https://cloud.google.com/architecture/security-foundations#a_defense-in-depth_security_model`

7. 12 Factor App: `https://12factor.net/`

7
Hybrid Cloud Use Cases

In the last decade, cloud computing has not just solved common challenges for enterprises, such as on-demand service provisioning, scaling, and reducing total cost of ownership – it has evolved into an engine of digital transformation by democratizing modern technology. With customer experience taking center stage, speed to market, resiliency, and availability are table stakes for any business to thrive. As organizations seek to disrupt the market through modern technologies such as Web 3.0, generative AI, or the metaverse, cloud computing becomes the de facto standard for business transformation. Just a decade ago, organizations that had the capital, resources, and wherewithal to build and maintain a Tier 4 data center had an uncanny edge over their competitors who operated within a Tier 1 data center. Cloud computing has democratized computing, along with access to modern technologies for businesses of any size, to innovate and deliver at scale.

Crucially, cloud computing has enabled enterprises to lead a technology-driven business transformation that is otherwise impossible or extremely difficult to develop a muscle on. For instance, developing an application with modern AI capabilities requires building a server infrastructure AI farm, which can be resource-intensive both in terms of effort and cost. Stack the ever-changing landscape of hardware technology on top and this can quickly become cost-prohibitive and unscalable. A cloud-based infrastructure not only provides on-demand access to modern hardware but more importantly allows teams to experiment, fail fast, and rapidly innovate.

In this chapter, we will explore a few case studies of enterprises that have embraced the cloud in various capacities, challenges with existing models, the driving factors for cloud adoption, and the business benefits that they realized.

In this chapter, we will go through the use cases of the following companies/businesses:

- Airbnb
- Carrefour
- Wendy's
- Capital One

Airbnb – leading business transformation through technology

Airbnb, founded in 2008, is an online marketplace with a mission to offer both short and long-term homestays and unique experiences to its consumers. The company offers a web-based platform that connects guests and hosts in various destinations across the world, where the hosts can list their properties, while guests can search, look up availability and prices, and book accommodation. Since its inception, Airbnb has had over 5 million hosts on its platform and has served over 1.5 billion guests across the world.

Disrupting the hospitality industry

Airbnb has reported a revenue of 8.4B USD in 2022 and boasts an 80B USD market capita [1]. For perspective, Airbnb's revenue was 400M USD in 2014 and has had a multifold YoY growth. Airbnb disrupted the traditional hospitality industry in several ways, including fundamentally changing the way people travel and book accommodations. In a way, Airbnb became a hospitality industry leader by just building a community platform on the internet while not having to own, operate, and maintain properties. Some of the key ways in which Airbnb disrupted the industry are as follows:

- **Introducing a peer-to-peer model**: Airbnb introduced a peer-to-peer model, allowing individuals to rent out their homes or spare rooms to travelers. This was a departure from traditional hospitality models, where travelers typically stayed in hotels, motels, or other commercial accommodations.

- **Diversified accommodation options**: Airbnb offers a creative range of accommodation options, including apartments, houses, condos, and even unique spaces, such as treehouses or houseboats. This diversity was a departure from how traditional hotels or resorts operated with standardized offerings. This also enabled Airbnb to create and offer unique experiences to their guests while also making it economically viable for the hosts, leading to a win-win-win strategy.

- **Think global, be local**: Airbnb provides travelers with a unique opportunity to experience a destination like a local. Staying in someone's home can offer a more authentic and one-of-a-kind experience compared to a standard hotel. This allowed Airbnb to scale beyond the traditional premises of a hotel and connect guests with their hosts.

- **Flexible reservations**: Airbnb introduced flexible booking options, including short-term and long-term rentals. This flexibility offered tremendous flexibility for travelers with varying needs, from simple weekend getaways to extended stays.

- **Community platform**: Airbnb built a sense of community and trust by allowing hosts and guests to leave reviews, feedback, and ratings. This system of feedback served as a means of trust to help both hosts and travelers make informed decisions. More importantly, Airbnb had an economic impact on communities by allowing hosts to earn income by renting out their spaces while also helping guests with unique experiences.

- **Digital platform**: Airbnb focused on creating an easy-to-use, scalable digital platform, making it extremely simple and easy for its community members to browse, book, and manage accommodations via just a browser or a mobile application. This allowed Airbnb to expand its presence globally, enabling travelers to find accommodations virtually in any corner of the world.

A business born in the cloud

Airbnb has a unique business model that is primarily reliant on a seamless, resilient, and scalable digital platform. Due to this, Airbnb needed a modern IT infrastructure that could scale on demand and help expand the business to support global operations with a particular focus on impeccable customer experience and speed to market. With a lean IT supporting the platform, it was critical to have the resources focus on core, high-value business functions rather than expending on mundane activities such as IT operations and ongoing maintenance. Airbnb was founded roughly 2 years after the launch of **Amazon Web Services (AWS)**. Cloud computing was an obvious choice for Airbnb as it offered the much-needed on-demand, managed, scalable, and resilient infrastructure to help them up and running in quick order. By being cloud-native, Airbnb was able to start with a simple cloud architecture for their platform while also being able to adapt and realize operational and financial efficiencies over time. Let's review how Airbnb evolved its services and efficiencies over time.

The first architecture

A huge part of Airbnb's success as a business venture can be attributed to its agility in adopting cutting-edge technology over time to adapt to changing trends, ensuring top customer experience, and seamlessly adapting to its business needs. At a time when the cloud was still niche, Airbnb leveraged cloud technology for two primary objectives – the ability to seamlessly scale as the business expands and operate with a super lean IT operations team. Airbnb leveraged some of the first cloud service offerings from AWS such as EC2, S3, RDS, DynamoDB, ElastiCache, and Route53 to build a simple and scalable yet resilient platform. This architecture was dubbed monorail due to the monolithic nature of the application that was powered by Ruby on Rails. The platform leveraged some of the basic cloud services offered by AWS *[2]*:

- **EC2**: Web servers, applications, and services
- **S3**: Store the ever-growing photos and videos of the property listings
- **ElastiCache**: Improve performance through data caching
- **RDS**: To handle transactional data
- **DynamoDB**: Metadata, NoSQL, and rollups

- **Route 53**: The following figure gives you an idea of Airbnb's initial cloud architecture:

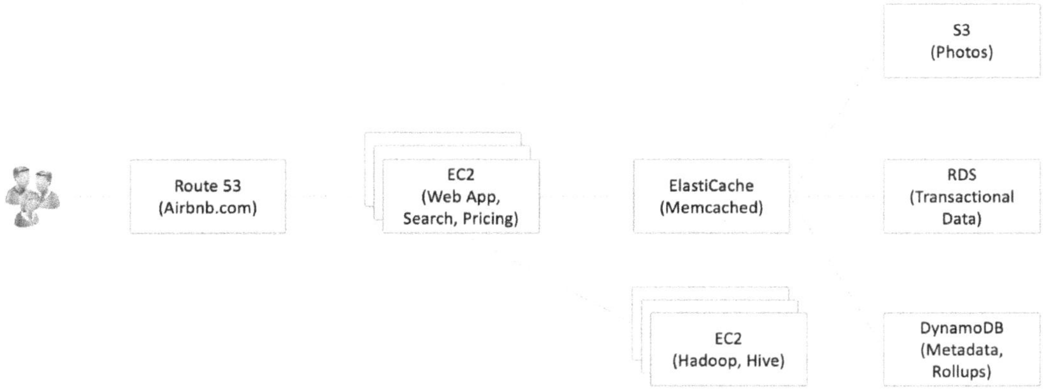

Figure 7.1 – Airbnb's initial cloud architecture

This was perfect for the initial demands and needs of the Airbnb platform as it took a few years for Airbnb to garner popularity and gain momentum. This monolith platform offered several benefits, such as simplicity, being easier to build, monitor, and deploy, and also reduced overhead, allowing the small team to quickly get Airbnb off the ground. The cloud platform was able to seamlessly scale on-demand to support the growth spurt at Airbnb as the total number of users more than doubled from 4 million to 9 million in 2013. Some of the first services include property search, pricing, and fraud prediction. It is important to note that Airbnb was able to continuously meet consumer demands with an extremely lean team, where this architecture was supported by just a five-member operations team.

Evolution to microservices

As Airbnb continued to globally expand and was entering a hyper-growth phase, the initial monorail platform offered some challenges. Airbnb was at an inflection point. For instance, it was not possible to scale monoliths infinitely, release new features quickly, and offer seamless developer collaboration, especially as the organization was growing in strength. In 2014, Airbnb went through a major rebranding exercise. This also meant the engineering team at Airbnb had to devote a significant amount of their resources to redesign every aspect of their platform. By 2016, Airbnb launched **Airbnb Experiences**, where local hosts or tour operators around the world can design and offer unique experiences for guests. Based on the overwhelmingly positive customer experiences and feedback, Airbnb also launched Airbnb Plus and Airbnb Collections. By being cloud-first, Airbnb was quickly able to pivot from a monolithic architecture to a cloud-native service-oriented architecture without any concern for tech debt. Not just that, the cloud enabled Airbnb teams to quickly experiment, deploy, and scale new features at scale *[3] [4]*.

With over a thousand engineers focused on delivering cutting-edge services, Airbnb was able to refactor the monorail into a service-oriented architecture, allowing for an API-driven approach that modularized independent service components, standardized communication protocols, and scaled services independently, resulting in easier maintenance. This provided better accountability and the ability to deliver new features faster and aid with business agility. This platform was also able to seamlessly cater to newer platforms such as mobile, and the results showed this. Airbnb experienced significantly lesser downtime of their platform due to reduced rollbacks and saw page performance improve by 10x.

From an architectural perspective, Airbnb weaned off core infrastructure services such as EC2 and moved to a Kubernetes platform to better align to the microservices paradigm. A very crucial improvement was that the microservices architecture based on Kubernetes allowed Airbnb to automatically scale individual services independently on demand, as shown in the following microservices architecture below *[5]*:

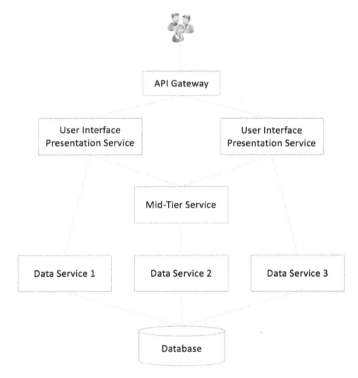

Figure 7.2 – Airbnb's microservices architecture

Several of the key incremental improvements enabled Airbnb to scale the platform to support a user base that contains hundreds of millions, investing in a common infrastructure with a combination of in-house and open source technologies. Some of the key architectural components are as follows:

- **API framework**: An in-house framework developed on Thrift over HTTP

- **Powergrid**: A **directed acyclic graph** (**DAG**) to orchestrate and manage tasks

- **OneTouch**: A Kubernetes framework that allows efficient management of services across environments

- **Spinnaker**: An open source continuous delivery platform

- **GraphQL**: A consolidated schema for data access

This was an important milestone in Airbnb's continuous digital transformation, thus embracing cloud technology to further business objectives *[6]*:

Multi-cloud adoption and transformation

As Airbnb continued to expand globally, the teams grew globally as well. Protecting mission-critical corporate applications running across on-premises as well as the cloud became a top priority. Airbnb.com was primarily hosted on AWS while some specific supporting services ran within the on-premises data center for latency considerations. For a while, Airbnb, like any corporate enterprise, leveraged traditional technologies such as VPN for their associates to connect to corporate applications. However, as teams traveled or connected to corporate applications and services from various locations, securing access while also allowing a seamless experience was a challenge. Restricting access purely over VPN meant it was either slow or the experience was inconsistent. Airbnb wanted to transform the way security was implemented by offering low latency connectivity to their associates, irrespective of their location, while also enabling them to work from anywhere – land or air – so long as they had access to the internet.

The solution came in the form of **BeyondCorp**, a security model developed by Google that leverages identity and context to evaluate trust for access decisions rather than using the corporate network as the perimeter *[7]*. Airbnb quickly adopted a multi-cloud strategy where Google Cloud would manage the network and security posture for Airbnb services, irrespective of where they ran. A high-level architecture of how Airbnb leveraged BeyondCorp's context-aware access is shown here:

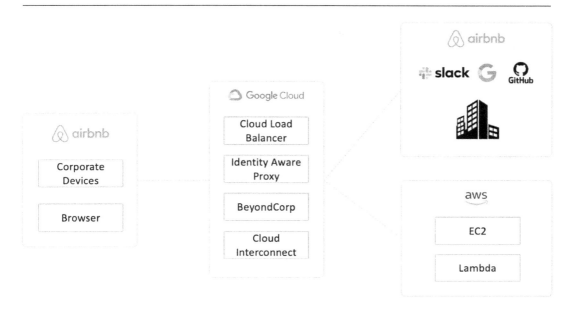

Figure 7.3 – Airbnb's multi-cloud architecture

The pandemic and economic slowdown – the optimization phase

Another key capability that cloud-based architecture enables for enterprises is the ability to rapidly experiment with new technology at a much lower risk threshold, while also keeping the costs in check. The Covid-19 pandemic had large-scale impacts on several industries and businesses across the world and Airbnb was no exception. However, early on, Airbnb formed a cloud FinOps team and began investigating its cloud usage for optimization avenues, partly in preparation for its IPO, and achieved significant cloud cost optimizations. The cloud governance and FinOps practices enabled Airbnb to respond to the global pandemic impact better than some of its peers, who were laying off scores of workers. Airbnb was able to optimize its cloud storage costs by approximately 27% and 60% in *OpenSearch* service costs *[8]*.

Let's look at some of the key cloud optimizations that Airbnb performed:

- **Identifying and visualizing the current cloud usage across the board while leveraging the tools that cloud providers offer**: In this case, Airbnb leveraged the cost allocation visualization engine known as AWS Cost Explorer and the data from AWS Cost & Usage Report tools. This helped Airbnb to visualize, understand, manage, and optimize its cloud stack at a granular level.

- **Identifying and optimizing large data storage across cloud environments**: Cloud providers offer various tiers of data storage options – from instant access to archival – to serve specific application needs. In this case, Airbnb leveraged AWS S3's intelligent tiering to optimize and align the right data storage needs with the right storage tier, resulting in significant storage cost savings.

- **Creating a flat network in the cloud**: This not only enabled cost savings but also resulted in low maintenance and improved performance efficiencies.

- **Identifying and leveraging the various savings plans and contracting vehicles in place**: By doing this, Airbnb was able to reap higher savings to run the same workloads. For instance, commitment to a certain baseline usage that is guaranteed to be used helped Airbnb realize significant cost benefits at discounted pricing.

- **Transferring to defined serverless platforms**: Moving from primitive dedicated compute infrastructure to serverless platforms with application-defined scale-out rules can yield a positive impact on cost savings.

- **Leveraging interactive log analytics and real-time applications**:As an ongoing FinOps best practice, Airbnb also leverages interactive log analytics and real-time application monitoring capabilities to continuously evaluate and optimize cloud costs.

By adopting a cloud-first cloud-native approach, Airbnb not only disrupted the hospitality industry through technology but also was successful in adapting to the dynamic market conditions while also being agile and customer-centric.

Carrefour's sustainable digital transformation journey

Carrefour, founded in 1959, is a multinational retail corporation that is one of the world's largest and well-known supermarket and hypermarket chains. As of 2024, Carrefour remains the eighth largest retailer in the world, with a global presence serving across 30 countries and operating over 12,225 stores. Carrefour operates various retail formats, including hypermarkets, supermarkets, convenience stores, and e-commerce platforms, while offering a wide range of products, including fresh food, groceries, electronics, clothing and home goods. Carrefour is considered an industry leader in leading some of the bold and successful digital transformation initiatives, including the development of modern e-commerce platforms and digital services, to enhance customer shopping experiences. Carrefour has also been involved in various sustainability and environmental initiatives, including commitments to reduce its carbon footprint, promote sustainable sourcing, and reduce food waste. Carrefour's success in the retail industry has made it a significant player in the global marketplace, offering a variety of products and services to consumers in many countries. Its continuous expansion and adaptation to changing consumer needs have allowed it to maintain its prominent position in the retail sector.

Carrefour's digital transformation is part of a broader effort to remain competitive in the ever-evolving retail marketplace, where digital technology and changing consumer behaviors play a significant role. This transformation allowed the company to meet the demands of an increasingly digital and connected customer base and to optimize its operations for efficiency and sustainability. Some of the key aspects of Carrefour's digital transformation initiatives are as follows:

- **e-commerce modernization**: Carrefour leveraged the cloud to significantly expand its e-commerce operations, allowing customers to shop for groceries and a wide range of products online. This includes both traditional e-commerce platforms and mobile apps, offering its customers the ability to shop creatively by ordering and receiving deliveries or choosing click-and-collect options. This allowed Carrefour to dynamically scale to meet consumer demand and offer personalized recommendations while also optimizing costs associated with operations and infrastructure maintenance.

- **Digital services**: Carrefour introduced various digital services to enhance the customer experience, including online ordering, home delivery, and features such as digital catalogs, shopping lists, and personalized recommendations. It also developed mobile applications that provide customers with convenient ways to shop, access discounts and promotions, and manage their loyalty cards. Carrefour also adopted and offered various digital payment methods, including mobile wallets and contactless payment options, to facilitate faster and more convenient transactions for customers.

- **Loyalty programs**: Carrefour has digitized its loyalty programs, offering customers personalized discounts and rewards based on their shopping habits and preferences.

- **Supply chain optimization**: Digital technology enabled Carrefour to improve the efficiency of its supply chain, reducing costs and forecast demand accurately ensuring the availability of products in stores and for online orders.

- **Omnichannel integration**: Carrefour has worked to integrate its offline and online channels to offer customers a seamless shopping experience. This empowered customers to shop flexibly which Carrefour defines as "*Whatever you want, Wherever you want, Whenever you want, and However you want*". This allowed Carrefour to reactivate lost customers, increase loyalty, and increase online sales.

- **Data insights**: Carrefour leveraged modern data analytics to gain insights into customer behavior, shopping trends, and inventory management. This data-driven approach helped the company make informed decisions and improve operations.

- **Environmental initiatives**: Carrefour leveraged digital tools to promote sustainability. In 2018, Carrefour's Chairman and CEO, Alexandre Bompard launched the *Act for Food* global program of concrete initiatives to help its customers and employees eat better – wherever they are – at affordable prices. For instance, the company uses technology to reduce food waste, optimize energy consumption, and support eco-friendly initiatives.

- **Customer engagement**: Carrefour employed digital channels to engage with customers through marketing, social media, and customer support, fostering a stronger brand-consumer relationship. This has been extremely effective and helped Carrefour build a strong brand value with consumers.

- **Partnerships for innovation**: Carrefour entered strategic partnerships with tech companies and startups to drive retail innovation. These collaborations have led to the development of new services and solutions.

The Carrefour omnichannel strategy

In April 2017, at its investor day in Paris, Carrefour presented its retail strategy and its vision toward *The Empowered Consumer* by offering seamless omnichannel experiences *[9]*. The primary focus was on ensuring Carrefour's commitment to transparency and establishing a benchmark for quality, standards, and consumer loyalty. This was a year where Carrefour recognized the age of the new consumer who is more urban, more digitized, and more mobile, drawing attention to the data that was shared. Some interesting observations from the market survey data included the following:

- The urbanization rate in 2014 was 54% and is projected to be 66% in 2050

- Digital penetration grew seven-fold just between 2000 and 2016

- 34% of all purchases made by consumers were on mobile devices

- 58% of consumers prefer to shop online for want of 24/7 availability

In response to these statistics, Carrefour invested in building a multiformat, omnichannel retail experience for its consumers that is not only convenient and seamless but also offers a pleasant shopping experience. As part of the multiformat mission, each of Carrefour's formats focuses on offering a unique experience. For instance, the hypermarkets ensured consumers could virtually get everything that they needed under one roof at a competitive price, while the supermarkets were strategically located close to households with a focus on offering fresh food. The convenience stores carried household essentials with extended shopping hours, whereas the *Cash & Carry* stores offered products at wholesale prices for a no-frills experience. Most importantly, the e-commerce shop bolstered the product catalog with the broadest assortment of product categories for a well-rounded, convenient, any-time, any-place shopping experience. The e-commerce platform, *Carrefour banque et assurance*, also offered value-added services such as booking travel experiences, car rentals, and insurance.

The omnichannel model capitalized on the unique opportunity to ensure e-commerce sustainability. For instance, Carrefour integrated its supply chain, CRM, HR, e-commerce, and digital marketing for a seamless omnichannel transformation, operationalized the backend order management that enabled consumers to store-pick across formats (hypermarkets, supermarkets, or convenience), offered home delivery, and provided click and collect in-store and pick-up points such as lockers. This was a crucial factor that helped Carrefour's consumers across its ecosystem. It did this through long-term loyalty, an increase in wallet share and shopping frequency, rejuvenating the customer base, and regaining lost consumers.

Another critical aspect of Carrefour's digital transformation strategy is building a cohesive data strategy gathering relevant customer and operational data. Carrefour laid the foundations for a **Data-as-a-Service** model that helps extract meaningful insights from its vast first-party data mashed up with third-party data. First-party data includes consumer and operational data Carrefour sources from its e-commerce applications, mobile app, loyalty programs, and social media, while third-party data involves anonymous data. This valuable data enabled Carrefour to improve customer focus by offering personalized recommendations, detecting customer churn, and increasing loyalty while also improving operational focus by detecting anomalies in real time at **point of sale (POS)** and stockouts, and improving demand forecasting.

A bold initiative augmented by cloud transformation

In 2018, Carrefour launched *Act for Food*, a global program of concrete initiatives that enabled its customers to eat better – wherever they are – at affordable prices. This program aligned with the corporate-wide transformation plan of striving to become the world leader in the *food transition* across geographies. **Food transition** is defined as a transition to a sustainable food system where food is produced and consumed without compromising the economic, social, and environmental foundations for the nutrition of future generations. In the months that followed, Carrefour made a bold, strategic move to leverage cloud technology as a foundational backbone to instill technology at the service of its business objectives. This meant that Carrefour capitalized on its core digital transformation philosophy to partner with hyperscalers to rapidly innovate, lead, and transform. Carrefour chose Google Cloud as its strategic partner to not just help with the digital transformation journey but, more importantly, to leverage Google's expertise in retail-centric solutions, data analytics, artificial intelligence, marketing, media transformation, and the modern digital workplace *[11]*.

Until its cloud transformation journey, Carrefour leveraged a mix of on-premises data centers, private clouds, and public clouds primarily to support its e-commerce across geographies. These choices were often made locally by Carrefours in the local geographies, resulting in a scattered landscape of service providers. Carrefour laid the foundation for its cloud transformation journey across four key pillars:

- **Defining a cloud vision and strategy**: The central idea of Carrefour's digital transformation was focusing all IT efforts on serving its customers better. Carrefour observed the rapid retail evolution trend and recognized early on that speed to market was an absolute priority and developed a vision and strategy for digital transformation in the cloud.

- **Clarity on purpose-built cloud service models**: Just like every enterprise is unique, so is the digital transformation. Carrefour defined the criteria around the use of different cloud service models – IaaS, PaaS, and SaaS. For instance, while a bulk of its applications can be customized and modernized on IaaS and PaaS, certain support functions such as HR and finance could quickly benefit from purpose-built SaaS applications.

- **Organizational alignment**: When enterprises embark on a major digital transformation journey, the traditional organization must evolve and adapt to support the same. Carrefour recognized the need for a **cloud center of excellence (CCoE)** to develop expertise in cloud operations, manage the new stack, identify the right solutions, define the roadmap, recruit cloud SMEs, and define reference architectural blueprints, while also infusing critical governance functions such as cloud FinOps.

- **Communication**: One of the primary reasons for Carrefour's success with its large-scale cloud transformation can be attributed to effective communication. Carrefour made its intention on cloud transformation public while also ensuring the vision and strategy are well communicated across the organization. This was instrumental in setting the organizational direction and the motivation for teams to march towards that larger mission.

As Carrefour set out on a mission to digitally transform its retail business and innovate on the cloud, it laid out some very clear value propositions tied to business challenges:

- **Seamless scale**: Both architecturally and operationally, maintaining a monolith e-commerce platform was tough on the IT teams, which made it difficult to adapt to business demands. Adopting a cloud-native approach promised to address this challenge.

- **Time to market**: Time to market is directly proportional to business agility in responding to market demands. As Carrefour was on a mission to digitally transform its business, cloud computing complimented the strategy by removing a lot of mundane yet critical on-premises decisions, such as picking the right infrastructure, procurement, software, and hardware compliance, as well as capacity planning, directly improving time to market.

- **Continuous innovation**: Adopting a cloud-native and **free open source software** (**FOSS**) strategy helped Carrefour take advantage of bleeding-edge technology while also rapidly experimenting with low risk. Carrefour also recognized the need for continuous innovation in the highly competitive retail landscape to thrive and sustain.

- **Availability**: In its existing on-premises environments, achieving a sustained high availability was extremely challenging from both resource, cost, and time constraints. For instance, a three 9's availability versus a four 9's availability can seem like a small difference on the surface but can result in an 8x impact on application uptime.

- **Sustainability**: One of the primary motivators for cloud transformation was Carrefour's unwavering focus on sustainability across the board. Carrefour's cloud strategy can enable it to achieve a significantly higher **power usage effectiveness** (**PUE**), optimize energy usage, and reduce its global carbon footprint.

- **Security**: As cyber threats continue to be on the rise, securing the IT infrastructure has become more complex than ever. Through its cloud strategy, Carrefour can tap into the cloud provider's security expertise and access modern cloud-native security solutions and defense-in-depth security architecture to manage, monitor, and secure its critical applications and data.

- **Efficiency**: Through its cloud strategy, Carrefour could focus all its resources on business priorities instead of building and running data centers. Carrefour adopted a multi-modal cloud based on the nature of the use case to improve overall efficiencies.

Transforming legacy IT to the modern cloud

Carrefour operates in dozens of countries and one of the major challenges it identified was that each Carrefour group in each of the geographies had its own IT, data centers, applications, and choice of technology. This served well for a while; however, over the years, various groups within the organization built up an assortment of applications, resulting in a scattered and heterogeneous infrastructure environment with redundant solutions and data silos. With exponentially growing retail market demands, several of these applications, infrastructure, and solutions were hitting their limits, necessitating a refresh for a scalable, resilient, and modern IT strategy for the future. As Carrefour was building toward the future of retail, it adopted a streamlined and phased approach toward IT transformation across various regions.

Program GearUp

The first phase of cloud transformation at Carrefour started in 2019, where the primary focus was to improve IT operations to drive performance and innovation. This program was codenamed GearUp. The GearUp program's idea was to focus on reinventing IT and ensuring business alignment. This comprised the following aspects:

- **Assessing the current state**: This involved interviewing the business stakeholders to understand the business aspirations and concerns while also assessing the current IT landscape across infrastructure, applications, and business processes

- **Strategy alignment**: Carrefour partnered with Gartner through workshops to gain insights on strategy and organizational alignment

- **IT roadmap definition**: This involved defining the near-term, mid-term, and long-term roadmaps for various IT projects

- **Stakeholder communication**: Carrefour presented and communicated the vision, strategy, and roadmap to business and IT stakeholders and got buy-in.

Based on the preliminary assessment, one key challenge that Carrefour had to address was reinventing the 60-year-old organization and adapting itself to the next generation of IT. Carrefour identified a set of 23 pain points within the existing IT operations. Here are some of the operational and process changes that Carrefour affected that had a direct positive impact on its business priorities:

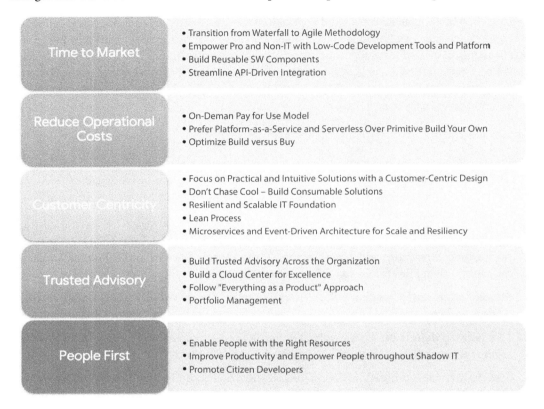

Figure 7.4 – Areas of focus for legacy IT transformation

Now that we've explored Carrefour's strategy in legacy IT transformation, let's review Carrefour Spain's digital transformation in the cloud.

Carrefour Spain's digital transformation

Carrefour's mission has been to transform the future of retail by offering the best shopping experience to its customers around the world with the best products at the best price. Carrefour Spain, the Spanish subsidiary, was one the first in the Carrefour group to embrace digital transformation with over 1,000 physical stores across the country and serving 1.4 million annual transactions online. To ensure Carrefour delivers the same high-quality service to its customers, irrespective of the shopping channel, it was crucial to collate data from multiple data streams and back-office functions relating to products, local inventory, pricing, and availability. Realizing the limitations of the existing on-premises IT infrastructure, the consumer demand for a seamless omnichannel shopping experience, and the potential to innovate with technology, Carrefour Spain decided to overhaul and modernize its aging IT infrastructure while also building a data-centric technology foundation for the future. Some of their primary objectives were as follows:

- **Consolidate and modernize the back office ERP infrastructure**

  Over the years, Carrefour had built up a flurry of applications and solutions on-premises to deal with its ERP requirements. This resulted in two major challenges – inconsistent data silos and legacy infrastructure that is not suited to support the business demand – resulting in a data sprawl and data silos. Carrefour Spain modernized its SAP on Google Cloud, which presented a perfect opportunity to standardize and consolidate its data streams and back-office business processes *[12]*. In 4 months, Carrefour was able to operationalize the first phase with a hybrid cloud infrastructure. With a cloud-based infrastructure for its ERP, Carrefour Spain was able to consolidate and integrate more than 2,000 data streams with a scalable infrastructure to collate, analyze, and act on the information in real time, which served as a foundational backbone for a data-centric infrastructure. This modernization also allowed Carrefour to quickly extend ERP functionality to integrate the **Internet of Things (IoT)** and ML capabilities for predictive analytics such as demand forecasting.

- **Modernize e-commerce to seamlessly scale and deliver new capabilities**

  Another key priority Carrefour Spain focused on was modernizing its e-commerce platform and infrastructure. The existing e-commerce platform was monolithic and was based on an aging on-premises infrastructure. The availability and resiliency of this platform were a huge concern, especially during the seasonal spikes in e-commerce traffic, as the company had to carefully assess and guess the capacity for on-premises infrastructure. Carrefour Spain replatformed its e-commerce on Google Cloud while taking advantage of the modern open source container technology Kubernetes, which helped deploy and scale seamlessly based on demand. This modern platform also allowed Carrefour Spain to deliver new capabilities to its customers rapidly instead of diverting resources to build, provision, scale, and manage the infrastructure. The results of this transformation were impressive and Carrefour Spain was able to scale seamlessly to accommodate and sustain a performance of over 20,000 operations per second, even at extreme traffic spikes of 4x the normal workload. The cloud-native platform also allowed them to deploy a wide variety of customer applications, from inventory to click and collect.

- **Build a cloud-centric foundation for the future**

  The cloud migration made a significant impact on Carrefour's IT teams, especially on the way they worked. For instance, the developers were able to focus on code and experiment rapidly instead of solving infrastructure capacity challenges and environment parity concerns and the operations team adopted modern cloud-native practices such as IaC to make quick and easy changes to environments in minutes. This was a significant productivity booster where the teams were able to build and iterate through multiple updates resulting in higher quality services.

Carrefour's IT architecture strategy

Carrefour's cloud transformation aimed to optimize the organization on three levels – infrastructure, application, and security modernization. To maximize the benefits of its Google Cloud adoption, Carrefour's cloud transformation journey involved a combination of *Google V1*, which focused on leveraging IaaS offerings for infrastructure modernization, and Google V2, which aimed at leveraging PaaS offerings for application transformation. This enabled Carrefour to optimize resource allocation and leverage the unique capabilities of each environment in the following ways:

- **Infrastructure modernization**: To enhance its operational efficiency, Carrefour transitioned from physical servers to serverless architectures, adopted DevOps processes, migrated from batch to real-time processing, and automated its deployment and testing procedures. These changes reduced operational complexity and increased scalability.

- **Application transformation**: Carrefour focused on migrating from a monolithic to a microservices architecture, adopting a **service-oriented architecture** (**SOA**) approach, and shifting from scheduled to real-time processes at the application level. They enhanced flexibility, agility, and the ability to scale individual services by breaking down their applications into smaller, more modular components.

- **Security modernization**: To guarantee the security of its applications and services in a hybrid cloud environment, Carrefour implemented a zero-trust model, granting access based on user identity and context. The company also moved control from the network to the application layer, strengthening its security measures. This approach offered fine-grained control over access rights, reducing the attack surface and improving data protection.

Carrefour defined and adopted an open platform strategy with a decoupled six-layered blueprint design that can support a wide range of application architectures and requirements. This is shown in the following figure *[13]*:

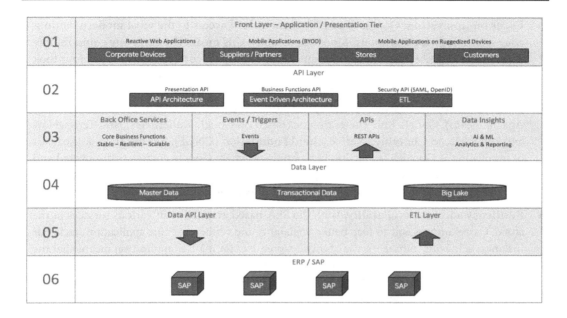

Figure 7.5 – Carrefour's six-layered blueprint design

By the end of 2019, the cloud transformation strategy yielded some impressive results for Carrefour.

- **Scale and agility**: The Spanish e-commerce modernization from an on-premises monolith to cloud-native microservices architecture gave Carrefour the utmost scale during seasonal peaks such as Black Friday. This also enabled the company to deliver new customer experiences quicker to market. For instance, Carrefour made roughly 400+ new feature deployments versus 52 in its on-premises environment. Another stark result was the data lake modernization on Google Cloud, where the on-premises data lake was capped at 700 TB and struggled to scale. The data lake in Google cloud was sustaining an incremental data volume of 2 TB per day while also serving 80+ applications and 100 million requests per month.

- **Speed to market**: Leveraging the agility of the cloud platform and scale, Carrefour was able to provision compute and platform resources in minutes versus having to procure, rack, and provision servers, which often took up to 3 months. Another major advantage was the flexibility to be "*casually pessimistic*" or "*over-optimistic*" on capacity requirements in the cloud-native environment. During the first COVID pandemic lockdown, Carrefour was able to launch a set of "*one-off*" websites and services across various countries it operated, leveraging cloud data centers across the world to provide essential goods to its customers. These were taken down once the pandemic period was over. A classic example of this was the *Les essentials Carrefour* website, which offered fixed-day home delivery of food bundles based on location and guaranteed availability of essential food products *[14]*:

- **Focus on innovation**: Google Cloud Platform offered access to the most modern cutting-edge technology for Carrefour. More importantly, this meant the company could rapidly experiment and test these capabilities quickly at lower risk, cost, and effort. Carrefour took advantage of pre-trained AI models such as Vision AI to incorporate features such as image recognition. Google was a synergetic partner to Carrefour's open source objectives where the company could benefit from several open source contributions such as Dataflow (based on Apache Beam), Google Kubernetes Engine (based on Google Kubernetes), and TensorFlow and adherence to **Container Native Cloud Foundation** (CNCF). For instance, at the heart of innovation is Google's leadership in technology, where Google engineers discovered and patched the microprocessor security vulnerabilities – **Spectre and Meltdown** – among others, such as Heartbleed and Rowhammer, across all of its cloud data centers with zero downtime.

- **Resiliency and high availability**: With the SLA-based availability of various services in the cloud, Carrefour was able to reap better availability and resiliency of the application stack. For instance, achieving a three 9's availability on-premises for a 3-tier application means that the entire stack must be accounted for full redundancy with a maximum downtime of less than 9 hours per year, which is extremely difficult to achieve and also cost prohibitive. Whereas, in a cloud environment, Carrefour was able to achieve this with limited effort and investment.

- **Sustainability in the cloud**: Sustainability is at the core of Carrefour's DNA and its partnership with Google ensures that Carrefour can achieve its sustainability goals quickly. Traditional data centers have an average **power usage effectiveness** (PUE) score of around 1.5, while Google Cloud's energy-efficient data centers have an average PUE score of 1.1. With transparency around carbon emissions associated with the choice of several cloud services, Carrefour could accurately measure its gross carbon footprint, track the emissions profile of cloud projects, and include carbon emissions data in reports and disclosures, helping it achieve its ESG goals.

Armed with the initial success of cloud migrations, Carrefour entered the next phase of digital transformation in the cloud, which focused on customer centricity. To accelerate Carrefour's transition to the cloud, the team began shutting down several of its on-premises data centers and migrated the applications to the cloud. Here are some of the key transformation strategies that Carrefour implemented:

- **Lift and shift VMware workloads**: Carrefour had a large VMware footprint that hosted a wide range of application workloads. Refactoring or rearchitecting all of these applications meant the teams would have to invest a lot of time and effort while also risking application compatibility and integrations. To help accelerate the cloud transformation, Carrefour leveraged Google Cloud VMware Engine, a native Google Cloud service offering that seamlessly migrates and runs VMware workloads on GCP *[15]*. This solution also offered flexible on-demand capacity and full operational compatibility and consistency with existing on-premises applications. This allowed Carrefour to harness the power of cloud infrastructure to optimize resources and costs, while also realizing efficiency gains. In its cloud-based environment, Carrefour was able to adopt FinOps best practices and techniques such as turning off non-prod environments automatically when not needed. Through this effort, Carrefour was able to cut the total cost of ownership by 30%.

- **Data and analytics transformation**: As part of its cloud transformation mission, the Carrefour team focused its attention on its core mission – to put customers first. To understand its customers at a much deeper level, Carrefour leveraged the Google Cloud data ecosystem to transform and modernize its data platform, internally known as project Darwin. Darwin enabled a single unified source of truth to a vast array of datasets securely and transparently. Google BigQuery became the cornerstone of this data platform and gave the company's data scientists reliable data access to help develop smarter AI/ML models. Furthermore, this enabled the teams to build a recommendation engine integrated with its e-commerce, helping offer personalized shopping experiences to its customers. The results of this transformation were huge:

  - With its adoption of modern AI/M capabilities and a new personalized recommendation engine, Carrefour was able to tailor and deliver personalized shopping experiences to its customers and saw an impressive 60% to 70% increase in online revenue during COVID-19.

  - Its data platform was scaled to serve and meet business demands and growth.

  - Carrefour leveraged Looker – an enterprise platform for BI, data applications, and embedded analytics – to not just visualize and analyze data in real-time, but also improve collaboration with its suppliers and partners by offering data-based insights.

- **API-led integration**: As Carrefour built digital services and platforms to offer a smooth and seamless online experience for its customers across channels, the consumer demand increased to billions of API requests. To better deal with the traffic spikes and deliver a scalable and low latency experience, Carrefour leveraged Apigee to standardize API integration and management. The Apigee platform enabled developers to build, manage, scale, and secure the APIs while also serving as a facade for the backend service APIs to provide security, rate limiting, quotas, and visibility. This also served as a huge productivity improvement for developers as they could focus on building services instead of worrying about service mechanics.

- **Sustainability at the core of digital transformation**: The Google Cloud partnership enabled Carrefour to achieve its goals towards sustainability. For instance, just by migrating workloads from its physical data centers to Google Cloud VMware Engine, Carrefour was able to reduce energy consumption by 35%. Another key initiative Carrefour co-created with Google Cloud is Carrefour's *Produce Assortment Solution*. This solution enabled the local stores to better regulate and manage their produce orders based on demands. This helped reduce food waste while also giving consumers timely access to the right produce.

Looking ahead – Carrefour's digital retail 2026 strategy

Carrefour is now defining a digital retail strategy for 2026, which is a result of the deep digital transformation it carried out since 2018. With a data-centric, digital-first approach, Carrefour aims to triple its e-commerce **Gross Merchandise Value (GMV)** by 2026 to reach 10 billion euros, where digital will contribute an additional 600 million euros to recurring operating income. To achieve this, Carrefour plans to increase investments in digital by 50% while also reaching carbon neutrality in its e-commerce activities by 2030 – 10 years ahead of the overall Carrefour group's objective for 2040. The data-centric, digital-first strategy will hinge on four key drivers:

- **Acceleration of e-commerce**: Carrefour intends to reinforce its retail leadership through creative digital formats such as express delivery (under 3 hours delivery), quick commerce (less than 15 minutes), social commerce, B2B, and live shopping.

- **Ramping up data and retail media**: Through the *Carrefour Links* platform, Carrefour anticipates that it will extract value from its rich first-party and third-party data. For instance, Carrefour's industrial partners can carry out marketing campaigns across multiple channels (stores, mobile apps, and websites), gain end-to-end visibility, and measure the impact.

- **Digitization of financial services**: Carrefour intends to leverage its strong presence and expertise in financial and insurance services and digitize the financial services activities products and services to enable new capabilities for B2C and B2B customers such as **buy now, pay later** (**BNPL**), micro-credits, and affinity insurance.

- **A deep transformation of traditional retail through digital**: Carrefour has migrated 30% of its applications to the cloud and intends to be fully cloud-based by 2026. By adopting a data-centric, digital-first strategy, Carrefour will drive digitization across its business processes to improve customer experience through operational efficiency and personalization.

Having reviewed Carrefour's digital transformation and its larger impact on the retail market, let's briefly explore how Wendy's is transforming consumer experiences and disrupting the restaurant industry.

Wendy's transforming consumer experiences

Headquartered in Dublin, Ohio, Wendy's is an American fast food restaurant chain and is the world's third-largest hamburger fast food chain. As the first restaurant brand that pioneered the pick-up window more than 50 years ago, Wendy's has always been at the forefront of innovation. In 1970, Dave Thomas – the founder of Wendy's – envisioned a new design element, the *Pick-Up Window* in its freestanding Wendy's restaurant, which was a breakthrough innovation that revolutionized the customer experience. Wendy's first modern drive-thru was also a catalyst that propelled Wendy's from a four-store local hamburger chain into a thriving global brand. Building on the legacy of design and innovation, Wendy's recently announced a new standard in global restaurant design – *Global Next Gen* – that promises to enhance customer experience at its restaurants through modern digital technologies and improve crew member experience *[16]*.

Global Next Gen

In February 2023, Wendy's shared its climate goal for 2030. As a leader in **Quick Service Restaurants** (**QSRs**), Wendy's aims to reduce its absolute scope 1 and 2 greenhouse gas emissions and scope 3 emissions by 47% *[17]*. One of the key actions toward this aggressive goal is the launch of Wendy's global next-gen design for its new restaurant builds, which is roughly 10% more energy-efficient than a traditional Wendy's common format restaurant. As part of its global next-gen strategy, every Wendy's business function, from operations to technology, would partner on the design and strategy, helping meet growing customer needs and expectations. Some of the key design features include a convenient and quicker delivery pick-up window for delivery drivers, offering dedicated mobile order pickup options, including dedicated parking spaces and shelving, a reimagined kitchen to improve point of sale efficiencies and faster order fulfilments, an optimized infrastructure to reduce energy usage, and a significant investment in next-generation technology to handle the growth in digital business and innovation [18].

Reimagining the restaurant experience through technology

Wendy's has been at the forefront of digital transformation by revolutionizing the restaurant industry by boldly reimagining its customer experience. From mobile ordering and contactless payment to personalized loyalty programs and AI-powered recommendations, Wendy's has been leveraging technology to create a seamless and delightful experience that meets the evolving needs of modern diners. Through strategic partnerships with cutting-edge technology providers, Wendy's has introduced a suite of innovative solutions that transform the way customers order, interact, and enjoy their meals. Let us review some highlights on how Wendy's has been innovating with emerging technologies.

Reinventing the drive-thru with generative AI

With 75% to 80% of Wendy's customers preferring the drive-thru, delivering a seamless drive-thru ordering experience has always been a challenge. Building on its technology partnership with Google, Wendy's embraced the modern Generative AI technology to develop a groundbreaking AI platform, the Wendy's FreshAI. FreshAI – the automated drive-thru ordering system – would feel as natural as interacting with a Wendy's crew member. The goal is to streamline the drive-thru ordering process and reduce the wait times for customers in the drive-thru lanes. With changing menus and thousands of customization probabilities, training an AI/ML model can be an insurmountable challenge. In this case, Wendy's leveraged various generative AI capabilities to customize and train the large language model so that it included phrases, synonymous language, and terms that are unique to Wendy's and its customers to offer a seamless restaurant experience. For instance, JBC refers to a Junior Bacon Cheeseburger, whereas a large chocolate milkshake refers to a large chocolate Frosty. Wendy's also pairs an AI-powered voice assistant with a visual order display to provide confidence in order accuracy for its customers. Through innovative restaurant technology, Wendy's aims to remove complexity from its drive-thru ordering and digital order pickup experience while also enabling its crew members to focus on serving fresh, fast, and quality food [19].

Unlocking value through data

As a society, just in the last decade, we have transitioned from data scarcity to data superfluity. This is no different for enterprises, and the challenge that most enterprises face today is the underutilization of data – that is, putting the right data to the right use. Wendy's had access to vast swaths of first-party as well as third-party data, and data is at the center of its vision to unlock new customer, crew member, and restaurant experiences. Wendy's leverages data to remove friction between its consumers and their restaurant experience. For instance, understanding whether a consumer wants their food as fast as possible or likes to try something new is critical to delivering the best experience. Insights into data allow Wendy's to deliver differentiated outcomes through personalized offers. Similarly, Wendy's taps into data from its franchises and business functions to improve operations for its franchise owners and restaurant teams.

Hybrid cloud with a bias toward the cloud

Like most enterprises, Wendy's has a substantial on-premises data center footprint that supports its mission-critical applications. Wendy's IT strategy, especially when delivering a new capability, has been to leverage a mobile-first and cloud-first design. The cloud-first strategy offers Wendy's the advantage of tapping into cutting-edge technology early, innovating, experimenting faster, and delivering new capabilities faster at much lower cost and risk. Wendy's partnership with Google Cloud enabled the company to deliver seamless experiences to its customers through cloud-native data analytics, pre-trained AI/ML models, and support for the hybrid cloud. Provisioning infrastructure with the right tools and technology is no longer the long pole in the tent, empowers the business, and lets the Wendy's team focus on core business functions.

Edge computing for an instantaneous customer experience

Wendy's has the unique advantage of having access to an enormous volume and variety of data spread across multiple locations. Processing the right data at the right time and activating it at the right place is crucial to long-term success. While some applications can benefit from historical data analytics, certain applications require real-time analytics. Wendy's refers to these analytics as "relevant time." With its distributed locations, Wendy's unlocked new value through edge computing. As Wendy's puts it, the holy grail of a QSR is that a POS system must be able to run within a restaurant, in the cloud, or at the edge as it provides enormous flexibility to set up a Wendy's restaurant virtually anywhere – urban, rural, and remote areas. A traditional POS is designed to take orders and process them. However, this isn't sufficient in today's digital world. With Google Anthos – a hybrid cloud solution – Wendy's can envision and perform AI functions at the edge to deliver instantaneous and personalized customer experiences [20].

Capital One – transforming banking through technology

Capital One is an American bank holding company headquartered in McLean, Virginia with operations primarily in the United States. It is one of the top 10 banks in the US by measure of total **assets under management** (**AUM**) and is the third largest issuer of Visa and Mastercard credit cards. Starting as a monoline bank with credit cards, Capital One expanded operations into auto loans and in 2005 entered the retail banking market. Capital One has been a disruptor in the financial services industry since the 1990s when it quickly identified that there was very little differentiation in the credit card services industry. When most of the industry was following a *one-size-fits-all* uniform pricing approach, as early as the 90s, Capital One leveraged the power of data and used statistical models based on publicly available credit and demographic data to understand its consumer base and tailored the credit card offerings to meet customer needs – giving the right product to the right customer.

Capital One leads digital innovation from the front and it can be seen evidently from its acquisition strategy to technology adoption. From an acquisitions point of view, Capital One augmented and bolstered its digital-first strategy through a series of acquisitions, such as ING Direct, to offer high-value digital banking services, Bankons, a mobile startup that creates geo-based offers, Bundle, a spend-data analytics company, Sail, a mobile point of sale swiping system, Confyrm, a digital identity and fraud alert service, and Wikibuy, a shopping comparison app *[21]*. Capital One was also one of the early adopters of cloud computing and has been at the forefront of digital transformation.

Capital One's cloud transformation journey

Capital One was one of the first financial services companies to experiment and exploit modern cloud technology to advance its digital transformation goals. Founded on the belief that the banking industry would be revolutionized by digital technology, Capital One's strategy has been to pair the tech innovations from leading technology companies with its risk management skills to build and deliver great customer experiences through the use of modern technology, including AI/ML and data. With over 65 million accounts, Capital One is more than just a credit card or a bank. Underpinning its business model is a technology-driven company. Capital One realized early on that their customers overwhelmingly interacted through digital channels to apply for products and services and, in turn, were serviced through digital channels. For instance, Capital One customers used its mobile apps twice as frequently as its web apps. To cater to its digitally savvy consumers, Capital One adopted a cloud-first strategy where the cloud allowed it to build great banking applications for its customers rather than divert attention and investments in building data center infrastructure.

Capital One modeled its IT strategy based on the following principles:

- Massively invest in top engineering talent
- Leverage the open source software stack and build software collaboratively
- Deliver software using agile methodologies and implement DevOps
- Adopt an API-first and microservices-based architecture
- Leverage big data and fast data for analytics

In the early 2010s, Capital One leveraged the cloud in an experimental mode to test out its capabilities and quickly leveraged the cloud across the enterprise. The company viewed cloud technology as a game-changer that allowed it to innovate and focus on delivering great customer experiences through technology. Capital One identified six key transformational benefits of the cloud *[22]*:

- **Velocity**: The cloud offers the ability to provision infrastructure just in time and on-demand, providing huge productivity gains and speed to market.

- **Elasticity**: With fluctuating consumer demand, cloud computing provides the capability to dynamically scale infrastructure capacity, offering a significant advantage over traditional on-premises deployments.

- **Availability**: As Capital One strives to offer capabilities over digital channels, high availability is table stakes. Cloud technology offers multiple layers of resiliency which can be extremely difficult and expensive to achieve on-premises.

- **Security**: Operating in digital channels will expose a cybersecurity threat. However, taking advantage of the cloud platform's defense-in-depth security enabled Capital One to manage security at a fine-grained level.

- **Access to technology**: The pace of innovation in the cloud was a crucial element in Capital One's IT strategy and it offered the much-needed access to modern technology.

- **Talent**: Capital One's forward-leaning approach to the cloud helped find and attract top talent in the industry to help deliver bleeding-edge solutions.

Capital One's cloud transformation journey has been marked by four phases of adoption *[24]*:

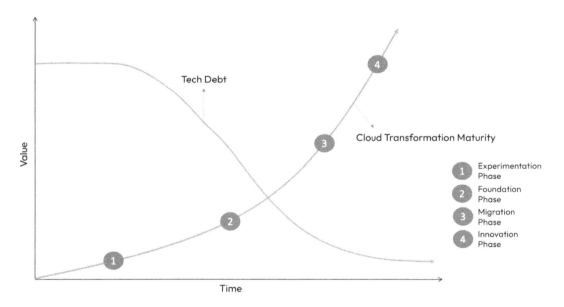

Figure 7.6 – Capital One's cloud transformation journey and phases

Let's explore these cloud transformation phases in a bit more detail.

The experimentation phase

Between 2013 and 2014, when cloud technology was still in its inception, Capital One embarked on a public cloud journey with AWS, primarily to experiment with the technology and operating model. In this phase, the innovation lab at Capital One – *The Capital One Lab* – created small-scale learning environments to prove the applicability of the technology and tools. The mission statement of the Capital One Lab reads as follows: *We explore the intersection of emerging technology and finance.* With a small footprint, a small number of software engineers participated in this experimentation phase. As a result of the successful trial, the recommendation was to continue the use of the public cloud to provision infrastructure capacity on demand and just in time, and leverage its high availability and elasticity to fast forward the pace of innovation.

The foundation phase

Circa 2015, Capital One deployed production-ready cloud-native applications on AWS, which marked a huge milestone. This marked a phase of training and upskilling a large number of IT associates to be able to develop and work in a cloud-native environment. Since Capital One also had significant investments in on-premises data centers, it was crucial to ensure the cloud applications could seamlessly integrate with on-premises environments to reduce the friction in application delivery processes. Establishing DirectConnect enabled Capital One to extend its data centers from on-premises to the cloud (AWS data centers), assisting in the transition to a cloud-first architecture for all new workloads. During this phase, Capital One also established a CCoE consisting of cloud-native specialist teams that included developers, solution architects, product teams, and technical account managers. The CCoE was instrumental in defining cloud engineering patterns and best practices in partnership with AWS while also helping cross-pollinate and train teams across Capital One. At the AWS annual conference, ReInvent 2015, Capital One shared its vision to reduce its data center footprint from eight (2014) to five by the end of 2016 and down to just three in 2018. This broad vision and objective rallied Capital One to focus on and leverage the public cloud to simplify infrastructure, innovate, and drive savings back into the business:

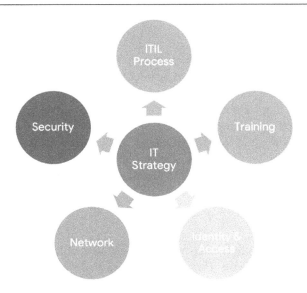

Figure 7.7 – The foundational elements of Capital One's cloud journey

The migration phase

The years that followed marked a phase of "great migration" at Capital One. The Capital One team continued to partner with AWS and a bunch of partners to assist with establishing patterns and processes to handle the cloud migration at scale. Capital One strategically adopted the 6 R's migration approach – *Rehost*, *Replatform*, *Refactor*, *Retain*, *Repurchase*, and *Retire* – to support the organization's vision of getting out of the data center business. For instance, Capital One preferred the *Rehosting* (lift and shift) strategy for applications where only minor changes were required without much differentiation, while *Replatforming* and *ReArchitecting* applications where there was a significant business impact. Capital One also benefited by adopting advancements in cloud technology during this phase by taking advantage of AWS platform offerings such as Amazon **Simple Queue Service** (**SQS**) to replatform message queues and Amazon **Relational Database Service** (**RDS**) to replatform traditional transactional databases, thus reducing the management complexities such as scaling, patching, backups, upgrading, and more while also unlocking higher performance efficiencies.

The innovation phase

As the AWS footprint grew and with Capital One having several years of cloud maturity, this phase marked the efforts toward innovation. Capital One leveraged cloud platforms to innovate the future of banking, as well as AI/ML capabilities for fraud detection, and offered personalized experiences through mobile assistants such as Eno. This phase also enabled Capital One to optimize its cloud investments, primarily to improve performance and cost efficiencies. Some of the early optimization efforts included tuning application infrastructure, implementing automation for infrastructure, and refactoring applications on PaaS offerings such as serverless offerings. Here are some key optimizations:

- Detecting unused capacity for application workloads running on AWS and optimizing the Linux distributions. This helped reduce the compute infrastructure usage and costs:

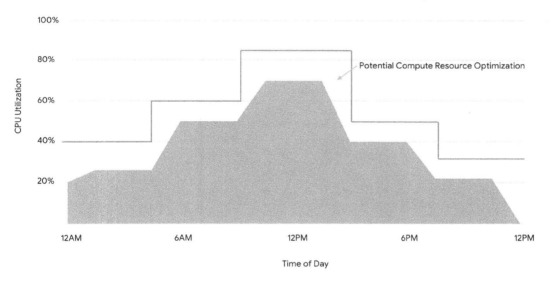

Figure 7.8 – An illustration of average compute resource usage in the cloud and its optimization potential

- Implementing IaC for dynamic just-in-time environment spin up and tear down in the cloud.

- Replatforming applications from traditional infrastructure (capacity-based) to serverless PaaS offerings (usage-driven). For instance, deploying a service on a compute instance (EC2) meant that Capital One had to pay for *everything in the box*, irrespective of whether the service was in use while also managing the infrastructure:

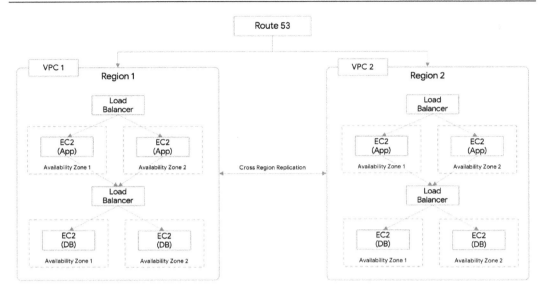

Figure 7.9 – Infrastructure-based application architecture

Refactoring this application and service to a serverless platform (Lambda) would mean that Capital One would only pay for when the service runs:

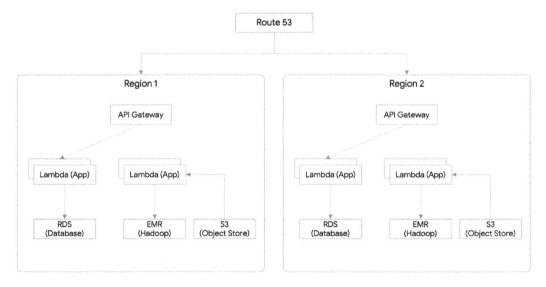

Figure 7.10 – Platform-based and serverless application architecture

Capital One's talent acquisition strategy

In this section, we will briefly explore how Capital One upskilled its talented IT workforce into cloud subject matter experts who were predominantly experts with on-premises technology. Seeking change, the leadership at Capital One created a unicorn job specification and hoped to hire top cloud talent from the market. This just didn't work because that unicorn just didn't exist. Capital One quickly realized that it could transform the extremely skilled, proactive, and dedicated talent they already had. In hindsight, Capital One articulates the steps that it put in place that worked wonders for them *[25]*:

1. **Acceptance:** This was a crucial first step where Capital One had to convince its talented engineers and leaders that they could learn modern cloud skills – in this case, AWS – and be able to upskill. Instilling the right level of confidence, creating a learning environment, laying out a clear path, giving ample time, and incentivizing were just enough.

2. **Training:** The team at Capital One swiftly started offering learning opportunities to its team through official classroom-led training.

3. **Getting their hands dirty:** Change is extremely hard and goes against human psychology. However, creating the right environment with blameless outcomes can be a powerful change agent. Capital One offered sandbox environments for its engineers to play around in the cloud helping create a solid learning environment.

4. **The two-pizza team:** The first engineering team that Capital One put together considered a good mix of IT folks from different expert areas, such as networking, database, system admins, application engineers, storage admins, and security engineers. This made perfect sense since cloud technology blurs the lines between these job roles, which are typically distinctly seen in a traditional on-premises set up.

5. **Cross-pollinate with external expertise:** It was essential to help cross-pollinate the home IT with some external coaching and hand-holding. This is where partnerships can bring a significant edge. Capital One brought in experts from AWS partners who were professionally certified to help with the initial rollouts. This had a transformative effect, where the Capital One team learned from watching, asking questions, and doing it themselves, getting them ready for the future.

6. **Making it real:** Setting a goal for the two-pizza team to build and deliver something real and in production was a key move. The objective here was to find a workload that is important but not too mission-critical. The key here was to ensure this identified workload didn't require too much customization of the cloud building blocks (in this case, AWS), as it may serve as a technical roadblock to start with.

7. **Scale learning with cellular mitosis:** Once the first team delivered a successful outcome, it was time to split this team – who now have the necessary experience – into two four-member teams while introducing four more engineers into each team. This helped scale the learning through hands-on and learning on the job. Capital One repeated this process until it had hundreds of skilled cloud engineers with the added side effect of a bunch of net new cloud applications.

8. **Cloud certification**: Capital One saw a direct correlation between engineer certification and the number of applications delivered on AWS. The certification process ensured that the engineers at Capital One understood the AWS language and had a broader understanding of the technology.

9. **Scaling certification and leadership**: Capital One advocates for a critical mass of 10% of the engineers to be certified and advocate for the platform after which the network effect takes hold. Grooming and motivating engineers to get certified resulted in creating a halo effect that also helped Capital One's perception not just internally but also externally.

10. **Recognize and reward**: The cloud (AWS) certification at Capital One was viewed as a great achievement. Recognizing and rewarding engineers publicly had a huge effect on team morale and motivation.

11. **Challenge yourself**: As a leader, it was also important to practice the preachings. At Capital One, leadership stepped up and took the certification challenge to have a broader and deeper understanding of the AWS lexicon.

12. **Redefining job families**: The Cloud had a far-reaching impact and is a transformation not just in the technology space but also across business functions, processes, and operations. Capital One redefined the job portfolio to reflect the same.

This holistic strategy helped Capital One not only acquire the right talent from the market but also harness its in-house talent by upskilling for cloud transformation. Now, let's explore how Capital One envisioned and pioneered creative mobile experiences for its consumers.

Re-architecting the Capital One mobile app on the cloud

The pinnacle of Capital One's cloud transformation effort was the re-architecture of its largest customer-facing mobile app. This was an ambitious project as this mobile app had a user base of tens of millions of customers. This was much more than a simple lift and shift and required a full re-architecture of the entire application, including the integration, orchestration systems, and operational support tooling. Building cloud-native software can often be a whole new ballgame as it requires a shift in mindset from traditional software development to cloud-native DevSecOps *[26]*.

The mission was simple: Capital One Mobile must be capable of keeping up with consumer demand, backed by an infrastructure that moves with the needs of the product.

One major advantage Capital One had was that the majority of the mobile application's existing architecture was "cloud-ready." For instance, the application leveraged microservices-based API-driven architecture (Capital One refers to this as micro experience APIs – more on this later), Netflix Zuul OSS for server-side load balancing, Netflix Hystrix OSS for service fault tolerance, Netflix Eureka as a service registry, and Ansible for operational automation. This meant that the team at Capital One only had to make minor adjustments to ensure AWS's cloud-native capabilities were fully leveraged *[27]*. For instance, from deploying service components within a single contained infrastructure on-premises, better scale and fault-tolerance can be achieved by deploying them on distributed infrastructure in AWS.

Capital One coined the concept of **Experience APIs (xAPIs)** and **Micro Experience**. xAPIs differ from regular APIs in that xAPIs focus on delivering a user experience flow, while a regular API can refer to servicing a resource or data model. Micro experience is essentially a collection of multiple xAPIs that can be put in a single deployable unit. For instance, a customer clicking on *Redeem Rewards* can be a micro experience that can comprise multiple micro experience APIs.

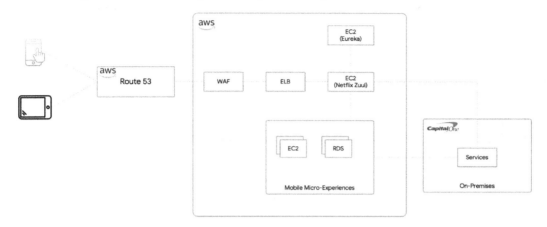

Figure 7.11 – Capital One's mobile application architecture

Having explored Capital One's mobile application architecture, let's review the challenges and learnings from their early cloud DevOps efforts.

DevOps challenges and learnings

The following are some of the Cloud DevOps best practices that we can glean from Capital One's major cloud transformation effort:

- Leverage cloud-native capabilities wherever possible to improve efficiencies. For instance, Capital One replaced the corporate GTM solution with AWS Route53 and migrated data stores from on-premises RDBMS to RDS.

- Develop a deployment pattern for service-based deployment instead of a full stack deployment to improve the frequency of micro releases and incremental deployments.

- Leverage **auto-scaling groups (ASGs)** to perform blue-green deployments. This has been critical to ensure real-world testing without a larger impact in case of issues.

- Build a golden image that is baked in with all application and server-level dependencies.

- Automate everything – build DevOps and SRE best practices while leveraging automation to reduce unnecessary human touchpoints and errors.

- Having a robust performance testing plan can help identify opportunities within the cloud environment for optimization. This includes testing software on different compute families and storage types for the best price-performance outcome.

- Treating server infrastructure as "cattle" versus "pets."

- Continuous tuning of application software based on scaling events or performance metrics can often expose application gaps and loopholes, while over-provisioned hardware or capacity could have obscured these issues on-premises.

- Leverage mock-test software for on-demand mock tests. Capital One leveraged the Mountebank OSS-based software solution.

- Build for functionality and architect for resiliency in the cloud.

Going all in on the cloud

In 2020, staying true to its goals, Capital One closed eight of its on-premises data centers and migrated completely to the cloud. In the process, it recycled 103 tons of copper and steel while also running 1,000s of applications on the cloud *[28]*. Capital One is uniquely positioned in the industry and operates as a digital bank, maintaining physical branches only in a few states, while offering access to its services through its 40,000 ATMs across the country. There are also Capital One Cafes, which serve as community hubs, and Capital One also provides technology access to its customers from virtually anywhere. Capital One is a proven example that a Fortune 100 company in a highly regulated industry such as financial services can take a legacy on-premises ecosystem to the cloud and deliver new customer experiences powered by data and AI.

Here are some key highlights on how the cloud has accelerated innovation for Capital One:

- Right off the bat, one of the key benefits that was realized was the ability to access compute resources almost instantly at virtually unlimited scale, while also having the flexibility to pay only for use. This reduced the lead time for the development environment from roughly 3 months to a few minutes. Applications could now use as much or as little resources to sustain and meet business demands.

- The data center exit helped Capital One realize a lower **total cost of ownership (TCO)** by leveraging the cloud economies of scale.

- Capital One went from quarterly and monthly application updates to releasing changes to production multiple times a day, which accelerated the speed to market, delivering new capabilities faster. It also observed a 50% reduction in the number of transaction errors and reduced critical incident resolution time.

- Capital One technologists could not have access to modern technology at will and leveraged real-time data streaming, ML, and the power of the cloud to solve unique problems to address business challenges.

- The cloud enabled extreme system availability and resiliency for its systems and applications. Most applications shifted to an active-active architecture with an automated failover without much effort and huge investments in infrastructure to support it. For instance, if one zone fails in the cloud, the workloads could be moved or served from another zone within the region and if an entire cloud region fails, the same workload could be spun up in a new cloud region.

This was improbable and almost impossible to achieve within the confines of a traditional data center. Capital One observed a 70% better disaster recovery in tests.

- The cloud has served as the backbone for customer-centric innovation for CapitalOne. A classic example is Eno – the intelligent assistant developed entirely using cloud technology such as Amazon EC2, Lambda, DynamoDB, and Kinesis. Eno's proactive insights help Capital One customers safeguard their accounts by looking out for unusual credit card charges, tracking spending, and sending useful insights if it finds a better offer. Another example is Capital One Shopping, a free tool that helps shoppers save money by comparing prices across sites, proactively locating active coupons, and offering price tracking and alerts. The cloud has enabled Capital One to experiment rapidly with new technology and offerings without much upfront investment and risk.

- The shift to modern architecture and processes such as RESTful APIs, microservices, and DevSecOps have transformed Capital One to be agile with business.

In conclusion, Capital One's case study serves as a fine example of how enterprises can leverage cloud as a catalyst to advance their business objectives. By leveraging the scalability, agility, and cost-effectiveness of the cloud, Capital One has been able to deliver innovative products and services faster, improve customer experiences, and gain a competitive advantage in the financial industry. Capital One's cloud journey serves as a testament to the immense potential of cloud computing and open source in driving business growth and success in the digital age.

Summary

As we explored in this chapter, cloud computing has evolved from a service model to being the epicenter of modern technology evolution. This presents a tremendous opportunity for enterprises and startups alike to disrupt the industry. In a sense, the cloud has transformed the level playing field, where customer experience is key to thriving. From the cloud transformation journeys that we explored and the business outcomes, let's consider some common takeaways.

Organizational vision is extremely critical and an often overlooked factor in a lot of transformative missions. Digitally transforming an enterprise through cloud technology is no different. We can see this from the clear goals that organizations such as Airbnb in the hospitality space, Carrefour in retail, and Capital One in financial services had for their teams. This sets the tone for the organization to rally behind a vision.

As we saw from the case studies, communication is an extremely important aspect that ensures the vision is communicated across business and IT functions. Carrefour's cloud strategy has communication as one of the primary drivers for a successful digital transformation. We also explored the importance of focusing on business outcomes rather than the underlying technology. For instance, the technology landscape is ever-changing and makes is easy for IT organizations to fall in love with the technology or infrastructure that they built over the years, which can have a detrimental impact on business outcomes. This is the cattle versus pets mindset.

From the Airbnb and Carrefour use cases, we can see how the cloud can be leveraged as a launchpad for innovation that serves as the cornerstone for successful enterprises. All modern technologies today, from digital assistants to generative AI, real-time data streaming to IoT, and blockchain to AR/VR, are built and delivered on the cloud. Gaining access early, experimenting with it, and driving customer experiences faster is extremely critical.

Dismissing lift and shift as a no-value cloud initiative is a common peril at most enterprises, especially today. However, this is entirely a myth, as we saw from Capital One's data center exits. Lift and shift presents a unique opportunity for established enterprises to get out of tech debt, serves as a learning launchpad, helps jumpstart the next phase of cloud maturity, makes companies attractive to the talent pool, and most importantly helps save resources, optimize costs, and meet ESG objectives.

Hybrid cloud is a tangible, low-hanging fruit strategy for most enterprises with a heavy on-premises footprint with a focus toward starting net new engagements on a cloud-first strategy.

In the next chapter, we will explore how to architect the next-generation enterprise cloud strategy with a particular focus on some of the prescriptive frameworks from major cloud providers and value realization.

Further reading

To learn more about the topics that were covered in this chapter, take a look at the following references:

1. `https://s26.q4cdn.com/656283129/files/doc_financials/2023/q2/3aec2916-f24a-4a9e-8a59-bdbcabe8c4bb.pdf`

2. `https://aws.amazon.com/solutions/case-studies/airbnb-case-study/`

3. `https://www.infoq.com/presentations/airbnb-culture-soa/`

4. `https://www.youtube.com/watch?v=Z3_V5ooxfxs`

5. `https://medium.com/airbnb-engineering/dynamic-kubernetes-cluster-scaling-at-airbnb-d79ae3afa132`

6. `https://medium.com/airbnb-engineering/building-services-at-airbnb-part-1-c4c1d8fa811b`

7. `https://www.youtube.com/watch?v=Sq9gp8KBsY0`

8. `https://aws.amazon.com/solutions/case-studies/airbnb-optimizes-usage-and-costs-case-study/`

9. `https://www.carrefour.com/en/news/investor-day-carrefour-omnichannel-experience`

10. `https://www.carrefour.com/sites/default/files/2020-01/investor_day_presentation_vfinal_v005pm_0.pdf`

11. `https://horizons.carrefour.com/tech/google-cloud-the-fuel-of-digital-transformation`

12. https://cloud.google.com/customers/carrefour

13. https://gcloud.devoteam.com/blog/peter-winkelmans-head-of-enterprise-architects-at-carrefour-driving-business-growth-through-cloud-infrastructure/

14. https://horizons.carrefour.com/e-commerce/launching-a-home-delivery-service-in-6-days

15. https://cloud.google.com/customers/carrefour-gcve

16. https://www.irwendys.com/news/news-details/2022/Wendys-Announces-Innovative-New-Global-Restaurant-Design-Standard-Global-Next-Gen/default.aspx

17. https://www.wendys.com/blog/wendys-reduce-greenhouse-gas-emissions-47

18. https://www.wendys.com/blog/blog-home/blog-wendys-innovative-new-qsr-design-approach

19. https://www.wendys.com/blog/how-wendys-using-ai-restaurant-innovation

20. https://www.forbes.com/sites/maribellopez/2023/01/12/wendys-cooks-up-new-experiences-with-ai-cloud-and-edge-computing/?sh=303f57ad6f1f

21. https://www.capgemini.com/wp-content/uploads/2017/07/capital-one-doing-business-the-digital-way_0.pdf

22. https://medium.com/capital-one-tech/we-re-a-disruptive-bank-a21f7cce25b6

23. https://medium.com/aws-enterprise-collection/capital-ones-cloud-journey-through-the-stages-of-adoption-bb0895d7772c

24. https://medium.com/capital-one-tech/serverless-is-the-paas-i-always-wanted-9e9c7d925539

25. https://medium.com/aws-enterprise-collection/a-12-step-program-to-get-from-zero-to-hundreds-of-aws-certified-engineers-287a4b45d39a

26. https://medium.com/capital-one-tech/moving-one-of-capital-ones-largest-customer-facing-apps-to-aws-668d797af6fc

27. https://medium.com/capital-one-tech/mobile-orchestration-innovation-on-the-edge-9835e4cbd69e

28. https://aws.amazon.com/solutions/case-studies/capital-one-all-in-on-aws/

8

Architecting a Cloud-Ready Enterprise

What do successful enterprises have in common? It's the fundamental ability to stay agile and relevant to meet consumer demands and expectations. As we explored in the earlier chapters, business ventures in the contemporary landscape are inseparable from the influence of technology. To put this into perspective, McKinsey research finds that the median age of the top 10 S&P companies in 2000 was 85 years and dropped to 33 years in 2018 [1]. What's even more interesting is the fact that the study estimates that the average tenure of an S&P 500 company would be a mere 12 years by 2027. In today's digital economy, as unicorn startups disrupt the marketplace through modern technology, the ability of enterprises to thrive and sustain inherently hinges on staying agile through the strategic use of technology.

In the previous chapter, we explored how enterprises can adopt a cloud strategy for digital transformation. In this chapter, we will discuss how to architect a cloud-ready enterprise that can improve an organization's ability to stay nimble, react and respond quicker to consumer demands, and stay ahead of the competition. In this chapter, we will explore the following topics:

- An opinionated hybrid cloud framework that can serve as a foundational blueprint for architecting a vendor-neutral cloud-ready enterprise

- Prescriptive cloud architecture frameworks from major cloud service providers – AWS, Google Cloud, and Azure

- Private and hybrid cloud strategies

Building a framework for a cloud-ready enterprise

Established enterprises typically have an existing data center with a significant infrastructure, technology, and software footprint and it is not practical to start on a clean slate. In the earlier chapters, we discussed how leadership plays a critical role in spearheading and chartering the course for a successful digital transformation and the importance of vision, will, and mindset shift. Now that we have established the need for an enterprise-wide digital transformation led by cloud technologies, it is important to redefine and architect the foundational building blocks to set up the IT organization for success. This brings us to the fundamental need for a prescriptive framework, regardless of the choice of a platform or provider. Several enterprises fall into the trap of adopting quick and dirty, one-off transformations that often fall flat due to the lack of a strong foundation, leading to undesirable outcomes in complexities, effort, and costs. For instance, consider Acme Corp., which invested in a modern data analytics solution without a strong data foundation, triggering huge complexities and costs in redesigning the data integration and semantic layers while still not having access to the right data to the right persona at the right time.

In this section, we will explore a provider-agnostic framework that helps redefine and architect a cloud-ready enterprise, regardless of the enterprise deployment platform. This is an opinionated framework that I have created, advocated, and prescribed for enterprise architects and IT leaders that follows and aligns with some common enterprise architecture frameworks. A typical enterprise IT footprint often comprises a combination of on-premises data centers with mission-critical applications, including legacy applications, business functions supporting SaaS, and possibly a mix of private and public cloud services. A common challenge that enterprises face in this model is getting to a cloud-native state, while also ensuring business continuity. According to the **Cloud Native Computing Foundation (CNCF)**, *"cloud-native technologies empower organizations to build and run scalable applications in modern, dynamic environments such as public, private, and hybrid clouds. Containers, service meshes, microservices, immutable infrastructure, and declarative APIs exemplify this approach." [2].* The cloud-native approach enables enterprises to build loosely coupled systems that are resilient, manageable, and observable, while also delivering high-impact changes frequently and predictably.

It is also a common practice for enterprises to start building net-new applications following a cloud-native architecture. However, without a cloud foundation and an ecosystem to support it, this can lead to a siloed, tough-to-integrate with existing on-premises systems and applications or worse yet result in increased complexity and effort. It will also prove prudent to broadly classify and identify applications into three primary buckets:

- **Legacy applications**: These are applications that serve primary business functions within the enterprise and are mission-critical to business. These often require a longer roadmap to fully transform to the cloud and are best suited to run within the existing on-premises environment.

- **Cloud-readiness**: These are applications that are architected and built using traditional software development methods but have the potential to be replatformed or refactored to run in a cloud environment.

- **Cloud native**: These are applications that are typically born in the cloud or applications re-architected from scratch to be cloud native.

Here are some primary objectives when architecting a cloud-ready enterprise:

- Improve business agility and speed to market through increased development velocity and developer productivity

- Reduce the IT effort and time to support business functions and growth – think infrastructure scaling, patching, DevOps, automation, upgrades, and maintenance

- Ensure application availability, scale, and resilience as table stakes

- Support an environment for innovation, prototyping, and rapid experimentation of new ideas with modern technology

- Ensure application portability and reduce dependency on underlying infrastructure and platform through the adoption of open standards and open technologies

Figure 8.1 describes the core constituents and the layers of an enterprise hybrid cloud framework:

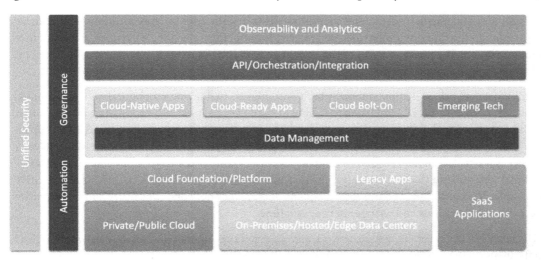

Figure 8.1 – Layers of an enterprise hybrid cloud framework

Now, let's review each of these layers in detail.

Cloud foundation layer

This is the most important foundational layer and comprises a combination of infrastructure and platform services. The primary objective of this layer is to decouple the underlying core infrastructure from application services to ensure portability and platform-agnostic deployments. Some key architectural components to consider within the cloud foundation layer are as follows:

- Network infrastructure modernization

- Compute infrastructure modernization

- Storage infrastructure modernization

- Cloud-native application design principles

Network infrastructure modernization

Regardless of a private cloud, public cloud, or multi-cloud strategy, the most critical factor to a successful digital transformation is network infrastructure. Unfortunately, this is also often the most overlooked aspect in several enterprises as businesses strive to deliver new products and services to their customers as efficiently as possible. In a traditional approach, the network perimeter was confined with a predictable boundary and fortified, following a single window access policy. This was much easier to construct, control, secure, and manage. However, in the digital era, network boundaries have expanded to cover a multitude of needs and opened up multiple entry and access points. For instance, introducing a SaaS service to meet a specific business need, adopting one or more public cloud platforms, corporate associates working out of global offices and remote locations, IoT devices connecting to corporate networks over modern protocols such as 5G, third-party access for suppliers and partners, deploying computing devices at the edge or store locations – all of these contribute to the blurring of network perimeter pronouncing a need for a network infrastructure modernization. The business value of the enterprise network has never been higher as the focus on digital transformation intensifies.

Traditional networks were fundamentally built on a premise that involves a physical network, routers, switches, hardware-based load balancers, network security devices, and protocol standards, often defined by individual network or device vendors. The data and management planes are tightly coupled in a traditional network infrastructure, necessitating huge efforts to device configurations whenever a change is warranted on the network. In contrast, modern cloud-based infrastructure relies on **software-defined networking (SDN)** principles, abstracting away the physical network infrastructure. SDN decouples the control plane from the data plane and enables network administrators to propagate network configurations and changes in near real time.

SDN enables a key capability where network administrators can operate and manage networks such as software using standard SDN APIs. Some key capabilities that SDN enables for enterprises are as follows:

- **Open standard**: SDN-based architectures usher in an open standard through open APIs to support multi-cloud and vendor-neutral interoperability. This also helps network operators to manage network services and control through APIs.

- **Network abstraction**: The primary advantage that SDN delivers is the abstraction of underlying networking hardware and technologies, thus enabling seamless connectivity and interoperability.

- **Network intelligence**: While traditional networks are fundamentally distributed and operate with limited awareness of the network state, SDN-based networks offer a centralized policy-based control that leverages artificial intelligence to manage network performance, bandwidth, and security.

This network modernization goes beyond just the data center. With the emergence of SD-WAN, enterprises can take a software-defined approach to provide secure and reliable access to business applications across the enterprise.

Compute infrastructure modernization

Traditional on-premises compute infrastructure in a typical enterprise often consists of a wide array of compute encompassing commodity general-purpose hardware infrastructure and specialized, proprietary hyper-converged infrastructure. Much of the focus for teams dedicated to managing traditional data center infrastructure involves maintenance and patching activities, managing hardware refresh cycles, and keeping the lights on. As business demands continue to rise for more modern, advanced, and powerful compute resources such as **high-performance computing (HPC)**, **graphical processing units (GPUs)**, and **tensor processing units (TPUs)**, managing and maintaining a data center is becoming cost-prohibitive for enterprises. Cloud platforms have democratized access to a wide variety of compute power that has transformed the way organizations rapidly experiment and use compute resources without long-term commitments, maintenance, and refresh overheads. The following are some best practices enterprises can adopt while designing for a cloud-ready compute infrastructure, particularly in the context of the hybrid cloud:

- **Virtualization and containerization**: By leveraging open standards virtualization and containerization technologies, organizations can create abstract compute environments that are independent of the underlying physical infrastructure. This allows for increased flexibility, portability, and reusability of compute resources.

- **Infrastructure as Code (IaC)**: IaC tools enable organizations to define their compute infrastructure as code, automating provisioning, configuration, and management. This streamlines the process, reduces errors, and ensures consistency across environments.

- **Standardization of compute instances**: Establishing standard instance types and configurations across both environments simplifies capacity planning, resource allocation, and cost management. Organizations can optimize their compute infrastructure by leveraging consistent configurations.

- **Centralized image management**: A centralized repository for operating system and application images ensures consistency, security, and compliance. By maintaining a single source for images, organizations can streamline the deployment and maintenance of compute environments.

- **Hybrid cloud management platform**: A hybrid cloud management platform provides a centralized dashboard for managing compute resources across on-premises and cloud environments. It enables seamless workload migration, resource optimization, and simplified administration.

Organizations can also benefit from implementing automated patching processes, establishing comprehensive monitoring and logging systems, and designing a unified **disaster recovery (DR)** and **business continuity plan (BCP)** that spans both on-premises and cloud environments.

Storage infrastructure modernization

As enterprises embrace the hybrid cloud to reap the benefits of both on-premises and cloud environments, it is imperative to modernize and standardize storage infrastructure to optimize for efficiency and flexibility. Typical on-premises storage solutions include **storage area networks (SANs)** for block-level storage, **network attached storage (NAS)** for file-level storage, and **object storage devices (OSDs)** for storing and managing enterprise data. Cloud-native storage services provide scalable, elastic, and cost-effective storage solutions by leveraging object storage for large datasets, block storage for high-performance applications, and file storage for traditional file-based workloads. Beyond the cloud-native storage solutions, enterprises can also adopt common protocols such as S3 APIs to access storage solutions across hybrid cloud environments while also leveraging storage gateways to seamlessly handle data types and protocols across on-premises and the cloud. The following are some best practices to standardize and modernize storage infrastructure for hybrid cloud environments:

- **Storage virtualization**: Abstract storage infrastructure resources from physical infrastructure using storage virtualization technologies to enable seamless data access and migration and improve resource utilization.

- **Data tiering**: In the context of storage infrastructure design, it is always a best practice to implement a tiered storage strategy based on data access, frequency, compliance, and performance needs. For instance, you can leverage high-performance storage for frequently accessed data and cost-effective storage for archival purposes.

- **Unified data management**: Implement a unified data management platform that provides a single pane of glass for managing storage across on-premises and cloud environments that offers centralized data visibility, control, and governance.

- **Data encryption and security**: Encrypt data at rest and in transit to ensure data confidentiality and security. Implement access control policies and audit mechanisms to prevent unauthorized access.

- **Backup and disaster recovery**: Establish a robust backup and DR strategy that includes both on-premises and cloud storage to ensure data protection and business continuity in the event of failures or disasters.

Having reviewed the core infrastructure components – network, compute, and storage – of the cloud foundation layer, let's explore how enterprises can architect and build modern applications while leveraging cloud-native principles.

Designing cloud-native applications

As cloud-native technologies catalyze a revolutionary shift in the way applications are developed, deployed, and managed, it is critical to establish a consistent, open, and portable platform that can support cloud-native architecture. Cloud-native is a software approach to building modern applications that are highly scalable, flexible, and resilient, where organizations can gain a significant competitive edge in delivering software applications such as increased efficiency, platform independence, speed to market, and reduction in technical debt and overall TCO. Traditional software application development follows a monolithic approach where all application functionality is in a single block structure and later passed down to an operations team for software delivery and management. Any small change to the application necessitated a long, full-blown regression test and deployment. In contrast, cloud-native applications advocate for a microservices architectural approach, where an application is broken down into smaller microservices that work in tandem to deliver an application function. This means development teams can work independently on their respective services, which can be managed, operated, and scaled independently.

At the forefront of this transformation stands the CNCF, which is an open source, vendor-neutral hub of cloud-native computing driving innovation, standardization, and community engagement. Subscribing to CNCF projects and standards can guarantee enterprises a rich set of technology offerings that adhere to the core principles of cloud-native architecture. Some popular and noteworthy CNCF projects include Kubernetes, Istio, Envoy, Fluentd, Helm, and Prometheus. More importantly, several major cloud providers are active contributors to CNCF. Adopting a cloud-native foundation is crucial for enterprises in the contemporary digital landscape and is quintessential for successful digital transformation, regardless of the deployment model – private, public, or hybrid cloud. At its core, cloud-native architecture has the following guiding principles:

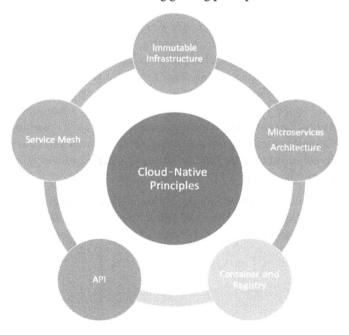

Figure 8.2 – Guiding principles of cloud-native applications

Let's go through these principles one by one:

- **Immutable infrastructure**: This principle is the first and foremost requirement for a cloud-native architecture and is where the underlying infrastructure is fully decoupled from the application. The application being deployed declaratively defines the underlying infrastructure requirements and can run on any infrastructure that satisfies this need. This advocates for the philosophy of *treat infrastructure as cattle versus pets*. For instance, monolithic applications have to adhere to very specific homogeneous infrastructure components, without which they will fail. In contrast, cloud-native applications are distributed in nature and can discard the underlying infrastructure in response to events such as hardware failures, planned or unplanned outages, or scaling events.

- **Microservices architecture**: Microservices architecture is a modern software design practice where an application is composed of small, independent services, each focused on a specific business capability. Unlike traditional monolithic architectures, microservices break down complex applications into modular, loosely coupled components, operate independently, communicate through well-defined APIs, and can be developed, deployed, and scaled independently. This promotes agility, scalability, and ease of maintenance, allowing organizations to adapt quickly to changing requirements and leverage diverse technologies for different parts of their applications.

- **Container and registry**: Containers are lightweight, portable, and self-sufficient units that encapsulate software and its dependencies, ensuring consistent and reliable execution across various computing environments. This provides an isolated and standardized runtime environment, allowing developers to package applications with all the necessary libraries and dependencies that can run independently, regardless of the underlying infrastructure. Containerization, popularized by technologies such as Docker, streamlines the development and deployment process, enhances scalability, and facilitates the creation of microservices architectures. Containers are instrumental in enabling efficient and consistent application delivery, from development to testing and production, fostering a more agile and reproducible software development life cycle.

- **API-first**: Cloud-native applications advocate for an API-first design and are the prescribed communication mode for microservices both within the application as well as cross-application communication. APIs help decouple application interdependencies and define a contract for request response.

- **Service mesh**: Service mesh is a dedicated infrastructure layer that facilitates communication, management, and control between microservices in a distributed application. It acts as a transparent, language-agnostic network that handles service-to-service communication, allowing for better observability, reliability, and security in a microservices architecture. Service meshes, such as Istio and Linkerd, provide features such as traffic management, load balancing, encryption, and monitoring, making it easier for developers to build resilient and scalable applications. They abstract away the complexities of network communication, allowing development teams to focus on building and maintaining the functionality of their microservices without getting entangled in networking concerns.

As described in *Figure 8.3*, a cloud-native application stack consists of the following layers:

- **Infrastructure**: This is the foundational layer and consists of computing resources, including operating systems, networks, and storage, all of which are typically managed by a cloud provider or platform.

- **Provisioning**: This is the first layer in the cloud-native stack and encompasses tools to configure, build, and harden the foundation for applications. This layer includes tools to automatically configure, create, and manage the underlying infrastructure, as well as tools for container image scanning and storage.

- **Runtime**: This layer provides the technologies and tools for containers to function, including access to cloud-native storage, cloud-native networking, and container runtimes.

- **Orchestration and management**: Cloud-native apps are inherently scalable and rely on automation. This layer consists of tooling to manage containerized services such as service orchestration, service discovery, scheduling, service proxy, API gateway, and service mesh.

- **Application definition and DevOps**: This is the top layer in the CNCF stack and focuses on tools for developing and deploying cloud-native applications. This includes databases, streaming, messaging, application definition, image builds, and CI/CD tools.

- **Observability and analysis**: Observability and analysis is one of the key layers of a cloud-native application, as it offers tools to measure, log, monitor, trace, and analyze every aspect of the application to detect and remediate anomalies:

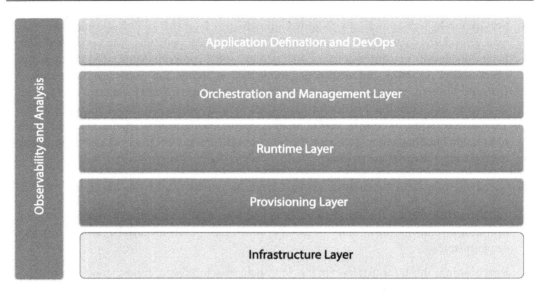

Figure 8.3 – Layers of a cloud-native application

As we have seen, while building cloud-native applications offers benefits such as scale, resilience, flexibility, and efficiency, enterprises must still have a plan for managing and integrating with legacy applications. Let's review some strategies that can help legacy applications coexist with their cloud-native counterparts.

Legacy apps

For enterprises embarking on a hybrid cloud strategy, careful planning and having a roadmap are essential to operate and maintain legacy applications. In an enterprise context, these are typically applications that cannot be easily rearchitected, replatformed, or refactored in a cloud-native environment but are still business-critical. As we reviewed the 6 R's of cloud migration in *Chapter 5, An Enterprise Journey to Cloud Transformation*, these applications would fall into the *retain until retired* category. Enterprises can employ several strategies based on specific business needs:

- **Data first approach**: In this approach, the critical data from legacy systems are extracted and migrated to a cloud-native database. This strategy can help enterprises unlock the data to take advantage of several cloud capabilities, including leveraging the data for artificial intelligence/ machine learning models, analysis, and reporting, thus reducing the dependency on legacy systems for peripheral needs.

- **Refactor**: Depending on the legacy application or system under consideration, enterprises can leverage code conversion or translation tools to migrate the application to a cloud-ready or cloud-native stack.

- **Re-architect**: If there are no imminent pressures, such as an impending contractual obligation renewal or a data center exit, enterprises can choose to re-architect and rewrite the legacy applications either natively on the cloud or replace them with a COTS or SaaS offering. This strategy can often be time-consuming but offers the benefit of starting from a clean slate.

- **Rehost or cloud adjacency**: This can often be the quickest option if there is an impending data center exit or the gravity of enterprise IT has shifted to a public cloud model. Rehosting the legacy system within a collocated data center adjacent to the public cloud can offer low latency connectivity from cloud services and improve operational efficiency and IT efforts to manage and maintain while also reducing the TCO. This can also be a mid-phase strategy while functionality from legacy systems is being re-architected natively on the cloud.

- **API black box**: Based on the type of legacy system, it will be prudent for organizations to implement an integration strategy through a middleware or API gateway that can enable connectivity to legacy applications without the need for lower-level or proprietary connectivity. For instance, a cloud service or cloud-native application can seamlessly interact with a legacy application through APIs, irrespective of where and how the legacy system runs.

Application development and operations

Now that we have a strategy identified for legacy applications, let's shift our focus to other categories of applications within an enterprise. We can broadly classify applications into four groups – cloud-native apps, cloud-ready apps, cloud bolt-on apps, and emerging tech apps. Let's briefly define these classifications:

- **Cloud-native apps**: These are *born in the cloud* applications that are architected and developed from the ground up as per cloud-native principles. When enterprises embark on a cloud transformation, this category will start small and eventually grow as applications are modernized.

- **Cloud-ready apps**: These are applications that can be refactored or replatformed with minimal efforts to ensure they are cloud-ready, but cannot take full advantage of cloud-native capabilities. For instance, certain components of the application, such as web servers, OS, load balancers, or databases, can be replatformed to cloud-native (as a service) components while the application itself remains predominantly unchanged. Generally, this is an intermediary stage as enterprises go through a phased cloud-native transformation. One of the key patterns in the cloud-ready evolutionary architecture is the *strangler fig* pattern *[3]*. Instead of completely rewriting an application, this pattern offers the ability to refactor parts of the application while still having them communicate with the original monolithic application.

- **Cloud bolt-on apps**: These are the category of applications that can take advantage of existing cloud solutions. Some examples include low-code or no-code solutions that can be quickly built on top of existing cloud applications or data, and purpose-built extensions for SaaS applications. These applications typically support specific business functions and needs that are quick to develop and deploy.

- **Emerging tech**: These applications are the innovation cornerstones of cloud transformation. Applications in this category leverage emerging technologies to deliver net new capabilities to an enterprise portfolio. Applications in this category are typically early adopters of emerging technology such as artificial intelligence, blockchain, robotics, AR/VR, and more. Successful adoption and rollout of these applications serve as a guiding post for other applications.

API orchestration, and integration layer

In the realm of cloud-native application architecture, API orchestration and integration play a pivotal role in harnessing the full potential of cloud computing. Cloud-native applications are composed of numerous microservices, each responsible for a specific function, and APIs enable seamless communication and data exchange between these services. In the context of the hybrid cloud, an API and orchestration layer plays a crucial role as it helps abstract the underlying infrastructure and services, allowing developers to focus on business logic rather than complex integrations. This abstraction empowers organizations to gain increased agility and flexibility in responding to changing business requirements.

The API orchestration and integration layer is also an integral part that helps improve the scalability and performance of applications. This is facilitated by managing API traffic, load balancing, and caching. By optimizing API interactions, this layer enhances application performance and ensures that systems remain responsive even under heavy load. As modern applications often rely on external services, such as payment gateways, analytics platforms, and social media integrations, the API orchestration and integration layer simplifies the process of integrating with these services by providing standardized interfaces and managing API credentials and authentication. This also helps streamline development and reduce operational complexity associated with third-party integrations.

Another significant advantage that an API orchestration and integration layer offers is security and governance controls. A well-architected API layer serves as a central point for traffic management, enforcing security policies such as authentication, authorization, and threat detection. The following are some considerations and best practices that can help unlock the benefits of cloud-native computing:

- **Define API standards**: Establishing clear API standards and governance is essential for scalability and interoperability. This includes defining consistent naming conventions, data formats, and security protocols. Enterprises should also consider industry best practices such as REST or GraphQL to ensure interoperability and maintainability.

- **Implement an API gateway**: An API gateway serves as the entry point for all API requests and provides features such as request routing, load balancing, authentication, and rate limiting. The gateway abstracts the underlying microservices from external consumers, providing a unified interface and enhanced security.

- **Build a service mesh**: For complex microservice environments, a service mesh can be invaluable. It provides service discovery, traffic management, observability, and security at the service-to-service communication level. Service meshes enhance the reliability and resilience of cloud-native applications.

- **Third-party integrations**: The API orchestration and integration layer should enable seamless integration with third-party services. It would be prudent for organizations to consider an API stack that offers a comprehensive suite of connectors and adapters to simplify connections with databases, external APIs, and messaging queues.

- **Governance**: Robust monitoring and analytics are vital for understanding API usage, identifying performance bottlenecks, and detecting security threats. Enterprises should implement tools to track API metrics, generate alerts, and provide insights for continuous improvement.

Observability and analytics layer

As cloud-native applications bring unprecedented flexibility and scalability to modern IT infrastructure, observability becomes an extremely important factor in ensuring the reliability, performance, and security of cloud-native systems. Observability refers to the ability to gain insights into the internal state of a system based on its external outputs. In the context of cloud-native applications, observability encompasses monitoring, logging, tracing, and metrics collection across the entire software stack, from individual microservices to underlying infrastructure components. Adopting comprehensive observability practices enables organizations to effectively detect, diagnose, and troubleshoot issues in real time, leading to improved system reliability and uptime. The following are some key factors to consider while architecting and designing the observability and analytics layer, especially for enterprises with a hybrid cloud strategy:

- **Centralized log aggregation**: The foundation of observability lies in centralized log aggregation. Enterprises should implement a unified set of tools that collect, store, and index logs from various sources, including applications, infrastructure, and network devices, across on-premises and cloud environments for a comprehensive view of system events.

- **Monitoring and metrics**: Establish robust monitoring capabilities to continuously monitor and alert on key performance metrics, such as CPU utilization, memory usage, and network latency. Enterprises can leverage monitoring tools that provide real-time dashboards, alerting, and historical trend analysis.

- **Distributed tracing**: For complex microservice architectures, implementing distributed tracing capabilities is essential, as it allows enterprises to track requests as they traverse multiple services, enabling them to identify bottlenecks, performance issues, and dependencies. For a higher level of governance and observability capabilities, organizations can also focus on implementing

business transaction management (BTM) capabilities alongside distributed tracing to garner insights into business transactions as they relate to backing IT services.

- **Infrastructure observability**: In the context of a hybrid cloud environment, monitoring the health and performance of infrastructure across both on-premises and the cloud is crucial. This includes monitoring metrics for compute instances, storage systems, and network resources. Enterprises should leverage cloud-native monitoring services or third-party tools to gain visibility into their infrastructure

- **Application performance management (APM)**: APM tools provide deep insights into application performance, including response times, error rates, and code-level analysis. By monitoring the end user experience, enterprises can proactively address performance issues and optimize application functionality.

- **Security monitoring and alerting**: Observability extends to security monitoring. Enterprises should implement tools to detect potential threats, such as suspicious network activity, unauthorized access attempts, and vulnerability exploits. Automated alerting and incident response mechanisms are essential for mitigating security risks.

Data management layer

As data continues to grow exponentially, designing a data stack in a cloud-native landscape is a strategic endeavor that demands a delicate balance between scalability, resilience, and value creation. Traditional on-premises data stacks are inherently siloed and are constantly challenged with rapid data growth, scale, data sprawl, data duplications, and adaptability. A cloud-native data management approach calls for an open data stack that is decentralized, API-driven, and prioritizes data modularity to support growing business needs. IDC estimates that the world datasphere will grow from 33ZB in 2018 to 175ZB in 2025, representing a 530% increase *[4]*. Another study by **Harvard Business Review (HBR)** indicates that less than 50% of structured data and less than 1% of unstructured data are being used for decision-making in organizations. This clearly indicates that data collection and data processing are not challenges within enterprises but activating and acting on the right data at the right time for the right value creation remains a major bottleneck. In a way, the emergence of cloud and modern technologies such as edge computing, mobile, IoT, and artificial intelligence/machine learning have only exacerbated the data challenge. For instance, in a typical enterprise, data sources that were once predominantly coming from corporate applications and systems are now encompassing data from SaaS applications, suppliers, partners, consumer devices, market trends, third-party data, and IoT devices. The core principles of a modern data strategy include a strategic shift from monolithic data platforms to flexible, purpose-built data clusters with federated data access and a move to democratize data ownership and access through data-as-a-product construct. Let's briefly review the core stages of a modern data analytics platform:

- **Data ingestion**: A modern data platform must support the ingestion of data from various sources, including real-time streaming, transactional systems, integration with SaaS systems, and structured, semi-structured, and unstructured data.

- **Data storage**: Traditional data organizations have a myriad of data platforms and technologies that span the landscape, including transactional systems, proprietary data formats, hyper-converged data warehouses, and hard-to-scale data lakes. This often means moving data constantly across systems, which results in data sprawl. Leveraging an analytics lakehouse approach that supports open file formats such as Avro, Apache Parquet, and Iceberg can standardize data storage, regardless of the underlying platform. Modern cloud data platforms must also support the separation of concerns for data storage and data processing tiers that can be independently scaled. The data storage layer must also enable a seamless read-write API for various data consumers.

- **Data processing**: This is the important layer, as it's where organizations must design for a data-as-a-product architecture. In a data mesh architecture, data is processed and moved between zones to enable consumption across the enterprise based on the business needs. A data mesh aims to connect the data producers directly to the business users to derive the greatest value. We will delve into the data mesh architecture in *Chapter 9, Facets of Digital Transformation*. Another key consideration in a cloud-native data processing platform is the ability to leverage serverless capabilities. For instance, in traditional data systems, the data processing layers scale proportionally with data storage. However, serverless data solutions can offer significant benefits from costs, time, and effort and elastically scale on demand for the duration of the data being processed.

- **Data consumers**: Decoupling the data layers enables a wide variety of application consumers to leverage the data from traditional BI analytical tools and data science. For instance, a reporting application can directly interface on the semantic layer of curated data, while a machine learning application can work on the raw data lake instead of duplicating it and accelerating the time to value.

- **Data governance**: Establishing unified data governance provides a centralized place to manage, monitor, and govern the data in a lakehouse and make it securely accessible to various data analytics and data science tools. This layer comprises three primary concerns:

  - **Data management**: This involves concerns such as data search, discovery, data lineage, data security, data access, and data quality

  - **Observability**: This involves data SRE, logging, monitoring, and alerting

  - **Data orchestration**: This involves automating data workflow orchestration, the authoring pipeline, scheduling, and monitoring

- **Data FinOps**: Data FinOps represents a strategic evolution in data management where financial considerations become integral to the decision-making process. As organizations navigate the complexities of the data landscape, implementing Data FinOps principles can lead to cost optimization, improved resource allocation, and a more accountable and strategic approach to data investments. It also helps organizations identify underutilized resources and optimize data workflows. More importantly, by understanding the cost implications of different data processes, organizations can prioritize investments in areas that deliver the most impact and value.

Automation and governance layer

Automation and governance is a cross-cutting layer that is pivotal to ensure that cloud-native applications are deployed and operated securely, compliantly, and cost-effectively for sustainable growth and success. Cloud-native applications, built to leverage cloud infrastructure and microservices architecture, require comprehensive automation practices to streamline deployment, scaling, and management. Additionally, governance frameworks ensure compliance, security, and cost efficiency, providing the necessary guardrails for successful cloud-native operations. The following are some of the best practices and considerations as enterprises embrace cloud-native practices in the context of a hybrid cloud environment:

- **IaC**: IaC plays a pivotal role by automating manual activities. By codifying infrastructure configurations using tools such as Terraform or Ansible, enterprises can automate infrastructure provisioning, management, and updates. This reduces manual errors, enforces consistency, and accelerates deployment processes.

- **Configuration management**: Configuration management tools, such as Puppet or Chef, enable enterprises to centrally manage and enforce desired application and system configurations. This ensures that environments remain consistent and compliant with established standards.

- **Continuous integration and continuous delivery (CI/CD)**: CI/CD pipelines automate the build, test, and deployment process, enabling faster and more frequent software releases. Implementing CI/CD tools enables organizations to streamline the software delivery life cycle and improve time to market.

- **Container orchestration**: Container orchestration platforms, such as Kubernetes, simplify the deployment, scaling, and management of containerized applications. By automating these tasks, enterprises can optimize resource utilization and reduce operational overhead.

- **Policy-driven governance**: Policy-driven governance is essential for maintaining control over hybrid cloud environments. By defining and establishing policies that govern resource usage, security, and compliance, enterprises can automate and enforce standards to prevent and mitigate risks. Policy engines can automatically monitor and enforce these policies.

Unified security layer

As organizations increasingly adopt hybrid cloud and cloud-native architectures to leverage the benefits of scalability, flexibility, and innovation, ensuring robust security across these environments becomes extremely crucial. Hybrid cloud environments, consisting of a mix of on-premises infrastructure and public/private cloud services, introduce complexity and challenges for security teams. Managing security policies, access controls, and identity management across disparate environments can become fragmented and challenging to maintain. Additionally, cloud-native applications, built on microservices architecture and containerization, introduce new attack vectors and security considerations, such as container vulnerabilities, API security, and orchestration platform security to name a few. Unified security refers to the cohesive approach of securing both traditional on-premises infrastructure and cloud-native applications under a single, integrated framework. A unified security layer provides consistent security policies, centralized visibility and control, integrated identity and access management, coordinated threat detection and response, and streamlined compliance management. The following are some best practices to consider while architecting a unified security layer:

- **Adopt a zero-trust architecture**: A zero-trust security architecture assumes that all users and devices are untrusted and grants access only based on explicit verification. Traditional enterprises operate on the principle of locked-down IT that is governed by a defined perimeter, which is easier to manage through security constructs such as VPNs. As the IT landscape expands outside of the traditional perimeters of IT, such as public clouds, integration with external services such as partner networks, IoT networks, and **bring-your-own-device** (**BYOD**) policies, and a globally spread out workforce, it has become harder than ever to secure a perimeter. A zero-trust architecture primarily pushes security from the network perimeter to the edge. More importantly, a zero-trust architecture eliminates VPN bottlenecks for enterprises, which can significantly improve performance and overall security.

- **Centralized security management platform**: Another key consideration for organizations with a hybrid cloud strategy is deploying a **security information and event management** (**SIEM**) solution that can integrate security tools and services across on-premises and cloud environments for centralized visibility and control.

- **Identity and access management (IAM)**: Establish a robust hybrid IAM solution with a central identity provider that integrates through open security standards with cloud service providers. It is also important to enforce **multi-factor authentication** (**MFA**), establish policy-driven access controls, and automate audits to review access privileges and risks.

- **Network security**: Implement granular network segmentation through **SDN** and deploy next-generation firewalls and **intrusion detection/prevention systems** (**IDS/IPS**) to protect against unauthorized access and malicious traffic.

- **Data security**: Favor strong encryption algorithms to encrypt data stored at rest across cloud storage services, databases, and on-premises filesystems. Establish security policies depending on your data sensitivity needs. For instance, consider using cloud-native **hardware security modules** (**HSMs**) to securely store and manage encryption keys while also meeting compliance requirements such as FIPS 140-2.

- **Security monitoring and audits**: Configure unified security event logging and monitoring across both on-premises and cloud environments. Leverage threat intelligence feeds and vulnerability scanning tools to identify potential threats. Establish security governance processes for incident response and forensic analysis and maintain auditable logs of security events and changes to the security posture.

Having explored the various layers of hybrid cloud infrastructure and how enterprises can architect a cloud-native framework, let's briefly review the prescriptive cloud architecture frameworks that are advocated by some major cloud service providers.

Cloud architecture frameworks from major cloud service providers

In this section, we will explore and review the cloud architecture frameworks prescribed for major CSPs. These frameworks are the result of years of cloud experience, are constantly updated, and reflect the best practices and guidelines to help organizations build a secure, resilient, and efficient cloud infrastructure. It also serves as a blueprint for enterprise architects and development and operations teams to align with industry best practices and adapt accordingly. Regardless of whether the enterprise strategy is to fully deploy on a single cloud, adopt a hybrid cloud approach, or a multi-cloud strategy, it will be prudent for enterprise architects to tailor a cloud strategy that remains compliant to open standards, mitigates vendor lock-ins, evaluates trade-offs, and ensures portability.

Since these frameworks can generally be found online and are maintained and constantly kept up-to-date by the respective cloud service providers, we will only briefly cover the philosophies advocated by each vendor and the focus areas. Although you will find that some of the pillars and concepts advocated by these cloud providers have a lot in common, it is important to acknowledge their unique points of view while also recognizing that these principles must be adapted to an organization's chosen cloud strategy. You can learn more about these frameworks by referencing the links provided at the end of the chapter, in the *Further reading* section.

AWS Well-Architected Framework

The **AWS Well-Architected Framework** is a set of best practices for designing and operating applications on the AWS cloud based on six key pillars – operational excellence, security, reliability, performance efficiency, cost optimization, and sustainability *[5]*. The framework is intended for CTOs, enterprise architects, developers, and operations team members and provides a consistent architectural approach to help reap the best value from AWS. It also enables cloud architects to build scalable, sustainable, and highly performant applications on AWS. The Well-Architected Framework also extends special guidance for various industry and technology domains – also commonly referred to as the AWS Well-Architected Lens – such as the architecting government lens, healthcare industry lens, hybrid networking lens, and machine learning lens, to name a few. AWS also offers the AWS Well-Architected tool – also known as the AWS WA Tool – as a service in the cloud that helps review and measure the application architecture against the best practices. This tool also offers recommendations to improve workload reliability, security, performance, and cost. The AWS Well-Architected Framework is organized into the following six pillars or categories:

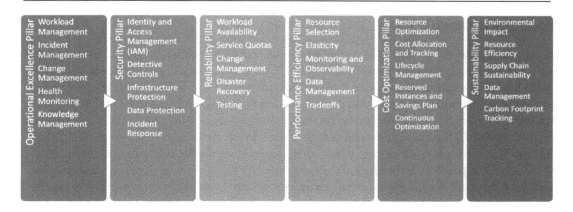

Figure 8.4 – A representation of the AWS Well-Architected Framework

Let's take a closer look.

Operational excellence pillar

The operational excellence pillar focuses on running and monitoring systems to deliver business value continually. This pillar advocates for automation, frequent testing, and refining operational procedures to enhance efficiency and maintain strong operational excellence. It includes treating infrastructure and operations procedures as code, making small and reversible changes, leveraging managed services, refining procedures regularly, and anticipating failures and learning from them.

Security design pillar

The security pillar of the AWS Well-Architected Framework focuses on safeguarding AWS workloads and protecting the confidentiality, integrity, and availability of data and systems. It encompasses five key constituents: IAM, detective controls, infrastructure protection, data protection, and incident response. IAM involves managing user access and permissions to ensure that only authorized individuals can access sensitive resources. Detective controls provide mechanisms to monitor and detect security events, such as malicious activity or unauthorized access attempts. Infrastructure protection includes measures to protect networks, compute resources, and storage systems from external threats. Data protection involves implementing encryption, data classification, and backup strategies to safeguard data confidentiality and integrity. Lastly, incident response focuses on establishing procedures for responding to and recovering from security incidents, minimizing damage and ensuring business continuity. By addressing these aspects, the security pillar aims to create a robust security posture that protects AWS resources and workloads from various threats.

Reliability design pillar

The reliability pillar of the AWS Well-Architected Framework emphasizes designing and operating systems that can withstand failures and recover quickly. It encompasses five constituents: workload availability, service quotas, change management, DR, and testing. Workload availability focuses on ensuring that systems are designed and deployed in a way that maximizes uptime and minimizes disruptions. Service quotas help organizations understand and manage the limits of AWS services to prevent reliability issues caused by exceeding these limits. Change management involves implementing processes to control and track changes to the environment, reducing the risk of unplanned outages. DR plans outline procedures for restoring systems and data in the event of significant disruptions. Finally, testing involves regularly validating recovery procedures and failover mechanisms to ensure that systems can quickly recover from failures and maintain business continuity.

Performance efficiency design pillar

The performance efficiency pillar of the AWS Well-Architected Framework guides organizations in selecting and optimizing cloud resources to achieve the desired performance levels while balancing cost and other considerations. It consists of five constituents: resource selection, elasticity, monitoring and observability, data management, and tradeoffs. Resource selection involves choosing appropriate compute, storage, and network resources based on workload requirements. Elasticity enables systems to scale resources dynamically to meet changing demand. Monitoring and observability provide insights into system performance, allowing organizations to identify bottlenecks and optimize resources accordingly. Data management focuses on optimizing data storage and access patterns for improved performance. Finally, tradeoffs emphasize the need to balance performance goals with factors such as cost, security, and availability, ensuring that the overall system meets the desired performance objectives efficiently.

Cost optimization design pillar

The cost optimization pillar of the AWS Well-Architected Framework focuses on strategies for managing and reducing cloud costs while maintaining service quality and meeting business needs. It encompasses five constituents: resource optimization, cost allocation and tracking, life cycle management, reserved instances and savings plans, and continuous optimization. Resource optimization involves maximizing resource utilization and eliminating waste. Cost allocation and tracking enable organizations to attribute costs to specific workloads or departments, facilitating accountability and informed decision-making. Life cycle management helps manage the life cycle of resources, reducing costs associated with idle or overprovisioned resources. Reserved instances and savings plans provide cost-saving mechanisms for predictable workloads. Finally, continuous optimization requires organizations to regularly review and adjust their cloud infrastructure and usage patterns to identify opportunities for further cost reduction. By implementing these best practices, organizations can optimize their AWS spending and maximize the value they derive from their cloud investments.

Sustainability pillar

The sustainability pillar of the AWS Well-Architected Framework emphasizes the importance of reducing the environmental impact of cloud computing. It encompasses five constituents: environmental impact, resource efficiency, supply chain sustainability, data management, and carbon footprint tracking. Environmental impact focuses on assessing and minimizing the carbon footprint of AWS workloads. Resource efficiency promotes the use of energy-efficient resources and the optimization of resource utilization to reduce power consumption. Supply chain sustainability encourages responsible practices and ethical sourcing in AWS supply chains. Data management involves managing data storage and disposal sustainably, including minimizing data storage volumes and implementing secure disposal methods. Finally, carbon footprint tracking enables organizations to monitor and report on their AWS carbon emissions, providing insights for further optimization and reduction initiatives. By addressing these aspects, the sustainability pillar helps organizations minimize their environmental impact and contribute to the responsible use of cloud computing resources.

The AWS Well-Architected Framework offers a comprehensive set of guidelines and best practices designed to guide organizations in architecting and operating cloud-based systems on the AWS platform that are reliable, secure, efficient, cost-effective, and sustainable. Now, let's explore the Google Cloud Architecture Framework.

Google Cloud Architecture Framework

The **Google Cloud Architecture Framework** provides best practice recommendations for IT leaders, architects, and cloud practitioners to design and operate a cloud topology on **Google Cloud Platform (GCP)** that's secure, efficient, resilient, high-performing, and cost-effective *[6]*. This framework advocates best practices and design recommendations that reflect the expanding capabilities of Google Cloud, industry best practices, community knowledge, and feedback from the industry. The Google Cloud Architecture Framework is organized into six key categories:

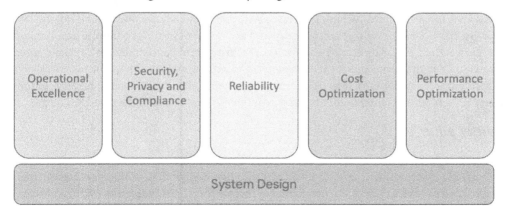

Figure 8.5 – Google Cloud Architecture Framework

System design pillar

The system design pillar forms the foundation of the Google Cloud Architecture Framework and offers a comprehensive set of design principles, architectural recommendations, and best practices to build a robust cloud foundation on GCP. This is a very broad set of system design principles that Google advocates and includes choosing cloud regions, managing cloud resources, designing foundational infrastructure (network, compute, storage), optimizing databases, data analytics, and implementing machine learning strategies for designing cloud workloads for sustainability. The system design pillar also delves deep into designing modern cloud-native architectures such as stateless and serverless architectures. It is important to observe that Google's Cloud Architecture Framework prescribes sustainability as a foundational aspect of system design instead of viewing it as a separate pillar.

Operational excellence pillar

The operational excellence pillar provides guidance on how to achieve operational excellence in the cloud. This pillar focuses on how to efficiently deploy, operate, manage, and monitor cloud workloads on Google Cloud. It covers topics such as automating deployments, setting up monitoring, alerting, logging, establishing cloud support and escalation processes, managing capacity and quota, planning for peak traffic and launch events, and creating a culture of automation. By following the best practices outlined in this category, organizations can improve the reliability, scalability, and efficiency of their cloud operations. This pillar also discusses the products and features of GCP that support the operational excellence objectives.

Security, privacy, and compliance pillar

The security, privacy, and compliance pillar of the Google Cloud Architecture Framework is an exhaustive set of principles that provides guidance on safeguarding cloud assets, data, and workloads within GCP. Some core security principles that Google has pioneered such as the multi-layered defense-in-depth security model, shared fate, and zero trust form the foundation of the security pillar. It covers a wide range of topics, including Google's advocacy of shared fate over shared responsibility, risk management, asset management, identity and access management, compute and container security, network security, data security, application security, compliance obligations, data residency and sovereignty requirements, privacy requirements, and logging and detective controls. By following the guidance in this category, organizations can protect their assets, maintain data privacy, and meet regulatory obligations, enabling them to operate confidently and thrive in the cloud.

Reliability pillar

Within the Google Cloud Architecture Framework, the reliability pillar offers guidance on designing and maintaining highly resilient services on GCP. This pillar focuses on how organizations can define, measure, and manage reliability goals, including defining **service-level indicators (SLIs)** and **service-level objectives (SLOs)** and managing error budgets to improve service reliability in the cloud. The reliability pillar also provides cloud design patterns and operational procedures to architect workloads for scale, high availability, and business continuity. By adhering to the reliability principles and best practices, organizations can design and implement systems that are highly available, resilient, and capable of recovering quickly from failures, ensuring a smooth operation of their cloud-based services.

Cost optimization pillar

The primary focus of the cost optimization pillar in the Google Cloud Architecture Framework is to maximize the enterprise business value of the cloud investments in Google Cloud. The cost optimization pillar provides strategies and techniques to help you manage and optimize costs in Google Cloud. It covers various aspects of cost management, including FinOps adoption and implementation, monitoring and controlling costs, and optimizing costs for specific services, such as compute, containers, serverless, storage, databases, smart analytics, networking, and cloud operations. By following the best practices, tools, and techniques provided in this pillar, organizations can optimize cloud costs while maintaining the performance and reliability of the applications.

Performance optimization pillar

The performance optimization pillar involves designing and tuning Google Cloud resources and services for optimal performance. Optimizing the performance of workloads in the cloud can provide numerous benefits for an organization, including increased efficiency, improved customer satisfaction, higher revenue, and reduced costs. The performance optimization pillar offers guidance on implementing performance optimizations, continuously monitoring and analyzing the performance of cloud resources, and optimizing compute, storage, networking, database, and analytics performance.

As we have discussed, the Google Cloud Architecture Framework provides a structured and comprehensive guide for organizations to build and operate enterprise-grade cloud-native solutions on GCP that meet the highest standards of quality, security, reliability, performance, cost efficiency, and agility. Now, let's explore Azure's Well-Architected Framework.

Microsoft Azure Well-Architected Framework

Similar to the cloud architecture frameworks from AWS and Google, Microsoft Azure prescribes a Well-Architected Framework that acts as a set of proven best practices and recommendations to maximize the business value for workloads deployed on Azure *[7]*. The Azure Well-Architected Framework serves as a guideline for organizations navigating the complexities of cloud architecture. By incorporating the principles outlined in each pillar, organizations can build resilient, secure, and cost-effective solutions in the Azure cloud. As technology continues to evolve, the framework remains a dynamic resource, guiding organizations on their journey to harness the full potential of cloud computing while also ensuring a solid foundation for digital transformation:

Figure 8.6 – Azure Well-Architected Framework

The Azure Well-Architected Framework is built on five core pillars, each addressing a critical aspect of cloud architecture.

Reliability pillar

The reliability pillar of the Azure Well-Architected Framework is built on key principles that contribute to the creation of robust and dependable cloud architectures on Azure. This pillar focuses on ensuring that cloud solutions designed in Azure are highly available, resilient, and able to recover from failures. It emphasizes the need for simple-to-design and implement systems that can take advantage of platform features and withstand component failures, network disruptions, and other unexpected events. This pillar encompasses key concepts such as fault tolerance, redundancy, and disaster recovery. By prioritizing reliability, organizations can minimize service interruptions and maintain business continuity. The framework provides guidance on implementing multiple availability zones, load balancers, automated failover mechanisms, and backup and recovery strategies to enhance the resilience and availability of cloud workloads, ensuring that critical applications and services remain accessible and operational.

Cost optimization pillar

The cost optimization pillar of the Azure Well-Architected Framework focuses on managing and reducing cloud costs while maximizing the business value of cloud investments. It provides strategies for optimizing resource utilization, leveraging cost-saving mechanisms, and implementing a cost-conscious culture. Key considerations include selecting appropriate cloud resources, implementing autoscaling and elasticity, utilizing reserved instances, and monitoring cloud consumption patterns. By adopting best practices in cost optimization, organizations can reduce wasteful spending, forecast and control cloud budgets effectively, and ensure that their cloud investments are aligned with their business objectives. The framework emphasizes the importance of continuous cost analysis, performance monitoring, and leveraging automation to identify and implement cost reduction opportunities.

Security pillar

The security pillar of the Azure Well-Architected Framework prioritizes the protection of cloud workloads from potential threats, data breaches, and compliance violations. It encompasses multiple layers of security measures, including IAM, network security, data encryption, and threat detection and response. The framework provides guidance on implementing Azure Security Center, utilizing **role-based access control** (RBAC), securing network traffic through firewalls and network security groups, and encrypting sensitive data at rest and in transit. By adhering to security best practices, organizations can establish a robust security posture, protect their cloud assets from malicious actors, and ensure compliance with industry standards and regulations such as ISO 27001, SOC 2, and HIPAA.

Operational excellence pillar

The operational excellence pillar of the Azure Well-Architected Framework focuses on building and maintaining cloud solutions that deliver operational efficiency, resilience, and the ability to respond to changes rapidly. It emphasizes the importance of automation, DevOps practices, and monitoring systems. Key aspects include automating infrastructure provisioning, implementing CI/CD pipelines, monitoring **key performance indicators** (KPIs), and conducting regular patch management. By prioritizing operational excellence, organizations can streamline their cloud operations, improve service reliability, reduce human error, and enhance the overall customer experience. The framework provides guidance on utilizing Azure Monitor, Azure Automation, and other tools to monitor workloads, automate tasks, and continuously improve the efficiency and effectiveness of cloud solutions.

Performance efficiency pillar

The performance efficiency pillar of the Azure Well-Architected Framework guides organizations in selecting and optimizing cloud resources to achieve desired performance levels. It involves balancing factors such as resource type, size, and scalability with cost and security considerations. Key concepts include selecting appropriate compute, storage, and networking resources, implementing autoscaling and elasticity mechanisms, and optimizing data access patterns. By focusing on performance efficiency, organizations can ensure that their cloud solutions can handle varying workloads, deliver consistent performance, and meet end-user expectations. The framework provides recommendations for monitoring performance metrics, identifying bottlenecks, and optimizing resource utilization through tools such as Azure Monitor and Azure Load Balancer.

The prescriptive cloud architecture frameworks from AWS, Google, and Azure have a lot of core principles in common, such as reliability, operational excellence, and cost optimization. All of the frameworks also provide guidance and best practices to achieve these objectives through platform-specific services. From a security perspective, AWS places a strong emphasis on operational security, and Azure focuses on security governance and compliance, while Google Cloud introduces the shared-fate model, which is uniquely different from the shared responsibility models. As organizations embark on a cloud transformation journey, sustainability can often be top of the mind for enterprise leaders. AWS emphasizes sustainability as a separate pillar while Google Cloud advocates for sustainability considerations as part of the foundational system design pillar. Regardless of the approach – single cloud, hybrid cloud, or multi-cloud – it will be prudent for enterprise architects to assimilate the best practices and guidance and develop a vendor-agnostic cloud framework that aligns with the organization's vision and objectives. Now, let's explore some of the private cloud and hybrid cloud strategies that are available.

Private and hybrid cloud strategies

While public clouds offer scalability and flexibility, there are instances where organizations opt for private cloud solutions to address specific needs related to security, compliance, regulatory controls, and restrictions. Private cloud strategies represent a nuanced approach to cloud computing, offering organizations a balance between the advantages of the cloud and the need for control, security, and compliance. Whether hosted on-premises or by a third-party provider, private clouds empower organizations to tailor their IT infrastructure to specific requirements, ensuring a flexible and secure foundation for their digital operations. A private cloud is a cloud computing model that is dedicated to a single organization. Unlike public clouds, which are shared among multiple users, a private cloud provides exclusive use of its resources to a single organization. This isolation offers enhanced control over data, security, and compliance. Several public cloud providers also offer private cloud solutions, allowing organizations to take advantage of a public cloud's principles, architecture, and skill set within their on-premises environment as well. However, as discussed previously, enterprises must carefully architect and design cloud frameworks that comply with open standards, open APIs, and open file formats. Let's review some of the popular private cloud and hybrid cloud offerings.

VMware Cloud Foundation (VCF)

VCF is an integrated platform that brings together VMware's virtualization, software-defined storage, and network virtualization technologies into a single stack. It is designed to deliver a consistent and standardized infrastructure across private and public clouds, facilitating a more agile and efficient IT environment. This can be a good choice for enterprises that have a significant VMware footprint within their IT landscape and want to maintain control over their infrastructure.

Let's look at some of the key components of VCF:

- **vSphere**: At the core of VMware Cloud Foundation is vSphere, VMware's flagship virtualization platform. vSphere provides the foundation for virtualized compute resources, enabling organizations to run and manage **virtual machines** (**VMs**) with high levels of performance and efficiency.

- **Virtual Storage Area Network (vSAN)**: VMware Cloud Foundation leverages vSAN for software-defined storage. vSAN enables the pooling of storage resources from direct-attached storage across server nodes, creating a highly scalable and resilient storage infrastructure without the need for external storage arrays.

- **NSX**: Network virtualization is achieved through VMware NSX, which allows organizations to create and manage virtual networks, providing agility and flexibility in the deployment of applications and services.

- **vRealize Suite**: The inclusion of the vRealize Suite enhances the management capabilities of VCF. It offers comprehensive cloud management, automation, and monitoring tools, enabling organizations to optimize resource utilization and enhance operational efficiency.

Major public cloud providers also offer VCF on public clouds, which can be hugely beneficial for organizations with a hybrid cloud strategy, imminent data center exits, or use cases such as cloud bursting. Some of the key benefits of VCF include unified infrastructure management, ensuring consistency across on-premises, private and public cloud environments, integrated management tools, automation, and accelerated deployment. However, the associated challenges, including initial investment, complexity, and dependencies on the VMware ecosystem, should be carefully considered and addressed during the planning and implementation phases.

OpenStack

OpenStack is a cloud computing platform that provides a set of software tools for building and managing both public and private clouds. It enables organizations to create and manage scalable **Infrastructure-as-a-Service** (**IaaS**) environments, offering flexibility, scalability, and customization. OpenStack, an open source cloud computing platform, has emerged as a transformative force in the dynamic landscape of cloud technology. Launched in 2010, OpenStack has rapidly evolved into a community-driven project, fostering innovation and collaboration. OpenStack is widely used for building private clouds within organizations, providing a secure and scalable infrastructure for internal needs. It also serves as the foundation for public cloud services offered by various service providers. Organizations often leverage OpenStack to build hybrid cloud environments, integrating private and public cloud services. This allows for flexibility in workload placement and facilitates a seamless experience across different cloud environments.

The following are some of the key components of OpenStack:

- **Nova (compute)**: OpenStack Nova is the compute component responsible for managing VMs and providing a scalable and on-demand compute service. It enables organizations to run instances of VMs, catering to various computing needs.

- **Swift (object storage)**: Swift is OpenStack's object storage component and is designed for storing and retrieving large amounts of unstructured data. It provides scalable, redundant, and durable storage capabilities, making it suitable for storing data objects such as images, videos, and backups.

- **Cinder (block storage)**: Cinder offers block storage services in OpenStack, allowing organizations to attach storage volumes to VMs. This provides additional storage capacity for applications and databases, offering high-performance block storage solutions.

- **Neutron (networking)**: Neutron is OpenStack's networking component and provides **Networking-as-a-Service (NaaS)**. It enables organizations to define and manage networks and connectivity within the cloud infrastructure, supporting diverse network topologies.

- **Keystone (identity)**: Keystone serves as the identity and authentication service in OpenStack. It provides a central directory of users and their permissions, ensuring secure access control and authentication across all OpenStack services.

- **Glance (image service)**: Glance is the image service component, allowing users to discover, register, and retrieve VM images. It facilitates efficient management of operating system images used for creating VMs.

- **Horizon (dashboard)**: Horizon is the web-based dashboard for OpenStack, providing users with a graphical interface to access and manage resources. It simplifies the user experience and allows administrators to monitor and control cloud resources.

OpenStack stands as a testament to the power of open source collaboration and community-driven development in shaping the future of cloud infrastructure. Its impact on private and public clouds, research, education, telecommunications, and hybrid cloud scenarios highlights its versatility and adaptability. As technology continues to advance, OpenStack's role in empowering organizations to build scalable, interoperable, and flexible cloud environments remains pivotal in the ever-evolving landscape of cloud computing. However, enterprises must consider the following challenges:

- **Complexity of deployment**: Deploying and configuring OpenStack can be complex, requiring expertise and careful planning. However, various distributions and deployment tools aim to simplify this process.

- **Evolving ecosystem**: The rapid evolution of the cloud technology landscape poses challenges in keeping OpenStack aligned with emerging technologies. The community actively addresses these challenges through regular updates and enhancements.

- **Competing technologies**: OpenStack faces competition from other cloud platforms and services, including proprietary solutions and alternative open source projects. The landscape continues to evolve with the emergence of new technologies.

AWS Outposts

In the era of cloud computing, organizations are continuously seeking innovative solutions that seamlessly blend the benefits of the cloud with on-premises infrastructure. **AWS Outposts**, introduced by AWS, represents an approach to bridging the gap between on-premises data centers and the cloud. AWS Outposts is an extension of the AWS cloud infrastructure that brings AWS services, compute, storage, and database capabilities to on-premises environments. It is designed to address scenarios where certain workloads, data, or applications need to reside within on-premises data centers due to specific requirements such as low latency, data residency, regulatory compliance, applications requiring ultra-low latency, and edge computing. AWS Outposts offer the following key benefits:

- **Hybrid cloud capability**: AWS Outposts enables organizations to build a truly hybrid cloud environment by seamlessly integrating on-premises infrastructure with the AWS cloud. This allows for consistent operations across both environments.

- **Fully managed service**: AWS Outposts is a fully managed service, meaning that AWS takes care of hardware installation, maintenance, and software updates. This eliminates the operational burden on organizations and ensures that the infrastructure is always up-to-date.

- **Native AWS services**: With AWS Outposts, organizations can leverage a wide range of AWS services locally, including compute instances (EC2), storage (S3, EBS), and databases (RDS). This ensures consistency with the AWS cloud and facilitates workload portability.

- **Local processing and low latency**: AWS Outposts brings compute and storage capabilities directly to the on-premises location, minimizing latency for applications that require local processing. This is particularly beneficial for latency-sensitive workloads.

- **Secure and consistent operations**: AWS Outposts extends AWS security and compliance to the on-premises environment. Organizations can apply AWS IAM policies, use AWS **Key Management Service** (**KMS**), and implement VPC peering for secure and consistent operations.

Here are some key considerations for enterprises that use this strategy:

- **Initial deployment complexity**: While AWS manages the hardware and software updates, the initial deployment of AWS Outposts may require careful planning and coordination with AWS. Organizations need to ensure that the on-premises environment meets the necessary prerequisites.

- **Cost considerations**: AWS Outposts involves costs for both the hardware and ongoing management by AWS. Organizations need to evaluate the TCO and determine whether the benefits justify the investment.

- **Integration with existing infrastructure**: Integrating AWS Outposts with existing on-premises infrastructure and networking configurations may pose challenges. Proper planning and collaboration with AWS are essential to ensure smooth integration.

- **AWS-centric cloud**: If the enterprise strategy is fully invested in AWS, this can be a great fit.

Google GKE Enterprise (Anthos)

GKE Enterprise, also popularly referred to as Google Anthos, is a modern cloud application platform that's designed to provide a consistent development and operations experience across hybrid and multi-cloud environments. Anthos enables organizations to build, deploy, and manage applications seamlessly across on-premises data centers, GCP, and other cloud providers. Google Anthos, stands at the forefront of this transformation, offering a comprehensive platform that facilitates application modernization, consistency across environments, and operational efficiency.

Here are some of the key features of GKE Enterprise (Anthos):

- **Multi-cloud and hybrid cloud support**: Google Anthos embraces a multi-cloud and hybrid cloud approach, allowing organizations to run applications consistently across different cloud providers, on-premises environments, and GCP. This flexibility provides freedom from vendor lock-in and supports diverse infrastructure needs.

- **Google distributed cloud edge**: The distributed edge feature lets enterprises add on-premises GKE clusters to their fleet, this time running on Google-provided and maintained hardware and supporting a subset of GKE enterprise features virtually anywhere.

- **Kubernetes-based container orchestration**: At the core of Google Anthos is Kubernetes, an open source container orchestration platform. Anthos leverages Kubernetes to automate the deployment, scaling, and management of containerized applications, fostering portability and scalability.

- **Anthos Config Management**: Anthos Config Management enables organizations to enforce policies and configuration settings consistently across their Kubernetes clusters, regardless of the underlying infrastructure. This centralized management streamlines operations and ensures governance.

- **Anthos Service Mesh**: Anthos Service Mesh is built on the open source Istio project, providing a unified and secure communication layer for microservices within applications. It enhances visibility, control, and security for microservices architectures.

- **Multi-cloud portability**: Google Anthos empowers organizations to build and manage applications that can run on multiple cloud providers, fostering a multi-cloud strategy. This mitigates the risk of vendor lock-in and provides the flexibility to choose the most suitable cloud services.

- **Migrate and modernize applications**: Google Anthos facilitates the modernization of existing applications by allowing organizations to lift and shift workloads or refactor applications into containers. This supports a gradual transition to cloud-native architectures.

- **Integrated DevOps and tools**: Anthos integrates with popular development tools, including Google Cloud Build and Google Cloud Code, providing developers with a familiar and streamlined environment for building, testing, and deploying applications.

Some considerations while adopting GKE enterprise (Anthos) are as follows:

- **Operational complexity**: While GKE enterprise simplifies aspects of hybrid cloud and multi-cloud operations, managing a hybrid environment can still be complex. Organizations need to invest in training and resources to effectively operate and maintain GKE enterprise.

- **Cost considerations**: Organizations should carefully assess the TCO of deploying and maintaining GKE enterprise on-premises. This includes hardware costs, licensing fees, and ongoing operational expenses, as enterprises would for on-premises infrastructure.

Azure Stack

Azure Stack is an extension of Microsoft Azure, the cloud computing platform by Microsoft. It allows organizations to deploy Azure services locally on their infrastructure, creating a consistent hybrid cloud environment. Azure Stack enables the development and deployment of applications that can run in both on-premises and Azure cloud environments. By providing a consistent Azure experience, Azure Stack empowers organizations with an Azure strategy to embrace a hybrid cloud strategy, supporting diverse workloads and scenarios.

Here are some of the key features of Azure stack:

- **Consistent Azure experience**: Azure Stack provides a consistent experience with Azure, allowing organizations to use the same **Azure Resource Manager** (**ARM**) templates, Azure portal, and Azure PowerShell commands. This consistency simplifies application development and deployment across environments.

- **Azure services on-premises**: With Azure Stack, organizations can bring a subset of Azure services into their data centers. This includes services such as Azure App Service, Azure Functions, Azure Blob Storage, and more. This enables the creation of applications that leverage cloud capabilities on-premises.

- **Hybrid cloud flexibility**: Azure Stack supports a hybrid cloud strategy, allowing organizations to run workloads locally and in the Azure public cloud. This flexibility is valuable for scenarios where certain workloads need to remain on-premises due to regulatory requirements, data residency concerns, or specific performance needs.

- **Integrated security and compliance**: Azure Stack inherits the security features and compliance certifications of Azure. This ensures that workloads running on Azure Stack benefit from the same level of security controls, identity management, and compliance standards as those in the Azure public cloud.

- **App services for containers**: Azure Stack supports containers through **Azure Kubernetes Service** (**AKS**) and **Azure Container Instances** (**ACI**). This allows organizations to modernize applications using containerized architectures while maintaining the flexibility to run them on-premises.

- **Edge and disconnected scenarios**: Azure Stack is suitable for edge computing scenarios where low-latency processing is crucial. It allows organizations to deploy Azure services in remote locations or areas with limited connectivity, ensuring a consistent computing experience.

The following are some key considerations:

- **Hardware compatibility and requirements**: Deploying Azure Stack requires compatible hardware that meets Microsoft's specifications. Organizations need to ensure that their existing infrastructure or new investments align with Azure Stack's requirements.

- **Operational complexity**: While Azure Stack simplifies certain aspects of hybrid cloud operations, managing a hybrid environment can still be complex. Organizations need to invest in training and resources to effectively operate and maintain Azure Stack.

- **Cost considerations**: Organizations should carefully assess the TCO of deploying and maintaining Azure Stack. This includes hardware costs, licensing fees, and ongoing operational expenses.

Summary

In this chapter, we discussed how enterprises with significant investments in their on-premises IT infrastructure can adopt cloud computing to accelerate and transform their business objectives. We explored how organizations can build the foundations of a hybrid cloud through an opinionated and vendor-agnostic framework, along with the core layers that constitute the framework. We also explored the cloud-native principles that organizations must consider while designing and developing modern applications in the cloud.

We then explored the different cloud architecture frameworks and the various pillars advocated by three major cloud service providers – AWS, Google Cloud, and Azure. Finally, we discussed some of the unique private cloud and hybrid cloud strategies and offerings that can be adopted by enterprises.

In the next chapter, we will discuss the various facets of digital transformation.

Further reading

To learn more about the topics that were covered in this chapter, take a look at the following references:

1. `https://www.mckinsey.com/~/media/McKinsey/Industries/Electric%20 Power%20and%20Natural%20Gas/Our%20Insights/Traditional%20 company%20new%20businesses%20The%20pairing%20that%20can%20 ensure%20an%20incumbents%20survival/Traditional-company-new- businesses-VF.pdf`

2. `https://landscape.cncf.io/`

3. `https://martinfowler.com/bliki/StranglerFigApplication.html`

4. `https://www.seagate.com/files/www-content/our-story/trends/ files/idc-seagate-dataage-whitepaper.pdf`

5. `https://docs.aws.amazon.com/wellarchitected/latest/framework/ welcome.html`

6. `https://cloud.google.com/architecture/framework`

7. `https://azure.microsoft.com/en-us/solutions/cloud-enablement/ well-architected/#reliability`

9

Facets of Digital Transformation

When is the right time to develop a cloud strategy? For some enterprises, the answer is as we adopt the cloud, while for several others, it is still unclear. In its *Cloud Strategy Cookbook*, Gartner advises organizations to develop a cloud strategy even before embarking on a cloud transformation initiative [1]. The cookbook recognizes the fact that a one-size-fits-all approach to the cloud is insufficient, considering the diverse needs and business objectives of modern-day enterprises. As modern technology continues to blur the line between business and IT, it is important to align the organization's cloud strategy closely with business objectives, to maximize the value derived from cloud investments and drive tangible outcomes. As organizations continue to adopt cloud computing –regardless of the deployment model, IaaS, PaaS, or SaaS – it is crucial to design and develop a digital strategy that will serve as the foundation for future business goals. The tools, processes, and technologies that supported a traditional IT ecosystem predominantly within the confines of a data center can no longer support the scale, diversity, complexity, and needs of a cloud-based ecosystem. Embarking on a cloud journey brings a paradigm shift to enterprise IT across functions. One fundamental example is the shared responsibility model of cloud where the cloud provider assumes the responsibility of managing and securing a portion of the stack while the consumer is responsible for the rest. This in itself is a major shift in enterprise IT operations, as the organization would now have little or no control over a significant portion of the infrastructure or application stack. Further, this also means that top-of-the-stack responsibility is guided and restricted as well, with a defined framework. For instance, most organizations today have some variant of a SaaS application in the IT ecosystem – think Microsoft 365 for office apps, Google Workspace for online productivity, Workday for HR, or Salesforce for CRM. All of these applications run within a cloud environment that is beyond the control of a traditional IT organization. This means that the organization has just expanded its IT footprint beyond the confines of the traditional data center, warranting a robust strategy for network connectivity, integration, application security, data security, and governance.

In this chapter, we will explore the various facets of digital transformation that can help set the foundation and tone for an organization's cloud strategy. Specifically, we will explore the following topics:

- How enterprises can build a security-first cloud foundation to ensure overall enterprise security including network, data, application, and asset management

- Learning to rethink infrastructure in a hybrid cloudscape with a focus on infrastructure modernization

- Strategies for building cloud-native applications with a focus on application modernization

- Leveraging cloud-native design to modernize data ecosystem

- Learning how to build a cloud governance model to optimize cloud infrastructure for costs, performance, and resource efficiency and maximize the value of cloud investments

Building a security-first cloud architecture

If we go by the measure of **Common Vulnerability and Exposures** (**CVEs**) published in the **National Vulnerability Database** (**NVD**) and maintained by the **National Institute of Standards and Technology** (**NIST**), we are witnessing a whopping 4.5x increase in the amount of CVEs just in the last 7 years. Per the data, roughly 100 CVEs were published in NVD each week on average in 2016, while that number jumped to 450 CVEs in 2023 *[2] [3]*. Security is everyone's business, and this is especially critical for modern enterprises as access to modern technology is democratized through the cloud. Building a security-first cloud architecture for enterprises is a crucial task in an era where cyber threats are becoming increasingly sophisticated. One common challenge enterprises typically face with cloud adoption is the shared responsibility model introduced by the cloud. Having a clear understanding of the shared responsibility model is extremely crucial to protecting and securing application workloads and data in the cloud. This can often be challenging as this shared responsibility model can be uniquely defined by each **cloud service provider** (**CSP**), the service model, and the cloud services being used. Before delving into security controls, let's review some common challenges organizations face during cloud transformation. According to the *Pandemic 11* report, the following are the top concerns that organizations face with cloud security *[4]*:

1. Insufficient identity, credential, access, and key management

2. Insecure APIs and interfaces

3. Cloud misconfiguration and inadequate change control

4. Lack of cloud security strategy and architecture

5. Insecure software development practices

In addition to this, enterprises face the following challenges further augmented by external threat vectors:

- **Constant changes to cloud services**: Due to the dynamic nature of cloud services, with new services being updated and launched regularly, enterprises must remain vigilant. To keep pace, organizations must have processes and security controls in place to validate and test against a baseline security configuration to maintain compliance with evolving requirements.

- **Leveraging multiple service tiers**: Enterprises typically have workloads that span multiple service types. This requires unification and validation of security controls of each service type while keeping the overall workload security requirement in consideration. For example, a payment processing service can leverage multiple service types (compute infrastructure, API platform, and payment gateway SaaS) while requiring a **payment card interface** (**PCI**) compliance obligation.

- **Data security**: As enterprise data grows beyond the on-premises environment and into the cloud, an important decision point for enterprises is data security. Depending on the regulatory requirements and data gravity, it is crucial for security organizations to define where data encryption keys are managed.

- **External threats**: As new security vulnerabilities and **advanced persistent threats** (**APTs**) continue to rise, this can pose a significant challenge. For instance, brute-force/**distributed denial-of-service** (**DDoS**) attacks, malware or ransomware attacks, and **man-in-the-middle** (**MITM**) attacks can all contribute to new attack vectors that enterprises will have to guard against.

Let us explore some of the foundational security principles that enterprises must account for while building a cloud foundation.

Foundational security principles

Architecting a secure cloud environment is extremely crucial for enterprises looking to leverage the benefits of cloud computing while ensuring the protection of data and applications. By implementing foundational security principles, organizations can establish a solid security posture, protect data and applications, and build trust with both internal and external stakeholders. Let's take a closer look at this:

- **Landing zone design**: The most fundamental aspect of cloud service deployment is landing zone design. A landing zone defines the foundational aspects of cloud deployment for an organization, such as organization policies, interconnectivity, resource management, security, networking, and **identity and access management** (**IAM**). A robust landing zone design is essential before organizations start deploying workloads on the cloud. It is also important to modularize the landing zone design and adapt with scalability and growth aspects in consideration.

- **Zero trust architecture** (**ZTA**): Zero trust security in the cloud is a comprehensive approach that eliminates implicit trust within cloud environments [5]. Instead of assuming that users or devices within a network are trustworthy, zero trust requires continuous verification and authentication for all access requests. This is achieved through mechanisms such as **multi-factor authentication** (**MFA**), least privilege access, and micro-segmentation. By limiting access to only what is necessary, zero trust minimizes the attack surface, reducing the risk of breaches.

- **Risk assessments**: It is essential to have periodical formal risk assessments to ensure that the security requirements of the organization meet both internal and external security obligations. This provides a summary of risks and the capability of the organization to detect and counter security threats. Some best practices include leveraging the **Cloud Security Alliance** (**CSA**) **Cloud Controls Matrix** (**CCM**) and **Cloud for Internet Security** (**CIS**) benchmarks for risk assessment.

- **Defining and adopting secure blueprints**: Automation is key to keeping up with the ever-changing security landscape. One of the primary responsibilities of a security organization is to define security blueprints for some common deployments in the cloud. These blueprints can standardize enterprise asset deployments while also enabling faster deployments and centralized governance.

- **Layered security design/shift-left security strategy**: Enterprises must adopt a layered **defense-in-depth** (**DiD**) security design by leveraging security features in each layer of the application or workload to limit the attack vector. Another strategy is to incorporate security best practices during the development and deployment stages; for instance, testing security issues in the application code, scanning container images during deployment, automatic scans, and detection of misconfigurations and security anti-patterns.

- **Automating deployment and security monitoring**: Automating deployments by taking human errors out of manual deployment activities cannot just increase development and deployment velocity but can, more importantly, improve the security posture of an organization. Similarly, it is a security best practice to invest in automated tools to scan infrastructure for vulnerabilities and automate the scanning of **continuous integration/continuous deployment** (**CI/CD**) pipelines.

- **Machine learning (ML) for security automation**: ML plays a pivotal role in enhancing enterprise cloud security by providing advanced capabilities for threat detection, **incident response** (**IR**), and overall risk management. As cloud environments become more complex, dynamic, and interconnected, ML-based security automation can help with advanced threat detection, **user and entity behavior analytics** (**UEBA**), and zero-day predictive analytics and improve the overall security of the workloads in the cloud.

- **Compliance with data sovereignty and data residency**: Based on the nature of the enterprise, it is important to comply with local regulations and data residency and data sovereignty requirements. Architecting applications ground up with compliance requirements can often save significant time and effort; for instance, hosting a workload in a secured cloud zone for the public sector, and leveraging confidential **virtual machines** (**VMs**) to prevent in-memory data exfiltration.

- **Compensatory controls**: With the shared responsibility model in the cloud, organizations should strive to mitigate risks with technical compensatory controls, contractual protections, and third-party attestations. For instance, leveraging cloud-native security controls for data-at-rest and in-transit encryption can be a compensatory technical control, and a **Business Associate Agreement** (**BAA**) or **Cloud Data Processing Addendum** (**CDPA**) can serve as a contractual protection [6].

- **Risk protection programs**: Finally, enterprises can also leverage cyber insurance programs to better understand, remediate, and achieve high levels of security posture.

- **Security audits and assessments**: Conduct regular penetration testing to identify and address vulnerabilities in the network infrastructure. Use automated vulnerability scanning tools to regularly assess the security posture of your cloud environment.

Automating cloud asset management

Having an accurate asset inventory and a good understanding of all cloud assets and their relationships are extremely critical to enterprise security. Asset management can quickly become complex to manage and secure as teams start building applications or moving workloads to the cloud. Automating asset management using **Infrastructure as Code (IaC)** tools such as Terraform can help meet enterprise security best practices. Security teams must also focus on implementing automatic asset monitoring and alerting to monitor assets for non-compliance and deviations from security blueprints. In the context of a hybrid cloud deployment model, enterprises can also leverage existing **security information and event management (SIEM)** systems as a **single pane of glass (SPOG)** to manage and monitor assets across the enterprise.

IAM

IAM is a critical component of securing enterprise resources, especially in the context of multi-cloud and hybrid cloud environments, where resources are distributed between on-premises data centers and CSPs. Implementing effective IAM practices helps organizations manage user access, protect sensitive data, and ensure compliance. Following are some best practices for IAM:

- **Centralized identity management (IdM)**: Implement a centralized IdM system that spans both on-premises and cloud environments. This centralization helps streamline user provisioning, de-provisioning, and access management processes, while also securely managing identities centrally.

- **Implement break glass procedures**: A break glass process in the cloud refers to an emergency access mechanism that grants temporary, privileged access to critical systems or data in the cloud in case of emergencies such as lockouts. This procedure is typically reserved for highly sensitive operations or when other access methods are unavailable. It is implemented with strict security controls to prevent unauthorized use. When activated, the break glass process allows designated individuals to bypass normal access restrictions, enabling them to quickly resolve critical issues or mitigate risks.

- **Federate access through single sign-on (SSO)**: Use secure federation protocols such as **Security Assertion Markup Language (SAML)** or **Open Authorization (OAuth)** for identity federation between on-premises and cloud environments, allowing users to authenticate once and access resources seamlessly.

- **Enable MFA**: Enforce MFA for accessing critical systems and data. This adds an extra layer of security, reducing the risk of unauthorized access even if credentials are compromised.

- **Protect super admin accounts**: Refrain from using existing user accounts and create new accounts for super admin access. Ensure break glass procedures are well documented, enabling MFA, augmented with physical security tokens and backup accounts.

- **Log everything**: Ensure all cloud activities are logged and integrated with a centralized SIEM. This also helps with audit access and adhering to compliance requirements.

- **Implement the principle of least privilege (PoLP)**: Overprovisioning user access is often the top security risk associated with misconfigured cloud resources and the risk of insider threat. Adopt PoLP or **just-in-time** (**JIT**) access policies across the organization. Implementing robust controls for privileged access such as session recording and monitoring can mitigate the risk of unauthorized actions.

- **Automate policy control**: Leverage cloud-native tools to automatically review access policies, permissions, and unnecessary privileges promptly to minimize security risks.

Network security

Extending networks outside of the traditional data centers can have implications on network security. On-premises networks often have a defined, predictable network perimeter or boundary that is easier to secure through network firewalls, **intrusion detection systems** (**IDS**), and physical routers. Ensuring robust network security, especially in hybrid cloud environments, is crucial for protecting sensitive data, maintaining compliance, and preventing cyber threats. Some best practices to secure hybrid cloud networks are as follows:

- **Segmentation and micro-segmentation**: Divide the network into segments to isolate different types of data and services. This limits the lateral movement of attackers if one segment is compromised. Implement micro-segmentation to apply granular access controls, especially in multi-tiered applications. This restricts communication between individual workloads.

- **Strive for a zero trust network**: The zero trust security model means that no one is trusted by default, regardless of where they are accessing the network from, unless accompanied by other levels of access checks such as identity checks, context, or trusted devices.

- **Secure cross-cloud connectivity**: Ensure secure connectivity between on-premises and cloud environments using **virtual private networks** (**VPNs**) or dedicated connections such as Google Cloud Interconnect, AWS Direct Connect, or Azure ExpressRoute. Encrypt data in transit using protocols such as TLS/SSL for web traffic and IPsec for site-to-site VPNs.

- **Secure the cloud perimeter**: Leveraging DiD network security strategy, define network firewall policies and rules at various hierarchical levels to permit or deny network traffic.

- **Automate network traffic inspection**: Leverage cloud-native tools such as cloud IDS, ML-based **next-generation firewalls** (**NGFWs**), firewall rules logging, and packet mirroring to inspect, monitor, and protect workloads in the cloud.

- **Application security**: Deploy **web application firewalls (WAFs)** to protect web applications from common security threats and vulnerabilities. Secure APIs with proper authentication, authorization, and encryption to prevent unauthorized access and data breaches.

- **Network monitoring and logging**: Implement continuous network monitoring to detect anomalies and potential security incidents promptly. Centralize logs from both on-premises and cloud environments for comprehensive visibility into network activities.

- **Implement a cloud access security broker (CASB)**: Implement a centralized CASB solution, especially with hybrid cloud and multi-cloud deployments, to monitor and manage the use of cloud services and to ensure compliance and data security.

Application security

Securing applications in hybrid cloud environments is essential for protecting sensitive data, ensuring compliance, and maintaining the integrity of business operations. It is essential for organizations to adopt a layered security approach while developing applications in the cloud and shift left with security practices. The following are some best practices for application security in a hybrid or multi-cloud environment:

- **Implement secure application development best practices**: Train developers on secure coding practices and leverage automated DevOps tools to mitigate common vulnerabilities in the application code such as injection attacks, buffer overflows, and **cross-site scripting (XSS)**.

- **Use security-hardened VMs or container images**: Enforce policies to only leverage security-hardened VM images and container images for application development and deployment. Leverage cloud-native offerings such as shielded VMs.

- **Automate application releases**: Due to the intricacy of complex application development environments, it is difficult to deploy, update, and patch them manually, especially when adhering to consistent security requirements. Automated deployment pipelines can eliminate manual errors, standardize development feedback loops, enable rapid product iterations, and secure application releases.

- **Implement DevOps security**: Especially with cloud-native application development, an attacker can compromise a CI/CD pipeline affecting the entire stack. Establish best practices such as binary authorization, securing artifact or container registries, container image vulnerability scanning, encrypting container images, and signature verifications in the CI/CD pipeline.

- **Patch management**: Keep all application components, frameworks, and libraries up to date with the latest security patches by implementing a robust patch management process. Organizations must define clear guidelines for patch frequency, prioritization, vulnerability scanning, and testing procedures and implement automated patch management tools to streamline and accelerate the deployment process.

- **Dependency scanning**: Regularly scan third-party libraries and dependencies for known vulnerabilities. Address and update any vulnerable components in your application stack. Also, have a process to validate third-party components – especially open source – are kept up to date and comply with enterprise security standards.

- **Implement dynamic application security testing (DAST)**: Use DAST tools to simulate real-world attack scenarios and identify vulnerabilities at runtime.

Data security

The importance of data security in the cloud cannot be overstated, as organizations increasingly rely on cloud services to store, process, and manage their data. It is imperative to implement robust security measures to protect against evolving threats, ensure compliance, and maintain data trust. The following are some best practices that enterprises can adopt to secure data in hybrid cloud environments:

- **Data classification**: Categorize data based on sensitivity and regulatory requirements and apply appropriate security measures based on the classification. Leverage automation tools to classify and secure data early in the data life cycle.

- **Implement comprehensive data governance**: Data governance is a combination of processes that ensures data is cataloged, secured, accurate, usable, and available. Establish robust data governance practices, including data stewardship and data life-cycle management. Based on the data gravity, implement data governance best practices such as data cataloging, automatic metadata harvesting, and enterprise data quality checks to identify and curate data assets.

- **Data encryption**: Encrypt data during transmission between on-premises and cloud environments. Implement encryption mechanisms purpose-built for data classifications. For instance, for **Federal Information Processing Standard (FIPS)** 140-2 level 3 data security, leverage a **hardware security module (HSM)** for key management.

- **Implement data loss prevention (DLP)**: Deploy DLP solutions to monitor, detect, and prevent unauthorized access and transmission of sensitive data. Implement data masking and redaction techniques to protect sensitive information and use tokenization to replace sensitive data with tokens, reducing the risk associated with handling and storing critical information.

- **Backup and disaster recovery (DR)**: Implement regular backups of critical data and ensure that the **DR plan (DRP)** includes procedures for data restoration. Incorporate procedures to backup mission-critical data in immutable, version-controlled, redundant storage to mitigate and prevent attacks such as ransomware.

- **Data retention policies**: Define and enforce data retention policies to ensure that unnecessary data is regularly purged, reducing the risk of exposure.

- **Manage secrets using a secrets manager**: Centralize and adopt a secrets manager solution to store and secure secrets such as application credentials, database passwords, API keys, account keys, and TLS certificates. Implement best practices such as automatic key rotation policies.

Data sovereignty and data residency

Data sovereignty and data residency requirements are often based on regional and industry-specific regulations. Different organizations can have different levels of requirements. As applications and data span across on-premises environments and the cloud, it is important to understand and govern how and where the data is stored, accessed, and processed to comply with regulatory requirements. Some best practices include the following:

- **Ensure data sovereignty**: For enterprises with data sovereignty requirements, it is essential to control and prevent data access by cloud providers. Some techniques include storing and managing encryption keys in an on-premises secrets manager, granting fine-grained access controls to key requests and access, and protecting data in use.

- **Manage operational sovereignty**: Implement policies in target cloud environments such as assurance programs to ensure enterprise workloads are only deployed to certain regions and zones and restrict cloud personnel access based on geographic and attestations to comply with regulations.

- **Manage software sovereignty**: Software sovereignty refers to the ability to quickly deploy or shuttle software applications anywhere regardless of the target environment. This is an important DevOps practice and consideration to ensure software sovereignty is maintained.

- **Manage data residency**: Data residency refers to where the enterprise data is stored at rest. This includes ensuring that the data is stored, backed up, and replicated only in authorized regions.

Now that we have learned how to build a security-first cloud foundation, let's explore how enterprises can rethink infrastructure in the cloud.

Rethinking infrastructure

The next facet of digital transformation is infrastructure modernization. Building a hybrid cloud infrastructure involves integrating on-premises and cloud resources to create a flexible and scalable IT environment. Enterprises will have to rethink infrastructure to achieve greater automation, consistency, and scalability, which are essential for managing dynamic IT environments effectively. One of the strategies enterprises can adopt is treating infrastructure resources as cattle instead of pets. This approach aligns with the principles of DevOps and is well suited for cloud-native and containerized applications, where the application's dependency on the underlying infrastructure is negligible. However, this is a paradigm shift in how enterprise IT traditionally views infrastructure, where infrastructure is irreplaceable and individually managed. We will classify infrastructure components as compute infrastructure, network infrastructure, and storage infrastructure.

Compute infrastructure

Compute infrastructure is a basic yet critical component that forms the backbone of an organization's ability to deliver scalable, flexible, and efficient computing resources. Regardless of the cloud strategy, here are some best practices that enterprises can adopt:

- **Standardize infrastructure**: It is imperative to define standardized configurations for servers, to ensure consistency across the infrastructure. Avoid manual configuration changes and rely on automated tools to identify and remediate configuration drifts to ensure infrastructure consistency.

- **Automate infrastructure**: Leverage IaC tools such as Terraform or Ansible to define and deploy infrastructure configurations in a repeatable and automated manner. Integrate infrastructure changes into CI/CD pipelines to automate testing, deployment, and rollback processes.

- **Decouple infrastructure**: Treat servers as immutable entities by replacing or updating entire instances rather than modifying existing ones. This reduces the risk of configuration drift and ensures consistency. Decouple application layers from the underlying infrastructure to ensure application portability and maximize the use of stateless serverless compute options. Consider instances as short-lived and disposable. Instead of troubleshooting and fixing issues on individual servers, replace them with new instances through automation. Implement caching logic while decoupling architectures and leverage features such as live migration to reduce dependency on infrastructure.

- **Build for scale**: Leverage auto-scaling groups or similar cloud-native features to automatically adjust the number of instances based on demand. This ensures scalability and responsiveness to varying workloads.

- **Compute choice**: Leverage multiple compute options and offer choice capabilities to support various maturity levels of DevOps teams. For instance, have a defined strategy to offer bare-metal solutions, VMs, container orchestration, and serverless technologies that DevOps teams can pick and choose.

- **Self-healing systems**: Design systems to be self-healing by automatically detecting and recovering from failures, reducing the need for manual intervention in case of infrastructure issues.

- **Declarative infrastructure**: Use a declarative approach to define the desired state of infrastructure. Declare what the infrastructure should look like and let automation tools bring it to that state.

- **Version control**: Version control infrastructure code to track changes and roll back to previous configurations if needed.

- **Testing**: Incorporate automated testing into your deployment pipelines to validate infrastructure changes before they reach production, including functional, security, and performance testing.

- **Continuous improvement**: Establish feedback loops based on infrastructure performance probes to continuously evaluate and improve the infrastructure. Monitor performance, gather feedback from incidents, and use that information to refine and enhance configurations.

Network infrastructure

Designing a network infrastructure for a hybrid and multi-cloud strategy involves creating a seamless and secure environment that integrates both on-premises and cloud resources. Establishing robust, redundant, and secure network connectivity between on-premises and cloud ecosystems is extremely crucial to offering low-latency **Quality of Service (QoS)** and improved customer experience. The following are some best practices:

- **Design virtual networks early**: Consider designing virtual networks early, considering long-term objectives with scope for extensions. Design a unified network architecture that spans all selected cloud providers. Consider factors such as bandwidth, latency, and data transfer costs in your design. This includes careful allocation of scarce network resources such as contiguous IP ranges to different cloud ecosystems, a strategy for IPv6 adoption, firewall configurations, and traffic routing, as changes to network configurations at a later stage can often be extremely difficult and challenging.

- **Redundant networks**: While establishing connectivity between on-premises and cloud ecosystems, consider establishing redundant network connections for fallback and network **high availability (HA)**. In case of extreme HA requirements, consider having the redundant networks provisioned through multiple **service providers (SPs)**.

- **Cloud interconnectivity**: Define a network strategy for connecting cloud and on-premises networks. Leverage direct connections or dedicated network links to establish high-performance, low-latency connectivity between on-premises infrastructure and each cloud provider. In the case of a multi-cloud strategy, consider having a cloud exchange design that can integrate and let services across multiple clouds communicate directly. Use VPNs for secure, encrypted connections over the internet, suitable for less sensitive data transfers.

- **Network QoS**: Implement network QoS measures to prioritize critical network traffic. Define policies for bandwidth allocation to ensure optimal performance for essential applications.

- **Unified DNS**: Implement a unified DNS strategy that allows seamless resolution between on-premises and cloud resources, leveraging DNS forwarding or integration with cloud DNS services. This is often a common challenge while resolving DNS across multiple clouds.

- **Unified network security policies**: Implement consistent security policies across on-premises and cloud environments. Utilize firewalls, **intrusion detection systems (IDS)/intrusion prevention systems (IPS)**, and encryption to secure data in transit. Utilize encryption protocols such as TLS/SSL for securing data in transit to ensure consistent encryption standards across all interconnectivity points.

- **Load balancing**: Have a strategy to design and implement load balancing across on-premises and cloud environments to distribute workloads efficiently and ensure optimal resource utilization. This is particularly helpful to design and architect highly available applications services across on-premises and cloud.

Storage infrastructure

Defining a storage infrastructure strategy requires a strong understanding of the various storage needs, data sovereignty requirements, and the data gravity of the enterprise. Designing a holistic storage infrastructure for a hybrid cloud strategy involves creating a flexible and efficient data storage environment that seamlessly integrates on-premises and cloud resources. The following are some best practices to design and architect a storage infrastructure:

- **Storage classification**: Understand the various storage needs and facilitate storage types based on workload, retrieval frequency, latency, IOPS, storage location, replication needs, capacity, and data formats. Leverage the storage type options to strike a price-performance balance based on the workload requirements.

- **Data transfer**: Leverage various storage transfer methods for bulk data transfers such as network-based transfers and appliance-based and software-driven data transfers, with consideration toward speed, data volumes, frequency of transfers, and latency.

- **Build for redundancy**: Leverage multiple levels of redundancy to design and protect data against equipment failure, data center failure, and data loss. For non-critical data (data that can be reproduced from source data), leveraging built-in cloud storage redundancy can be sufficient. However, for business-critical data, plan on building additional data replication and backup strategies.

- **Storage strategy**: Although certain kinds of storage types are flexible to be used for multiple purposes, cloud-based storage types offer purpose-built storage for various application needs. Leverage persistent disks (HDDs, SSDs) for general application workloads, object storage for unstructured data at scale, and file storage for the **Network File System (NFS)** and **network-attached storage (NAS)**.

- **Storage life-cycle management**: Optimize the use of object storage by enabling automatic life-cycle management policies. For instance, classify less frequently used data from more frequently used and move the data to the right storage class. Implement automated data life-cycle management policies to move, archive, or delete data based on predefined criteria to optimize storage costs and performance.

- **Cloud-based content-delivery network (CDN)**: Leverage a cloud-based CDN to cache and serve static data to optimize cost and access latency.

- **Data encryption**: Establish consistent data encryption methods to encrypt data at rest and in transit. Leverage encryption methods and key management techniques based on the data type and data sensitivity.

- **Metadata management**: Implement effective metadata management strategies to enhance data discoverability and accessibility across hybrid storage environments.

- **Data replication and synchronization**: Implement data replication and synchronization mechanisms to ensure consistency and availability across on-premises and cloud storage environments. Use cloud storage gateways to facilitate seamless communication between on-premises storage systems and cloud storage services.

Having reviewed how enterprises can reimagine and rethink infrastructure modernization encompassing compute, network, and storage, let's now explore how organizations can develop and modernize applications in the cloud.

Application modernization strategy

The next critical facet of digital transformation is application modernization. As organizations transition toward cloud-native application development and deployment, it is essential to implement a robust application modernization strategy. Application modernization is not a one-size-fits-all approach and depends on each organization's long-term digital transformation objective and the choice of cloud strategy. However, there are some foundational principles that organizations can adopt to improve business agility, scale, resilience, and reduce tech debt. Application modernization can fall into two broad categories – traditional application modernization and cloud-native application DevOps.

Traditional application modernization

While it is easier to envision and build new applications in the cloud-native paradigm, it is not always feasible to re-architect and rewrite legacy applications. As organizations focus on application modernization, it is important to clearly define a strategy for existing legacy and traditional monolith applications within the enterprise. The following are some best practices:

- **Prioritize and plan migrations**: Classify applications using the 6Rs approach, publish a near-term, mid-term, and long-term migration wave roadmap for the legacy application modernization, and have this communicated to the stakeholders within the enterprise. This is often an important first step that sets the tone for the cloud transformation.

- **Fit assessment**: Perform an exhaustive fit assessment to help identify good candidates for migration and blockers based on the target state objective. For instance, certain legacy applications earmarked for rewrites can be left on-premises in case of a hybrid cloud strategy, while the same can be rehosted, collocated, or migrated to the public cloud for organizations with a phased transformation approach or data center exit strategy.

- **Leverage containers for modernization**: For traditional applications built using Java and .NET stack, leverage containers to modernize them for the cloud. This strategy can often be leveraged by enterprises as a mid-stage strategy before the applications can be fully re-architected for cloud-native.

- **Strategy for virtualization**: In conventional enterprises, applications commonly run on various virtualization technologies that are often proprietary in nature. These technologies may include VMware, Hyper-V, or **Red Hat Virtualization** (**RHV**). As cloud platforms rely on open virtualization standards such as **Kernel-based VM** (**KVM**) and Xen, enterprises must define a clear strategy to standardize virtualized applications.

- **Abstract using an API gateway**: In certain situations, some legacy applications may not be ideal targets for rationalization, modernization, or migration. However, as organizations continue to modernize and build cloud-native apps, they will have to seamlessly integrate with these applications. An API management solution can serve as an abstraction layer, expose the legacy application capabilities as standard RESTful APIs, insulate client-facing applications from shifting backend services, and make them consumable by modern applications and cloud services. This strategy also allows enterprises to quickly build peripheral applications and deliver new capabilities such as mobile apps while also allowing the underlying application to be modernized over time. API management also brings security, analytics, and scalability to legacy services.

Cloud-native DevOps

Cloud-native application development is a set of principles and practices for building and running applications in the cloud that are designed to take advantage of the unique characteristics of cloud computing platforms. DevOps is a set of practices that emphasizes collaboration between developers and operations teams to ensure that applications are built and deployed quickly and efficiently and that they are reliable and scalable. Cloud-native application DevOps is a powerful way to build and run applications in the cloud that are agile, scalable, resilient, and efficient. Let us explore some best practices for building cloud-native applications:

- **Microservices architecture**: Build applications using microservices architecture for better scalability, flexibility, and maintainability. Leverage container and container orchestration technologies such as Docker and Kubernetes for packaging applications and automate deployment, scaling, and management of application services.

- **APIs and service mesh**: Implement APIs to enable communication between microservices and consider using a service mesh for managing service-to-service communication. Implement an API-first approach to accelerate application design to govern, analyze, and gain visibility into all application APIs across hybrid and multi-cloud environments.

- **Build for interoperability**: Plan for interoperability between on-premises and multiple cloud environments for flexibility and risk mitigation. Design applications to allow for easy data movement between different cloud providers. Leverage a declarative approach to managing policies across environments.

- **Scale with serverless**: Leverage serverless architectures for application functions to reduce operational overhead and improve resource utilization. A serverless computing platform offers automated scaling of resources based on traffic, eliminating the need for infrastructure management and capacity planning. It encourages the design of applications that respond to events and asynchronous communication patterns.

- **Modernize DevOps**: Adopt DevOps practices for application development and implement CI/CD pipelines to automate testing, deployment, and release processes for faster and more reliable software delivery. Leverage secure software supply chain practices for software delivery such as serverless CI/CD pipelines and artifact registries to store, manage, and secure container images, implementing binary authorization for gating deployments and AI-assisted IDE plugins to enhance code quality and developer productivity. Use IaC to define and manage infrastructure, allowing for consistent and repeatable deployments declaratively abstracting the target deployment platform.

- **Architect for resilience**: Design for failure by building in redundancy and failover mechanisms in a distributed environment. Implement chaos engineering principles to proactively test and improve system resilience.

- **Data management**: Choose cloud-native databases and storage solutions that are scalable and compatible with cloud services. Consider event sourcing and **Command Query Responsibility Segregation (CQRS)** for data consistency and scalability.

Let's now explore how to modernize the enterprise data ecosystem in the cloud-native landscape.

Data modernization

The next facet of digital transformation in the cloud is data management. Cloud-native data management represents a strategic imperative for enterprises aiming to harness the full potential of modern IT architectures. By adhering to the principles of cloud-native design, integrating advanced technologies, and prioritizing security and compliance, organizations can build a resilient and flexible data infrastructure that adapts to the evolving demands of the digital landscape. The journey toward effective cloud-native data management in hybrid clouds is not just a technological evolution; it is a strategic investment in the future of data-driven enterprises. As enterprise data continues to exponentially grow – from new data sources such as social media, IoT devices, and market trends that were once non-existent and non-critical for business functions, it is extremely critical for enterprises to have a clear and robust data strategy. This is affirmed by the emergence of new data-management functions and roles such as **chief data officer (CDO)** and **chief data and analytics officer (CDAO)** within enterprises. Modern data also takes a unique paradigm shift where more and more data that an enterprise handles today tends to be unstructured and semi-structured. According to an IDC survey, the world datasphere will be 175 ZB by 2025, with 80% of that data being unstructured [7]. In an article titled *What's Your Data Strategy?*, **Harvard Business Review (HBR)** opines that only less than 50% of the data is used by enterprises to make business decisions and less than 1% of the unstructured data is even tapped into for analysis [8]. This means organizations are now better at collecting and storing massive amounts of data with no means of value realization from it. The following are some foundational data modernization principles that enterprises can adopt:

- **Build for platform agnostic**: Open data formats have revolutionized modern data lake architectures, allowing for full data interoperability, portability, and flexibility and preventing vendor lock-in. Open formats facilitate seamless data exchange between various systems, making it easier to integrate analytics, processing engines, and other tools into an enterprise's data lake environment while also enhancing data accessibility by enabling multiple applications and analytics tools to read and write data in a consistent format. As data lake architectures evolve, open formats support the integration of new data sources and the adoption of emerging technologies. This adaptability is crucial for enterprises seeking to future-proof their data lake infrastructure.

- **Facilitate schema evolution**: Choose open formats that can support schema evolution, allowing for changes to data structures over time without requiring a complete reorganization of the data lake. This is an important flexibility as enterprises often need to adapt to evolving business requirements. The choice of open formats also provides efficient compression algorithms, reducing storage costs and improving performance. For example, Parquet and **Optimized Row Columnar** (**ORC**) are columnar storage formats that offer excellent compression ratios and are suitable for large-scale data lakes.

- **Single-copy data lake architecture**: Building a single-copy data lake architecture involves creating a unified and centralized repository for diverse data sources, reducing redundancies and promoting data consistency. One common challenge enterprises face today is data sprawl and data silos. For instance, the same dataset gets copied multiple times for multiple use cases for multiple departments, resulting in exponential growth in data volumes, data pipelines, data governance, data inconsistency, and data security challenges. This also causes *data untrust syndrome*, where businesses can no longer guarantee the trust of the data source. One strategy enterprises can leverage is a federated data mesh architecture where data is offered as a service by business data domains.

- **Unlock data value through AI**: As unstructured data continues to grow, legacy platforms and tools are not equipped to realize value. Embedding AI capabilities across the data ecosystem can be extremely powerful in unlocking the power of the data. As the AI landscape continues to evolve rapidly, organizations must pivot and adapt AI strategies and emerging technologies. For example, organizations can offer relevant, real-time, personalized recommendations leveraging AI to their customers based on browsing activity and user actions.

- **Consolidate and unify tools**: Have a strategy to consolidate and unify data platforms and tools that are leveraged within the enterprise. This can be standardizing proprietary data warehouse platforms, rationalizing data lakes, and consolidating analytical tools, which can result in streamlined processes, reduce tech debt, and improve overall productivity.

Digital native data management spans seven major areas – *ingesting, processing, storing, analyzing, activating, securing,* and *governing.*

The following are some of the best practices that enterprises can adopt to define a modern data strategy:

- **Data ingestion**: Efficient data ingestion is a critical component of modern data architecture, ensuring the seamless and timely flow of diverse data into a centralized repository. Best practices for data ingestion involve adopting scalable, event-driven architectures that enable real-time or near-real-time data processing of data from a myriad of data sources – from legacy systems to SaaS. Implementing schema-on-read approaches, such as Apache Avro or Parquet, ensures flexibility in handling diverse data types. Orchestrating data pipelines with open standards such as Apache Kafka enables the reliable and secure movement of data across systems. It is essential to prioritize data quality checks, validation, and error handling during the ingestion phase to maintain the integrity of the data. Metadata management practices and documentation of data lineage contribute to a comprehensive understanding of the ingested data, aiding in governance and compliance efforts. It is also essential to embrace a modular and scalable approach to accommodate evolving data sources and changing business requirements, ensuring the adaptability and sustainability of their data ingestion processes.

- **Data processing**: Effective data processing in modern data architecture can enable organizations to derive valuable insights from vast and varied datasets. Best practices for data processing involve leveraging distributed data processing frameworks such as Apache Spark or Apache Flink to handle large-scale data processing tasks. Implementing strategies for real-time streaming, bulk data transfers, data partitioning, and parallel processing can enhance performance by utilizing the full processing capacity of the underlying infrastructure. In-memory processing and caching mechanisms, when applicable, contribute to faster query response times. As part of the data processing stage, it would be prudent for organizations to prioritize fault tolerance by designing robust error handling, retry mechanisms, and checkpointing strategies to ensure the resilience of data processing workflows. Integration with data orchestration tools such as Apache Airflow can streamline workflow management and scheduling. Embracing serverless computing and cloud-native technologies enables automatic scaling based on demand, optimizing resource utilization and costs.

- **Data storage**: In adherence to the principle of a single-copy data lake architecture, a data storage strategy is critical to accommodate the growing volumes and diversity of data. Organizations can leverage cloud-based storage solutions for scale, durability, and cost effectiveness to plan out a data lakehouse. Develop a robust strategy for structured, semi-structured, and unstructured data storage across relational and NoSQL, in-memory cache, and object storage. Implementing data partitioning and indexing strategies can optimize query performance, particularly in large datasets. Regularly archiving and tiering data based on usage patterns contributes to cost optimization. Organizations should also consider the use of data lakes as a centralized repository for diverse data types, promoting flexibility and agility in data storage with version control and documentation to enhance data lineage and metadata management.

- **Data analytics**: Fostering a data-driven culture can help drive an organization's competitive advantage, where analytics insights are seamlessly integrated into decision-making processes. This involves the adoption of advanced analytics and modern ML techniques to derive actionable intelligence from vast datasets. Leveraging open, distributed computing frameworks such as Apache Spark enables scalable and parallelized data processing for complex analytics tasks. Data democratization through self-service and AI-powered analytics tools can empower business users to explore and analyze data independently. Continuous monitoring of analytics performance and user feedback loops enables iterative improvements and optimization.

- **Data activation**: In the context of modern data architecture, data activation is the critical step in transforming insights into actionable outcomes. It is important to democratize the activation of data for a multitude of persons within enterprises. Some strategies include building a unified semantic layer that can serve data for analytics on a wide range of analytics platforms and tools. Enterprises can also leverage modern AI capabilities in analytics such as **generative AI (GenAI)** and serve data for non-traditional business users for ad hoc reporting and rapid insights needs.

- **Data security**: Ensuring robust data security is paramount in cloud-native modern data architecture, given the increasing complexity and volume of data, coupled with evolving cybersecurity threats. Best practices for data security include implementing strong encryption mechanisms for data at rest and in transit and leveraging SSL/TLS for secure data transfers, incorporating a DiD security strategy including implementing unified access controls and IdM to enforce PoLP, ensuring that users have access only to the data necessary for their roles regardless of access methods, and DLP mechanisms such as data masking and anonymization to safeguard **personally identifiable information** (**PII**) and sensitive data during analysis and sharing.

- **Data governance**: Unified data governance is fundamental to the success of modern data architecture, ensuring that data is managed, protected, and utilized responsibly. Some best practices for data governance involve establishing clear policies and standards for data quality, privacy, and security. Organizations should define ownership and accountability for data across different **business units** (**BUs**), fostering a culture of responsibility and stewardship. Implementing a comprehensive metadata management strategy can also aid in understanding and tracking the lineage of data, enhancing transparency and compliance. Regularly auditing and monitoring data access, usage, and changes contributes to maintaining data integrity and security.

Having reviewed how to modernize the data ecosystem in the cloud, let us explore how to optimize cloud costs and implement cloud governance to maximize business value from cloud adoption.

Cloud optimization and cost governance

As cloud-native continues to drive innovation across the enterprise, optimization and governance are essential to strike the right balance between innovation and cost control, leading to sustainable, responsible, and successful long-term cloud adoption. FinOps represents a culture of collaboration among finance, operations, and engineering teams to manage cloud expenses effectively. According to McKinsey, by 2030, value drivers could enable the cloud to deliver more than 3 trillion dollars in **earnings before interest, taxes, depreciation, and amortization** (**EBITDA**) value across the Forbes Global 2000 companies [9]. The study also defines how enterprises can maximize cloud value captured across three dimensions:

- **Rejuvenate**: This dimension defines the potential value enterprises could derive from IT cost efficiencies across cloud spending, including application development, infrastructure, and maintenance. IT cost optimization involves optimizing cost across application development, IT maintenance, and infrastructure, improving business resilience, and leveraging advancements in the latest cloud technologies to improve overall IT operations.

- **Innovate:** This dimension defines the value, including revenue uplift, that enterprises can derive from unlocking modern technologies in the cloud such as advanced analytics, IoT, and automation. Enterprises can tap into new use cases to drive innovation and accelerate **time to market (TTM)** by easing and democratizing access to technology.

- **Pioneer:** The pioneer dimension involves experimenting with nascent emerging technologies and exploring new business models. For instance, experimenting with modern cloud technologies such as blockchain, quantum computing, **augmented reality/virtual reality (AR/VR)**, and GenAI can help enterprises pioneer change and digital disruption.

According to the *Flexera 2023 State of the Cloud Report*, 82% of enterprises specify managing cloud spend as the top organizational challenge *[10]*. Let's review the cloud FinOps framework, which enterprises can leverage to stay on top of cost governance and maximize the value realized in the cloud.

The cloud FinOps framework is a set of best practices and guidelines that organizations can follow to optimize the financial management of cloud resources. It aims to align the objectives of finance, operations, and technology teams, ensuring cost effectiveness in cloud operations. Adopting FinOps early on and establishing this as a practice within the organization can be instrumental in maximizing business value from cloud investments. At the heart of the cloud FinOps framework is fostering a FinOps culture across the organization that promotes collaboration and shared responsibility for cloud costs. The framework typically consists of the following key pillars with a FinOps **Center of Excellence (CoE)** at its core. Modern enterprises with a mature cloud adoption should strive to establish a FinOps CoE whose primary objective should be to maximize value from cloud investments by educating and empowering people, leveraging continual advancements in cloud technology, and establishing standardized processes while also maintaining a goal toward maintaining and improving overall performance, productivity, and efficiency. Leadership involvement and support are important to drive a culture of collaboration and are extremely critical to the success of a FinOps CoE, which otherwise can alienate teams instead of working together toward a common objective. Let's look into each of these FinOps phases in detail.

The inform phase

The *inform* phase is the first step in an organization's FinOps journey. It is a critical phase that involves collecting data from various sources to gain insights into an organization's cloud usage and spending patterns. As the popular management quote goes, "*You cannot improve what you cannot measure.*" The *inform* phase is essential for measuring and gaining a clear understanding of an organization's cloud spend. This data can then be used to create reports, identify anomalies, benchmark spending against peers, allocate costs to the appropriate BUs, and create taxonomies and tags for cloud resources. This can then be used to make informed decisions about how to optimize the overall cloud spend. One of the primary goals of this phase is to gather detailed cloud resource allocation information that enables the FinOps team to associate cloud resource utilization and costs with enterprise cost centers and business stakeholders. This visibility aids in accountability assignment, the avoidance of unexpected costs, the identification of opportunities for improvement, and the demonstration of the business value of the cloud to stakeholders.

The following are some best practices that are typically performed in the *inform* phase:

- Estimate overall cloud costs based on **total cost of ownership** (**TCO**)
- Create reports that provide insights into cloud usage and spending patterns
- Empower teams to make informed business decisions with visibility into performance, costs, and anomalies through cloud cost management and advisor tools
- Allocate costs to BUs by creating taxonomies, tags, and project hierarchies
- Leverage unified cloud cost management tools to report, benchmark, and forecast costs
- Utilize migration tools and services offered by cloud providers to discover and assess on-premises resources to plan your migration and modernization
- Benchmark cloud spend against peers

The optimize phase

The next phase in the FinOps framework is the *optimize* phase. This phase involves identifying and acting on opportunities to optimize an organization's cloud spending while also maintaining the same level of performance for workloads. Insights gained from the *inform* phase will be used to guide optimization efforts. A FinOps team can leverage multiple automation techniques to optimize cloud costs and resources. These techniques can include the use of committed-usage discounts, such as reserved or committed instances and long-term commitments to reduce costs, the evaluation of a cloud environment and the right-sizing of resources, adopting equivalent cloud-native capabilities such as serverless, and the utilization of tools to automatically scale down or shut off unnecessary resources. Specifically, the following are some activities that this phase focuses on:

- **Key performance indicators (KPIs)**: Metrics that will help track progress and measure the success of optimization efforts
- **Leveraging cloud-native recommendation services**: This can help to improve cloud cost effectiveness, performance, reliability, and security
- **Outcomes**: What do you want to achieve with your optimization efforts?
- **Optimizing usage**: This includes identifying and eliminating unnecessary or underutilized resources
- **Optimizing rates**: This includes negotiating better prices with your cloud providers
- **Business cases**: These documents will justify the need for your optimization efforts and help you secure funding

The operate phase

The *operate* phase is the last stage of the FinOps framework. It involves establishing a standard framework for an organization's ongoing cloud cost management and cloud governance so that the organization can maintain optimal cloud usage and cost efficiency over the long term. In this phase, the focus will be on organizational and cultural adoption of FinOps best practices. The following are some best practices for the *operate* phase:

- Establish guardrails across cloud resources to help ensure cloud compliance, avoid misconfigurations, and practice consistent resource policy governance

- Implement cloud cost management, budgets, and alerting policies at organizational as well as project levels to mitigate cost runoffs

- Use cloud-native resource insights and best practices to optimize ongoing and future cloud adoption

- Leverage the **Cloud Adoption Framework (CAF)** and **Well-Architected Framework (WAF)** to adopt best practices to improve the cloud journey

- Enable team collaboration by educating teams on FinOps best practices to learn new skills to maximize value and efficiency

- Create a plan to incentivize teams that best leverage and adopt FinOps best practices

Summary

In this chapter, we explored the various facets of digital transformation and best practices that enterprises can leverage to build a solid cloud foundation regardless of the deployment model. We reviewed how enterprises must start with a build-out of a security-first cloud foundation to ensure holistic enterprise security encompassing network, data, application, and asset management. We also learned how to rethink infrastructure modernization in a cloud-native ecosystem.

We then explored strategies that enterprises can leverage to modernize the application landscape and data ecosystem. Finally, we reviewed best practices to optimize cloud costs, maximize value, and improve cloud resource efficiency and performance.

In the next chapter, we will explore how enterprises can lead and innovate in the cloud, leveraging emerging technologies.

Further readings

To learn more about the topics that were covered in this chapter, take a look at the following references:

1. `https://www.gartner.com/smarterwithgartner/the-cloud-strategy-cookbook`

2. `https://www.f5.com/labs/articles/threat-intelligence/the-evolving-cve-landscape`

3. https://cve.mitre.org/

4. https://cloudsecurityalliance.org/press-releases/2022/06/07/cloud-security-alliance-s-top-threats-to-cloud-computing-pandemic-11-report-finds-traditional-cloud-security-issues-becoming-less-concerning/

5. https://cloudsecurityalliance.org/zt

6. https://csrc.nist.gov/glossary/term/compensating_security_control

7. https://www.forbes.com/sites/forbestechcouncil/2022/02/03/the-unseen-data-conundrum/?sh=7ad20637fccd

8. https://hbr.org/webinar/2017/04/whats-your-data-strategy

9. https://www.mckinsey.com/capabilities/mckinsey-digital/our-insights/projecting-the-global-value-of-cloud-3-trillion-is-up-for-grabs-for-companies-that-go-beyond-adoption

10. https://info.flexera.com/CM-REPORT-State-of-the-Cloud

10
Leading and Innovating with the Cloud

In the digital age, innovation is quintessential for companies to thrive and keep pace with digital advancements. Aside from leveraging the cloud for the obvious benefits such as IT cost optimization, scale, and operational convenience, the true value of cloud computing lies in leveraging the cloud as a launchpad to drive innovation and lead digital disruption. According to a study by McKinsey, 75% of predicted cloud value comes from boosting innovation. Enterprises have an estimated $770 billion worth of cloud value that can be acquired through innovation-driven growth, faster product development, and hyper scalability, as compared to $430 billion through cost and risk reduction [1]. Companies such as Airbnb, Carrefour, Netflix, and Uber have leveraged the power of the cloud to not just innovate but also to differentiate and disrupt their respective industry. Iconic brands such as McDonald's and Tiffany & Co. are reinventing themselves to connect with their customers, fans, and culture, leveraging advancements in modern technology. For instance, McDonald's launched a Fan-to-Fan campaign to tap into the TikTok trend of menu hacks to empower its customers to customize menus and make a new food creation that will then feature on menus across the nation [2]. This campaign was a huge hit as it spotlighted its fans' creativity and brought McDonald's closer to its consumers.

Most enterprises start their cloud journey with a lift-and-shift approach to rationalize applications. However, as enterprises achieve higher levels of cloud maturity and strive to put technology at the service of their business, greater value can be unlocked. As we discussed in *Chapter 7, Hybrid Cloud Use Cases*, Capital One is a classic example of how enterprises can innovate and deliver greater business value at higher levels of cloud maturity. In an industry where the credit card business had a one-size-fits-all approach with very little differentiation, Capital One was a pioneer in the adoption of cloud technology to restructure its IT workforce and disrupt the credit card industry. Capital One leveraged cloud computing to rapid experiment, develop, and deploy innovative services to its consumers. Capital One fundamentally disrupted the industry by altering traditional approaches to working through digital technology, with an unflinching focus on digital.

Capital One launched Capital One Labs with a mission to innovate and develop digital products in partnership with venture capitalists and academics. This was a game changer for Capital One that allowed it to explore and experiment with new ideas in modern technology without impacting ongoing projects and at low risk. Key highlights of how Capital One Labs delivered value to business over the years include the following:

- The launch of Spark Pay in 2013, which allowed merchants to accept payments from customers on mobile devices.

- In 2014, Capital One launched and experimented with café-styled branches that offered complementary services to its customers to improve customer loyalty and intimacy.

- Capturing the mobile trend early on, Capital One exploited the omnichannel approach and launched cutting-edge services from mobile payments, **near-field communication** (**NFC**), QR codes, and **peer-to-peer** (**P2P**) payments.

- Capital One embraced social media as a channel to engage with its customers online, create brand awareness, and run targeted campaigns.

- Tapping into the potential of big data and analytics, Capital One offered targeted personalized recommendations and services to its customers, while also launching unique services such as the *Purchase Eraser* and *Mobile Deals*. Capital One conducts over 80,000 big data experiments a year *[3]*.

The success of Capital One Labs, as the Capital One CTO, Monique Shivanandan, says, is down to the following: "*We combine technology people, data analysts, marketing people, brand managers and product managers in the labs to be sure we're focused not just on cool technology but innovative products and services to delight the customer.*" *[4]*

In this chapter, we will explore some strategies on how enterprises can disrupt and innovate in the cloud, including the following:

- How organizations can innovate in the cloud by setting up innovation **centers of excellence** (**CoEs**)

- Innovating with emerging technologies in the cloud including big data, serverless, **artificial intelligence** (**AI**), **extended reality** (**XR**), edge computing, blockchain, and quantum computing

- Responsible uses of emerging technologies

Innovating with the cloud

We would be hard-pressed to find an enterprise that doesn't have at least one form of organization whose charter is to focus on innovation. This often goes by various names – innovation hubs, innovation labs, research hubs, business accelerators, and innovation CoEs. For companies that operate in highly regulated industries or have traditional approaches, innovation centers serve as a safe place to experiment and iterate on new projects and technologies. This is an important area of investment for enterprises. However, many organizations still struggle to derive value from these innovation centers.

Consumer expectations continue to rise, and it is extremely important to meet consumer demands for businesses to thrive. Cloud computing has become the de facto hub for innovation and digital disruption, from advanced hardware, **artifical intelligence (AI)/machine learning** (ML), XR, edge computing, and **generative AI (GenAI)** to quantum computing.

In the pursuit of innovation, setbacks are an unavoidable consequence. However, organizations often invest significant resources, including protracted experimentation effort that makes the process of innovation unsustainable. Cloud computing alleviates this challenge by providing on-demand access to cutting-edge technologies and resources while also facilitating rapid experimentation without a need for significant upfront investments.

Following are some primary reasons why innovation labs struggle to succeed and deliver value:

- **Lack of alignment with business priorities**: In some cases, innovation centers are set up with a model that doesn't have a clear strategy aligned with the organization's business priorities.

- **Lack of governance**: Oftentimes, there are no defined processes or governance for innovation labs where top-of-the-funnel experiments are streamlined and moved to the next logical step.

- **Thinking too far out**: One of the cardinal sins innovation centers make is to have extremely aspirational thinking too far out into the future, which can lead to unrealistic expectations.

- **Disconnected from reality**: Oftentimes, innovation labs – especially when they are set up autonomously or decentralized, lead to siloed experimentation that is disconnected from real consumer needs.

- **Lack of key performance indicators (KPIs)/metrics**: Not all experiments have to yield results or success. However, a lack of KPIs and metrics to track the performance and results of innovation labs can be disastrous. Defining clear tangible **returns on investment (ROIs)** with leadership and stakeholder buy-in is extremely important.

As organizations continue to innovate in the cloud, let's understand how enterprises can set up innovation centers to drive the cloud transformation.

Setting up innovation labs

Innovation centers offer enterprises the space to explore, ideate, experiment, and achieve market disruption. The core objective of an innovation center is to accelerate digital innovation by rethinking customer experience, improving operational efficiencies, and testing new business models through the use of modern technologies. Innovation centers also help enterprises stay abreast with the latest digital advancements and upcoming technologies in the market. There is no universal approach to jumpstart an innovation program, as every enterprise is unique. Some organizations may choose to invest in a centralized digital lab, while others may choose to have smaller steering groups in a decentralized manner. Setting up a dedicated innovation center or lab can bring a range of tangible and intangible benefits to enterprises. For instance, with an unwavering focus on innovation, labs can be a source of fresh ideas that can explore and experiment while also accelerating the speed of innovation. Intangibly, a dedicated innovation lab projects the organization's focus and investment, which often attracts top talent, enhances the risk-taking ability of the business, and cultivates a positive culture loop of innovation. More importantly, innovation labs equip enterprises with the edge of a start-up – rapidly experiment and launch. Depending on the focus of innovation, innovation labs can be set up as either centralized, decentralized, or autonomously. While setting up innovation labs, enterprises must have a clear purpose and vision for them. The following diagram illustrates various innovation lab constructs that organizations can leverage depending on the vision:

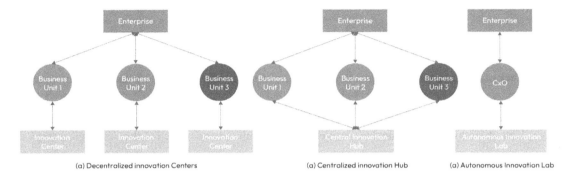

Figure 10.1 – Innovation lab models

Let's look into what each of these models are:

- **Decentralized innovation centers**: In this model, individual **business units** (**BUs**) within the enterprise fund their own respective innovation labs. One major benefit of this model is that the innovation labs are much closer to the BUs and hence are in sync with the business requirements. However, care must be taken to not mimic, replicate, or duplicate efforts across innovation labs, resulting in wasted time, effort, and cost. This model can also introduce some complexities with overall governance, funding, and management.

- **Centralized innovation hub**: A centralized digital innovation hub often offers better control and governance over its operations. It also serves as a centralized technology-focused lab across multiple BUs.

- **Autonomous innovation lab**: An autonomous innovation lab typically reports to a CXO often with a targeted mission, working largely independently. An autonomous innovation center can co-exist with a centralized or decentralized innovation lab with a specific purpose that is often distinct. For example, an autonomous innovation center can help enterprises explore newer markets or new business models.

Regardless of the model, there are some key considerations, as shown in the following screenshot, that organizations must consider to ensure innovation labs deliver consistent long-term value to business:

Vision & Governance   Talent & Partnerships   Innovate & Deliver

Define & Communicate Purpose	Staff with Cross-Functional Team	Deliver Quick Wins
Leadership Commitment	Partner with Business Units	Implement Feedback Loop
Establish Governance Model	Hire Strategically	Embed Innovation Outcomes
	Engage with Diverse Partners	

Figure 10.2 – Pillars of innovation labs

Let's explore the pillars of innovation labs in detail.

Vision and governance

Defining a clear vision provides the innovation lab with a guiding purpose and defines why the lab exists and what it aims to achieve. The vision serves as a compass for strategic decision-making and helps the lab prioritize projects, allocate resources, and make the right choices. This overarching goal helps to align activities and initiatives with an enterprise's common objective. Governance structures are often overlooked but help in the effective allocation of resources, funding, talent, and time. Governance frameworks are instrumental in managing risks associated with innovation projects. They enable the assessment of potential failure impacts, implementation of risk mitigation strategies, and the creation of an environment that fosters experimentation while minimizing adverse outcomes. Defining performance metrics helps assess and measure the impact of the innovation. It is also important to have governance defined around ethical considerations, especially while innovating with modern technologies, to ensure projects adhere to ethical standards, data privacy regulations, and other legal and moral guidelines. Let's explore the key constituents of the *vision and governance* pillar:

- **Define and communicate purpose**: Defining a clear purpose and focus is critical for an innovation center. This will serve as the north star for the innovation lab to ensure its focus on the right business priorities. This will also prevent the innovation lab from picking extremely futuristic projects with no logical business outcome or getting involved in routine projects.

- **Leadership commitment**: To foster a culture of innovation, visionary leadership and buy-in are extremely crucial to long-term success. Innovation should ideally be driven top-down, and it is imperative for leaders to fund and nurture innovation labs and be champions of initiatives across the organization. Executive sponsorship and involvement are foundational to the success of the innovation center.

- **Establish a governance model**: Establishing a centralized governance model across people, processes, and technology is another extremely crucial foundational element for an innovation lab. Governance frameworks help ensure that the innovation lab operates efficiently and maximizes its impact. For instance, this is extremely crucial when experimenting with modern technologies involving AI/ML, as mismanaged or uncontrolled rollout and adoption can pose significant risks to an organization's ethical operations and brand reputation.

Talent and partnerships

From a people perspective, having a top talent pool and forging strategic partnerships play crucial roles in the success and sustainability of an innovation lab. Talented individuals bring creativity and innovative thinking to the lab and often possess an entrepreneurial mindset, which is essential for driving innovation. This mindset involves a willingness to take risks, learn from failure, and pursue opportunities that lead to positive outcomes. Innovation requires continuous learning and adaptation. Their diverse skill sets and perspectives contribute to the generation of novel ideas and solutions. Forging strategic partnerships with a wide range of entities, from academic universities and actively contributing to open source community projects to technology start-ups and hyperscalers, offers access to external resources, expertise, and opportunities that can significantly enhance the lab's innovation capabilities. Let's explore the key components of the *talent and partnerships* pillar:

- **Staff with cross-functional teams**: A diversified team with cross-functional experts is a powerful catalyst for innovation. In a diverse team, individuals bring unique backgrounds, cultural insights, and approaches to the table, challenging conventional thinking and sparking a broader range of ideas. A diverse team is better equipped to understand and cater to a wide range of end users, ensuring that innovative products and services are more inclusive and reflective of the diverse needs of a global audience. The synergy of diverse talents also promotes a culture of openness and adaptability, which are crucial elements in navigating the dynamic landscape of innovation.

- **Partner with BUs**: One of the primary risks that innovation labs face is operating in a siloed fashion, which can cause a drift in the lab's focus from business priorities. It is imperative to have business stakeholders closely involved with innovation labs to select, scope, and execute innovation projects. By collaborating closely with BUs, the innovation center can gain valuable insights into specific business challenges, market dynamics, and customer expectations that the organization faces. This direct connection ensures that creative solutions are not developed in isolation but are grounded in a deep understanding of the business context. Engagement with BUs can form a symbiotic relationship to promote a culture of cross-functional collaboration, breaking down silos and encouraging the exchange of ideas between different parts of the organization.

- **Hire strategically**: Strategic hiring is a linchpin in cultivating an innovative environment within an organization. This requires innovation centers to strategically recruit talent, to not only seek individuals with the necessary technical skills but also to find talent who bring diverse perspectives, creative thinking, and a passion for problem-solving. Hiring strategically also helps identify candidates who exhibit an entrepreneurial mindset, adaptability, and a willingness to embrace change – essential qualities in the dynamic landscape of innovation.

- **Engage with diverse partners**: Establishing strategic partnerships allows the innovation lab to integrate into broader ecosystems, such as industry networks, research institutions, and start-up communities, fostering a collaborative environment that supports ongoing innovation. For instance, by collaborating with academic institutions, enterprises gain access to cutting-edge research, emerging technologies, and a pool of talented individuals at the forefront of their fields. This collaboration facilitates the transfer of academic insights into practical applications, accelerating the development of innovative solutions. Concurrently, universities benefit from real-world industry challenges, offering students and researchers opportunities to apply theoretical knowledge in a practical setting. Collaborating with hyperscalers grants enterprises access to cutting-edge technologies, scalable infrastructure, and a vast array of cloud-based services and tech talent. This partnership enables enterprises to leverage hyperscalers' advanced capabilities, such as AI, ML, and big data analytics, empowering them to solve complex problems and innovate more efficiently. Additionally, enterprises benefit from hyperscalers' global reach and reliability, ensuring a robust and secure foundation for their digital initiatives. In a more mature model, organizations partner with open communities while also contributing back to them. Several modern technological advancements are a result of the innovation labs of tech-savvy organizations.

Innovate and deliver

Innovation labs are all about experimentation and delivering cutting-edge technology solutions that can deliver incremental business value and disrupt the market. This pillar is instrumental in demonstrating value and delivering on the core promise of an innovation lab. Let's review the core constituents of the *innovate and deliver* pillar:

- **Deliver quick wins**: As innovation centers typically tend to work on longer gestational projects, it is also very important to deliver quick wins and incremental value to BUs. Leading innovation centers have short-term and long-term missions and are designed to operate with speed and flexibility, allowing teams to rapidly prototype, test, and iterate on new ideas. By focusing on short-term achievable goals, innovation labs can deliver tangible outcomes that showcase immediate value to the business. Quick wins not only demonstrate the feasibility and impact of innovative solutions but also generate momentum and enthusiasm among stakeholders.

- **Implement a feedback loop**: Innovation centers thrive on experimentation and the iterative process of trial and error. However, to optimize resource allocation and maximize impact, it's essential to strategically prioritize the most viable and feasible projects. It is also equally important to sunset projects and initiatives that don't prove feasible or add value. Innovation labs must establish a robust feedback loop within BUs, fostering a continuous cycle of improvement and refinement. By actively engaging with stakeholders, customers, and end users, innovation labs collect valuable insights and feedback on prototypes, concepts, and initial implementations. Organizations can employ practices such as A/B testing and canary testing methods to roll out new features faster to the market and look at feedback data analytically to make the best decision at a much lower risk. This iterative process allows for the identification of strengths, weaknesses, and areas for enhancement and also ensures that the innovation lab can rapidly iterate on ideas, refining them based on real-world input. Establishing a feedback loop is not merely a technical process; it's a cultural shift that promotes openness, collaboration, and a commitment to continuous improvement, positioning the innovation lab as a dynamic hub for innovation within the organization.

- **Embed innovation outcomes**: An innovation center achieves its highest maturity when it successfully disseminates its innovative practices beyond its immediate boundaries and integrates them deeply into various BUs and functions, instead of standalone projects. One of the approaches is to become knowledge hubs, offering training programs, resources, and expertise to teams across various departments, to standardize and institutionalize successful approaches. This not only streamlines operations but also fosters a shared language and mindset around innovation, positioning the entire organization to navigate challenges and seize opportunities with agility and efficiency.

Innovation is not a one-size-fits-all approach and must be defined uniquely based on the organization's DNA. With the exponential evolution in technologies, innovation labs help businesses keep pace with market demands and, more importantly, help shield them from obsoleteness. Cloud computing has democratized access to emerging technologies to businesses of all sizes, where an SMB or a start-up can offer a new feature or capability to the market that took several years of time, experience, and effort for a large enterprise. In the next few sections, we will review some of the ways enterprises can leverage the cloud to innovate with emerging technologies.

Innovating with big data and serverless

The convergence of digital technologies, the expansion of connected devices, and the growing complexity of data types contribute to the exponential evolution of data in enterprises today. The proliferation of connected devices, the IoT, social media, clickstream data, logs, and multimedia-rich applications has intensified the diversity and volume of data being generated. According to a study by **Harvard Business Review (HBR)**, organizations use less than 50% of their structured data for business decisions, while less than 1% of unstructured data is even tapped in *[5]*. The following aspects define big data – also described across 7-Vs *[6]*:

1. **Variety**: Refers to the variety of data sources and data across multiple formats – structured, semi-structured and unstructured

2. **Volume**: This is the primary factor distinguishing big data, with growing data volumes across transactions, files, signals, and events

3. **Velocity**: Speed at which data is processed, accessed, and analyzed in batch and real-time streams

4. **Veracity**: Defines the quality, accuracy, and credibility of data in the system

5. **Value**: The ROI and value of big data

6. **Variability**: Refers to the ability to analyze data contextually to predict context-based outcomes

7. **Visibility**: Presentation of data for multiple personas in a meaningful way

As advancements in the cloud continue to lower the barriers to collecting massive datasets, scalable storage, and real-time data processing at significantly lower investments, emerging technologies such as serverless data processing, real-time streaming, and AI/ML for predictive analytics help unlock massive business opportunities. In the following sections, let's look at some ways enterprises across industries are leveraging the power of big data and emerging technologies to innovate.

Banking and financial services

Big data plays an extremely important role in the banking and financial services sector and has revolutionized banking. By leveraging large datasets, companies can gain valuable insights into customer behavior, optimize operations, manage regulatory compliance, reduce costs, and improve customer experience. Following are some innovative uses of big data:

- **Fraud detection**: Banks are leveraging AI- and ML-based big data analytics to identify and flag suspicious activity such as money laundering or identity theft by analyzing patterns before it occurs.

- **Risk management**: With vast amounts of historical market data, financial institutions can better assess risk associated with investments and loans by using predictive analytics models. Predictive analytics help model and assess credit risk, improving the accuracy of credit scoring and lending decisions.

- **Robo advisors and algorithmic trading**: Financial institutions use big data and ML algorithms for algorithmic trading to analyze market data in real-time and make split-second trading decisions, optimizing investment strategies. This has also helped portfolio managers assess a wide range of factors for asset allocation strategies and diversification techniques.

- **Regulatory compliance**: Leveraging big data analytics augmented with AI/ML, financial institutions can ensure compliance with complex regulatory requirements such as compliance reporting, documentation, and monitoring activities to adhere to financial regulations.

- **Cybersecurity**: With the ever-growing threat of cybersecurity, continually evolving advanced analytics help detect and respond to cybersecurity threats in real time, protecting sensitive financial data.

Retail

Data is the cornerstone for retail, as retailers can tap into vast quantities of first-party and third-party data to drive innovation. The following are ways retailers are innovating with big data:

- **Customer segmentation and personalization**: Retailers use big data analytics to segment customers based on their preferences, behaviors, and purchase history. This enables personalized marketing campaigns, product recommendations, and targeted promotions, leading to a more tailored and engaging consumer shopping experience.

- **Demand forecasting**: Big data analytics help predict customer demand and optimize inventory levels by analyzing historical sales data, market trends, and external factors. Accurate demand forecasting is extremely critical and can directly impact a retailer's bottom line to help make more accurate inventory decisions, reducing stockouts and overstock situations.

- **Dynamic price optimization**: Retailers can leverage intelligence from big data to dynamically adjust prices based on various factors such as demand, competitor pricing, and market conditions. Dynamic pricing strategies help optimize revenue, maximize competitiveness, and respond in real-time to changes in the market.

- **Supply chain visibility**: Big data provides retailers with end-to-end visibility into their supply chains. This includes tracking the movement of goods, monitoring supplier performance, and identifying potential disruptions. Improved supply chain visibility enhances efficiency, reduces costs, and ensures smoother operations.

- **Fraud detection and prevention**: Big data analytics help detect fraudulent activities and prevent losses due to theft and other suspicious activity. Advanced analytics models analyze patterns to identify anomalies in transactions, reducing the risk of fraud.

- **Sentiment analysis (SA)**: Retailers tap into big data analytics to monitor social media for insights into customer sentiments, preferences, and trends. This information helps in shaping marketing strategies, understanding brand perception, and engaging with customers on social platforms.

- **In-store analytics**: Big data analytics is applied to in-store data, including foot traffic patterns, dwell times, and heatmaps. This information can be leveraged to optimize store layouts, improve product placements, and enhance the overall in-store experience.

Healthcare

In the healthcare industry, enterprises are leveraging big data to drive innovation, enhance patient care, improve operational efficiency, and advance medical research. The following are ways in which enterprises are innovating with big data in healthcare:

- **Predictive analytics for disease prevention**: By analyzing large datasets, including patient records, environmental factors, and population health data, healthcare organizations can identify patterns and trends that may indicate potential disease outbreaks, enabling proactive measures for prevention.

- **Clinical decision support systems (CDSS)**: Analyzing vast amounts of patient data helps in creating **decision support systems (DSS)** that offer insights into personalized treatment plans, drug recommendations, and diagnostic insights.

- **Population health management**: By identifying high-risk groups, monitoring health trends, and optimizing preventive care strategies, population health management improves overall healthcare outcomes of the overall population.

- **Electronic health record (EHR) analysis**: Enterprises use big data analytics to extract valuable insights from EHRs. This includes identifying trends in patient demographics, treatment outcomes, and disease patterns, enabling healthcare providers to make informed decisions and enhance patient care.

- **Genomic data analysis**: Big data is instrumental in analyzing genomic data for personalized medicine. By examining genetic information on a large scale, healthcare organizations can identify genetic markers, understand disease predispositions, and tailor treatment plans based on individual patients' genetic profiles.

- **Real-time patient monitoring**: Big data facilitates real-time patient monitoring, especially for patients with chronic conditions. Connected devices and wearables collect continuous streams of health data, allowing healthcare providers to monitor patients remotely, identify potential issues, and intervene proactively.

- **Patient engagement and behavior analysis**: Big data analytics is applied to understand patient behaviors and engagement patterns. By analyzing patient interactions with healthcare apps, websites, and educational materials, healthcare providers can tailor engagement strategies and improve patient adherence to treatment plans.

Now that we have reviewed how various industries are innovating with big data and cloud-based serverless technologies to advance business objectives, let's explore how enterprises are innovating with AI.

Embedding AI across the enterprise

AI is transforming enterprises across various industries, bringing about transformative changes in how businesses operate, make decisions, and interact with their customers. With AI embedded across the IT estate from chips to apps, the application of AI/ML has become indispensable for enhanced decision-making, automation of repetitive tasks, personalizing customer experiences, fraud detection and prevention, SA, and supply chain optimization. According to a study by IDC, global spending on AI is estimated to exceed $301 billion. Cloud computing has democratized the use and application of AI across the spectrum – from offering purpose-built GPUs and TPUs to running AI models that can be used on-demand with a pay-for-use model, APIs for pre-built AI models, **automated ML** (**AutoML**), and AI SDKs. Furthermore, the emergence of GenAI is revolutionizing creativity and is proving to change the way businesses operate.

Following are some ways enterprises are innovating with AI:

- **AI-enabled APIs and SDKs**: Leveraging pre-built AI models and SDKs allows developers to quickly incorporate AI capabilities into applications such as **natural language processing**

(**NLP**), image recognition, and SA into their applications. For instance, application developers can now embed ML models directly into applications to enable capabilities such as real-time decision-making, personalized recommendations, and predictive analytics.

- **Chatbots and virtual assistants**: AI-powered chatbots and virtual assistants are integrated into applications to enhance customer interactions and support services. These applications leverage NLP to understand user queries and intent and provide relevant responses or assistance.

- **AI-infused security**: AI plays a pivotal role in bolstering enterprise security by offering advanced capabilities in threat detection, prevention, and response. From intelligent authentication and access control to behavior analysis and malware detection, AI technologies fortify the cybersecurity posture of enterprises, providing a robust and adaptive defense against the growing sophistication of cyberattacks. AI-driven security systems leverage ML algorithms to analyze vast datasets, identify patterns indicative of malicious activities, and detect anomalies in real-time, providing a proactive defense against cyber threats.

- **IT operations**: AI is transforming IT operations by introducing intelligent automation, enhancing efficiency, and enabling proactive management. From predictive analytics for issue prevention, intelligent **incident management** (**IM**), capacity planning, automated troubleshooting, remediation, and optimization, the application of AI is enhancing the overall efficiency of IT processes while also contributing to a more resilient and responsive IT infrastructure.

- **Associate productivity**: AI is integrated into employee productivity tools to enhance collaboration, automate administrative tasks, and streamline workflows. This includes features such as intelligent scheduling, document summarization, and automated data entry.

Enterprises across industry verticals are harnessing the power of AI to innovate and introduce new capabilities, described as follows:

- **Financial services**: In the realm of financial services, innovative applications of AI are revolutionizing traditional practices and reshaping the industry. AI-driven fraud detection and **threat intelligence** (**TI**) systems analyze vast datasets and transactions to identify unusual patterns indicative of fraudulent activities in real time; AI-based robo-advisors are transforming wealth management, offering algorithm-driven investment advice tailored to individual preferences and risk profiles; credit scoring and underwriting processes benefit from predictive analytics, allowing financial institutions to make more accurate lending decisions; chatbots and virtual assistants powered by NLP help enhance customer interactions, provide personalized support, answer queries, and even facilitate transactions.

- **Retail**: In retail, AI is driving innovation across various aspects of operations, customer experiences, and supply chain management. AI is enabling innovative retail experiences from personalized shopping recommendations, visual search, dynamic pricing optimization, intelligent demand forecasting, churn prediction, micro inventory management, **augmented reality** (**AR**) for try-on experiences, customer SA, automated shelf checking, and shrink reduction.

- **Manufacturing**: AI is making significant strides in the manufacturing sector, introducing innovative applications that enhance efficiency, productivity, and overall operational performance. The application of AI is enabling modern use cases from predictive maintenance, **quality control (QC)**, **robotic process automation (RPA)**, digital twins for simulation, collaborative robots, AI-driven maintenance scheduling, and additive manufacturing processes.

- **Healthcare**: AI is ushering in transformative changes in the healthcare industry, offering innovative solutions to improve patient care, enhance diagnostics, and streamline operations. Some notable advancements in AI include diagnostic imaging, predictive analytics for patient outcomes, drug discovery and development, virtual health assistants, remote patient monitoring, clinical documentation, genomic data analysis, and medication adherence management.

GenAI

GenAI is emerging as a transformative branch of AI technology, pushing the boundaries of innovation across various industries. Through its ability to create novel content, audio, images, video, and even entire virtual environments autonomously that mimic human creativity, GenAI is unlocking unprecedented opportunities. Unlike traditional AI systems that analyze and interpret data, GenAI generates new content based on patterns learned from training data. This is primarily achieved through **deep learning (DL)** models such as **generative adversarial networks (GANs)**, **variational autoencoders (VAEs)**, and transformer-based architectures such as **Generative Pre-trained Transformer (GPT)**. As GenAI continues to evolve, its impact on industry verticals is poised to grow, unlocking new possibilities and driving innovation in the digital era. Following are some innovative applications of GenAI across industries:

- **Healthcare**: In healthcare, GenAI is facilitating medical image synthesis, drug discovery, and personalized treatment planning. Researchers can employ generative models to generate synthetic medical images for training diagnostic algorithms and simulating medical scenarios. Additionally, GenAI has the potential to drive advancements in drug discovery by accelerating the design and synthesis of new molecules and helping summarize clinical notes that can provide care providers with timely access to critical health information.

- **Financial services**: With the power of GenAI, investment advisors can generate meaningful and actionable insights from publicly available information such as news, analyst reports, and annual reports. Financial institutions can employ GenAI to generate synthetic financial data for training predictive models and simulating market scenarios, enabling more accurate risk management and investment strategies. GenAI is also finding applications in financial document synthesis, where vast amounts of financial documents are searched, synthesized, and summarized for faster document processing times.

- **Retail**: In a competitive retail world, GenAI is helping retailers reimagine customer experiences. By engaging with consumers through guided, tailored, and personalized shopping experiences, retailers have the potential to improve conversion rates while improving customer satisfaction. Retailers can generate personalized product configurations and offer customizable products and design services based on customer specifications and preferences. By deploying GenAI-powered virtual personal shoppers that assist customers in finding products based on their preferences, budget, and style, retailers can use NLP and **computer vision** (**CV**) techniques to understand customer queries and recommend relevant products, providing personalized shopping experiences both in-store and online. Retailers can also leverage GenAI to automate and create compelling content for marketing campaigns and product catalogs by generating text, images, audio, and videos that resonate with their target audience, driving engagement and brand awareness.

- **Media and entertainment**: In the entertainment industry, GenAI is revolutionizing content creation. It enables the automatic generation of scripts, music, and visual effects for movies, video games, and **virtual reality** (**VR**) experiences. It unleashes creativity for creators and assists in generating novel ideas, composing music, and creating stunning visuals. By automating repetitive tasks, it frees up creators to focus on higher-level conceptualization and exploration.

- **Manufacturing**: GenAI is emerging as a technology to optimize manufacturing processes by designing more efficient components and reducing waste. For instance, it enables the creation of digital twins, virtual representations of real-world systems, allowing for improved quality control. By automating design tasks, GenAI can accelerate product development cycles and foster innovation.

- **Marketing and advertising**: GenAI plays a crucial role in marketing and advertising campaigns by creating compelling content, including advertisements, product descriptions, and promotional materials at unparalleled speed and scale. Brands can leverage generative models to generate personalized marketing campaigns tailored to individual consumers, thereby improving engagement and conversion rates.

XR

XR is an umbrella term that encompasses AR, VR, and **mixed reality** (**MR**). XR experiences transform reality through the use of technology by augmenting or overlaying it with the virtual world, to create immersive user experiences[7]. XR is radically transforming interactive and immersive customer experiences for industries across several industries. Following are some innovative uses of XR across industry verticals:

- **Entertainment and gaming**: Entertainment and gaming are probably the most well-known applications of VR and AR. XR places the gamer in the center of a virtual experience based on the context – from live music events and sporting events to worlds of fantasy, offering an immersive gaming experience.

- **Manufacturing**: In engineering and manufacturing, having a skilled workforce is extremely crucial. Training resources on complex engineering tasks and risky equipment can often be expensive and time-consuming. XR tools offer a solution by reducing costs and preventing injuries, making them a valuable investment. In realms where certain manufacturing functions can be inherently hazardous, AR offers a solution by enabling workers to execute these tasks from a safe distance. One example is **computer-aided design** (**CAD**), where designers and clients can immerse themselves in life-size plans while drafting, allowing for superior exploration of design space.

- **Retail and consumer-packed goods (CPG)**: AR and VR have the potential to offer immersive, tailored shopping experiences for shoppers both in-store and online. For instance, in-store shoppers can visualize and experience the item or product in a variety of settings, especially in a complex or guided selling experience. AR is also helping bring online shoppers closer to an in-person experience while also proving to reduce product returns. XR and 3D technologies are boosting consumer confidence in online purchases.

- **Healthcare**: XR is enabling innovative applications of technology in healthcare, including remote patient monitoring, customized rehabilitation programs, simulating drug trials, surgical training, and collaboration. One application of XR is in medical imaging, which allows medical professionals to visualize and represent traditional 2D images in 3D for faster and more accurate diagnosis. Another fine example of XR is in surgical training, which helps surgeons practice complex surgeries and develop new surgical techniques without risking lives.

- **Education and learning**: Educational institutions and corporate learning environments can offer AR and VR for immersive learning experiences with virtual field trips, historical recreations, and interactive educational modules that enhance engagement and understanding. XR is proving to boost training speed, engagement, and knowledge retention. AR gives learners a hands-on, real-world experience without the need for a classroom, including gamification, in which lessons are made entertaining, and can further enhance learning outcomes.

Edge computing

Enterprises across industries are harnessing the potential of edge computing to drive innovation. Edge computing involves processing data closer to the source of generation, reducing latency and improving real-time decision-making, while also reducing the need for signals and event data transmission to centralized locations for processing. With the evolution of distributed cloud edge compute, the adoption of edge computing plays an important role in shaping the future of decentralized and intelligent computing architectures. Edge computing also enhances security and privacy by processing sensitive data locally. Following are some innovative applications of edge computing:

- **IoT**: In the realm of IoT, edge computing addresses the challenges of managing a vast number of devices generating data. By processing data on the edge, enterprises can reduce the load on centralized cloud servers and enhance the efficiency of IoT applications. This is particularly critical in scenarios with limited bandwidth or where real-time responses are essential. For instance, retail locations can process real-time data captured by cameras, point of sale (POS), and sensors to reduce shrinkage.

- **Real-time analytics and insights**: Edge computing facilitates real-time data processing and analysis, enabling enterprises to extract valuable insights without the latency associated with sending data to centralized servers. This is crucial in industries such as finance, where split-second decision-making is essential, or in manufacturing, where instant adjustments can optimize production processes.

- **Customer engagement**: Edge computing can power real-time inventory management, enabling retailers to track products and manage stock levels efficiently. It also supports customer engagement through applications such as tailored recommendations, personalized real-time offers, and cashierless checkout experiences, enhancing the overall shopping experience.

- **Healthcare diagnostics and monitoring**: Edge computing is transforming healthcare by supporting real-time diagnostics and patient monitoring. Medical devices and wearables equipped with edge processing capabilities can analyze health data locally, providing timely insights for healthcare professionals and facilitating remote patient monitoring.

- **Smart manufacturing**: Edge computing is a cornerstone of Industry 4.0 initiatives, empowering smart manufacturing processes. By processing data at the edge, manufacturers can implement predictive maintenance, monitor equipment health, and optimize production efficiency, contributing to a more agile and responsive manufacturing ecosystem.

- **Energy management and smart grids**: In the energy sector, edge computing is applied to manage smart grids efficiently. It enables real-time monitoring of energy distribution, load balancing, and the integration of renewable energy sources for a more resilient and responsive energy infrastructure.

- **Edge-to-cloud integration**: Enterprises are innovating by integrating edge computing with public cloud services. This distributed edge hybrid architecture allows for a seamless flow of data between the edge and the cloud, offering the advantages of local processing and storage, coupled with scalability and centralized management capabilities of the cloud.

Blockchain

Blockchain applications go beyond cryptocurrencies and bring new opportunities for digital transformation. With a decentralized network, immutable recordkeeping, smart contracts, transparency, and traceability, blockchain is enabling creative applications for enterprises across industries. Following are some innovative applications of blockchain across industries:

- **Supply chain management**: Across industries, blockchain can enhance transparency and traceability in supply chains. Enterprises can record every transaction and movement of goods on a blockchain, providing a secure and immutable ledger that can be helpful in verifying product authenticity, reducing fraud, and optimizing supply chain processes. This is an extremely important application of blockchain that can improve consumer confidence while shopping anything from high-value goods such as fashion to produce.

- **B2B smart contracts**: Smart contracts, self-executing contracts with the terms of the agreement directly written into code, can be implemented on blockchain platforms without the need for an intermediary. Enterprises utilize smart contracts for automating and executing contractual agreements, reducing the need for intermediaries and ensuring trust in the execution of business processes. This process can be streamlined further through industry-specific blockchain consortiums.

- **Identity management and credentialing**: Blockchain provides a secure and decentralized way to manage digital identities. Enterprises can leverage blockchain for identity verification, authentication, and access management to help prevent identity theft, streamline onboarding processes, and enhance overall security. This finds an interesting use in healthcare professional credentialing where authenticity can be verified.

- **Asset tokenization**: Tokenization of physical and digital assets, representing ownership or rights on a blockchain. This can include real estate, art, stocks, or other assets. Tokenization enhances liquidity, facilitates fractional ownership, and simplifies the transfer of assets.

- **Immutable healthcare records**: Blockchain can be used to create secure and immutable records of healthcare data. Patient records, treatment histories, and other healthcare information can be stored on a blockchain, ensuring data integrity, accessibility, and privacy.

- **Intellectual property (IP) and royalties**: Blockchain can be leveraged to manage and track IP rights and royalties. This ensures that creators receive fair compensation for their work and simplifies the complex royalty distribution process in industries such as music, publishing, and entertainment.

- **Food safety and traceability**: In the food industry, blockchain can be utilized to enhance food safety by providing end-to-end traceability of produce. Each step in the supply chain, from farm to table, is recorded on the blockchain, enabling quick identification, product provenance, and resolution of food safety issues.

- **Quality assurance (QA)**: Blockchain can be used to record and verify the quality of products in manufacturing. Each step of the manufacturing process is documented on the blockchain, providing a secure and unalterable record of production, which is particularly important in industries with strict quality standards.

Quantum computing

Quantum computing serves as a proof point for the exponential evolution of emerging technology. As breakthroughs are accelerating, hyperscalers such as Google and companies such as IBM and D-Wave are already offering commercial cloud offerings (**Quantum-as-a-Service** or **QaaS**). Although niche, this is a space with a limitless potential that can help advance several fields of science and technology to reach milestones that were once deemed impossible. For instance, in an experiment by Google, its 70-qubit quantum computer can execute a task in moments that would normally take 47 years to complete by the world's fastest supercomputer *[8]*. For the foreseeable future, as advancements in quantum computing develop, **high-performance computing (HPC)** will take a more significant role in the cloud arena. This is another classic example to show how cloud economies of scale and limitless innovation shape the future of how enterprises operate, as the QaaS model will yield the maximum value for businesses.

In a study by McKinsey, it is estimated that, by 2035, the conservative value for businesses in pharmaceuticals, chemical, automotive, and finance industries will be up to nearly $700 billion *[9]*. In the pharma sector, drug discovery, research, and development typically take years to come to fruition while also costing billions of dollars. Quantum computing can be a game changer that can fast-track the R&D process and the clinical supply chain. Similarly, in the chemical and automotive industry, even a small percentage of improvement in R&D, production, and supply chain optimization can result in multi-billion dollar savings while also improving overall efficiency.

Responsible uses of emerging technologies

Leveraging emerging technologies responsibly is crucial for enterprises to ensure ethical practices and compliance with regulations, establish brand trust with customers, and also gain the trust of stakeholders. As enterprises continue to adopt emerging technologies, it is extremely important to ensure the technologies are used responsibly. Responsible technology adoption not only mitigates risks in technology adoption but also positions enterprises as ethical leaders in the evolving digital landscape. The following are principles that enterprises can adopt to leverage emerging technologies responsibly:

- **Ethical considerations**: Prioritize ethical considerations in the development and deployment of emerging technologies. Establish ethical guidelines and frameworks to guide decision-making, addressing issues such as privacy, transparency, bias, and fairness.

- **Compliance with regulations**: Stay informed about relevant laws and regulations pertaining to emerging technologies in the industry and region of operation. Ensure that the implementation of technologies complies with data protection, security, and other regulatory requirements.

- **Data privacy and security**: Prioritize data privacy and security as first principles across the enterprise by implementing robust measures to protect sensitive information. Adopt encryption, secure access controls, and data anonymization techniques to safeguard user data and maintain confidentiality.

- **Promote transparency**: Foster transparency in the use of emerging technologies by clearly communicating how they are employed and for what purposes. Establish accountability mechanisms within the organization to ensure responsible use and decision-making related to technology adoption.

- **Diversity and inclusion**: Promote diversity and inclusion in the development and deployment of emerging technologies. Ensure that diverse perspectives are considered to mitigate biases and enhance the inclusivity of technology solutions.

- **Human-centric design approach**: Adopt a human-centric design approach that prioritizes the well-being and experiences of end users. Consider the societal impact of technologies and strive to create solutions that enhance human lives while minimizing negative consequences.

- **Responsible AI practices**: While leveraging AI, adhere to responsible AI practices. Implement governance measures to address biases, ensure explainability, and monitor AI systems for unintended consequences. Establish governance frameworks for AI decision-making.

- **Education and training**: Provide education and training programs for employees to enhance their awareness of responsible technology use. Foster a culture of ethical decision-making and equip teams with the knowledge and skills necessary to navigate ethical challenges.

- **Sustainability**: Consider the environmental impact of emerging technologies. Strive to adopt sustainable practices and minimize the ecological footprint associated with technology deployment, especially in areas such as cloud computing and data centers.

Summary

In this chapter, we discussed the importance of innovation and how enterprises can lead, disrupt, and innovate with emerging technologies in the cloud space. We explored the various kinds of innovation labs that organizations can leverage to build their innovation CoEs. We also explored the three pillars of an innovation center that serve as guiding principles to ensure innovation centers can deliver consistent long-term value to the business.

We then discussed how the convergence of cloud-native big data and serverless technologies plays a central role in modernizing the application and data ecosystem for enterprises across industry verticals. Finally, we explored the role of various emerging technologies such as AI, GenAI, XR, blockchain, and quantum computing in the context of industries and how enterprises can innovate responsibly in the cloud.

In the next chapter, we will explore the importance of ESG standards and sustainability for a modern enterprise and how enterprises can leverage cloud computing as a driver toward achieving ESG objectives.

Further reading

To learn more about the topics that were covered in this chapter, take a look at the following references:

1. `https://www.mckinsey.com/capabilities/mckinsey-digital/our-insights/five-fifty-cloudy-with-a-chance-of-billions`

2. `https://www.fastcompany.com/90850282/mcdonalds-marketing-cultural-moments-addictive-fries`

3. `https://www.sogeti.com/globalassets/uk/reports/sogetiuk_vint4_your_big_data_potential_wp.pdf`

4. `https://www.computerworld.com/article/2711618/how-enterprise-it-gets-creative.html`

5. `https://hbr.org/webinar/2017/04/whats-your-data-strategy`

6. https://www.researchgate.net/figure/The-7Vs-of-Big-Data-Volume-Velocity-Variety-Variability-Veracity-Value-and_fig1_341622174#:~:text=by%20Virginia%20Niculescu-,The%207Vs%20of%20Big%20Data%3A%20Volume%2C%20Velocity%2C%20Variety%2C,%2C%20Veracity%2C%20Value%2C%20and%20Visibility

7. https://channellife.com.au/story/ar-vr-and-3d-tech-boost-consumer-confidence-in-online-purchases-report

8. https://www.earth.com/news/quantum-computer-can-instantly-execute-a-task-that-would-normally-take-47-years/

9. https://www.mckinsey.com/capabilities/mckinsey-digital/our-insights/quantum-computing-use-cases-are-getting-real-what-you-need-to-know

11
ESG and Sustainability

The **United Nations Climate Change Conference (COP28)** in Dubai closed with an agreement that signaled the *beginning of the end* of the fossil fuel era, by forging a just and equitable transition to renewable energy, underpinned by deep emission cuts and scaled-up finance *[1]*. **ESG** stands for **environmental, social, and governance** and encompasses a set of criteria used to measure the sustainability and ethical impact of a company's operations. As ESG principles gain prominence across industries, they are not just a nice-to-have but have become a core necessity for businesses to thrive. Sustainability has become a key goal for CEOs across industries due to the convergence of stakeholder expectations, regulatory pressures, competitive advantages, and a broader recognition of the need for businesses to play a role in addressing global challenges. As CEOs prioritize sustainability, businesses are not only responding to external pressures but also recognizing the strategic value and long-term viability that sustainable practices bring to their organizations.

Sustainability and ESG-related legislation and regulations are on the rise globally across a wide spectrum of themes, from climate disclosure, supply chain due diligence, **diversity, equity, and inclusion (DEI)**, to manufacturing and a circular economy. For instance, in 2022, the U.S. **Securities and Exchange Commission (SEC)** proposed a rule that would enhance and standardize climate disclosure requirements provided by public companies. With the new regulation, organizations would be required to furnish specific climate-related disclosures in their registration statements and annual reports, including essential metrics pertaining to climate-related financial impact and expenditure. As part of the European Green Deal – which strives to be the first climate-neutral continent – **European Union (EU)** law requires all large companies and all listed companies to disclose information on ESG *[2]*. As ESG and **corporate social responsibility (CSR)** standards are evolving across various regions, such as the **European Sustainability Reporting Standards (ESRS)**, the **International Sustainability Standards Board (ISSB)**, and the **Taskforce on Nature-related Financial Disclosures (TNFD)**, global organizations with operations across regions will have a need to comply with the regulations.

In this chapter, we will cover the following topics:

- The principles of ESG and sustainability
- The value of integrating ESG for enterprises
- Building and adopting an ESG reporting program
- Leveraging the cloud as an ESG enabler

Definition of ESG and sustainability

ESG refers to a set of criteria that investors and other stakeholders use to evaluate a company's impact on the planet beyond just its financial performance. The business benefits of incorporating ESG considerations into enterprise practices are diverse and can positively impact various aspects of a company's operations. ESG principles help evaluate the sustainability and ethical impact of an organization's operations. Here's a breakdown of the ESG components.

Environmental impact

This dimension assesses how a company manages its impact on the environment – impact on climate, biodiversity, and its usage of natural resources:

- **Climate change**: Efforts to reduce greenhouse gas emissions, energy efficiency, and renewable energy usage
- **Resource usage**: Sustainable sourcing of raw materials, energy management, water management, fuel management, and waste reduction
- **Biodiversity**: Initiatives to protect biodiversity and ecosystems, efforts to reduce the environmental impact of products, and material sourcing

Social impact

The social dimension focuses on a company's relationships with its employees, customers, communities, and other stakeholders:

- **Employee relations**: Efforts toward employee health, safety and well-being, implementing fair wages, labor practices, diversity and inclusion
- **Community engagement**: Social responsibility, philanthropy, and contributions to community development
- **Customer relations**: Product safety, quality, ethical marketing, fair advertising, fair disclosure, and product labeling
- **Human rights**: Respecting human rights in supply chain and corporate operations

Governance

Governance examines the systems and structures that guide an organization, including its leadership, transparency, and accountability:

- **Board structure**: Independence of the board, diversity, and its effectiveness
- **Risk management**: Accident and safety management, systemic risk management practices
- **Executive compensation**: Fair and transparent executive pay practices
- **Anti-corruption measures**: Policies and practices to prevent corruption and bribery
- **Shareholder rights**: Protection of shareholder rights and fair treatment

These ESG principles are often used as a framework for evaluating the sustainability and ethical practices of businesses as investors, rating agencies, and other stakeholders are increasingly incorporating ESG factors into their decision-making processes. Companies that demonstrate strong ESG performance are often viewed as more resilient, responsible, and attractive to investors who prioritize sustainable and socially responsible investments.

The value of ESG for enterprises

Integrating ESG into business practices can lead to enhanced brand reputation, improved risk management, cost reduction, increased access to capital, and long-term resilience, ultimately contributing to the overall success and sustainability of enterprises. Following are some key reasons why sustainability is rising to the top of the agenda for enterprises.

Stakeholder expectations

As ESG principles take center stage, both internal and external stakeholder demands continue to drive business priorities. The following are some key stakeholder expectations:

- **Investor demand**: There is a growing demand from investors for companies to demonstrate not only financial performance but also ESG responsibility. Many investors now consider sustainability factors as critical indicators of a company's long-term viability.
- **Customer preferences**: Consumers are becoming more environmentally and socially conscious. Companies that align with sustainable practices may gain a competitive edge by attracting customers who prefer products and services from environmentally and socially responsible companies.
- **Employee expectations**: The workforce, especially younger generations, increasingly seek employers that share their values. Companies that prioritize sustainability can attract and retain top talent by fostering a purpose-driven and socially responsible work environment.

Competitive advantage

Another major consideration that drives business value is the competitive edge that ESG goals of a business command in the industry:

- **Innovation and differentiation**: Sustainability can drive innovation within a company, leading to the development of new products, services, and processes. Companies that prioritize sustainability often foster a culture of innovation to develop environmentally friendly products and processes, leading to long-term competitiveness. CEOs recognize that a commitment to sustainability can set their companies apart in the market and enhance their competitiveness.

- **Brand reputation**: Consumers and other stakeholders value companies with strong sustainability credentials. CEOs understand that a positive reputation for environmental and social responsibility can enhance brand loyalty and trust, positively influencing purchasing decisions.

Long-term business viability

Long-term business viability is another major value that ESG helps drive, resulting in the following:

- **Resilience and adaptability**: CEOs are increasingly recognizing the need for long-term resilience and adaptability in the face of global challenges. Sustainable business practices contribute to the overall resilience of a company by considering long-term impacts on the environment, society, and governance.

- **Resource efficiency**: Sustainable practices, such as energy efficiency and responsible resource management, contribute to cost savings and operational efficiency, supporting the long-term financial health of the company.

- **Employee productivity**: Companies with strong social practices, including fair labor standards, diversity, and employee well-being programs, often experience higher employee satisfaction and productivity, reducing turnover and recruitment costs.

Risk mitigation

With rising global demands for ethical responsibility, business partners are more inclined to work with organizations that share common ESG objectives. Adopting ESG principles can help mitigate risks in the following ways:

- **Climate and environmental risks**: Climate change and environmental degradation pose significant risks to business sustainability. Enterprises recognize the need to incorporate sustainability practices to mitigate environmental risks, ensure long-term operational continuity, and avoid potential legal and financial challenges.

- **Supply chain resilience**: Sustainability efforts, such as responsible sourcing and supply chain transparency, contribute to building resilient supply chains that are less vulnerable to disruptions.

Regulatory landscape

Finally, as the regulatory landscape continues to evolve and mandate enterprises across the world to adhere to ESG principles and reporting, it becomes an indispensable business value.

Governments worldwide are increasingly implementing and tightening regulations related to environmental and social issues. CEOs understand that aligning their companies with sustainability goals is not just a matter of ethical responsibility but also a strategy to comply with current and future regulatory requirements.

Now that we've discovered how ESG can drive long-term business value for organizations, let's explore how organizations can build and adopt an ESG sustainability program.

Building a sustainability program

Building an effective ESG sustainability program requires a strategic and comprehensive approach. This involves collecting ESG data from various data sources, defining metrics, measuring, benchmarking, and reporting them. In this section, we will review popular ESG reporting standards and frameworks and build a sustainability program.

ESG reporting standards and frameworks

ESG standards and frameworks provide organizations with a structured approach to evaluating and improving their performance in key areas that impact the environment, society, and governance. Today, various frameworks and standards exist – voluntary reporting, regulatory, and benchmarking – to guide organizations in integrating ESG principles into business operations. An ESG consulting firm, *Governance and Accountability Institute Inc.* in a research study reports that the largest companies in the S&P 500 are approaching 100% ESG reporting, while mid-cap companies making up the smallest half of the Russell 1000 continue to close the gap with 82% publishing reports in 2022.

So, why are ESG frameworks and standards important? Without a framework or a standard to adhere to, benchmarking and measuring where a company stands on its ESG score is extremely difficult and also leaves room for goals that are either too far out without intermediary milestones or arbitrary objectives or lead to unintended practices such as greenwashing, among others. Greenwashing refers to the practice when a company uses misleading advertising or language to market itself or its products as sustainable or environmentally friendly. This can lead to consequences such as fines or even damage to brand reputation. For instance, a company can set a lofty, decades-long goal of achieving carbon neutrality or net zero by 2050, or enter into superficial targets such as buying carbon credits or carbon offsets. Carbon offsets are programs where companies invest in green emission reduction projects and in return get a certificate for carbon credit, instead of reducing carbon emissions themselves.

Although several ESG frameworks and standards are evolving across different regions, the selection of a framework is guided by the organization's materiality assessments, stakeholder expectations, regional or geographical presence, and industry needs. Next are some of the popular ones.

Sustainability Accounting Standards Board (SASB)

SASB is a non-profit organization originally founded in 2011 with a focus on sustainability accounting and environmental, social, and corporate governance. As of 2022, the SASB standard definition responsibility was assumed by the ISSB of the **International Finance Reporting Standards** (**IFRS**) Foundation. SASB standards empower organizations to offer industry-specific disclosures to stakeholders regarding sustainability risks and opportunities that have the potential to impact cash flows and influence investor decisions. SASB has recognized 77 industries and defined sustainability issues that are most relevant to investor decisions within each industry.

ISSB

As part of the IFRS Foundation, ISSB has released two sustainability disclosure standards, with a goal to create a unified set of global disclosure standards that can be used to report ESG data to investors. *IFRS S1* relates to general requirements for sustainability-related financial information, and *IFRS S2* relates to climate-related disclosures.

Global Reporting Initiative (GRI)

GRI is a voluntary reporting framework and is one of the most internationally recognized standards and frameworks. GRI standards offer guidance to organizations in the generation of their own sustainability reports *[3]*. GRI standards are designed to be modular, delivering an inclusive picture of an organization's material topics, their related impacts, and how they are managed across three standards:

- **Universal standards**: Help report on human rights and environmental due diligence, in line with intergovernmental expectations that apply to all organizations

- **Sector standards**: Help enable consistent reporting on industry or sector-specific standards

- **Topic standards**: Help adapt to universal standard revisions and disclosures

Carbon Disclosure Project (CDP)

CDP is a non-profit charity organization that runs the global disclosure system for investors, companies, cities, states, and regions to manage their environmental impacts *[4]*. Organizations leveraging CDP respond to a CDP questionnaire and in turn receive a CDP score. CDP is considered a gold standard for corporate environmental reporting and is fully aligned with the **Task Force on Climate-related Financial Disclosures** (**TCFD**) recommendations *[5]*. As of October 2023, TCFD was disbanded and integrated into the IFRS Foundation to take over the monitoring and progress of companies' climate-related disclosures.

International Integrated Reporting Framework

The International Integrated Reporting Framework, now integrated into the IFRS Foundation, aims to bolster the adoption of integrated reporting *[6]*. The framework aims to improve the quality of information that is accessible to investors and financial capital providers, promote a unified and efficient corporate reporting approach, enhance accountability and stewardship for a wide range of capitals, and encourage decision-making that prioritizes generating enterprise value in the short, medium and long term.

EU Corporate Sustainability Reporting Directive (CSRD)

The EU's CSRD established a reporting framework called ESRS. This framework includes environmental, social, governance, and cross-cutting requirements to enhance the breadth, depth, and uniformity of the EU's ESG reporting while also improving the reliability and usefulness of sustainability information to investors [7]. The framework has finalized 12 ESRS standards, with 2 cross-cutting standards that apply to all sustainability matters and 10 topical standards covering a wide range of environmental, social, and governance matters:

- **Environmental standards**: *ESRS E1* for climate change, *ESRS E2* for pollution, *ESRS E3* for water and marine resources, *ESRS E4* for biodiversity and ecosystems, *ESRS E5* for resource use and circular economy.

- **Social standards**: *ESRS S1* for the organization's workforce, *ESRS S2* for workers in the value chain, *ESRS S3* for affected communities, *ESRS S4* for consumers and end-users.

- **Governance standards**: *ESRS G1* for business conduct.

- **Cross-cutting standards**: *ESRS 1* establishes general requirements, and *ESRS 2* establishes general disclosures.

United Nations Global Compact

The United Nations Global Compact lays out five defining features for corporate sustainability, including operating responsibly, strengthening society, committing to leadership at the highest level, reporting progress, and taking local actions. The United Nations Global Compact also offers a dynamic management framework – the United Nations Global Compact Management Model – as a guide on four areas: human rights, labor, environment, and anti-corruption.

Having reviewed the various ESG standards and reporting frameworks that offer a structured approach to ESG reporting, let's explore the concept of double materiality and its impact on businesses.

Double materiality assessment and reporting

The concept of double materiality recognizes the bidirectional relationship between a company and its external environment concerning ESG factors. It underscores the importance of considering both how external factors affect a company and how the company, through its actions and decisions, impacts the broader ESG landscape. This is essential for companies aiming to integrate sustainability into their core business strategies and operations. Double materiality is the intersection or union of financial materiality and impact materiality. While financial materiality is a well-established concept in traditional financial reporting, it has evolved in the context of ESG reporting. Financial materiality in the realm of ESG describes the economic value creation of a company through ESG and sustainability initiatives. Impact materiality describes the impact of a company's decision on the environment and external stakeholders.

Double materiality can be seen in various industries and sectors whenever companies make strategic decisions. For instance, when a manufacturing company sources raw materials for its production, impact materiality can describe how the implementation of sustainable sourcing practices on both the upstream and downstream value chain impacts the environment, and financial materiality describes the company's financial implications in areas such as material costs, consumer loyalty, and brand reputation.

Every organization is unique from the perspective of organizational context, industry, and operations, and so is the approach to double materiality. However, there are some best practices that organizations can consider, such as conducting a double materiality assessment and leveraging a standard framework for double materiality reporting. Conducting a double materiality assessment is often akin to a research project that helps identify which environmental, social, and governance issues are impactful and relevant to its business. This can often be done through a careful selection of stakeholder groups within the company to identify and describe material topics for double materiality assessment consideration. Organizations can also conduct interviews with stakeholders to understand their views on impacts, risks, and opportunities, which can then be summarized to arrive at the financial and impact materiality. Following is an example of a double materiality assessment conducted by **Sanofi** – a French multinational pharmaceutical and healthcare company headquartered in Paris, France *[8]*. This matrix captures the 16 material topics that Sanofi identified in 2022 mapped across the impact materiality in the *y* axis against its impact materiality in the *x* axis:

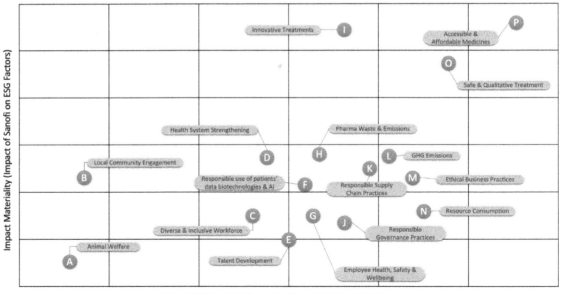

Figure 11.1 – Illustration of Sanofi's double materiality assessment

Regardless of whether double materiality assessment is mandated by regulations, it offers enterprise stakeholders and boardrooms deeper visibility and insight into its impact on ESG and business value.

Adopting an ESG reporting program

Regardless of the chosen ESG standard and framework, the accuracy and transparency in the collection and measurement of ESG data, automation of the ESG process, and auditability are core to successful ESG adoption and reporting. Similar to the implementation of dedicated IT software systems for various business functions such as HR, ERP, and finance, ESG reporting also requires a dedicated software system. Organizations can benefit from having a specialized ESG software platform to capture ESG data across multiple dimensions and measure emissions data and sustainability initiatives. ESG reporting software can help organizations stay organized by automating data capture directly from multiple sources, benchmarking, and transparently reporting while also staying compliant with ever-changing regulatory requirements. Following is a four-stage approach that organizations can leverage to simplify and streamline ESG reporting:

Figure 11.2 – ESG reporting life cycle

Let's learn more about each of these stages:

- **Collect**: Data collection is the first step in sustainability reporting. ESG data collection is instrumental in providing organizations with the information needed to make informed decisions, manage risks, build trust, and contribute to a sustainable and responsible business environment. This involves seamlessly collecting and integrating data across multiple enterprise data sources, systems, and applications into a single unified repository of truth.

- **Measure**: The next step in ESG reporting is measurement and benchmarking. Measurement provides organizations with quantifiable metrics to assess ESG performance. These metrics help evaluate the effectiveness of sustainability initiatives, identify areas for improvement, and set benchmarks for future progress. Measurement enables companies to compare their ESG performance against industry peers, sector benchmarks, and best practices. This comparative analysis helps organizations understand their relative standing and areas where they may need to catch up or lead.

- **Report**: Reporting is often the critical step that helps organizations report ESG standings to internal or external stakeholders. Regardless of whether it is voluntary reporting or responding to an audit or regulatory requirement, transparency and accuracy in ESG reporting are extremely crucial, as stakeholders increasingly use ESG information reported to make informed decisions. This is also an opportunity for organizations to communicate their commitment to ESG values, which is more likely to attract capital, build a positive brand image, and also attract and retain top talent.

- **Analyze**: The *analyze* stage helps organizations gain visibility into ESG metrics and convert them into actionable strategies and performance benchmarks. With visibility into ESG metrics through a dashboard, enterprise leaders can have the ability to access, filter, and visualize ESG data to make better decisions, faster. Leveraging predictive analytics, organizations can model different targets and outcomes, for the right targeted business outcomes.

Cloud computing as an ESG enabler

Cloud computing can contribute to ESG objectives in several ways, aligning with sustainable and responsible business practices, spanning environmental considerations, social impacts, and governance. Leveraging cloud services allows organizations to optimize resources, enhance collaboration, innovate responsibly, and adopt more sustainable and efficient IT practices. Following are some ways in which cloud computing helps advance sustainability and ESG objectives for organizations.

Environmental factors

As enterprises strive to achieve larger and bolder objectives such as carbon zero and carbon net neutrality, cloud computing offers a seamless pathway to realize those visions. By leveraging the cloud provider's green data centers, energy-efficient computing options, and out-of-the-box ESG reporting capabilities that continuously evolve, organizations can realize long-term business value while also focusing resources on larger and core business objectives. The following are some environmental factors that can help organizations deliver on ESG commitments.

Energy efficiency

By leveraging cloud providers' energy-efficient infrastructure, applications, and services, enterprises can take advantage of infrastructure consolidation and optimization while also aligning technological advancements with environmental responsibility. Following are some examples of how hyperscalers can help with energy efficiency:

- **Green data centers**: Hyperscalers invest in green data center technologies, utilizing renewable energy sources, water replenishment plans, energy-efficient hardware, and advanced cooling systems to minimize environmental impact. **Power usage effectiveness** (**PUE**) is often used as a popular metric to measure data center efficiency. PUE is defined as the metric that describes how efficiently a data center uses energy. An ideal PUE score of 1.0 indicates a perfectly efficient data center in which 100% of the facility's power is delivered to IT equipment. The average annual PUE for a typical data center is 1.58 *[9]*. Let's compare this metric to some of the popular cloud provider's data centers. For instance, **Amazon Web Services** (**AWS**) has a PUE of 1.2, with Azure at 1.12 and Google Cloud at 1.10 (the lower the score, the better its efficiency) *[10] [11]*. What does this mean for enterprises? By running workloads in the cloud, organizations could see a significant positive impact on their ESG goals. Beyond energy, major cloud providers also have net zero goals, implementing water stewardship and replenishment plans and zero waste toward a goal of a circular economy. More importantly, as hyperscalers invest heavily and constantly work toward larger sustainability goals, these benefits can be shared and leveraged by enterprises.

- **Infrastructure consolidation**: Cloud providers operate large-scale data centers with efficient server consolidation, leading to better resource utilization and reduced energy consumption per workload compared to on-premises infrastructure. Several cloud providers also offer transparent metrics on data center regions and zones that operate on green energy, low carbon intensity, or **carbon-free energy** (**CFE**). This allows organizations with sustainability goals to pick a cleaner region with a better CFE percentage to run their workloads. For instance, Google publishes carbon data for all its cloud regions by displaying the CFE % and the local electricity grid's carbon intensity, and AWS publishes the electricity map.

Reducing the carbon footprint

With cloud economies of scale, serverless technologies, elastic scaling, and reducing e-waste, organizations can significantly reduce overall carbon emissions. Following are some key factors that can help reduce the carbon footprint:

- **Economies of scale**: Cloud providers achieve economies of scale by leveraging multi-tenant models, allowing multiple organizations to share computing resources on the same infrastructure. This reduces the overall carbon footprint as compared to individual organizations managing their own data centers. A traditional data center consumes substantial amounts of energy, resulting in significant carbon emissions. In contrast, the aggregation of workloads in the cloud increases server utilization and drives economies of scale, incorporating newer efficient servers and utilizing recycled or reclaimed water to cool cloud data centers. According to a study published in the **World Economic Forum** (**WEF**), the transition to cloud computing between 2021 and 2024 should prevent at least 629 million metric tons of CO_2 from entering the atmosphere.

- **Dynamic scaling**: Cloud services enable organizations to scale resources up or down based on demand. This elasticity helps avoid over-provisioning, leading to lower energy consumption during periods of lower demand. At a very basic level, traditional data centers operate on the principle of oversizing to accommodate traffic spikes – sometimes even as high as 3x idle capacity. In contrast, with cloud computing's elastic on-demand scale, server efficiencies are dramatically improved, resulting in a much more efficient overall data center operation. Enterprises can further improve efficiencies by picking fully managed services and offerings in the cloud, such as serverless and instanceless services due to higher packing, deployment, and operational efficiencies associated with them.

- **Reducing e-waste**: By relying on cloud services, organizations may reduce the need for maintaining and disposing of physical IT equipment, contributing to the reduction of electronic waste (e-waste).

Sustainability impact dashboards

Several hyperscalers offer sustainability dashboards that can provide insights into an organization's carbon emissions. This can help enterprises measure, track, report, and act on sustainability objectives. For example, Google Cloud offers an out-of-the-box dashboard that gives a high-level overview of gross carbon emissions from electricity associated with the usage of Google Cloud services, broken down by services, projects, and regions. Similarly, Azure offers the Emissions Impact Dashboard to gain transparency into carbon emissions. This helps organizations make targeted decisions to help create new efficiencies around cloud usage.

Social factors

Social factors within ESG are integral to creating a responsible and sustainable business model. Enterprises that prioritize social considerations demonstrate a commitment to ethical practices, employee well-being, community engagement, and customer satisfaction, contributing to long-term success in an increasingly socially conscious business environment. The following are some examples of how the cloud helps drive positive social impact:

- **Facilitating remote collaboration**: By nature, cloud computing is available across the world to support both businesses and workforces in accessing cloud services from virtually anywhere. Cloud solutions such as virtual desktops, **unified communications as a service** (**UCaaS**), and productivity workspace tools have facilitated flexible and remote working. Consider a cloud solution such as a SaaS ERP application that can be accessed through just a browser with an internet connection versus a traditional on-premises closed ecosystem. Opening up security firewalls and access can often be extremely tricky, while cloud services are designed ground up for open security. From a social impact perspective, cloud computing services support remote work by providing employees with access to applications, data, and collaboration tools from anywhere. This contributes to a positive social impact by fostering work-life balance while also reducing commuting-related environmental impacts.

- **Global collaboration**: Cloud-based collaboration tools and platforms also facilitate global collaboration – an important social dimension, allowing organizations to work with diverse teams and partners, contributing to social and cultural diversity objectives. In a way, the cloud has leveled the playing field to enable the best person for the job role regardless of their location.

- **Accessibility and diversity**: Cloud technology has democratized access to modern applications and services for people with disabilities or special needs, who are no longer hindered by the obligation to attend an office and continue to have the same access to resources and opportunities to progress their careers.

Governance factors

Although governance features last in ESG, corporate governance is the foundational element that anchors and drives environmental and social aspects. The realm of corporate governance encompasses various elements, including corporate structure, the composition of the board, ethical business practices, and anti-corruption measures. Let us review some key aspects of corporate governance as it pertains to ESG principles.

Data security and privacy

Data security and privacy are critical components of the ESG framework, playing a vital role in governance and ethical business practices. As companies continue to prioritize ESG principles, robust data protection measures become essential to ethical business conduct, garnering stakeholder trust, and overall corporate responsibility:

- **Data protection and compliance**: Data security and compliance are critical components of governance within an organization. Cloud providers invest heavily in robust security measures, data encryption, and compliance certifications. Adopting cloud services can help organizations enhance data protection and governance practices, aligning with ESG principles.

- **Regulatory compliance**: Cloud providers often offer comprehensive tools, reports, and visibility into compliance to help organizations comply with data protection regulations, contributing to good governance and adherence to legal and ethical standards. These tools and out-of-the-box reports improve transparency and simplify the process of audits, tracking, and compliance with industry regulations.

- **Logging, monitoring, and auditing**: Cloud platforms typically offer comprehensive logging and auditing features that enable organizations to track user activities, changes to configurations, and system events, supporting transparency and auditability. With real-time monitoring capabilities, organizations can proactively identify and address potential governance issues for better decision-making and risk mitigation.

Business continuity (BC)

BC is crucial in the context of ESG as it ensures that enterprises can maintain operations during disruptions, safeguarding stakeholders' interests and contributing to social responsibility. By prioritizing BC, companies demonstrate their commitment to resilience and risk management, fostering trust with investors and communities:

- **Disaster recovery (DR) and resilience**: Cloud services provide robust DR capabilities, including features for backup, DR, and redundancy, ensuring BC in the face of unforeseen events. This resilience aligns with ESG objectives by minimizing disruptions to operations.

- **Enhanced risk assessment**: Cloud computing enables organizations to assess and manage risks more effectively, including risks related to data breaches, system downtime, and other potential disruptions. By leveraging cloud-based tools and services, companies can enhance their overall risk management practices, promoting better governance.

Supplier risk management

Supplier risk management is a vital aspect of ESG as it ensures ethical and sustainable practices throughout the supply chain. By assessing and mitigating risks related to suppliers, companies demonstrate commitment to social responsibility, fair labor practices, and environmental standards. It also enhances governance and strengthens stakeholder trust, contributing to a more responsible and sustainable business ecosystem:

- **Due diligence for cloud providers**: Organizations can conduct due diligence on **cloud service providers (CSPs)** to assess their security practices, compliance certifications, and commitment to ethical business conduct. This supports governance by ensuring that third-party relationships align with organizational values and standards.

- **Contractual agreements**: Cloud computing contracts often include terms related to data protection, security, and compliance. Effective governance involves reviewing and negotiating contractual agreements with cloud providers to align with organizational governance objectives.

Now that we reviewed how the cloud contributes to an organization's overall ESG objectives, let's review how organizations can incorporate ESG and sustainability principles while designing and building applications in the cloud.

Building sustainable applications in the cloud

Building sustainable cloud applications involves considering environmental, social, and economic factors throughout the application's life cycle. Sustainable cloud applications aim to minimize their environmental impact, promote social responsibility, and contribute to long-term economic viability. Although moving from traditional on-premises data centers to the cloud can aid in achieving an organization's sustainability goals, it is not the end of the sustainability journey. To continue and advance the sustainability promise, top-down leadership commitment is quintessential in driving and embedding ESG principles within applications ground up. Following are some design principles and architectural best practices that can help instrument sustainability at the core of every application:

- **Choose sustainable cloud providers**: Choose cloud providers who share the same commitment to sustainability and operate green data centers. Providers who invest in renewable energy sources and energy-efficient infrastructure contribute to a lower overall environmental impact that can directly benefit the organization's ESG goals. Consider cloud providers that transparently report on their carbon footprint, water usage efficiency, water replenishment, circular economy, and waste reduction. Choose providers who publish annual sustainability reports that detail their environmental initiatives *[12]*.

- **Optimize cloud resources**: Carefully optimize the allocation of computing resources, storage, and network bandwidth to minimize over-provisioning and resource waste. Ensure application architecture design leverages cloud services that allow for dynamic scaling to match demand.

- **Energy-efficient computing**: Leverage cloud providers and services that prioritize energy efficiency in their data centers. While deploying workloads in the cloud, choose regions and availability zones that use CFE, low carbon intensity, and renewable energy sources.

- **Design for efficiency**: Prefer fully managed services and serverless and instanceless architectures while designing applications over build-you-own. Manually installed and deployed applications are less efficient than provider managed.

- **Optimize code**: Encourage development teams to write efficient and optimized code to reduce resource consumption. This includes minimizing unnecessary computations, optimizing algorithms, and using caching strategies.

- **Iterative development**: Embrace an iterative development process that allows for ongoing enhancements and optimizations. Regularly reassess and update your application to incorporate the latest sustainable practices and technologies.

- **Internal training**: Educate your development team on sustainable practices and the environmental impact of technology. Promote a culture of awareness and responsibility within the organization. Educate and provide users with information on the sustainability features of the application to encourage environmentally conscious usage patterns and promote the positive impact of using sustainable technology.

- **Data compression and deduplication**: Implement data compression and deduplication techniques to minimize storage requirements, storage encryption, and hash processing and reduce unnecessary data movement, bandwidth consumption, and data transfer costs.

- **Data lifecycle management (DLM)**: Define DLM policies to automatically archive or purge data that is no longer needed. This helps control storage costs and improves efficiency.

- **Continuous monitoring**: Implement monitoring tools to continuously assess the performance and resource utilization of your application. Identify opportunities for optimization and efficiency improvements.

- **Cost management**: Regularly review and optimize cloud costs. Utilize cloud provider tools and third-party solutions to identify cost-saving opportunities and ensure efficient use of resources. Several cloud providers offer recommender services that tie into ESG data to identify wasteful resources and also recommend alternative options to promote efficiency.

- **Security and compliance**: Implement strong encryption practices for data in transit and at rest for better governance practices. Secure sensitive data to protect user privacy and comply with data protection regulations. Ensure that the application complies with relevant environmental and social responsibility standards and adheres to industry-specific regulations and certifications.

- **Inclusivity and accessibility**: To promote social responsibility, design applications with inclusivity and accessibility considerations. Ensure that user-facing applications are accessible to users with diverse abilities and backgrounds.

- **Ethical use of data**: Implement ethical data practices, ensuring responsible data collection, usage, and storage. Clearly communicate privacy policies and obtain user consent for data processing.

- **Support for non-profits**: Consider offering cloud resources or services to non-profit organizations or initiatives that align with sustainability and social responsibility goals.

- **Open source contributions**: Contribute to open source projects that focus on sustainable and ethical technology practices. Share expertise and best practices with the community to advance responsible technology development.

- **Feedback loops**: Establish feedback loops to gather insights from both internal and external users and stakeholders. Use this feedback to make continuous improvements to applications, addressing sustainability concerns and meeting user expectations.

By integrating these considerations into the fundamental design, development, and operation of cloud applications, organizations can contribute to building sustainable, environmentally friendly, and socially responsible solutions. The goal is to create technology that not only meets functional requirements but also aligns with broader ESG principles and promotes a positive impact on the world.

Summary

In this chapter, we have discussed the various principles governing corporate ESG and how cloud computing contributes to an organization's overall ESG objectives. We also explored the various ESG regulatory reporting standards, including double materiality, and the value of integrating ESG principles. Further, we reviewed how enterprises can leverage cloud computing as an ESG enabler and build sustainable cloud applications by choosing providers committed to sustainability, optimizing resource allocation, using energy-efficient computing, and designing for efficiency.

By integrating these considerations into cloud application design, development, and operations, organizations can create technology that aligns with broader ESG principles and promotes a positive impact on the world.

Further reading

To learn more about the topics that were covered in this chapter, take a look at the following references:

1. https://unfccc.int/news/cop28-agreement-signals-beginning-of-the-end-of-the-fossil-fuel-era

2. https://commission.europa.eu/strategy-and-policy/priorities-2019-2024/european-green-deal_en

3. https://www.globalreporting.org/standards/

4. https://www.cdp.net/en

5. https://www.fsb-tcfd.org

6. https://www.integratedreporting.org/resource/international-ir-framework/

7. https://finance.ec.europa.eu/capital-markets-union-and-financial-markets/company-reporting-and-auditing/company-reporting/corporate-sustainability-reporting_en

8. https://www.sanofi.com/en/investors/environment-social-governance/our-double-materiality-assessment

9. https://www.statista.com/statistics/1229367/data-center-average-annual-pue-worldwide/

10. https://www.nutanix.dev/2023/05/04/digging-into-data-center-efficiency-pue-and-the-imp

11. https://www.google.com/about/datacenters/efficiency/

12. https://www.weforum.org/agenda/2021/09/the-next-big-cloud-competition-is-the-race-to-zero-emissions/

Index

packtpub.com

Subscribe to our online digital library for full access to over 7,000 books and videos, as well as industry leading tools to help you plan your personal development and advance your career. For more information, please visit our website.

Why subscribe?

- Spend less time learning and more time coding with practical eBooks and Videos from over 4,000 industry professionals

- Improve your learning with Skill Plans built especially for you

- Get a free eBook or video every month

- Fully searchable for easy access to vital information

- Copy and paste, print, and bookmark content

Did you know that Packt offers eBook versions of every book published, with PDF and ePub files available? You can upgrade to the eBook version at packtpub.com and as a print book customer, you are entitled to a discount on the eBook copy. Get in touch with us at customercare@packtpub.com for more details.

At www.packtpub.com, you can also read a collection of free technical articles, sign up for a range of free newsletters, and receive exclusive discounts and offers on Packt books and eBooks.

Other Books You May Enjoy

If you enjoyed this book, you may be interested in these other books by Packt:

Multi-Cloud Handbook for Developers

Subash Natarajan, Jeveen Jacob

ISBN: 9781804618707

- Understand the core structures and implications of cloud-native and multi-cloud apps
- Explore key principles and patterns to build agile, scalable, and future-proof apps
- Master cloud-native essentials: service mesh, DDD, and API-centric approaches
- Implement deployment pipelines with advanced IaC, CI/CD, DevSecOps, and GitOps techniques
- Manage and monitor data, security, compliance, and identity access in multi-cloud scenarios
- Optimize your cloud costs with shift-left and FinOps practices
- Get ready for the future of cloud-native and multi-cloud technology

Achieving Digital Transformation Using Hybrid Cloud

Vikas Grover, Ishu Verma, Praveen Rajagopalan

ISBN: 9781837633692

- Design and build a foundation for hybrid cloud platform
- Leverage Kubernetes, containers, and GitOps for hybrid cloud
- Use architectural pattern blueprints to deliver applications on hybrid cloud
- Enable communication between applications hosted on different clouds
- Rollout zero-touch provisioning and monitoring in a hybrid architecture
- Enhance stability and scale up or down without rebuilding apps
- Understand principles of hybrid cloud security for application stack
- Design cost-optimized systems based on the economics of hybrid cloud

Packt is searching for authors like you

If you're interested in becoming an author for Packt, please visit `authors.packtpub.com` and apply today. We have worked with thousands of developers and tech professionals, just like you, to help them share their insight with the global tech community. You can make a general application, apply for a specific hot topic that we are recruiting an author for, or submit your own idea.

Share your thoughts

Now you've finished *Enterprise-Grade Hybrid and Multi-Cloud Strategies*, we'd love to hear your thoughts! Scan the QR code below to go straight to the Amazon review page for this book and share your feedback or leave a review on the site that you purchased it from.

`https://packt.link/r/1804615110`

Your review is important to us and the tech community and will help us make sure we're delivering excellent quality content.

Download a free PDF copy of this book

Thanks for purchasing this book!

Do you like to read on the go but are unable to carry your print books everywhere?

Is your eBook purchase not compatible with the device of your choice?

Don't worry, now with every Packt book you get a DRM-free PDF version of that book at no cost.

Read anywhere, any place, on any device. Search, copy, and paste code from your favorite technical books directly into your application.

The perks don't stop there, you can get exclusive access to discounts, newsletters, and great free content in your inbox daily

Follow these simple steps to get the benefits:

1. Scan the QR code or visit the link below

https://packt.link/free-ebook/9781804615119

2. Submit your proof of purchase

3. That's it! We'll send your free PDF and other benefits to your email directly

www.ingramcontent.com/pod-product-compliance
Lightning Source LLC
Chambersburg PA
CBHW080615060326
40690CB00021B/4707